The UK Eco

A Manual of A

CONTRIBUTORS

Chapter 1

M.C. Kennedy *B.Sc. (Econ.) (London)*
Lecturer in Economics, University of Manchester

Chapter 2

Richard Harrington *B.Sc. (Econ.) (Wales), M.Sc. (Econ.)*
(London)
Senior Lecturer in Economics, University of Manchester

Chapter 3

Christopher J. Green *B.A. (Oxford), Ph.D. (Yale)*
Sir Julian Hodge Professor of Banking and Finance,
Cardiff Business School, University of Wales College of Cardiff

Chapter 4

Malcolm C. Sawyer *B.A. (Oxon.), M.Sc. (Econ.) (London)*
Professor of Economics, University of York

Chapter 5

Geraint Johnes *B.Sc. (Bath), M.Sc. (Lancaster), Ph.D. (Lancaster)*
Lecturer in Economics, University of Lancaster
and
Jim Taylor *B.A. (Liverpool), M.A. (Liverpool), Ph.D. (Lancaster)*
Professor of Economics, University of Lancaster

Prest and Coppock's

The UK Economy

A Manual of Applied Economics

Twelfth Edition

Edited by

M. J. Artis, B.A., F.B.A.

Professor of Economics, University of Manchester

Weidenfeld and Nicolson
London

First published 1966
Second impression 1967
Third impression 1968
Second edition 1968
Second impression 1969
Third edition 1970
Second impression 1971
Fourth edition 1972
Fifth edition 1974
Sixth edition 1976
Seventh edition 1978
Eighth edition 1980
Ninth edition 1982
Tenth edition 1984
Eleventh edition 1986
Reprinted 1987, 1988
Twelfth edition 1989

First published in Great Britain by
George Weidenfeld and Nicolson Limited
91 Clapham High St, London SW4 7TA

ISBN 0 297 79691 7   paperback

Printed in Great Britain at The Bath Press, Avon

Contents

TABLES

Chapter 1

Chapter 2

Chapter 3

Chapter 4

Chapter 5

TABLES IN THE STATISTICAL APPENDIX

FIGURES

ABBREVIATIONS

(1) Economic Terms

BOF Balance for Official Financing
CAP Common Agricultural Policy
CCFF Compensatory and Contingency Financing Facility
CET Common External Tariff
c.i.f. Cost including Insurance and Freight
CPI Consumer Price Index
EAP Enlarged Access Policy
ECU European Currency Unit
EER Effective Exchange Rate
EFF Extended Fund Facility
f.o.b. Free on Board
GDP Gross Domestic Product
GNP Gross National Product
IPD Interest Profits and Dividends
MCA Monetary Compensation Amount
MLH Minimum List Headings
MTFS Medium Term Financial Strategy
nie Not included elsewhere
PAYE Pay as you Earn
PDI Personal Disposable Income
PPP Purchasing Power Parity
PRT Petroleum Revenue Tax
PSBR Public Sector Borrowing Requirement
R&D Research and Development
REX Real Exchange Rate
RPM Resale Price Maintenance
SDRs Special Drawing Rights
SIC Standard Industrial Classification
SITC Standard Industrial Trade Classification
TFE Total Final Expenditure at Market Prices
VAT Value Added Tax

(2) Organizations, etc

CBI Confederation of British Industry
CSO Central Statistical Office (UK)
DE Department of Employment
DTI Department of Trade and Industry
EC European Community
EEC European Economic Community
EFTA European Free Trade Area

EMCF	European Monetary Co-operation Fund
EMS	European Monetary System
FAO	Food and Agriculture Organization
GATT	General Agreement on Tariffs and Trade
IMF	International Monetary Fund
MC	Monopolies and Mergers Commission
NEB	National Enterprise Board
NEDC(O)	National Economic Development Council (Office)
NIESR	National Institute of Economic and Social Research
OECD	Organization for Economic Cooperation and Development
OPEC	Organization of Petroleum Exporting Countries
OSA	Overseas Sterling Area
SEA	Single European Act
SEM	Single European Market
TUC	Trades Union Congress
UN	United Nations
UNCTAD	United Nations Commission for Trade and Development

(3) Journals, etc.

AAS	*Annual Abstract of Statistics* (HMSO)
AER	*American Economic Review*
BB	*National Accounts (Blue Book)* (HMSO)
BEQB	*Bank of England Quarterly Bulletin*
BJIR	*British Journal of Industrial Relations*
BOUIES	*Bulletin of the Oxford University Institute of Economics & Statistics*
CJE	*Cambridge Journal of Economics*
CSO	*Central Statistical Office*
DEG	*Department of Employment Gazette* (HMSO)
EC	*Economica*
EJ	*Economic Journal*
ET	*Economic Trends*
ET(AS)	*Economic Trends (Annual Supplement)* (HMSO)
FD	*Finance and Development*
FES	*Family Expenditure Survey* (HMSO)
FS	*Financial Statistics* (HMSO)
FSt	*Fiscal Studies*
FSBR	*Financial Statement and Budget Report* (HMSO)
GES	*Government Economic Service*
GHS	*General Household Survey*
HMSO	*Her Majesty's Stationery Office*
IFS	*International Financial Statistics*
IRAE	*International Review of Applied Economics*
JIE	*Journal of Industrial Economics*

JPE	*Journal of Political Economy*
JRSS	*Journal of Royal Statistical Society*
LBR	*Lloyds Bank Review*
MBR	*Midland Bank Review*
MDS	*Monthly Digest of Statistics* (HMSO)
MS	*The Manchester School of Economic and Social Studies*
NIER	*National Institute Economic Review*
NWBQR	*National Westminster Bank Quarterly Review*
OEP	*Oxford Economic Papers*
OREP	*Oxford Review of Economic Policy*
QJE	*Quarterly Journal of Economics*
RBSR	*Royal Bank of Scotland Review*
REST	*Review of Economics and Statistics*
SJPE	*Scottish Journal of Political Economy*
ST	*Social Trends* (HMSO)
TBR	*Three Banks Review*
TI	*Trade and Industry* (HMSO)

Foreword to the Twelfth Edition

With this edition we have broken with the tradition of a two-year cycle; the interval between this edition and the last is three years. Much has happened in this time, as is reflected in the rewritten chapters. At the same time there has been a change of personnel. In this edition we welcome Professor Taylor and Dr Johnes, who have taken over the Labour chapter from Professor Metcalf and Dr Richardson, and Professor Sawyer who has taken over the Industry chapter from Mr Cable.

The approach adopted in the book, however, remains the same, continuing to reflect the standards set by the original editors for whom the volume is still named. They summarized this approach in the Foreword to the first edition as follows:

> The central idea behind this book is to give an account of the main features and problems of the UK economy today. The hope is that it will fulfil two functions simultaneously, in that it will be as up to date as possible and yet will not be simply a bare catalogue of facts and figures. There are many sources of information, official and otherwise, about the structure and progress of the UK economy. There are also many authors to whom one can turn for subtle analyses of the problems before us. Our effort here is based on the belief that there is both room and need for an attempt to combine the functions of chronicler and analyst in the confines of a single book.
>
> The contributors to these pages subscribe rather firmly to the belief that economists should practise, as well as preach, the principles of the division of labour. The complexity of a modern economy is such that, whether one likes it or not, it is no longer possible for any individual to be authoritative on all its aspects; so it is inevitable that the burden of producing work of this kind should be spread among a number of people, each a specialist in his or her particular field. Such a division carries with it obvious dangers of overlap and inconsistency. It is hoped that some of the worst pitfalls of this kind have been avoided and there is reasonable unity of purpose, treatment and layout. At the same time, it is wholly undesirable to impose a monolithic structure and it is just as apparent to the authors that there are differences in outlook and emphasis among them as it will be to the reader.
>
> The general intention was to base exposition on the assumption that the reader would have some elementary knowledge of economics – say a student in the latter part of a typical first-year course in economics in a British university. At the same time, it is hoped that most of the text will be intelligible to those without this degree of expertise.

We may not have succeeded in this; if not, we shall try to do better in the future.

Chapter 1, 'The Economy as a Whole', is concerned with questions of applied macroeconomics: fluctuations in output and expenditure and the determinants and management of demand. Chapter 2, 'Money and Finance: Public Expenditure and Taxation', begins with a description of the inter-relationship between fiscal and monetary policy and the background to each, which is provided on the one hand by the institutions of the financial system and on the other by the structure of the government's accounts. It describes the activities of the institutions making up the financial markets and the way in which the Bank of England influences and supervises them, emphasizing the global nature and international dimensions of financial activity. The discussion of the government's accounts covers all the main heads of expenditure and revenue and describes the many recent changes that have taken place. Chapter 3, 'The Balance of Payments', deals with the importance of foreign trade and payments to the UK economy and discusses the behaviour of, and policy towards, the exchange rate, including the prospect of entry into the European Monetary System. It then looks at current problems and policies in this field, and ends with a discussion of recent developments in the field of international economic policy co-ordination and of the world debt problem. Chapter 4, 'Industry', summar-izes recent UK industrial performance and discusses competition and mergers policy, privatization, R&D and technology policy, and the per-formance of the nationalized industries. The clash of theoretical paradigms governing the approach of economists to these questions is made very clear. The last chapter, 'Labour', analyses employment and unemployment among the UK workforce in considerable detail and then discusses problems of pay and income distribution.

Certain themes, inevitably, crop up in more than one chapter; North Sea oil, for example, is treated as it influences the balance of payments and the exchange rate in Chapter 3, as it influences the structure of produc-tion in Chapter 4, and as it affects the fiscal balance in Chapter 2. The EEC similarly makes an appearance in more than one chapter, as does the problem of inflation and that of world debt. The aim has been to avoid straightforward duplication of treatment of the same theme in different chapters, allowing instead for complementary treatment of different aspects of the same theme and, where appropriate, for alternative interpretations of the same theme to make their appearance.

Each chapter is accompanied by a list of references and further reading. The Statistical Appendix at the end of the book includes tables dealing with different aspects of the UK economy. There is an index, as well as the detailed list of headings and subheadings given in the Contents pages.

It is pleasant to acknowledge the great help given to this enterprise by those who have rendered secretarial assistance.

University of Manchester   M.J.ARTIS
May 1989

1

The economy as a whole

M.C.Kennedy

1 INTRODUCTION
1.1 Methodological Approach

This chapter is an introduction to applied macroeconomics. It begins with a brief description of the national income accounts, and goes on to discuss growth and fluctuations, aggregate demand, inflation and macroeconomic policy. It does not pretend to give all the answers to the questions raised, but aims to provide the reader with a basis for further and deeper study.

In principle there is no essential difference between applied economics and economic theory. The object of applied economics is to explain the way in which economic units work. It is just as much concerned with questions of causation (such as what determines total consumption or the level of prices) as the theory which is found in most elementary textbooks. The difference between theoretical and applied economics is largely one of emphasis, with theory tending to stress logical connections between assumptions and conclusions, and applied economics the connections between theories and evidence. Applied economics does not seek description for its own sake, but it needs facts for the light they shed on the applicability of economic theory.

At one time it used to be thought that scientific theories were derived from factual information by a method of inference known as *induction*.[1] It was supposed that general laws about nature could be deduced from knowledge of a limited number of facts. From the logical point of view, however, induction is invalid. If ten people have been observed to save one-tenth of their income it does not follow that the next person will do likewise. The conclusion may be true or false, but it does not rest validly on the assumptions. Inductive propositions of this kind simply have the status of conjectures and require further empirical investigation.

More recently it has come to be accepted that scientific method is not so much inductive as *hypothetico-deductive*. A hypothesis is proposed to explain a certain class of events. It will generally be of the conditional

---

[1] For an introduction to the problems of scientific method the reader is referred to P.B. Medawar, *Induction and Intuition in Scientific Thought* (Methuen, 1969) and K.R.Popper, *The Logic of Scientific Discovery* (Hutchinson, 1959) and *Conjectures and Refutations* (Routledge and Kegan Paul, 1963). For a treatment of methodological problems in economics, see I.M.T. Stewart, *Reasoning and Method in Economics* (McGraw-Hill, 1979), M.Blaug, *The Methodology of Economics* (Cambridge University Press, 1980) and D.M.McCloskey, 'The Rhetoric of Economics', *Journal of Economic Literature*, June 1983.

form 'if p then q', from which the inference is that any particular instance of p must be accompanied by an instance of q. Thus the hypothesis is tested by all observations of p; corroborated whenever p and q are observed together; and falsified if p occurs in the absence of q.

It will be clear that this concept of scientific inference places the role of factual information in a different light from the inductive approach. Facts, instead of being the foundation on which to build economic or scientific theories, become the basis for testing them. If a theory is able to survive a determined, yet unsuccessful, attempt to refute it by factual evidence, it is regarded as well tested. But the discovery of evidence which is inconsistent with the theory will stimulate its modification or the development of a new theory altogether. One of the purposes of studying applied economics is to acquaint the theoretically equipped economist with the strength and limitations of the theory he has studied. Applied economics is not an attempt to bolster up existing theory or, as its name might seem to imply, to demonstrate dogmatically that all the factual evidence is a neat application of textbook theory. Its aim is to understand the workings of the economy, and this means that it will sometimes expose the shortcomings of existing theory and go on to suggest improvements.

The discovery that a theory is falsified by factual observations need not mean that it must be rejected out of hand or relegated to total oblivion. Economists, as well as natural scientists, frequently have to work with theories that are inadequate in one way or another. Theories that explain part but not all of the evidence may be retained until some new theory is found which fits a wider range of evidence. Frequently the theory will turn out to have been incomplete rather than just wrong, and when modified by the addition of some new variable (or more careful specification of the *ceteris paribus* clause), the theory may regain its status. The reader who sees inconsistencies between theory and facts need not take the line that the theory is total nonsense, for the theory may still hold enough grains of truth to become the basis for something better.

It is often argued that our ability to test economic theories by reference to evidence is sufficient to liberate economics from value judgements, i.e. to turn it into a *positive* subject. This position has more than an element of truth in it: when there is clear evidence against a theory it stands a fair chance of being dropped even by its most bigoted adherents. Nevertheless, it would be wrong to forget that a great deal of what passes for evidence in economics is infirm in character (e.g. the statistics of gross domestic product or personal saving), so that it is often possible for evidence to be viewed more sceptically by some than by others.

The discussion of economic policy which also figures in this chapter is partly normative in scope, and partly positive. The normative content of policy discussion involves the evaluation of goals and priorities. But the means for attaining such goals derive from the positive hypotheses of economics. They involve questions of cause and effect, to which the answers are hypothetical and testable by evidence. The combination of normative objectives and positive hypotheses leads to recommendations for policy. But in making such recommendations, the economist treads on thin ice. This is partly because his positive knowledge is not inevitably correct, but also because it is seldom possible to foresee and properly appraise all the side-effects of his recommendations, some of which have implications for other policy goals. When economists differ in their advice on policy questions it is not always clear how much the difference is due to diagnostic disagreements, and how much to value judgements. Indeed it is seldom possible for an economic adviser to reveal all the normative preferences which lie behind a policy recommendation. Policy judgements have to be scrutinized carefully for hidden normative assumptions, and the reader of this chapter must be on his guard against the author's personal value judgements.

1.2   Gross Domestic Product

Most of the topics discussed in this chapter make some use of the national accounts statistics. A complete explanation of what these are and of how they are put together is available elsewhere.[1] It will be useful, however, in the next few pages to introduce the reader to the main national accounting categories in so far as they affect this chapter.

Gross domestic product (GDP) represents the output of the whole economy, i.e. the production of all the enterprises resident in the UK. In principle, it can be assembled from three separate sets of data – from output, from income and from expenditure. The three totals should, in principle, be equal – a point which may seem surprising when it is recalled that spending and output are seldom equal for an individual firm. But the convention in national accounting is to count all *unsold output* as part of investment in stocks, and to regard this both as expenditure and as income (profits) in kind. Thus the three estimates are made to equal each other by the device of defining expenditure and income differently from their everyday meanings.

The two principal estimates of current price GDP – the expenditure- and income-based estimates – are shown in table 1.1. The expenditure-based method classifies expenditure by four types of spending unit: persons, public authorities, firms and foreign residents.[2] Purchases by persons are described as consumers' expenditure, but this excludes the purchase of new houses which are deemed to have been sold initially to 'firms'. Fixed investment represents purchases by firms of physical assets which are additions or replacements to the nation's capital stock. The preface 'gross' warns us that a year's gross investment does not measure the change in

---

[1]   See, for example, the introduction in CSO, *United Kingdom National Accounts, 1988 Edition* (HMSO, 1988) and the CSO Handbook (the 'National Income Blue Book'), *United Kingdom National Accounts: Sources and Methods* (3rd edition, HMSO, 1985).
[2]   The distinctions between types of spending units are not always clear-cut, e.g. expenditure by self-employed persons is partly consumers' expenditure and partly investment.

TABLE 1.1

GDP at Current Prices, UK, 1987

FROM EXPENDITURE

	£bn	% of TFE[1]
Consumers' expenditure	258.4	49
General government final consumption	85.8	16
Gross domestic fixed investment	70.8	14
Investment in stocks	0.6	0
Exports of goods and services	107.5	21
Total final expenditure at market prices (TFE)	523.1	100
less Imports of goods and services	−112.0	
less Adjustment to factor cost	−62.2	
Gross domestic product at factor cost (from expenditure)	348.9	
Statistical discrepancy	3.4	
Gross domestic product at factor cost (average estimate)	352.2	

FROM INCOME

	£bn	% of domestic income[1]
Income from employment	226.3	63
Income from self-employment	33.0	9
Income from rent	24.8	7
Gross trading profits of companies	65.6	18
Gross trading surpluses of public corporations and other public enterprises	6.4	2
Imputed charge for consumption of non-trading capital	3.2	1
Total domestic income	359.4	100
less Stock appreciation	−4.9	
Gross domestic product at factor cost (from income)	354.5	
Statistical discrepancy	−2.3	
Gross domestic product at factor cost (average estimate)	352.2	

BY INDUSTRY (FROM INCOME)

	£bn	% of total[1]
Agriculture, forestry and fishing	5.9	2
Energy and water supply	24.2	6
Manufacturing	85.6	23
Construction	21.5	6
Distribution, hotels and catering, repairs	49.0	13
Banking, finance, insurance, business services and leasing	63.9	17
Education and health	31.7	8
Other services	93.3	25
Total (after providing for stock appreciation)	375.1	100
Adjustment for financial services[2]	−20.5	
Gross domestic product at factor cost (from income)	354.5	

Source: BB, 1988, tables 1.2, 1.3 and 2.1

1 Details may not add to totals because of rounding.
2 Deduction of net receipts of interest by financial companies.

the size of the capital stock during the year because it fails to allow for the erosion due to scrapping and wear and tear. The concept of gross capital formation is also carried through into the definition of domestic product itself, indicating that the value of *gross* domestic product makes no allowance for capital consumption. The other category of investment is investment in stocks or, as the CSO puts it, the value of the physical increase in stocks. This makes no distinction between voluntary and involuntary stock changes.

The sum of exports, consumers' expenditure, government final consumption and gross investment is known as total final expenditure at market prices (TFE). These expenditures contain two elements which must be deducted before arriving at GDP at factor cost. The first is the import content, which is foreign, not domestically produced, output. The simplest way of removing imports is to take the global import total as given by the balance of payments accounts and subtract it from TFE, and this is the usual method. Estimates do exist, however, for the import content of the separate components of final expenditure in the input–output tables – although these are drawn up much less frequently than the national accounts.

The second element of total final expenditure which must be deducted to obtain the factor cost value of GDP is the indirect tax content (net of subsidies) of the various expenditures. This is present because the most readily available valuation of any commodity is the price at which it sells in the market. This value will overstate factor incomes earned from producing the commodity by the amount of indirect tax; it will understate factor income if the price is subsidized. The deduction of indirect taxes (net of subsidies) is known as the *factor cost adjustment*, and is most conveniently made globally since it can be found from the government's records of tax proceeds and subsidy payments. Annual estimates of its incidence on the individual components of TFE can be derived from the National Income *Blue Book*.[1]

The income-based estimate arrives at GDP by summing up the incomes of all the residents of the UK earned in the production of goods and services in the UK during a stated period. It divides into income from employment, income from self-employment and profit, and income from rent. These are factor incomes earned in the process of production and are to be distinguished from *transfer incomes*, such as pensions and sickness benefits, which are not earned from production and which, therefore, are excluded from the total. The breakdown of factor incomes for 1987 is illustrated in table 1.1.

The income breakdown of GDP contains two items which may need further explanation. The first is the imputed charge for consumption of non-trading capital. This represents the capital consumption of non-trading activities. It is added to their income (which comes mainly from invest-

---

[1] *BB*, 1988, table 1.2.

ments) so that it can be valued gross of depreciation on the same basis
as the profit income of all other companies.[1] The other item is the adjustment for stock appreciation which appears here because changes in the
book value of stocks have been credited to profits. The problem of adjustment for stock appreciation arises because the change in the book value
between the beginning and end of the year may be partly due to a price
change.

A firm holding stocks of wood, for example, may increase its holding
from 100 tons on 1 January to 200 tons on 31 December. If the price
of wood was £1.00 per ton at the beginning of the year and £1.10 at the
end of the year, the increase in the monetary value of stocks will show
up as (£1.10 × 200) − (£1.00 × 100), which equals £120. This figure is
inflated by the amount of the price increase and fails, therefore, to give
an adequate record of what the Central Statistical Office (CSO) calls 'the
value of the physical increase in stocks'. In order to rectify this, the CSO
attempts to value the physical change in stocks at the average price level
prevailing during the period. If, in the example, the price averaged £1.05
over the period, then the value of the physical increase in stocks would
be shown as £1.05(200–100), which equals £105. The difference of £15
between this and the increase in monetary value is the adjustment for
stock appreciation.

GDP by income can be rearranged in terms of the industries in which
the incomes were earned. This beakdown is available annually and gives
an up-to-date picture of the industrial composition of total output, showing,
for example, that manufacturing production is less than one-quarter of
the value of GDP. The industry breakdown is shown in table 1.1.

The expenditure and income estimates are derived from different and
largely independent sets of data. They never add up to exactly the same
total, and the difference between them is known as the *residual error*.

An output-based estimate of GDP can, in principle, be compiled by
adding up the *net output* or *value added* of all the firms and productive
units in the economy. To obtain such a total it would be necessary to
find the *gross output* of each firm in the economy and to subtract from
it the value of *intermediate input*, i.e. goods and services purchased from
other firms. In practice this herculean task cannot be accomplished in the
time-span of a single year. But the CSO has enough data on gross output
to estimate changes in value added in real terms (i.e. at constant prices).
A new departure in 1987 was the publication of an average estimate of
GDP derived partly from output data. The value of GDP by output was
not found directly, but was derived by applying the deflator for expenditure-
based GDP to the volume estimate of GDP by output – see section 1.3
below.

This means that there are now four estimates each year for GDP in
current prices: the expenditure, income, output and average estimates.

---

[1]   This corrects the impression given in previous editions. See *BB*, 1987, p. 5, n44.

The difference between the expenditure and income estimates is the residual error (and was 1.6% of GDP in 1987), and the differences between these two estimates and the average estimates are termed the 'statistical discrepancies'.

Gross domestic product is the most widely used of several aggregates, the others being GNP and National Income. The relationships between the various aggregates in 1987 were:

		£bn *(current prices)*
	GNP at market prices	420.7
less	Net property income from abroad	−5.5
equals	GDP at market prices	414.5
less	Factor cost adjustment	−62.2
equals	GDP at factor cost (from expenditure)	352.2
plus	Net property income from abroad	+5.5
equals	GNP at factor cost	357.8
less	Capital consumption	−48.2
equals	Net national product at factor cost ('national income')	309.5

GNP, like GDP, may be valued at market prices or factor cost. It differs from GDP by including net interest, profits and dividends earned by UK residents from productive enterprises owned overseas. The other concept, Net National Product, differs from GNP by the amount of capital consumption, this being the CSO's estimate of depreciation. It is also the figure which must be subtracted from gross investment to find net investment. GDP and the gross concept of investment are in much more frequent use than net product and net investment because they relate directly to employment. When a machine is being produced it makes no difference to the number of workers employed whether it is to replace one already in use or whether it adds to the capital stock.

1.3 Gross Domestic Product at Constant Prices

If we wish to compare the *volume* of goods produced in different periods we must use the estimates of GDP at constant prices, the expenditure side of which is presented in the Statistical Appendix, table A-1. These constant price or real estimates show the value of GDP (expenditure-based) for each year in terms of the prices ruling in 1985. Similar estimates are available for the output-based total together with its main industrial components. The components of both these GDP estimates are derived almost entirely from movements in volume, the various quantities for each year being added together by means of the value weights obtaining for 1985. With the income figures, however, the only way of obtaining a constant price estimate is to take the value of GDP by income and deflate it by the implied price index (or 'deflator') for GDP. This index is simply the result of dividing GDP at current prices by GDP at constant prices (both on the expenditure basis). This means that for GDP as a whole there are three independent estimates of the constant-price total, all of them published.

There are often sizeable discrepancies between the three estimates of GDP at constant prices. In 1987, for example, GDP in constant prices was put by the expenditure estimate at 106.5% of the 1985 level, whereas the income and output estimates were 107.9 and 107.7 respectively. Since 1980 the largest spread between the three measures was 2.3% of GDP (in 1984) and the average difference was 1.2%. These discrepancies in the level of GDP also mean that the annual rate of change is not known unambiguously. The decline in GDP from 1979 to 1981, for example, was put at 2.7% by the expenditure-based estimate, but at 4.2% by the output estimate. An inspection of the annual changes in GDP since 1980 shows that, on average, the spread between the highest and lowest estimates of the change was 1.0%; in 1982–3 the spread was 2.1%.

Gross domestic product is an important entity in its own right and changes in its real amount are the best estimates available of changes in total UK production. Even so, it must be remembered that it leaves a good deal out of the picture by excluding practically all productive work which is not sold for money. The national income statistics neglect, for example, the activities of the housewife, the do-it-yourself enthusiast and the so-called 'black economy', even though they must add millions of hours to UK production of goods and services.[1] It is also important to recognize that GDP stands for the production of UK residents, not their expenditure. As an expenditure total it measures the spending of all persons, resident or foreign, on the goods and services produced by the residents of the UK. Thus if national welfare is conceived as spending by UK residents, it is incorrect to represent it by GDP. The total appropriate for this purpose is GDP *plus* imports *minus* exports. This total is referred to as total domestic expenditure, or 'absorption', and is equal to the UK's total use of resources. It is the sum of personal consumption, government consumption and gross investment.

2   ECONOMIC GROWTH AND FLUCTUATIONS
2.1   The Growth of the Economy

In 1937, the level of GDP at factor cost was £110 billion (at 1985 prices); by 1987 it had approximately trebled in size, to reach £327 billion – an average growth rate of 2.2% per annum. The population of the UK had grown from 47 million to 57 million, so that domestic output per head was about $2\frac{1}{2}$ times as high in 1987 as it had been 50 years earlier.

The growth of GDP over long periods of time must be contrasted with short-lived bursts of expansion due mainly to cyclical increases in the use

---

[1] On 11 April 1989, the House of Commons gave a first reading to a private member's bill demanding the inclusion of unpaid work by women in the estimates of GDP.

of existing resources. Between 1972 and 1973, for example, real GDP 'grew' by nearly 8% according to the average estimate. This was accompanied by a rise in employment of about 2.5%, by longer working hours, and by a more intensive use of existing plant and machinery. An increase in GDP of this order could not have been sustained over a long period without running up against the constraints set by the existing labour force and the level of capacity. It is best, therefore, to reserve the term 'economic growth' for long-term increases in the economy's ability to produce, or *productive potential*, which, at any one time, depends on the quantity and quality of the economy's factors of production, and the skills with which they are combined. The traditional way of measuring productive potential is by recording actual GDP for a period when the economy's resources are fully employed. This may be done using either a standard unemployment percentage or a standard vacancy rate. Unemployment, it is argued, represents the availability of unusual labour resources, whilst the number of vacancies indicates the difficulty of obtaining labour. Since the 1970s, the economy has become much more inflationary at given levels of unemployment than it used to be, and the levels of unemployment which were normal in the 1950s and 1960s have no longer been achieved. In table 1.2, therefore, the growth rate is measured between years of similar unemployment rates up to 1960, after which the benchmark years are chosen as years with similar vacancy rates. The vacancy statistics are incomplete and not quite ideal – see section 4.4 below – but they are probably more consistent over time than the unemployment statistics.

TABLE 1.2
Economic Growth, UK, 1900–87 (percentage increases per annum)

	GDP (output estimate)	GDP per person employed	Employed labour force	Capital (excluding dwellings)
1900–13	1.5	0.6	0.9	1.7
1922–38	2.3	1.2	1.1	1.7
1950–60	2.6	2.2	0.4	2.8
1960–69	2.8	2.5	0.3	4.3
1969–78	1.9	1.8	0.1	3.6
1978–87	2.0	2.0	0.0	2.2

Sources: 1950–87: *BB*, 1988 and earlier; 1900–38: C.H.Feinstein, *National Income, Expenditure and Output in the United Kingdom, 1855–1965* (Cambridge University Press, 1972).

The causes of long-term economic growth have been much discussed and debated. Growth must depend upon increases in the quantity and quality of the two main factors of production – labour and capital – and on the efficiency with which they are combined. Increases in the supply of labour come mainly from increases in the population of working age, including net migration, changes in the participation rate and in hours worked. The quality of labour must in large degree depend upon the facilities available for education and training, the opportunities taken of them, and the degree to which they match the changing demands for skills arising out of new technology and the structure of aggregate demand. The mobility of labour from job to job and from area to area is probably an important factor in economic growth in so far as it reflects the degree to which the labour force can adjust to economic change.

One obvious influence on the growth of labour productivity is the rate of increase in the nation's stock of capital, both in quantity and in quality. Some indications of the growth of the UK capital stock are given in table 1.2, where it can be seen that the rate of increase, like that of productivity, has tended to rise during the course of this century. The stock of capital, however, is extremely difficult to measure. This is partly because the figures of depreciation in the national accounts are based on data collected for tax purposes; and also because the type of capital equipment used changes drastically as a consequence of technical innovation.

The quality of the capital stock is, perhaps, even more important and even more difficult to measure. According to one widely accepted view, the quality of capital depends, by and large, upon its age structure. This view looks upon the capital stock as a series of vintages of gross investment, each new vintage containing machines of higher quality than the previous one. Scientific and technical progress are embodied in new machines, not old ones, so that the most recent equipment is likely to be the most efficient.

The other main influences on the rate of economic growth are the competitive climate, the facilities available for scientific and technological advance, and the propensity to save. When new investment depends partly on the level of interest rates, it must be feared that continuously high interest rates will inhibit the growth process. On the side of demand, both the average pressure of demand and the size of fluctuations deserve attention. It can certainly be argued that a very low average pressure of demand, such as we had during the 1930s, was inimical to innovation and investment. It hinders investment because capital equipment is under-utilized; and its continuation for any length of time will depress business expectations. High demand, on the other hand, will generally have the opposite effect. It may also encourage managers and workers to devise new and better ways of working with existing equipment, thereby making technical progress of a variety which is not embodied in new types of machine. This effect has sometimes been described as 'learning by doing', and fits in with the view that the scale of production problems that have to be solved is itself a stimulus to their solution. But high demand pressure may also work the other way. Easy profits and a sellers' market can diminish the incentive to innovate and lead to lazy attitudes to production. Extreme pressure of work can promote mental and physical exhaustion.[1]

---

[1] For a recent discussion, see C.H.Feinstein, 'Economic Growth since 1870: Britain's Performance in International Perspective', *OREP*, Vol. 4, No. 1 (1988).

2.2 Fluctuations Around the Growth Path

The long-term growth of the economy has been interrupted by periodic booms and cyclical collapses. During the nineteenth century these appeared to follow a fairly uniform cycle, with a peak-to-peak duration of seven to ten years, and a tendency for 'full employment' (roughly defined) to return at each cyclical peak. After the First World War this pattern ceased, and for nearly twenty years there were well over one million unemployed. Unemployment reached nearly 10% of the labour force in the downturn of 1926 and 17% (3.4 million) in 1932.

The period from the Second World War until the early 1970s was one of continuously high employment, with only the mildest fluctuations in GDP, employment and unemployment. The unemployment rate (UK, excluding school-leavers) never exceeded an annual figure of 2.4%, and, during peak periods of activity, was as little as 1 or 1½% of the employed labour force. During this period, declines in real GDP never exceeded 1.0%, and in most recessions GDP simply rose at a slower-than-average rate of increase. This period was also characterized by a much lower average rate of inflation than has been experienced since 1970.

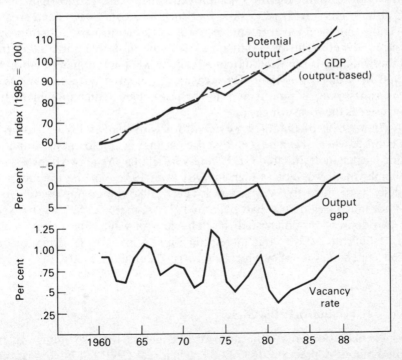

Figure 1.1   Actual and Potential Output, the Output Gap and Vacancies, UK, 1960–88

Since 1970 business recessions have become much more severe. There was a sharp downturn in 1973–75, and by 1977 unemployment had reached 5% of the labour force. The vacancy rate, which indicates the degree of labour shortage in the economy, was at an exceptionally high level in the boom of 1973. By 1979 the economy had recovered to about the same level of vacancies as in earlier periods of boom – see figure 1.1. After that, there was a major slump, with unemployment rising from 5% of the labour force in 1979 to 11% in 1985. But whilst unemployment remained extremely high throughout the 1980s, there was a gradual rise in the vacancy percentage, which by 1988 was almost back to its 1979 peak.

What was potential output? It is difficult to answer this question because of the conflicting course of unemployment and vacancies. Throughout the 1970s and 1980s, GDP could have been higher if the numbers unemployed had been brought down to the levels of the 1960s. But the vacancy figures indicate that there were shortages of labour, even at times when unemployment was very high. Thus the inference must be that for various reasons – lack of skills, difficulty in moving – the unemployed were unable to fill the available vacancies – see section 4.4. If potential output was measured, as it used to be, by reference to unemployment, its level in recent years would be much higher than the graph illustrated in figure 1.1. There would be a substantial output gap in 1988. But the implication would be that jobs could be found for the unemployed which were in the right places and of the right sort. It is possible that such jobs could have been created by central and local government – e.g. for work on infrastructure improvement, roads, etc. Thus it is difficult to estimate or define potential output without making a political statement about what is optimal. Figure 1.1 should be seen in this light. By measuring potential output in terms of the vacancy rate, it puts it at a lower level than if unemployment had been used as the measuring rod.

A comparison of the 1979–81 downturn with that of 1929–32 is given in table 1.3, where it can be seen that the declines in employment, manufacturing output and estimated GDP were very similar in the two depressions. Unemployment was not as high in 1981 as in 1932, but the number rose steadily in the next five years, and by early 1986 the unemployment rate was not much less than it had been in 1932. A major difference between the two depressions concerned the behaviour of wages and prices, which were falling in 1929–32 but increasing rapidly in 1979–81. Inflation has posed a dilemma for policy which was not present in the 1930s.

2.3   Expenditures in the Cycle

Business recessions occur because of declines in total spending. In the United States' depression of 1929–32, when real GNP fell by almost one-third, the mainspring of the recession was a decline in fixed investment which spread, through falling incomes, to personal consumption. The accompanying decline in US imports led to falling world trade and production, and thus to depression in the export industries of other countries.

In the United Kingdom in 1929–32, the decline in GDP was much smaller

TABLE 1.3

Output and Employment in Three Recessions (percentages)

	1929–32	*1973–5*	*1979–81*
Unemployment rate: peak year	8.0	2.7	4.8
trough year	17.0	3.9	9.5
Change in employment	−3.7	0.0	−5.5
Change in GDP (output estimate)	−4.8	−3.4	−4.2
Change in manufacturing production	−10.8	−8.1	−14.6
Change in prices per annum	−6.8	+22.0	+16.0

Sources: C.H.Feinstein, *National Income, Expenditure and Output in the United Kingdom, 1855–1965* (Cambridge University Press, 1972); *ET(AS)*, 1988; *BB*, 1988.

and largely confined to exports. These fell by 32%, which in absolute amount was enough to account for the whole of the decline in total final expenditure. There were mild declines in fixed investment and stockbuilding and offsetting increases in consumers' and government expenditure (see table 1.4).

TABLE 1.4

Expenditures in Three Recessions

	Level in 1929 (£bn at 1938 prices)	*Change 1929–32*	*Level in 1973* (£bn at 1985 prices)	*Change 1973–5*	*Level in 1979* (£bn at 1985 prices)	*Change 1979–81*
Consumers' expenditure	3.77	+0.07	179.9	−0.6	193.8	0.0
Government consumption	0.44	+0.03	62.5	+4.7	69.9	+1.3
Fixed investment	0.46	−0.06	55.8	−2.4	56.5	−8.1
Investment in stocks	0.03	−0.03	6.9	−10.3	3.3	−6.5
Exports of goods and services	0.99	−0.32	69.0	+3.0	88.8	−0.6
TFE	5.69	−0.32	375.4	−10.0	412.9	−12.6
GDP (expenditure)	4.22	−0.24	259.6	−3.6	282.3	−7.7

Sources: Feinstein, *op. cit.; BB*, 1988.

If the recession of 1929–32 was led by exports, those of 1973–5 and 1979–81 were more domestic in origin. The 1973–5 recession was primarily a stock recession, whilst in 1979–81 there was a large decline in fixed investment as well as in stockbuilding, together with a much smaller decline in exports.

Periods of recovery have usually been led by a revival of fixed investment. In 1975–79, the main stimuli came from exports and stockbuilding, and the same pattern was repeated between 1981 and 1983, with fixed investment not recovering until 1984. Real GDP regained its 1979 level in 1983. But the level of the workforce in employment did not recover until 1987, and unemployment, although falling, was still very much higher in 1989 than it had been ten years earlier.

3   DEMAND AND THE MULTIPLIER

The proximity of national output to its full-employment potential is determined by the level of total expenditure on goods and services, which, in the simplest terms, can be divided into two main categories: the 'autonomous' items, which are not affected by the current level of national income, and the 'dependent' items, which are related to current or to lagged income. In elementary accounts, the former category is represented as investment, and is said to be determined by business expectations of the rate of return, the rate of interest, and by the stock of unexploited technological potential. Consumption, on the other hand, is dependent on income itself, so that the line of causation runs from investment to income to consumption, with investment acting as the primary generator of movements in total output.

When this model is extended to the 'real world', it is necessary to add exports and government expenditure to the autonomous elements of demand, and to allow for imports and the factor cost adjustment as dependent items; investment in stocks is partly autonomous and partly dependent.

3.1   Consumers' Expenditure

Consumers' expenditure is the largest single element in aggregate demand. It accounts for nearly half of TFE (see table 1.1) and, after the removal of its import and indirect-tax content, for about the same fraction of GDP at factor cost. Consumption is one of the more stable elements of demand. It fell slightly in 1973–75, but held up well in the recession of 1979–81. Its total amount is so large in relation to GDP that quite small percentage variations in its level can have important effects on output and employment. An understanding of consumption behaviour, therefore, and an ability to predict it, are important objectives for economic analysis.

The starting point for the early studies of consumer behaviour was the well-known statement by Keynes:[1] 'The fundamental psychological law upon which we are entitled to depend with great confidence both *a priori* from our knowledge of human nature and from the detailed facts of experience, is that men are disposed, as a rule and on the average, to increase their consumption as their income increases, but not by as much as the increase in their income.' Keynes was suggesting that current income was the principal, although not the only, determinant of consumers' expenditure in the short run. The marginal propensity to consume (the ratio of additional consumption to additional income) was positive, fractional and reasonably stable.

Keynes' statement has sometimes been taken to mean that the aggregate consumption function can be expressed as a linear relationship with a positive intercept and slope (the MPC) of less than unity. Short-term relationships often obey this pattern, although they are not really satisfactory.

---

[1]   J.M.Keynes, *General Theory*, p. 96.

If, for example, annual figures of consumption for 1970–79 are related to real personal disposable income, the resulting regression equation is:

$$C = £33.3\text{bn} + 0.72Y \tag{1}$$

where C stands for consumers' expenditure and Y for personal disposable income in 1985 prices. The intercept is positive and the slope is well short of unity.[1] The equation implies that the APC must fall – and the savings ratio rise – as the level of income increases. But when these implications are tested using the equation to predict the APC in years outside the sample period – and when income levels were quite different – the results are not at all satisfactory:

	APC predicted by equation (1)	Actual APC	Error (%)
1955	1.02	0.96	6
1965	0.94	0.91	3
1975	0.89	0.88	1
1985	0.87	0.91	−4

In 1955 and 1965, when income was much lower than in the sample period, the APC is overpredicted, whereas in 1985, when income was higher, the equation underpredicts. It is clear, then, that the equation exaggerates the extent to which the APC varies with income; and it is also possible that it omits other factors which are also important in determining the level of consumption.

As a matter of history, the APC has fallen a little over the long period, but not as fast as would be predicted by equation (1). Real incomes per head doubled between the 1930s and the 1980s, and the savings ratio rose from about 5% to 10%:

	Savings Ratio (%)	APC
1920–29	1.5	0.985
1930–39	4.8	0.952
1950–59	3.7	0.963
1960–69	8.1	0.919
1970–79	11.0	0.890
1980–87	10.2	0.898

Source: Feinstein, op. cit.; *ET(AS)*, 1988; *BB*, 1988.

On a year-to-year basis, the savings ratio tends to move in cycles, although as figure 1.2 makes clear, the cyclical recovery after 1981 was exceptional, with the savings rate falling each year.[2] The normal procyclical behaviour of savings, which can be seen in the correlation with the vacancy rate for earlier years, may be interpreted as evidence for the life-cycle and permanent income hypotheses – both of which stress the dependence of saving and consumption on 'permanent' or expected lifetime income, rather than

---

[1]   The standard error of equation (1) is £1.3bn or 0.7% of the average level of consumption; $R^2 = 0.985$.
[2]   It should be noted that figures for the savings ratio are prone to substantial revision: that for 1976 was put at 14.6% in 1980, but is revised in *ET(AS)* 1989 to 12.1%.

current income. In support of these theories, it is claimed that when the economy is in recession, incomes are below permanent income, so that consumption will be high relative to measured income. This explanation would be more convincing if permanent income was a known quantity. But in the absence of that knowledge, there must be some doubt as to whether the causation does not lie with other cyclical variables, such as the interest rate or the rate of inflation. These are both correlated with the savings rate.[1]

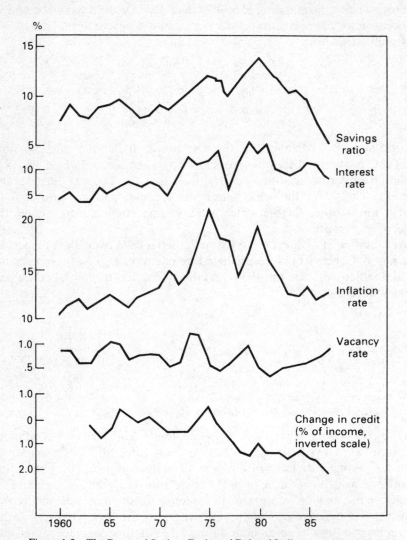

Figure 1.2   The Personal Savings Ratio and Related Indicators, UK, 1960–87

[1]   The correlation coefficient (*r*) between the savings rate and the variables in figure 1.2 are: interest rate (on Treasury bills) 0.73, inflation rate 0.71, vacancies as per cent of work force −0.20 and change in consumer credit as per cent of disposable income 0.07.

The case for including the rate of interest as an influence on saving is partly that it is a pecuniary incentive to save, and partly that high mortgage rates exert a squeeze on spendable incomes in much the same way as higher taxes. The other side of the coin is that the holders of building society deposits are better off, but their MPCs are likely to be low.

The inflation rate was first seen as a possible influence on saving in the 1970s, when peaks in the inflation and savings rates tended to coincide. The inference was drawn that inflation had eroded the purchasing power of liquid assets, with the consequence that people attempted to replenish their wealth by saving more. But the increased savings rate may also have arisen from the inclusion in personal income of the profits of unincorporated businesses. These profits are included gross of stock appreciation, which naturally tends to be high in periods of inflation. The effect is to raise personal sector income without any effect on consumption, and, although this is a consequence of inflation, it is not a wealth effect of the kind envisaged. It has also been pointed out that the personal sector's main non-liquid asset is house property, and this increased in value during the 1970s.[1] Finally, it should be borne in mind that the inflation rate is correlated with the level of interest rates, so that causation may have been indirect rather than direct – running from inflation to interest rates to saving, but not perhaps directly from inflation to saving.

The availability of credit is partly a cause and partly a consequence of consumer buying, so that it is difficult to interpret the inverse correlation with the savings rate shown in figure 1.2. But in recent years there has been so much aggressive selling of credit that it seems plausible to regard it as the principal cause of the fall in the savings ratio from 10.5% in 1984 to 5.4% in 1987 (and to 4.1% in 1988, according to the first estimates).

The salient influence on consumption and saving is undoubtedly income itself. It is not clear that *permanent* income, or expected lifetime income has quite the influence that is sometimes claimed for it. Much depends on the ability to borrow in the expectation of future income being higher than at present; and the supposition that saving is undertaken to provide for retirement (which is the main assumption of the life-cycle hypothesis) carries more conviction when applied to the well-to-do than to the poor. The evidence favours interest rates and credit as additional variables, but there must be doubts about the separate influence of inflation.[2]

In forecasting the level of consumption, the key magnitude is the *marginal*, rather than the average, propensity to consume. Here, the life-cycle

[1]   For a further treatment, see K.Cuthbertson, 'The Measurement and Behaviour of the UK Savings Ratio', *NIER*, February 1982. For more general discussions, see J.Thomas, 'The Early History of the Consumption Function' and A.Spanos, 'Early Empirical Findings on the Consumption Function, Stylized Facts or Fiction: A Retrospective View', *OEP*, January 1989, and R.L.Thomas, 'The Consumption Function', in D.Demery, N.W.Duck, M.T.Sumner, R.L.Thomas and W.N.Thompson, *Macroeconomics* (Longman, 1984).
[2]   The classic reference is F.Modigliani and R.Brumberg, 'Utility Analysis and the Consumption Function', in K.Kurihara (ed.), *Post-Keynesian Economics* (Allen and Unwin, 1955). See also R.Ferber, 'Research on Household Behaviour', *AER*, 52, 1962.

hypothesis gives its own theoretical insight. The hypothesis assumes that the object of saving is to provide for consumption during retirement. An individual of representative age (say 38) who receives an increase in his income of £1 per year will plan to save just enough to maintain a constant annual addition to his spending. If he or she expects to go on receiving the extra income until he retires at age 65 and if he also expects to live for a further 12 years after retirement (the life expectation of a 65-year-old man), then his extra £1 will be earned for a further 27 years but will be needed for spending over a period of 39 years. These two periods are the key to his MPC, which will be $27/39 = 0.69$, whilst his marginal propensity to save will be 0.31. The calculation assumes that he disregards the interest on his savings, that the increase in income had not been previously anticipated, and that he expects it to be a permanent addition to his income. It also assumes that he is not interested in leaving further bequests to his children, and that he is disposed to make calculations of the kind suggested. On these rather stringent assumptions it is possible to deduce that a 'representative' increase in aggregate income (i.e. one which is spread evenly across age groups) might involve an MPC in the region of 0.7, which is, of course, well below the APC.

It is difficult to know whether the life-cycle hypothesis can be accepted at face value, given the large number of individuals who appear to spend all that they have and who rely on the state pension for retirement. It may apply more closely to the well-off in late middle age than it does to the mass of consumers. The correspondence between the implied MPC and regression estimates which put the figure close to 0.7 (as in the example above) is probably a coincidence. In general, it seems clear that factors such as interest rates and the availability of consumer credit have their part to play. But the savings rate varies so little between one year and the next that it is probably unwise to expect an MPC which is very different from the APC. This is why in estimating the multiplier in section 3.5 below the assumed MPC is 0.9.

3.2   Fixed Investment

Fixed investment or gross domestic fixed capital formation consists of business investment in plant and machinery, and housebuilding in both the public and private sectors of the economy. Its breakdown by industry is shown in table 1.5, where it can be seen that investment by the service industries is much larger than in manufacturing. Manufacturing investment, however, is the most volatile element in the total. In the recession of 1979–81, for example, manufacturing investment fell in real terms by 35% compared with a total decline in private fixed investment of 10%.

The explanation of investment is not without difficulties. New capital stock is purchased and old stock replaced in the expectation of profits in the future. It is not difficult to show formally that an investment project

TABLE 1.5

Gross Domestic Fixed Capital Formation, UK, 1987 (£bn)

	Private sector	*Public sector*	*Total*
Dwellings	12.4	2.8	15.2
Manufacturing	9.5	0.3	9.9
Energy and water supply	3.7	2.6	6.3
Distribution, hotels, catering, repairs	7.1	0.0	7.1
Banking, finance, insurance, business services, leasing	12.1	0.5	12.7
Other	14.5	5.2	19.6
Total	59.3	11.5	70.8

Source: BB, 1988, p. 133: current prices. Detail may not add to totals because of rounding.

is profitable if its marginal efficiency exceeds the rate of interest, or if its present value exceeds zero. But these calculations have to be based upon *forecasts* of revenues and costs which extend for years, even decades, into the future. When so much depends upon vulnerable and uncertain guesses about the future it must be expected that investment expenditure will not be as readily explicable as consumption.

Two of the models which are often advanced to explain investment behaviour make their own special assumptions about expected future income. The acceleration principle is sometimes justified on the assumption that the future growth of income will be equal to the past rate of growth, and on this basis it is suggested that investment is proportional to the change in income:

$$I = a\Delta Y$$

where I is investment, ΔY the change in income and a is a constant coefficient. A related model is the capital stock adjustment principle which explains investment as an attempt to adjust the capital stock from its actual level to a desired level based on the expected level of output. It also assumes that there is a fixed relationship between output and the amount of capital equipment needed to produce it. The model can be expressed by the equation:

$$I = aY - K$$

where K is the actual level of the capital stock, and a is the assumed constant capital–output ratio.[1] Neither of these models says anything explicit about costs or interest rates, and although they are right to focus on income

---

[1] Because K^*, the desired capital stock, is equal to aY^* where Y^* is expected income. Hence $I = K^* - K = aY^* - K$. And if Y^* is assumed to equal current income, Y, then $I = aY - K$. It is also possible to attach a coefficient to K on the assumption that investment demand in a single period is a constant fraction of $K^* - K$, i.e. $I = b(K^* - K) = abY^* - bK$. Replacement investment may also be allowed for on the assumption that it is proportional to income.

expectations, they are still very crude. Another theory altogether is the
view that investment can be predicted by the level of business profits,
the idea being that firms simply spend what they can afford.

Whatever the theoretical merits of these models it is possible to assemble
data that relate to them, and this is done in figure 1.3, where the top
graph is manufacturing investment in constant prices. The figure illustrates
that manufacturing investment is indeed correlated with the change in
income, where this is taken as the three-year change in real GDP at factor
cost up to the previous year. (The three-year change in manufacturing
output would have given a similarly good correlation.) Figure 1.3 also shows
the relationships between investment and the level of manufacturers' real
profits. What we have done here is to estimate a price deflator for profits
by dividing manufacturing investment in current prices by manufacturing
investment in constant (1985) prices. Profits are gross profits before adjustment for stock appreciation. A correlation also exists for the capital–output
ratio, where the ratio shown on the graph is the capital stock at the end
of the previous year divided by manufacturing output in that year (both
at 1985 prices). Finally, the graph shows the long-term interest rate on
government securities, and for this there is virtually no correlation at all.[1]

The question now arises as to whether we can interpret any of these
correlations as causal. The correlation with the change in income, might
seem to give a strong case for the acceleration principle. But the correlation
may have more to do with the phasing of the business cycle than with
the causation of investment. If peaks in the cycle occur every four or five
years because of investment booms, then the fastest changes in GDP will
occur in the two or three years between the trough and peak of the cycle.
Peaks in investment and the rate of change of GDP are bound to be correlated.

In the case of the profits hypothesis, a similar argument applies. Profits
will be high when sales are high, and this will happen when autonomous
spending is at its peak. Manufacturing investment is, of course, an important
element in autonomous spending, and when it reaches a peak income will
tend to be high and so will profits. So we are now arguing that it is not
profits which cause investment, but investment which causes profits. But
there *could* be causation in both directions.

The correlation with the lagged capital stock is slightly better than the
other two. It could be simply a mechanical result of low investment leading
to low economic activity and, therefore, to a high ratio of capital to output.
The fact that we have incorporated a lag in the correlation does not completely remove this objection, since periods of low and high economic
activity tend to occur for several years at a time. There are other objections
too, namely that the stock-adjustment principle makes the naive assumptions

---

[1] The correlation coefficient (r) between investment and the variables in figure 1.3 are:
three-year change in GDP 0.65, profits 0.76, capital output ratio −0.79, long-term interest
rate −0.11.

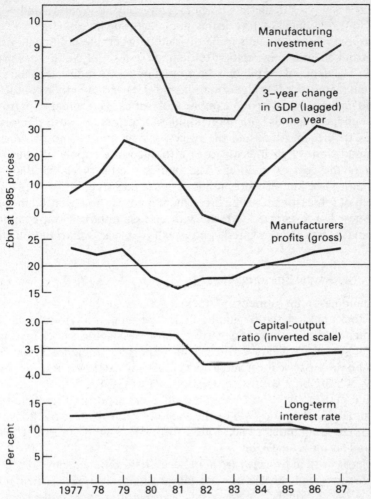

Figure 1.3   Manufacturing Investment and Related Indicators, UK, 1977–87

that next year's sales will be equal to this year's and that one year's sales are the relevant consideration in plant and machinery designed to last for many years.

To the question of what actually caused manufacturing investment over the period shown, we can give only a tentative answer. We doubt whether the correlation with ΔY gives any real credence to the acceleration principle. We think there is a bit of truth in both the profits and the capital–stock adjustment models, although it would not be surprising if the correlations overstated the importance of the variables. Finally, we believe on *a priori* grounds that interest rates are an influence even though there is not much correlation. The main econometric models of the UK have used both profits and interest rate variables to explain investment, besides making some use of the capital stock adjustment and acceleration principles. But at the end of the day it is still uncertain whether anybody has a robust and reliable model for explaining and forecasting manufacturing investment.

Housing investment needs to be divided between the public and private sectors and examined in relation to demand and supply influences in both sectors. The demand for public-sector building comes indirectly from population characteristics (family formation and size) and directly from the policies and financial position of the public authorities. The demand for private-sector building depends both upon population factors, the costs of mortgage credit, expected income, and the prices of new houses and of substitute accommodation. High interest rates also affect the supply of housing by adding to the cost of building. The building industry claims that a 1% rise in mortgage interest rates reduces house construction by 6–7%.[1] The problem of forecasting housing investment is eased, however, by the statistics of new houses started, which, with an assumption about completion times, makes it possible to predict housing for at least a short period ahead.

3.3   Stocks and Stockbuilding

Stockbuilding or investment in stocks is a change in a level – the level of all stocks held at the beginning of the period. In any one year, stock investment can be positive or negative, whilst the change in stock investment between successive years can exert an important influence upon GDP. The increase in stock investment in 1975–7, for example, and the decline in 1979–80 were both equivalent to about 3% of GDP.

At the end of 1987 the total value of stocks held in all industries was approximately £96bn or 27% of the value of GDP in a year. Stocks held by manufacturing industry accounted for nearly £44bn, and by wholesale and retail business for £32bn.[2]

Stocks of work in progress are held because they are a technical necessity of production, whilst stocks of materials and finished goods are held mainly out of a precautionary motive. They are required as a 'buffer' between deliveries and production; or, more precisely, because firms realize that they cannot expect an exact correspondence between the amount of materials delivered each day and the amount taken into production, or between completed production and deliveries to customers.

For these reasons it seems plausible to assume that firms carry in their minds the notion of a certain optimum ratio between stocks and output. If stocks fall below the optimum ratio, they will need to be replenished; if they rise above it, they will be run down. The reasoning here is the same as that of the stock-adjustment principle which we have already mentioned in connection with fixed investment. The principle holds quite well for some periods, and is illustrated in figure 1.4. It can be seen that peaks in stock investment coincided with low levels of the stock–GDP ratio until

---

[1]   *Financial Times*, 2 March 1989.
[2]   *BB*, 1988, table 14.1.

about 1983, after which stock investment has been low despite a falling stock–output ratio.[1] This was partly due to the ending of stock relief in the budget of 1984.

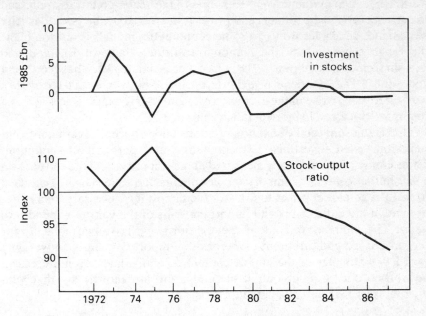

Figure 1.4   Investment in Stocks and the Stock–GDP Ratio, UK, 1972–87

The stock-adjustment principle is only the beginning of an explanation of investment in stocks. It makes no allowance for interest rates or price expectations, both of which are relevant to the preferred stock–output ratio. Nor can it account for unplanned movements in stocks, which for finished goods will occur when sales deviate from their expected levels.

3.4   Government Consumption, Exports, Imports and Indirect Taxes

Of the two remaining components of TFE, government consumption is primarily determined by the social and political objectives of the central government and local authorities, and partly by macroeconomic and financial policy. Until 1979, it was unusual for government spending to be affected by macroeconomic policy, the preferred instrument of control being changes in tax rates. But the advent of financial targets for the PSBR, and of expenditure control by cash limits, were a change of some significance. Between 1979 and 1987 the rise in government consumption has been only about 1% per annum.

Exports of goods and services are determined by two principal factors:

---

[1]   The correlation (*r*) is −0.63 for 1972–83, but only −0.24 for 1972–87.

by the level of overseas income and by export prices, measured in terms of foreign currency. The latter, in turn, are influenced by the exchange rate for sterling. UK exports correlate quite closely with the volume of world trade in manufactures, and exports to particular countries are linked to national GNP. The influence of prices is measured by the price elasticity of demand, which according to some econometric models is not too high: the range suggested by the National Institute, Bank of England and Treasury models is −0.6 to −0.8, but other estimates vary between −0.4 and −2.8.[1] The 3% drop in exports during 1980 was associated with a particularly sharp rise in the exchange rate and in UK export prices. Export trends are discussed in more detail in chapter 3.

TFE is the sum total of exports of goods and services, government consumption, fixed investment, stockbuilding and personal consumption. These elements are normally measured at market prices and they all contain a substantial content of imported components and materials. To proceed from TFE at market prices to GDP at factor cost it is necessary, therefore, to remove the indirect-tax and import contents of the various expenditure items. The indirect-tax content (net of subsidies) is known annually for the various expenditure items, whereas the import content is known only for TFE. Estimates of the import content for individual expenditures can be worked out by input–output methods, and are shown, together with their indirect-tax contents, in table 1.6 below.

TABLE 1.6

Domestic Output Content of Total Final Expenditure at Market Prices

	Consumers' expenditure	Government consumption	Gross domestic fixed investment	Exports of goods and services	Total final expenditure
	Percentage of market price totals:				
Indirect taxes (less subsidies)	18	6	7	4	12
Imports of goods and services	21	13	34	24	22
Domestic output content	61	81	59	72	66

Sources: BB, 1988, table 1.2 and p. 29.

The main determinants of imports are the level of GDP and competitive factors, such as price, quality and delivery dates. It is probably this last group which is responsible for the upward trend (see chapter 3) in the ratio of imports of goods and services (at constant 1985 prices) to TFE:

1950–54	14.0%
1955–59	14.7%

[1] See S. Brooks, 'Systematic Econometric Comparisons: Exports of Manufactured Goods', *NIER*, August 1981, p. 70, and A. P. Thirlwall, *Balance of Payments Theory and the United Kingdom Experience* (London 1980), pp. 204, 210–11, 230–1, 237–8.

1960–64	15.6%
1965–69	16.6%
1970–74	19.0%
1975–79	19.4%
1980–84	20.6%
1985–87	22.5%

These are average relationships. The marginal import content of TFE is probably higher. Between 1982–4 and 1985–7, for example, imports rose by £54.4bn (in 1985 prices) compared with a rise in TFE of £147.6bn. This suggests a marginal propensity to import with respect to TFE of about 0.34. Strictly speaking, this estimate presupposes that there were no other influences such as relative price changes affecting imports during the period. But it is probably a better guide to the influence of expenditure changes than the average relationship.

3.5 Personal Income and the Multiplier

Any increase in GDP will normally give rise to a multiplier process. The initial rise in income leads to higher consumption, and thus to higher GDP. Successive rounds of higher income and consumption will lead to the eventual establishment of an 'equilibrium' level of GDP, this being the level which GDP finally settles at. The multiplier process is the succession of income changes, whilst the 'multiplier' itself is defined as the ratio of the total or cumulative increase in GDP to its initial or 'first-round' increase.

In elementary models, the multiplier may be found quite simply because no distinctions are made between GDP and personal income, and because taxation, undistributed profits and the import contents of expenditure are ignored. On these lines, it can be seen that an initial increase in GDP of 100 units, combined with a marginal propensity to consume of, say, 0.5, will lead to an eventual increase in GDP of 200 units. This is because the initial rise in GDP will cause personal incomes to rise by the same amount, so that consumption will then increase (after a time-lag) by 50 units. This, in turn, raises personal incomes in the consumer-goods industries by 50 units so that consumption in the third round of the multiplier will increase by 25 units. Each increment of income leads to a rise in consumption half as large again, so that the sequence of period-to-period additions to GDP will be:

$$100, 50, 25, 12.5, 6.25, 3.125, \ldots \text{etc.}$$

It is not difficult to see that if all the terms are added together they sum to 200, which is the equilibrium rise in GDP. And since this is twice the original increase, the multiplier is 2. This value may also be found from the formula:

$$\frac{\Delta Y}{\Delta I} = \frac{1}{1 - \text{MPC}} = \frac{1}{1 - 0.5} = 2$$

where ΔY is the final increase in GDP and ΔI the initial increase.[1]

The multiplier for the UK follows the same principles as the simple model. But its calculation is complicated by a number of factors, one of which is the distinction which must be drawn between GDP and personal income. This may be illustrated by a direct comparison for 1987:

GDP (£352.2bn)	equals	Income from employment and self-employment (£259.3bn)	plus	Rent, total profits and trading surpluses, and imputed charge for capital consumption (£96.8bn)	minus	Stock appreciation (£4.9bn)
Personal income (£347.9bn)	equals	Income from employment and self-employment (£259.3bn)	plus	Personal receipts of rent, dividends and interest (£33.9bn)	plus	Transfer incomes (£54.8bn)

The main point here is that personal income and GDP are similar in total, but different in composition. Their main common element is employment income. But personal income includes a large transfer element – mainly pensions and social security benefits – which do not figure in GDP because they are not payments for production. Personal income from rent and profit is only a small part of total domestic rent and profit.

To arrive at an estimate of the UK multiplier we may begin by assuming an initial increase in GDP of £100m. This will be the domestic output content of a larger increase in TFE at market prices, the difference being due to the import and indirect-tax contents of the expenditure. The coefficients in table 1.6, for example, suggest that an increase in government expenditure of £123m would be needed to generate a rise in GDP of £100m.

A series of assumptions must now be made as to the size of various 'withdrawals' or leakages between the first and second round increases in GDP. The first stage in the calculation concerns the likely increase in personal income. This will depend on the way in which new GDP is divided between employment incomes and profits, on how much of the latter is distributed to the personal sector as dividend income, and also on how much transfer incomes decline as a result of lower unemployment and other national social security benefits. It can be assumed that the increase in GDP is divided between employment income and profits in its usual ratio

---

[1]   The formula assumes that ΔI is a sustained increase in the level of investment expenditure. An unsustained or 'one shot' injection of new investment would lead only to a temporary rise in GDP.

about 4:1. Thus £80m will go directly into personal income in the form of income from employment, and £20m to profits. Most of the rise in profits, however, will find its way into undistributed profits (say £7m) and corporate taxes (£7m), so that only £6m finds its way into personal incomes. But we also have to allow for a reduction in transfer incomes arising from lower unemployment benefits, and this would be of the order of £4m.[1]

Thus the total increase in personal income will be £80 + 6 − 4 = £82 million, which gives us the first in a series of coefficients needed to derive the multiplier (see table 1.7).

The remaining stages of the calculation involve the marginal rate of direct taxation (including national insurance and pension contributions), the marginal propensity to consume, and the marginal indirect tax and import contents of consumption. Once these are allowed for, it is possible to arrive at the second round increase in GDP, which is the domestically produced element of the rise in consumption.

TABLE 1.7
Stages in the Multiplier Estimate

	£m	Assumed marginal relationships
1st-round increase in GDP	100	
Increase in personal income	82	$b_1 = 0.82$
Increase in personal disposable income	56	$b_2 = 0.68$
Increase (after a time-lag) in consumers' expenditure at market prices	50	$b_3 = 0.9$
Increase in consumers' expenditure at factor cost	41	$b_4 = 0.82$
Increase in domestically produced consumption at factor cost (equals 2nd-round increase in GDP)	25	$b_5 = 0.61$

The marginal rate of taxation for standard rate taxpayers is 25%, but national insurance contributions add a further amount, so that the total leakage comes to about 32% for people on average incomes;[2] and it is this rate which is assumed to hold for an across-the-board rise in personal income. The marginal propensity to consume can be put at 0.9, as suggested in section 3.1; and the marginal rate of indirect tax on consumer goods and services can be taken as equal to the average rate of 0.18 − as given in table 1.6. Finally, the marginal import content of consumption (at market prices) can be estimated at 0.32 (this being the average rate times a factor of 1.5 which is the ratio of the estimated marginal import content of TFE to the average content).

The upshot of the calculation is that the second-round increase in GDP is only £25m, or 0.25 times the initial increase. It follows that the third,

---

[1]   Derived by assuming that every 1% rise in GDP leads to a 0.5% increase in employment, and from official estimates of the cost of unemployment benefit. See *Treasury Economic Progress Report*, February 1981.
[2]   See the tax and insurance rates reported in *The Guardian*, 15 March 1989, p. 1.

fourth and later increases will all be 0.25 times the previous rise, so that the sequence of period-to-period changes in GDP will be as follows:

$$£100, 25, 6.25, 1.6, 0.4, 0.1 \ldots 0 \text{ million}$$

This series sums to a cumulative increase of £133m, so that the multiplier is 1.33. Its value may also be found from the expression:

$$\frac{1}{1 - 0.25} = 1.33$$

where 0.25 can be described as the marginal propensity to purchase new domestic output. It represents the five coefficients b_1, b_2, b_3, b_4 and b_5 all multiplied together.[1]

It should be noted that we have defined the multiplier as the ratio of the eventual increase in GDP to the initial increase in GDP, and not to the initial increase in market price expenditure. This is in order to keep the numerator and denominator both in terms of domestic output. The multiplier so defined applies much more directly to employment than the ratio of the change in GDP at factor cost to a change in market price expenditure.[2]

These calculations are based on the usual multiplier assumptions that there are unused resources of capital and labour, and that interest rates are held constant through a policy of monetary accommodation. The multiplier estimate is not meant to be precise, but is seen as indicating the right general order of magnitude. In practice, there are other effects of an increase in GDP besides the multiplier which also have to be taken into account. The most basic of these is the effect of higher income on stockbuilding. Any increase in demand will be met initially from stock, so that there will be some unplanned stock decline at the start of the process, and this may be reversed later as production is stepped up to replenish stocks and to meet the higher level of demand.[3]

The value of the multiplier is also affected by variable exchange rates. Rising imports lead to a lower exchange rate and hence to higher demand for UK exports which, in turn, generate incomes and consumption. The effect on the exchange rate, however, can be prevented by a rise in interest rates.

The multiplier calculation above can be used to estimate the effect on GDP of a £1bn increase in government expenditure, and the results com-

---

[1] Thus $0.25 = \frac{82}{100} \cdot \frac{56}{82} \cdot \frac{50}{56} \cdot \frac{41}{50} \cdot \frac{25}{41} = b_1 b_2 b_3 b_4 b_5$ and the multiplier is $\frac{1}{1 - b_1 b_2 b_3 b_4 b_5}$.

[2] This discussion has followed an early estimate of the multiplier in W.A.Hopkin and W.A.H.Godley, 'An Analysis of Tax Changes', *NIER*, May 1965, the main difference being the estimate of the marginal import content of consumption.

[3] In some cases there may be oscillations in GDP. On this the classic reference is L.A. Metzler, 'The Nature and Stability of Inventory Cycles' in R.A.Gordon and L.R.Klein (eds.), *Readings in Business Cycles* (Allen and Unwin, 1966).

pared with those given by recent versions of large econometric models. On the reasoning given, a £1bn rise in government expenditure at market prices will involve an indirect tax and import content of at least £0.19bn (see table 1.6), with the consequence that the initial rise in GDP at factor cost will be £0.81bn. The multiplied effect will be this amount times 1.33, which is £1.08bn – or 0.23% of 1988 GDP at current prices. The main lag in the process is between the increases in personal incomes and consumption, and is likely to be fairly short. Thus most of the effect can be assumed to come through within six months of the initial rise in spending. The comparison with the main econometric models is as follows:

Change in GDP, per cent, arising from a £1bn increase in government expenditure:

	1st year	2nd year
Multiplier calculation above	0.23	0.23
Treasury model	0.24	0.24
London Business School	0.23	0.32
Bank of England	0.22	0.26
National Institute	0.36	0.37

The rough calculation above compares quite closely with the results of four large-scale econometric models. But the econometric models are able to allow for feedbacks from the exchange rate and exports as well as for stock effects, so that the results are not wholly comparable. The large difference between the National Institute and Treasury models is somewhat surprising.[1]

3.6 The Effects of Tax and Interest Rate Changes

The multiplier calculations may also be used to estimate the effects on the economy of changes in taxation. The effect of a change in income tax may be illustrated by reference to a reduction of 1p in the basic rate. This is estimated by the Treasury to reduce revenue by £1,725m.[2] Personal disposable income would be raised by an equal amount, so that the *initial*, or multiplicand, effect upon GDP can be found using the coefficients estimated in table 1.7:

	£m
change in tax revenue	−1,725
increase in personal disposable income	+1,725
increase in consumers' expenditure at market prices	+1,553
increase in consumers' expenditure at factor cost	+1,273
initial increase in GDP	+777
multiplied increase in GDP	+1,033

The initial increase in GDP of £1,273m is simply the change in tax revenue multiplied by the marginal propensity to consume (b_3 in table 1.7), along with the coefficients b_4 and b_5 which remove the indirect-tax and import

---

[1]   See P.G.Fisher, S.K.Tanna, D.S.Turner, K.F.Wallis and J.D.Whitley, 'Comparative Properties of Models of the UK Economy', *NIER*, August 1988.
[2]   Treasury, *Autumn Statement*, November 1988.

contents of the increase in consumers' expenditure. The multiplier effect raises this by 1.33 to a figure which, with current price GDP at an estimated £500bn (in 1989), is equivalent to a gain in total output of approximately 0.21%. This is the deviation in GDP from what it would have been in the absence of the tax reduction.

Changes in indirect taxation affect consumption by altering prices and the level of real personal disposable income. The effects of a change in VAT, for example, can be estimated approximately provided we know the effect on tax revenue. If taxes are reduced, the fall in revenue as a proportion of consumers' expenditure is equal to the proportionate change in prices. The latter leads to an increase in real personal disposable income, from which the effects on consumption and GDP may be estimated.[1] For a 1% fall in VAT, the Treasury estimates that revenue declines by £1,830 million.[2] Real personal disposable income will increase by this amount times the ratio of disposable income to consumption (i.e. the reciprocal of the APC). This leads to changes in consumption and GDP which can be found from coefficients already given for the multiplier:

	£m
change in tax revenue	−1,830
increase in real personal disposable income	+1,926
increase in real consumers' expenditure at market prices	+1,733
increase in real consumers' expenditure at factor cost	+1,421
initial increase in GDP	+867
multiplied increase in GDP	+1,153

Here the effect of a 1% cut in VAT is equivalent to about 0.2% of GDP.

When discussing the effects of tax reduction it is important to remember that all changes in the budget balance have to be financed either by borrowing from the public or by increasing the money supply (or by some mixture of the two). The effects described above must, strictly speaking, assume that the method of financing is such that the money supply is increased sufficiently to prevent any increase in the rate of interest. (This means that the results relate not to fiscal policy *per se* but to fiscal policy accompanied by this particular financing mix.) If fiscal changes are allowed to give rise to an increase in the rate of interest, as they would if entirely financed by borrowing, then some expenditures – those sensitive to interest rates like investment and purchases of consumer durables – will be reduced (or 'crowded out').

The effects of *monetary policy* have in the past been the subject of a good deal of scepticism, although on purely *a priori* grounds it is difficult to see how higher interest rates can fail to have some effect on both invest-

---

[1]   In terms of algebra we can denote the revenue change as ΔT, so that the change in consumer prices is $\Delta T/C$, where C is current consumption. The proportionate change in real disposable income, $\Delta Y/Y$, is equal to $-\Delta T/C$, and the absolute change, ΔY, is equal to $\dfrac{-Y}{C}\cdot\Delta T$.

[2]   *Op. cit.*

ment demand and consumer durables. The effects are certainly more difficult to estimate than those of tax changes. The National Institute, however,
claims to have estimated substantial effects from changes in interest rates,
an increase of 2% giving rise to the following effects on expenditures and
employment:

	After 4 qtrs. (change %)	After 8 qtrs.[1] (change %)
Consumption	−0.8	−1.0
Fixed investment	−2.3	−3.0
Stockholding (% of GDP)	−0.2	−0.1
Imports	−1.5	−2.1
GDP	−0.5	−0.7
Employment	−0.3	−0.5

These effects include the multiplier and other feedbacks.

3.7   Economic Forecasts

The analysis of movements in demand leads on naturally to the question
of how GDP may be predicted over short periods of time. The first economic
forecasts were developed by the Treasury in the late 1940s, and were used
as an aid to demand management. Indications of their content were sometimes revealed in Budget speeches. Since 1968, they have been published
and, with the Industry Act of 1975, the Treasury has been obliged to publish
them twice yearly in the Autumn Statement and the Financial Statement
and Budget Report (FSBR). The published forecasts extend about 15
months ahead; that for March 1989, for example, goes forward to the
first half of 1990.

The first problem encountered in constructing a forecast is that of establishing GDP estimates for the period extending from the last known figures
to the month in which the forecast is assembled. A forecast made in February, for example, has to be made with the benefit of quarterly GDP figures
which do not go beyond September of the previous year. A GDP estimate
has to be assembled for the October–December quarter on the basis of
monthly information which includes exports, imports, retail sales, industrial
production and employment. Difficulties can arise because of various gaps
in coverage, and because different indicators sometimes tell conflicting
stories, as, for example, when the employment and industrial production
figures move in different directions.

Once the base period is established, the forecast proper (i.e. the part
relating to the future) can be started. The methods by which this is done
need not be described in detail. But for six months to a year ahead the
task is made easier by the presence of a number of forward indicators
which provide fairly direct information on the prospects for particular sec-

---

[1]   *NIER*, August 1988, pp. 20–1. For an earlier discussion, see D. Savage, 'The Channels
of Monetary Influence: A Survey of the Empirical Evidence', *NIER*, December 1980.

tors of demand. The CBI, for example, conducts regular inquiries into whether its members intend to invest more or less in the next twelve months than in the previous period. The Department of Industry has its own inquiry, in which business is asked to estimate the percentage change in prospective investment. There are new order series for engineering, machine tools and shipbuilding, which provide a forward view of production (for investment or export) in these industries. There are also figures for new orders received by contractors for private construction work, whilst in the field of housing investment figures are collected for orders received by contractors, for new houses started, and Building Society commitments and advances on new dwellings.[1] Government current expenditure and the government component of fixed investment can be predicted from information provided by government departments and the nationalized industries. Direct information, therefore, covers a fairly significant proportion of the autonomous element in total demand, and can be processed to provide forecasts for 6 to 12 months ahead. Some help towards the personal income and consumption forecasts is available from the record of recent wage settlements, whilst government forecasters will also have estimates of the pay and employment of public employees.

For longer-term forecasts, and for the more obviously endogenous components of GDP, the forecaster needs to have an integrated model, in which the relationships are either estimated econometrically or arrived at in some systematic way. The Treasury has a very large econometric model at its disposal, in which there are more than 1,000 equations. At the risk of simplification, this may be described as a highly complex and disaggregated multiplier model, with accelerator relationships for the main investment items, and with exports linked to world production and relative prices. The model includes links between wages, prices and the exchange rate, and it also makes some use of interest rates as a determinant of investment. Imports are determined by GDP and competitive factors.[2]

The Treasury's model is in a constant state of revision, if only because there are many different ways of formulating consumption and investment functions, and it is not an easy matter to judge which of them is best. Thus, although the model is in constant use, it may be assumed that parts of it will be questioned by those responsible for getting the forecast right. The model, therefore, does not dictate the forecast to the exclusion of all argument and discussion, and there is plenty of room for judgement. There are often events which a model is not able to handle (strikes and fuel shortages, for example) and which necessitate judgemental estimation of their effects upon economic activity.

The main upshot of the government forecasting work is a table in considerable detail of the course of GDP and its components, quarter by

[1]   These figures are all published in *Economic Trends*.
[2]   See T. Burns, 'The Interpretation and Use of Economic Predictions', *Proceedings of the Royal Society*, Series A, 407, 103–125 (1986).

quarter, over a period of two to three years. The published version is less detailed and provides estimates by half-years.

The accuracy of forecasts is a matter of some interest to policy-makers since they are still used to guide decisions on monetary policy, taxation and public expenditure.[1] Their accuracy is also an important test of the methods and hypotheses which lie behind them. Table 1.8 gives the main Treasury forecasts (published at budget time) for GDP, consumption and fixed investment since 1979. The horizon chosen is the period from the second half of the previous year to the second half of the current year; thus, for the case of the 1988 forecast, the period runs from the second half of 1987 to the second half of 1988.

As the table shows, GDP forecasts have achieved an average level of accuracy of a little over 1%, and with some tendency to under-predict. The GDP forecast for 1988 received a good deal of criticism chiefly because, in keeping with this tendency it under-predicted the growth of demand by about $1\frac{1}{2}$% during a period when the rate of inflation was increasing and there was a large balance of payments deficit. But as the table shows, the 1988 forecast was not the worst forecast of the last ten years.

The errors in the forecasts of component expenditures tend to be larger than those for GDP itself. The Treasury publishes average errors for the calendar year forecasts (e.g. 1988 over 1987), and these show the mean absolute errors for the most recent ten-year period to be 1% for GDP, consumption and government expenditure, 2% for exports, $2\frac{1}{2}$% for imports and 3% for fixed investment; the average error in forecasting the change in stock investment is put at $\frac{1}{2}$% of GDP.[2]

4 INFLATION
4.1 Meaning and Measurement

Inflation is defined variously as *any* increase in the general level of prices or as any *sustained* increase. In this chapter we shall use the wider definition since it enables us to include short-lived increases in the general price level, such as those of 1920, 1940 and 1951–2, within the sphere of discussion.

In measuring the rate of inflation we have a choice of index numbers. The appropriate index of the prices charged for all goods produced in the UK economy is the implied deflator for total final expenditure, so called because it is obtained by dividing the value of TFE at current prices by TFE at constant (1985) prices. The TFE deflator includes export prices. If an index is required to measure the prices of goods purchased by UK residents, the best general measure is the implied deflator for total domestic expenditure, since this is an average of the prices paid for consumption and investment goods, both privately and publicly purchased. Yet another implied index is the GDP deflator, which is a price index for value added

---

[1]   Burns, *op. cit.*, p. 117.
[2]   *FSBR*, 1989–90, p. 38.

TABLE 1.8

Treasury Forecasts, 1979–89 (% changes to 2nd half-year from 2nd half of previous year)

	GDP			Consumption			Fixed Investment		
	Forecast	Actual	Error (F–A)	Forecast	Actual	Error (F–A)	Forecast	Actual	Error (F–A)
1979	−0.5	2.4	−2.9	1.2	2.9	−1.7	−0.5	6.1	−6.6
1980	−3.1	−4.2	1.1	1.0	−0.2	1.3	−5.0	−9.3	4.3
1981	−0.2	.9	−1.1	−0.8	.4	−1.2	−1.0	−6.9	5.8
1982	−1.5	1.7	−0.2	0.7	2.2	−1.5	4.1	8.1	−4.0
1983	4.2	2.5	−1.7	2.0	4.4	−2.4	3.1	3.5	−0.4
1984	3.5	1.2	2.3	3.1	1.0	2.1	6.6	8.0	−1.4
1985	3.5	3.8	−0.3	3.4	4.5	−1.1	4.1	1.5	2.6
1986	3.3	3.1	.2	3.8	5.2	−1.4	5.7	4.6	1.2
1987	2.8	4.8	−2.0	3.3	5.9	−2.6	4.7	6.1	−1.4
1988	2.3	3.8	−1.5	2.9	5.9	−3.0	5.7	9.9	−4.2
1989		2.0			2.2			4.3	
Mean absolute error			1.3			1.8			3.2
Bias (mean algebraic error)			−0.6			−1.1			−0.4

Source: *FSBRs*, 1979–80 to 1989–90; *ET(AS)*, 1989.

in the UK, i.e. wages and profits per unit of output. This index leaves out the effect of import prices and indirect taxes, except in so far as these affect wages and profits.

If we are chiefly interested in the prices paid for consumer goods and services, we have a choice between the implied deflator for consumers' expenditure (the CPI) and the index of retail prices (RPI). The former, like all implicit indices, is not compiled directly from price data but is found by dividing the current value of consumers' expenditure by the volume estimate as measured at constant prices.[1] By contrast, the index of retail prices (the cost-of-living index) is compiled directly from price data. It registers the prices of a collection of goods and services entering a typical shopping basket. The composition of the basket has been revised from time to time so as to keep up with changes in the pattern of expenditure. Being a base-weighted index it gradually becomes outdated in coverage. In periods of inflation, it will tend to exaggerate the increase in the cost of living because consumers will switch their expenditure patterns towards those goods which are rising less rapidly in price. In early 1988 the RPI became the subject of criticism because it includes the interest cost of mortgages. Since interest rates were being increased to counter inflation, the paradoxical effect was that counter-inflationary policy raised inflation. A more basic defect is that mortgage payments are not purchases of goods and services but transfers between persons. When the mortgage rate is increased, income is simply transferred from borrowers to savers. Transfer payments do not figure in the various implicit deflators such as the CPI.

There is nothing new about inflation. The retail price index in 1980 was approximately 25 times its level at the beginning of the century. Prices fell in only 13 out of the last 80 years (notably in 1920–23 and 1925–33). During the rest of the period they generally rose, with a particularly fast inflation during and immediately after the First World War (13% per annum during 1914–20). The rate of price increase was much lower in the Second World War because of widespread price controls. In the period after the war the average rate of increase was still quite low – 3% per annum in the 1950s and 4% in the 1960s – despite the high level of employment. It was not until the 1970s that inflation became really serious, with a record 24% increase in 1975 and an average rate for the whole decade of 13%.[2] The rate of inflation was falling after 1980, and down to 3% in 1986. But by the spring of 1989, the increase in the RPI was 8% on a year earlier.

4.2   The Inflationary Process

To explain inflation in an open economy like the UK it is necessary to take account of at least three independent types of impulse. These are

---

[1]   The volume or constant price estimates are derived from base-weighted quantity indices.
[2]   This is the average of annual increases. The compound rate for 1970–80 was 14%.

(i) increases in world prices and UK import prices; (ii) excess demand in the home economy, and, in particular, the degree of labour shortage, and (iii) the independent influence of 'wage pushfulness'.

The influence of import prices is important because imports of goods and services account for more than 20% of TFE. Some imports are in competition with home production, so that if their prices are raised home buyers may switch to domestic substitutes. But a large part of UK imports cannot be made at home at all. Certain foods, most raw materials and many of the semi-manufactures are in this category, and as demand for these goods is highly inelastic, increases in world prices for such commodities are followed by increases in the level of UK costs and prices. UK prices will also rise if there is an increase in the world price of oil, which is the one major primary commodity it produces at home. Many of the most violent inflations in the UK can be traced to changes in the world prices of primary commodities.

The main domestic element in the inflationary process is the degree of excess demand (i.e. demand less supply at going prices) in the various markets for goods and, particularly, for labour. Wages and prices in individual markets may be expected to increase whenever demand runs ahead of supply. Their *rate of increase*, moreover, is likely to be related to the degree of excess demand in the market. In goods markets where there is excess supply there will be some tendency for prices to fall; and, in slack labour markets, wages may fall in real terms. The balance of excess supply and excess demand in the labour market used to be measurable by either the rate of unemployment or the vacancy percentage. But in the last two decades these two series have lost their old relationship to each other so that there is now some uncertainty about comparisons of the pressure of demand over long periods of time. There have also been a number of definitional changes to the unemployment figures. (See section 4.4 below.)

A third element in the inflationary process is, perhaps, more controversial, and is the potentially independent force of wage-pushfulness. It is included as a separate force because wages are widely fixed by bargaining between the representatives of powerful groups, the union and the firm or employers' federation, each of which has the ability to influence the bargain by threatening to interrupt production and employment. Whilst there are reasons to expect that the pressure of demand for labour will normally be an influence in the bargaining process, we cannot exclude the possibility that alterations in the strength of the union, in the loyalty of its members and in its readiness to strike may act as an independent force (i.e. independent of market forces) in determining wage increases.

Import price changes, variations in demand pressure and, at times, wage-push are the main *exogenous* elements in the model. But the inflationary process cannot be understood without reference to the inter-reactions between them (figure 1.5). Of these, the most important is the wage-price spiral. Higher wages mean higher average costs of production and these lead, inexorably, to higher prices. This will happen either because business firms tend to set prices by a constant mark-up over variable costs or because they seek to maximize profits. Higher prices lead, again after a time-lag, to higher wages since trade unions will tend to claim compensation for increases in the cost of living, or in other words to restore the real wages of their members. The other main inter-reaction in the system is that running from domestic prices to the exchange rate and back to import price. As domestic costs and prices rise, exporters have to increase their prices too. If the foreign demand for exports (or the home demand for imports) is elastic, this leads to a deterioration in the balance of payments which induces a decline in the exchange rate. When this happens, the sterling price of imports increases, and domestic costs and prices go up further.

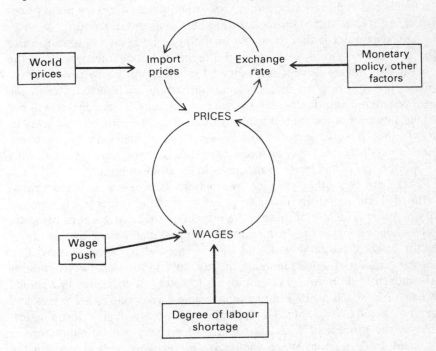

Figure 1.5   Inflationary Processes

The model as it stands makes no allowance for a direct influence of excess demand upon price increases. This omission is justified for the 1960s where various investigations found no evidence for such a relationship.[1] Later on, however, some correlation was observed between profit margins and output. The margins of non-oil industrial and commercial companies fell by about four percentage points in the downturns of 1973–5 and 1978–81,

---

[1]   For example, L.A.Dicks-Mireaux, 'The Inter-Relationship between Cost and Price Changes, 1945–1959', *OEP* (NS), Vol. 13(3), reprinted in R.J.Ball and P.Doyle (eds.), *Inflation* (Penguin, 1969). The model of figure 1.5 is an extension of the relationships investigated by Dicks-Mireaux.

and they rose in the ensuing recoveries.[1] These are fairly small changes, and the main influence of demand pressure still seems to run through the labour market.

A second objection to the model might be that there is no reference to the quantity of money. This lack of an explicit reference, however, does not rule out monetary causation of inflation since additions to the quantity of money can lead to increases in wages through the medium of excess demand, and excess demand has a prominent place in the model. This amounts to saying that monetary inflation is a variety of demand-pull inflation. An increase in the money supply will act through interest-rate reductions or more directly through credit availability to increase the demand for goods and services, and hence create excess demand. There is, however, no place in the model, for an influence of money upon prices which is not transmitted through the medium of excess demand.

A further point is that increases in the price level always tend to raise the demand for money because of the higher value of transactions. If the quantity of money is kept unchanged the effect will be to raise interest rates, thus lowering the levels of real output and employment, reducing excess demand and dampening the rate of inflation. These effects will not occur, however, if the central bank is aiming to hold interest rates constant. It will then have to *increase* the money stock in line with the demand. Inflationary processes may be initiated in various ways, but they are usually supported through permissive increases in the stock of money.

There are two other possible interactions between wages and prices, both of them operating through the effect of rising prices upon *expected future prices*. The first of these is the possibility that expectations of future price changes, rather than compensation for past increases, may be a major factor in wage bargaining. It has been suggested by some writers[2] that the expectation of a price increase of, say, 10% in the next twelve months will induce trade unions and employers to settle for increases in nominal wages of as much as 10% more than would have occurred if prices had been expected to be stable. This hypothesis assumes a degree of sophistication in the process of wage bargaining which may not be characteristic of many trade unions. Wage claims are more likely to be based on the *actual* than on the *expected* rise in the cost of living. But the employers' side must not be neglected, and there may be something in the idea that the propensity of firms to grant wage increases is influenced by their expectations of price increases on the part of their competitors.

There is also a possible link between price expectations and the level of demand. As consumers become aware that prices are going to rise, they may react by attempting to buy now rather than later (effectively

---

[1]   See the discussion in *NIER*, November 1982, pp. 21–2.

[2]   E.S.Phelps, 'Phillips Curves, Expectations of Inflation and Optimal Unemployment Over Time', *EC*, N.S. 34, 254–81, and M.Friedman, 'The Role of Monetary Policy', *AER*, Vol. 58(1), pp. 1–17.

switching out of money into goods). The consequence will be to lower the savings ratio (which, as we have seen, did not happen in the 1970s) and to raise the velocity of circulation of money (which also did not happen). In general, this seems to be a mode of behaviour which is more characteristic of much faster inflations than those so far experienced in the UK.[1] But the fact that such behaviour can develop adds to the danger of inflation getting out of hand and provides a powerful case for stopping it as early as possible.

4.3   Imported Inflation

Nearly every major increase or decrease in the UK price level has been associated with a major change in import prices (see table 1.9). Import prices rose rapidly in 1940 at the beginning of the Second World War; and again in 1951 with the Korean War. Between 1972 and 1975 they rose by 112% as a result of a very fast rise in fuel prices, together with price increases for basic materials and food, beverages and tobacco. There are strong grounds for believing that this was the main factor responsible for the protracted spiral of price and wage increases in the 1970s.

The main effect of a rise in import prices is to increase costs of production which, in turn, means higher final prices. With imports comprising some 22% of TFE, it can be expected that each rise of 1% in import prices will lead to an initial rise in finished goods prices of 0.22%, and these will be raised further by the response of wages.

TABLE 1.9
Major Changes in UK Import Prices since 1940

	Change in import prices (%)	Change in retail prices (%)
1940	39	17
1951	33	9
1972–5	112	58
1976	22	17
1977	16	16

Sources: retail prices: *ET(AS)*, 1989, *BLS*; import prices:
   LCES, ET(AS), 1989, *AAS*.

Imported inflation is not readily curable because, unless the exchange rate can be raised, there is not much prospect of offsetting the effect on final prices other than by inducing large reductions in total demand and employment. Between 1972 and 1974 the dollar prices of primary commodities in world trade rose by 130%, and this was accompanied by rapid increases in prices in all the main industrial countries: 39% in Japan and

---

[1]   See, for example, A.J.Brown, *The Great Inflation* (London, 1955) and P.Cagan, 'The Monetary Dynamics of Hyperinflation' in M.Friedman (ed.), *Studies in the Quantity Theory of Money* (Chicago, 1956).

Italy, 27% in France and 13% in Germany. The UK increase, at 44%, was higher than elsewhere because of high internal demand pressure and the indexation of wages under stage III of Mr Heath's incomes policy. The much lower inflation in Germany was partly attributable to an 18% appreciation of the Deutschmark which went some way to offset higher import prices.[1]

4.4   Excess Demand, Unemployment and Vacancies

Whilst external influences have been responsible for most, if not all, the major inflationary episodes in UK economic history, there is not much doubt that the degree of labour shortage has been the main internal influence. The measurement of this pressure is not without difficulties. For many years it was taken for granted that a reasonably reliable measure of demand pressure was given by the unemployment percentage. Involuntary unemployment in a particular labour market is equal by definition to the excess of supply over demand at the going rate of pay. The degree of excess supply in the whole economy is measured by the unemployment percentage.

A direct index of excess demand is given by the number of unfilled vacant jobs. The figures here are less complete than those for unemployment. The unemployed have an incentive to register because, as a rule, they are entitled to claim unemployment benefit. Unfilled vacancies, however, are reported by employers only if they believe it worth their while to notify them. They may prefer to recruit through the local newspapers rather than through job centres. And an employer who has already notified the job centre of vacancies for a particular kind of worker will not need to register new vacancies because the original notice will be sufficient to attract applicants. Thus the vacancy statistics are bound to be incomplete, and it is officially recognized that only about one-third of all new vacancies are notified to the Department of Employment.

For many years the unemployment and vacancy statistics moved in a close, consistent relationship to each other. The same unemployment percentage was always observed against the same given vacancy rate, and changes in the two percentages were the same in absolute magnitude. It was possible, therefore, to regard either measure as an index of excess demand, whilst the unemployment percentage also served as an indication of the degree of personal and social distress caused by lack of work.

Since the mid-1960s, however, the measurement of excess demand has become problematical because of a gradual change in the relationship between the unemployment and vacancy statistics. A given level of vacancies is now associated with much higher unemployment than before. The extent of the change can be seen from the following comparisons:

---

[1]   These statistics are taken from the *National Institute Economic Review*.

	Unfilled vacancies, UK		Unemployment, UK	
	(000s, percentages in brackets)			
1965–6 (average)	262	(1.0)	346	(1.5)
1973–4 (average)	302	(1.2)	598	(2.1)
1979	241	(0.9)	1,296	(4.1)
1962–3 (average)	147	(0.6)	497	(2.2)
1971–2 (average)	139	(0.6)	794	(2.8)
1975–6 (average)	139	(0.5)	1,121	(3.7)
1982–4 (average)	134	(0.5)	3,060	(10.3)

The figures illustrate a continuing tendency for unemployment to increase relative to a given vacancy percentage. Thus the unemployment rate associated with a vacancy rate of 0.6% (as experienced in the recession period of 1982–4) has increased from 2% in the early 1960s to 10% in the early 1980s – a rise of eight percentage points. By 1988, the ratio of unemployed relative to recorded vacancies was 3.1 compared with only 1.3 in 1965–66, and if 1988 unemployment had been recorded on the older definition, the ratio would have been higher still (at around 3.7 or 3.8).

The reasons behind this very large change in the numbers unemployed relative to vacancies are not as well understood as they ought to be. One obvious possibility is that the unemployed have become more mismatched – both by region and by skill – to the available vacancies. What could have happened is that the recessions of 1973–5 and 1979–82 led to substantial shake-outs of unskilled and marginal labour, whilst the demand recoveries that followed were concentrated on labour with highly specific skills. Thus the unemployed were not equipped to fill the vacancies. This problem could have been made worse by the exceptionally large flow in recent years of unskilled and unqualified school-leavers on to the workforce. And the mismatch of skills would have been intensified by regional mismatch, and by the great difficulties encountered in moving from low rent areas – mainly in the North – to areas such as the South-East where there are vacant jobs but a shortage of cheap, rented accommodation.

The mismatch explanation is, however, contested. It has been shown that the degree of mismatch measured proportionately between unemployment and vacancies in 18 occupational groups and nine regions has not greatly altered. But if the *number* of unemployed is much larger, then the *magnitude* of the mismatch is more serious than before.[1] It has also been questioned whether measurements based on a small number of occupational groups and regions (the only available data) is sufficient to deal adequately with the question. On balance it seems likely that a rather complex blend of skill plus regional mismatch, combined with a housing problem, is responsible for a large part of the shift in the U–V relationship.

A related reason for the rise in U relative to V is that unemployment has become less involuntary. The argument is not that large numbers of

---

[1] R. Layard, *How to Beat Unemployment* (Oxford University Press, 1986), pp. 55–8. But see also A. Wood, 'How much Unemployment is Structural?', *Oxford Bulletin of Economics and Statistics*, February 1988, and the reply by R. Jackman and B. Kan.

workers have voluntarily opted for the dole, but rather that once they have been made redundant (through no fault of their own) they have chosen to remain unemployed for a longer period than they might have before. The difficulty of finding a job when there are very few vacancies leads to a loss of interest in applying; and repeated rejections discourage further applications (the 'discouraged worker effect'). Furthermore, the sheer rise in the amount and generality of unemployment will have had the effect of breaking down the old social stigma attached to being on the dole.[1] Finally, in the late 1960s and early 1970s, there was some rise in the level of unemployment benefit relative to average earnings, and this would have tended to prolong the period of unemployment once a worker is made redundant.

There are also statistical reasons for the change in the U–V ratio. Between 1966 and 1981, the ratio of recorded to actual unemployment increased. Thus for male unemployment the ratio of the registered unemployed to the numbers shown as unemployed in the population census increased to 56% in 1966 to 71% in 1971 and around 100% in 1981.[2] This effect, however, will have been counter-acted after 1981 by the series of statistical revisions to the official unemployment figures. The main changes were the effect in 1981 of removing from the register people on special employment and training schemes, the change in 1982 from a registered to a claimant basis for the figures, and the re-start interviews initiated in 1986. The Unemployment Unit calculates the effects of these and other changes made since 1981 to have been about 900,000 by August 1988.[3]

It is not easy to make sense of what has happened. But the main statistical conclusion is that the unemployment rate can no longer be taken as a consistent inverse indicator of excess demand in the labour market. If a single indicator has to be used to measure the pressure of demand for labour, there is not much doubt that the vacancy figures are to be preferred.

4.5   Demand-pull Inflation

There is ample evidence of the influence of the pressure of demand for labour upon the rate of inflation. Numerous studies in the 1950s and 1960s showed a strong negative relationship between the level of unemployment (which is inversely related to excess demand) and the rate of change of money wage rates. One of the earlier studies of this kind, and certainly

---

[1]   The term 'hysteresis' is sometimes given to the process whereby a variable such as unemployment is determined by its past history and where there is no tendency to return to its former value.

[2]   For further discussion, see *NIER*, November 1983, pp. 39–41; and A.Evans, 'Notes on the Changing Relationship between Registered Unemployment and Notified Vacancies: 1961–1966 and 1966–1971', *EC*, May 1977; S.J.Nickell, 'The Effect of Unemployment and Related Benefits on the Duration of Unemployment', *EJ*, March 1979; A.B.Atkinson and J.S.Flemming, 'Unemployment and Social Security and Incentives', *MBR*, 1978, and R.Layard and S.Nickell, 'The Causes of British Unemployment', *NIER*, February 1985.

[3]   *Unemployment Bulletin*, Autumn 1988. See also the discussion in chapter 5 of this book.

the most influential, was published in 1958 by Professor A.W.Phillips.[1] This examined the relationship between unemployment rates and wage increases for nearly a century, and on the basis of data for 1861–1913, suggested that wave increases were associated with different rates of unemployment as follows:

Unemployment rate	1.0	2.0	3.0	4.0	5.0
% change in wage rates	8.7	2.8	1.2	0.5	0.1

The relationship became known as the *Phillips Curve*.[2] It implied a non-linear, marginal 'trade-off' between the rate of wage increase and unemployment.

One of the more remarkable features of the Phillips Curve, and one which distinguished it from most similar studies, was that it was found to be highly reliable in predicting increases in wages during much later periods of time than the years 1861–1913 which had been used to derive the equation. Thus Phillips was able to show a very close correspondence for 1948–57 between the wage changes implied by his relationship and those that actually took place. The Phillips Curve was also accurate in predicting wage increases over the period 1958–66, which was after the study had been published. During these eight years there was not a single error in excess of 2.5% and the mean error (regardless of sign) was only 1.1%; furthermore, the positive and negative errors tended to offset each other. These predictive successes, however, have to be seen in the light of what was an exceedingly stable level of unemployment compared with the experience from which Phillips had started. In 1861–1913 unemployment rates ranged from 1 to 11% whereas in 1948–66 they were between 1 and 2.3%. Thus it could be argued that postwar experience up to 1966 tested only a small part of the Phillips relation.

After the mid-1960s, the pure Phillips Curve became increasingly unreliable as a guide to the rate of wage inflation. It under-predicted by about 4.5% per annum in 1967–9, by 10–12% in 1970–3, and by more than 20% in 1974 and 1975. For several years there was no recognizable relationship between statistics of the unemployment percentage and the rate of wage increase. It is important, therefore, to ask whether the breakdown of the Phillips relationship can be explained, and here several factors come to mind:

---

[1] A.W.Phillips, 'The Relation between Unemployment and the Rate of Change of Money Wage Rates, 1861–1957', *Economica*, November 1958, although A.J.Brown, *op. cit.*, had illustrated the same relationship.

[2] The equation for the schedule was:

$$\frac{\Delta W}{W} = -0.900 + 9.638 U^{-1.394}$$

It can also be expressed in logarithmic terms as

$$\log \frac{\Delta W}{W} + 0.9 = 0.984 - 1.394 \log U$$

where $\frac{\Delta W}{W}$ is the percentage rate of wage change and U is the unemployment rate (Phillips, *op. cit.*).

(i)   First, it is the upwards pressure of excess demand (as represented
      by vacancies) rather than the downwards pressure of excess supply
      (indicated by unemployment) which is the crucial determinant of
      rising wage inflation. In the 1950s, when unemployment and vacan-
      cies moved closely together, it did not matter greatly if unemploy-
      ment was taken to represent (inversely) the degree of labour
      shortage. But as unemployment has drifted away from its old
      relationship to vacancies, it has also ceased to be a consistent indi-
      cator of the degree of labour shortage.

(ii) A second factor is the omission from the pure Phillips equation
      of the causal influence of price changes. This would not have mat-
      tered so much in the 1950s and early 1960s when inflation was
      moderate. But the omission became serious with inflation at the
      rates experienced in the 1970s and early 1980s.

(iii) A connected factor was that wage increases became more sensitive
      to price increases as a result of learning to live with inflation. A
      growing number of trade-union negotiators would have been led
      to insist on full compensation for price changes in wage negotia-
      tions, whilst others would have sought negotiations at more fre-
      quent intervals. There may have been some tendency to follow
      the 'expectations-augmented Phillips curve', with expected rather
      than actual price changes being taken as the basis for wage awards.

(iv) A fourth factor is the influence of 'wage-pushfulness', which, as
      we discuss below, appears to have been more prevalent in the
      period after 1970.

(v)   Finally, the Phillips relationship was partly obscured by a number
      of attempts, notably in the late 1960s, 1972–3 and 1975–8, to control
      wage increases by incomes policy.

These factors help to explain why the old wage-increase–unemployment
relationship failed to hold after the mid-1960s. The principle behind the
Phillips relationship is that wage rates tend to rise most rapidly when there
is a high pressure of demand for labour. Evidence for this can be found
by comparing increases in earnings with the vacancy percentage.

Earnings and the vacancy rate: As a first approximation, this relationship
may be examined in terms of the extent to which earnings (and wage rates)
forge ahead of the change in retail prices. This tends to be much larger
when the vacancy rate is high – as in 1974, 1979 and 1988 – than in periods
of recession as in 1975–7 and 1981–2. The evidence is presented in figure
1.6 where the earnings and wage rate changes are measured at end-year
(October–March average compared with a year earlier) and the rise in
retail prices is the calendar year increase – an effective lag of six months.
The reason for the lag is the assumption that the earnings index is similar
to an index of negotiated wage rates. As such, its level in one particular

month is likely to be an average of wage negotiations by different groups of workers over a 12-month period. This means that one-twelfth of the index will have been negotiated 12 months ago, one-twelfth this month, and the 'average' group will have negotiated six months before the date of the index. For a wage rate index recorded at the end of December, the relevant price index is that for the calendar year. Hence we may say that the end-1989 rise in wage rates is governed by the rise in retail prices between 1988 and 1989, and also by the vacancy rate for 1988. In figure 1.6, the excess of the earnings change over the lagged price change is referred to as 'real earnings', although it is, of course, conventional to measure real earnings without the lag. The figure illustrates how the rate of increase in 'real' earnings – or the extent to which earnings forge ahead of prices – is depressed by a low vacancy rate and increases when the vacancy rate rises.[1]

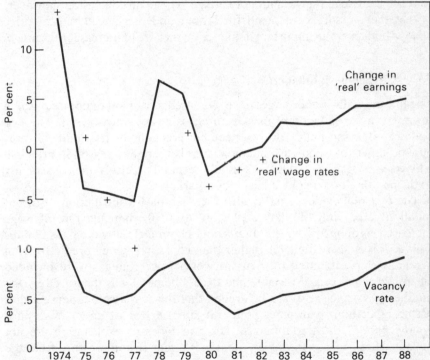

Figure 1.6   The Vacancy Rate and Changes in 'Real' Earnings and Wage Rates, UK, 1974–88 (Change from a year earlier in end-year (Oct–March average) money earnings and money wage rates *less* the calendar year rise in the retail price index.)

A possible drawback to the presentation in figure 1.6 is that the 'real earnings' series assumes implicitly that there is a one-to-one relationship between increases in prices and increases in money earnings. Bearing in mind that some negotiating groups may, as a rule, fail to achieve a full cost-of-living increase, it is also interesting to consider the change in money

---

[1]   Over the 1980–88 period, which was free of the effects of incomes policy, the correlation between the increase in 'real' earnings and vacancies was 0.8.

earnings as the dependent variable, and to express it as a function of the vacancy rate and price change. This results in a multiple regression equation as follows:

$$\dot{E} = 7.68V + 0.74\dot{P} - 3.00IP + 3.06CU - 0.74 \tag{2}$$

This is the equation for increases in end-year money earnings ($\dot{E}$) from 1975 to 1988, with V standing for job vacancies as a percentage of the workforce in each calendar year, $\dot{P}$ for the annual rate of increase in prices, IP for incomes policy in 1975–7, and CU for the 'catch-up' effect after the policy had broken down. The equation fits well, and its mean absolute residual is about 0.6% of the level of earnings.[1] It suggests that the coefficient on prices may not be unity, as implied in figure 1.6, but is nearer $\frac{3}{4}$. It also suggests that the rate of increase in earnings rises by about 0.8% for each 0.1 rise in the vacancy percentage. The main conclusion, however, is that the pressure of demand for labour and the lagged rate of price change both exert an important influence on the rate of increase in earnings.

4.6   Wage-push Inflation

The question of whether wages have increased as a result of unions pushing up wages independently of market forces is more controversial. The evidence for demand-pull, however, need not preclude the possibility of sporadic outbursts of wage-push inflation. Nor is there any reason in principle why wage-bargaining procedures should respond precisely and consistently to the pressure of demand in the labour market.

The first real evidence in favour of a wage-push contribution to recent inflation came with the 'pay explosion' of 1970 when the rate of wage increase was about 12% faster than could be predicted by the pure Phillips Curve. It was also about 7% higher than could have been predicted from a relationship estimated by Artis in which price changes were included as an additional causal variable and excess demand was measured by the number of vacancies.[2] It can be argued that this was a consequence either of the relaxation of incomes policy in late 1969 or of direct wage-push on the part of the trade unions. The two types of explanation are not unconnected because the government was under strong pressure from the unions to bring incomes policy to an end.

In the next few years there was further evidence of wage-push inflation in terms of a tendency for money wage rates to press ahead of prices. This was certainly true of the old wage rate index for manual workers. If this index is deflated (without a lag) by the retail price index to arrive at an index of real wage rates, then a very conspicuous rise in real wages

---

[1] $R^2 = 0.96$, standard residual error 0.98% of earnings, Durbin–Watson $= 1.98$; t-statistics 3.5, 10.2, 2.8 and 2.8 in order.

[2]   M.J.Artis, 'Some Aspects of the Present Inflation', *NIER*, February 1971, reprinted in H.G.Johnson and A.R.Nobay (eds.), *The Current Inflation*, Macmillan, 1971.

appears in the early 1970s – as is shown by the following comparison of five-year periods:

1960–65	3%
1965–70	7%
1970–75	23%

This, however, is not the story told by other indicators. The index of average weekly earnings (again deflated by the RPI) shows much the same real gain in 1970–75 as in 1965–70, and if the national accounts data of wages and salaries are deflated by prices they also fail to show a significant jump in real wages in 1970–75. This was a case of conflicting evidence. There was, however, a history of confrontation and industrial unrest in the 1970–75 period and the very sharp rise in the number of industrial disputes was at least suggestive of wage-pushfulness.

4.7   Inflation since 1970

The inflation rate rose sharply in the 1970s partly because of a number of exogenous disturbances and partly because the main inflationary mechanism – the wage–price spiral – became stronger as a result of an increased sensitivity of wages to prices. In the early 1970s, the main exogenous disturbances were the 'wage explosions' of 1970 and 1972, when wages rose much faster than could be attributed to their normal relationship with prices or with the pressure of demand. The 1970 explosion may have been partly or wholly a 'catch-up' from incomes policy, whereas the explosion of 1972 seems to be either inexplicable or attributable to direct union push associated with discontent over the Industrial Relations Act of 1971 and the policies of the Conservative government. The sharp rise in the numbers involved in industrial disputes bears witness to this explanation.

Between 1972 and 1975, fresh factors took over. Undoubtedly, the most important was the colossal rise in oil and other import prices. The increase of 112% in import prices must, with imports comprising 22% of TFE, have added well over 20% to the level of retail prices. But the inflation was helped, rather than hindered, by Stage III of Mr Heath's incomes policy, where under the 'threshold agreements', wages were effectively linked one-to-one with prices. This was in 1974, and the linkage was continued during the first half of 1975. But, as figure 1.6 shows, the inflation of 1973 and 1974 was greatly helped by an extremely high pressure of demand for labour, with vacancy rates higher for two years than they had ever been before. High rates of monetary expansion (or, more particularly, low real rates of interest) helped the rise in the pressure of demand, but could hardly be regarded, as some commentators believed at the time, as the sole cause of the inflation.

After 1975 there was a sharp decline in the inflation rate for three years, and by 1978 the rate had fallen 16 points to 8%. This decline was partly

TABLE 1.10

Inflation and inflationary pressures 1960–88

	(1) Change in retail prices (%)	(2) Change in average weekly earnings (%)	(3) Unemployment percentage	(4) Unfilled vacancies percentage	(5) Days lost in industrial disputes (m)	(6) Change in import prices (%)	(7) Change in exchange rate (%)	(8) Change in money stock (£M3) (%)
1960–64 (average)	2	5	1.8	0.8	3	1	0	—
1965–69 (average)	4	7	2.0	0.9	4	4	−3	6
1970	6	12	2.6	0.7	11	4	−1	9
1971	9	11	2.6	0.5	14	5	0	14
1972	7	13	2.9	0.6	24	5	−4	28
1973	9	14	2.0	1.2	7	28	−9	27
1974	16	18	2.1	1.2	15	46	−3	11
1975	24	27	3.1	0.6	6	14	−8	6
1976	17	16	4.2	0.5	3	22	−14	8
1977	16	9	4.4	0.6	10	16	−5	8
1978	8	13	4.4	0.8	9	4	0	15
1979	13	15	4.1	0.9	29	7	7	12
1980	18	21	5.1	0.5	12	10	10	18
1981	12	13	8.1	0.3	4	8	−1	16
1982	9	9	9.6	0.4	5	8	−4	9
1983	5	8	10.5	0.5	4	9	−7	11
1984	5	6	10.7	0.6	27	9	−4	10
1985	6	9	10.9	0.6	6	5	−1	13
1986	3	8	11.1	0.7	2	−4	−9	21
1987	4	8	10.0	0.8	4	3	−2	23
1988	5	9	8.1	0.9	4	1	6	21

Sources: *ET(AS)*, 1989; *ET*, February 1989; *DEG*, March 1989.

Notes: Col. (2) earnings in whole economy linked to earlier indices. Col. (3) UK unemployed excluding school-leavers as percentages of mid-year workforce. (N.B. There are discontinuities in the definition of unemployment after 1979.) Col. (6) unit value of merchandise imports on balance of payments basis. Col. (7) sterling exchange rate index. Col. (8) end-year, seasonally adjusted.

attributable to the lower pressure of demand in 1976 and 1977, but the main factor responsible was the introduction in July 1975 of an incomes policy which won the consent of the trade union movement. Phase I of the policy, set a limit of £6 a week on wage increases, whilst Phase II which began in July 1976 imposed a limit of 5%.[1] Thus the rise in average weekly earnings fell from 27% in 1975 to 9% in 1977.

The rise in the inflation rate between 1978 and 1980 can be traced to a number of influences, of which the first was the revival of demand pressure in 1978 and 1979. Oil prices rose sharply between 1978 and 1980, with the OPEC price more than doubling between these two years. Possibly the most serious factor, however, was the withdrawal of union co-operation with incomes policy and the wage increases associated with the 1978/9 'winter of discontent'. But a further four percentage points were added to retail prices by the budget decision of June 1979 to raise VAT from 8 to 15%. Without this increase the task of reducing inflation in the next three years might well have proved easier.

Between 1980 and 1986 the inflation rate fell by 15 percentage points, although the decline would have been less without the VAT increase. Although world primary product prices were falling at this time (in terms of dollars), UK import prices (in sterling) were rising each year at a fairly steady 8–10%. The cause of the reduced rate of inflation in this period was primarily internal, and can be traced to very high unemployment and the low level of the vacancy rate (see figure 1.6). The figures for industrial disputes also show a marked reduction in this period.[2]

After 1986, the rate of inflation was creeping up again, mainly as the consequence of the gradual rise in the pressure of demand for labour. Thus by the end of 1988, earnings were increasing at $9\frac{1}{2}$% a year compared with $7\frac{1}{2}$% two years earlier; profit margins were increasing too; and a sharp rise in mortgage interest rates was estimated to have added about $1\frac{1}{2}$% to the index of retail prices in less than a year.

5   MACROECONOMIC POLICY
5.1   Demand Management 1944–74

It is traditional to state that the two principal objectives of short-term macroeconomic policy are the maintenance of high employment and a stable level of prices. This tradition, however, belongs to normative thought. It is open to any elected government to break with tradition if it chooses. Thus the period since the end of the Second World War can be divided into two, or perhaps three, sub-periods. In the first of these,

---

[1]   The earnings equation on p. 46 puts the effect of the policy as a reduction in earnings of about 3% a year for three years.
[2]   For further discussion of recent inflation, see, in particular, P.Rowlatt, 'An Analysis of the Recent Path of UK Inflation', *Oxford Bulletin of Economics and Statistics*, November 1988.

the era of demand management, which lasted from 1944 to about 1974, governments of both the main political parties sought to achieve both high employment *and* price stability. In the third period, starting in 1979 and continuing under Mrs Thatcher's third term of office, price stability has been the main macroeconomic objective, and the employment objective has taken a very low priority. Between these two periods, from 1974 to 1979, the situation was, perhaps, more like the third than the first. The huge inflation of 1974 and 1975, and the balance of payments difficulties which followed, were major constraints on the Labour government's economic policy. Unemployment, which was high by the standards of the earlier period, was allowed to rise.

During the demand management era, governments developed a systematic approach to the problem of maintaining high employment. The objective was announced by the White Paper on *Employment Policy* (Cmd. 6527) issued in 1944 by the wartime coalition government. The White Paper stated that:

> The Government believe that, once the war has been won, we can make a fresh approach, with better chances of success than ever before, to the task of maintaining a high and stable level of employment without sacrificing the essential liberties of a free society.

The White Paper recommended that there should be a permanent staff of statisticians and economists in the Civil Service with responsibility for interpreting economic trends and advising on policy. The execution of employment policy was to be examined annually by Parliament in the debate on the Budget. The White Paper foresaw that high levels of employment were likely to endanger price stability, and pointed out the need for 'moderation in wage matters by employers and employees' as the essential condition for the success of the policy.

For nearly thirty years the task of maintaining a high level of employment proved to be less difficult and less inflationary than had been feared. Employment levels were higher than the authors of the White Paper had hoped for, and inflation, at 3% per year in the 1950s and 4% in the 1960s, was remarkably moderate.

As was noted in section II, however, the postwar economy passed through a series of fluctuations, minor until the 1970s, with the annual unemployment rate varying within a narrow range. Part of the reason for these fluctuations could be found in the different views taken by successive governments (or sometimes by the same government at different times) as to the most desirable pressure of demand. The aim of high employment was always in some measure of conflict with the balance of payments and with price stability. The conflict with the balance of payments arose because governments were unwilling to make use of independent instruments of policy, such as exchange-rate devaluation or import controls, for dealing with the external balance. Thus fiscal and monetary measures which affect employment were sometimes directed towards the required balance of payments, with the consequence that the employment objective took second place. This conflict was most noticeable in two periods: from 1956 to early 1959 when the Conservative government was aiming at a long-term balance of payments surplus (and when there was also concern about inflation), and the period of eighteen months preceding the devaluation of sterling in November 1967.

The employment objective was equally in conflict with that of price stability. Here there is no independent instrument of control to parallel the variability of the exchange rate. Incomes policy, in the sense of voluntary or compulsory guidelines for the rate of increase in wages and prices, was seldom found to be particularly successful and certainly not successful enough to permit nice percentage adjustments to the permitted rate of inflation. Thus the absence of an independent instrument for controlling inflation implied a genuine conflict of aims. This, together with the balance of payments, helps to explain why the target level of employment was not wholly stable from year to year, but tended to fluctuate according to circumstances and the priorities of the government of the day.

It follows that the decision on what level of employment to aim for was normally made on the basis of a compromise with the objectives of price stability and the balance of payments. But once the employment target was settled, the problem of how to attain it could be seen as a largely technical issue.

One of the initial difficulties in any attempt to control employment is that there are significant time-lags between the onset of a recession and the period when remedial action takes effect. The employment statistics are about a month behindhand; civil servants may take up to six months to advise the appropriate action; Parliament may take three months to enact it; and even after the policy is put into force, the full economic effects may not appear for some months afterwards. Thus a strategy based solely upon the observation of recent economic performance can involve a significantly long time-lag (of twelve months or longer) between the observed need for a change in policy and the effects of that change upon the level of employment.

It was partly for this reason that demand management in the UK was guided by forecasts rather than by direct response to the current situation. With correct forecasts, the problem of delay between the need for intervention and its effects could be taken care of.

There was another reason, too, for relying upon forecasts. This was the need to tailor (or 'fine-tune') the amount of intervention to the future size of the problem rather than to what is currently observed. The mere observation of high unemployment or excessive inflation in no way guarantees that it will continue in the same degree of seriousness. The problem may get worse or better. Quite clearly it was essential to form some view of what will happen in the future before deciding the degree and the direction of policy intervention required. Failure to produce a correct forecast of the course of employment over the next twelve to eighteen months could result in an *inadequate* degree of corrective policy action. Or it could be *destabilizing*,[1] in the sense that the effect of intervention is to remove the level of output still further from target than it would have been without it.

Thus the system adopted for managing the economy was for the Treasury to keep a constant watch on the main economic time series and to make forecasts of GDP, employment, prices and the balance of payments for a period running 12–18 months ahead. The forecasting exercises took place three times a year. Of these, the most important were those preceding the public expenditure decision in the autumn and the pre-budget forecast in February.

On receipt of the forecast, the Chancellor of the Exchequer would decide whether the situation foreseen was acceptable – in terms of employment, inflation and the balance of payments – or whether it needed adjustment. The adjustments might consist of changes in government expenditure or in tax rates, although the Treasury took the view that public expenditure was not a suitable instrument for fine-tuning because (a) it was difficult to control its timing, and (b) because its level was determined by political and social objectives which were independent of the employment goal.[2] Thus the more usual instruments of demand management were changes in tax rates, particularly income and indirect taxes. For changes in these, a tax 'ready reckoner' was drawn up to indicate the GDP and other effects of given variations. This followed the principles set out in sections 3.5 and 3.6 on the multiplier. Thus, the Chancellor could decide by how much taxes should be raised or lowered in order to achieve what he saw as the most satisfactory level of demand.

The system of demand management improved over the years as a result of developments in economic statistics – particularly the production of quarterly GDP accounts with seasonal adjustments – and a gradual improvement in forecasting methods.

5.2   Criticisms of Demand Management

Demand management came in for a great deal of criticism even when employment was held high with comparatively little inflation. There were business objections to the frequency of tax changes, although these were heard more often when taxes were raised than when they were lowered. Opposition spokesmen in Parliament were reluctant to concede the need for tax cuts because of their electoral advantage to the other side. There were complaints of 'stop–go' and, later, of 'too much fine tuning' although these terms were never very carefully defined. Amidst all the clamour it was difficult to distinguish criticisms of the technical proficiency of demand management from differences about the objectives which it was seeking to attain.

---

[1]   A more accurate term would be 'perverse' since policy does not necessarily aim to stabilize anything.
[2]   J.C.R.Dow, *The Management of the British Economy, 1945–60* (Cambridge University Press, 1964), pp. 180–1.

The criticisms divided into five main groups: (i) that the economy fluctuated considerably despite the advocacy of 'stable' employment in the
1944 White Paper; (ii) that the technical apparatus of demand management
was inadequate to its task; (iii) that economic policy was in some sense
destabilizing; (iv) that demand management was not really necessary; and
(v) that it was inflationary.

(i) On the first of these points there is no doubt that the course of the
economy was not perfectly stable for most of the period when demand
management was practised. What is not so clear, however, is the extent
to which this instability (or 'stop–go' as it was called) reflected changes
in objectives, or failures to achieve a constant objective. For even if the
economy does proceed in cycles, it is quite possible that these could have
been brought about deliberately. This could have happened because
governments periodically changed their minds about the best level of
employment at which to run the economy. The conflicts or presumed conflicts between economic objectives are sufficiently obvious to make it doubt-
ful whether the target pressure of demand would have always been the
same. The evidence seems to suggest that the target fluctuated quite significantly.

Government targets for GDP over this period can be taken from the
'post-budget forecasts', i.e. the forecasts made at the time of the budget
but with allowance for the effects of the budget itself. These forecasts were
tantamount to targets for GDP since they represented levels of output
and employment which could and would have been altered if the Treasury
had so wished. Each forecast level of GDP implied a specific use of potential
output, and this may be found by applying it to an estimate of productive
potential. This is done in table 1.11 where productive potential is taken
as representing a 1.0% unemployment rate for 1955–67, and, for reasons
outlined in section 2, a 0.9% vacancy rate after 1968. The table shows
a fall in the planned use of potential output of about 6% between 1955
and 1959, increases in 1960 and the election year of 1964, and a fairly
steady target from then until 1970. The main feature of the period after
1970 was the very high intended pressure of demand in 1973 and 1974
(the 'Barber boom') and the sharp contraction in 1975.

The principal conclusion is that there were, quite definitely, fluctuations
in the level of productive potential at which governments sought to run
the economy. Whether these can be traced to electoral ambitions is less
clear, since not all the election years were years of high targeted demand
pressure. It is, perhaps, disputable whether a government gets more votes
from high employment than it does from tax give-aways in a year of
depression. The other explanation offered is that years of high demand
led to balance of payments difficulties and inflation, to which the various
Chancellors responded with phases of demand deflation.

(ii) As regards the technical apparatus of demand management the key
question is whether, and by how much, it failed to achieve the target levels
of employment and GDP which governments were aiming for. Since the

TABLE 1.11

Short-term Targets and Forecast Errors, UK, 1955–78

		Forecast use of potential output (target pressure of demand)[1] %	Forecast change in GDP from year earlier[2] %	Actual change in GDP from year earlier[3] %	Error (forecast less actual) %
1955	(years)	100	2.9	3.7	−0.8
1956	,,	99	1.1	1.4	−0.3
1957	,,	98	1.3	1.6	−0.3
1958	,,	95	−0.4	−0.2	−0.2
1959	(4th qtr)	94	2.8	7.1	−4.3
1960	,,	98	3.1	3.8	−0.7
1961	,,	97	1.8	1.9	−0.1
1962	,,	98	3.9	1.0	2.9
1963	,,	97	4.6	6.9	−2.3
1964	,,	101	5.4	4.3	1.1
1965	,,	100	2.7	2.6	0.1
1966	,,	99	2.0	1.3	0.7
1967	,,	98	3.1	2.0	1.1
1968	(2nd half)	99	3.6	4.9	−1.3
1969	,,	100	1.9	2.2	−0.3
1970	,,	101	3.6	2.3	1.3
1971	,,	99	1.1	1.4	−0.3
1972	,,	103	5.5	3.5	2.0
1973	,,	105	6.0	5.9	0.1
1974	,,	105	2.6	−0.6	3.2
1975	,,	98	0.0	−2.1	−2.1
1976	,,	99	3.9	4.0	−0.1
1977	,,	98	1.5	2.2	−0.7
1978	,,	99	3.0	3.5	−0.5
	Mean absolute error			1955–67	1.1
				1968–78	1.1
	Bias (mean algebraic error)			1955–67	−0.2
				1968–78	+0.1

Notes and Sources:
1　Potential output for 1955–67 is estimated as the level of GDP which would sustain an unemployment rate of 1.0%, and for 1968–86 as the level needed to keep the vacancy rate at 0.9 to 1.0%. The rate of growth of potential output is taken as 2.9% per annum for 1955–68 and 2.2% for 1968–78.
2　M.C.Kennedy, 'Employment Policy – What Went Wrong?', in Joan Robinson (ed.), *After Keynes* (Blackwell, 1973), and *Financial Statement and Budget Reports* (HMSO).
3　Average estimate of GDP, *ET(AS)*, 1989.

target level of GDP is equivalent to the government's forecast, this question is essentially a matter of how accurate the forecasts were.[1] If the Treasury fails to forecast the increase in GDP correctly, then it will be led into

---

[1]　Forecasting accuracy is not always simple to interpret: there may be strikes or other events of an unforeseeable nature which affect the accuracy of the forecasts without necessarily discrediting the methods by which they are derived.

taking the wrong measures. The result will be that the target level of GDP is missed by the same amount as the forecast is in error.

The question of the accuracy of Treasury forecasts is answered most satisfactorily for those forecasts which have been published or described with sufficient clarity to permit comparisons with the outcome. For 1968 and after, the forecasts were published as part of the *Financial Statement and Budget Report*. But before then, the forecasts have to be inferred from budget speeches and official documents or, in some years, from forecasts made by other bodies at the same time. Nevertheless, the task is worth attempting even though the data on the earlier forecasts is imperfect.[1]

The main point to emerge from an inspection of the early Treasury forecasts is that, whilst they were not as accurate as might have been hoped, they led policy seriously astray on only four or five occasions. There is not much doubt that the 1959 forecast, when the error was 4%, was the worst. It meant that an unforeseen recovery in total output was coupled with an expansionary Budget, and the result was a much higher level of employment at the end of the year than the government had actually intended. By contrast, the forecasting error in 1962 went the other way, with the result that there was a recession despite the policy aim of a roughly 4% rise in output. The error was put right in 1963, although the recovery went further than intended. The forecast of 1974 was another example of a seriously mistaken forecast.

Taking the whole period from 1955–74, the average error in Treasury forecasts (regardless of sign) was 1.1% of GDP. This implies an average deviation of about 0.4% between the actual and desired unemployment rate, and was equivalent to an error between the appropriate rate of income tax and the actual rate of about 4p in the £. The size of the forecast errors must be seen, however, against the background of conflicting and by no means accurate estimates of GDP itself. There is some evidence that the forecasts have become more accurate after 1975.[2]

(iii) A number of writers also sought to show that demand management was 'destabilizing'. This term might be taken to mean that policy increased the *amplitude* of the business cycle; or that it reduced the average *level* of output around which fluctuations took place; or, as discussed here, that policy had the effect of removing the economy further from target than it would have been if it had been left alone.[3] To demonstrate that demand management was destabilizing it is necessary to state assumptions as to the target level of output and the level which output would have attained

---

[1] The same qualifications carry through to the series for the Forecast Use of Potential Output.

[2] Burns, *op. cit.*

[3] For reviews of these and other studies of short-term policies, see G.D.N.Worswick, 'Fiscal Policy and Stabilization in Britain' in A.K.Cairncross (ed.), *Britain's Economic Progress Reconsidered* and M.C.Kennedy, *op. cit.*

in the absence of discretionary intervention. Some of the assumptions that
have been used for this purpose have been questionable. Thus one authority
has claimed that policy was destabilizing because it could be shown that
'policy-off' changes in GDP (i.e. after deducting the effects of changes
in taxation and government spending) were less widely scattered round
the average annual increase in GDP than policy-on (i.e. actual) changes
in GDP.[1] The implication is that the average increase was the target.
But sensible governments will strive for faster increases than average when
the economy is in recession, and for slower increases in times of boom.
And, as we have seen from table 1.11, there is no evidence to support
the assumption that either the target growth of demand or target use of
potential was constant.

The stabilizing effectiveness of short-term policy was also investigated
in terms of the stability of GDP around its trend. It was shown by Artis[2]
that for the 1958–70 period the dispersion of quarterly levels of observed
GDP from their time-trend was larger than the dispersion of estimated
'policy-off' GDP. Policy-off GDP was found by deducting the cumulative
effects of all tax changes introduced after a particular base year from its
own (different) time-trend. The results indicated that policy was 'destabilizing' in the sense of this particular method of measurement. But, as the
author made clear, there was never any presumption that trend GDP coincided with target GDP.

The main conclusion seems to be that there has not, as yet, been any
convincing demonstration that demand management was destabilizing in
the sense that, in general, it took the economy further from target than
would have been the case with no policy at all. Such a demonstration would
have to make acceptable assumptions about both the objectives of economic
policy and the effects of policy instruments. It is not difficult, however,
to accept that policy was destabilizing in particular years: in 1959, for example, the economy would have remained nearer to the government's target
if an expansionary budget had not coincided with an investment boom
which was not foreseen in the Treasury forecast. But this was an example
of exceptionally poor economic forecasting in one particular year.
The general picture, as we have seen, was one of fairly close proximity
between actual GDP and target. The average forecast error of 1.1%
implies also that policy could not have been destabilizing by a large
amount.

The associated criticism that there was 'too much fine tuning' may also
be discussed briefly. If this means simply that the economy would have
held very nearly as close to target levels of output during the demand
management period (1944–74) without the intrusion of minor alterations
in tax rates, then the point must carry some weight. For there is not much

[1]   B.Hansen, *Fiscal Policy in Seven Countries, 1955–65* (OECD, Paris, 1969).
[2]   M.J.Artis, 'Fiscal Policy for Stabilization', in W.Beckerman (ed.), *The Labour Government's Economic Record, 1964–70* (Duckworth, 1972).

doubt that the effects of the tax changes were quite small in terms of their effects on GDP.

(iv) A fourth point is not so much a criticism as an observation. It is that much of the exercise of demand management was unnecessary because the post-war investment boom, and the recovery and liberalization of world trade, would have happened anyway, and there was no real need for the degree of intervention that took place. This suggestion acts as an antidote to the widely-held belief at the time that full employment owed its existence to Keynes, the 'Keynesian revolution', and the post-war enlightenment of the UK Treasury. It has been shown that the rise in GDP towards its full employment potential between the pre- and post-war periods can be largely accounted for by investment and exports.[1] This is not an easy view to refute, although the investment boom may, itself, have been helped by the mood of optimism induced by the declared aim of maintaining high and stable employment. The investment boom after 1918 did not last as long, and it can be argued that in the USA, where monetary rather than fiscal policy was the instrument, there were still substantial fluctuations in employment. But even if the amount of intervention was excessive for the reasons given, it would have still been appropriate for the Treasury to have kept a watching eye on the economy.

(v) During the period of fast inflation in the 1970s demand management came in for some further criticisms. One of these was that the very fast expansion of demand during 1973, and the high level of demand pressure, was responsible for the acceleration in the rate of inflation. There is, of course, something in this view, but the inflation of 1973–5 was caused mainly by the rise in oil and other import prices (see section 4).

The more general criticism is that demand management was just a bit too inflationary throughout the 1950s and '60s. The Phillips curve and similar studies had all suggested that a *critical rate of unemployment* existed, at what was then estimated to be some $2\frac{1}{4}\%$ of the workforce, where money wage rates would rise at about 2% per annum, or by just enough to equal the normal rise in output per person. A number of economists[2] had advocated that this should be the target rate for policy, but in the Treasury it was believed that this was too high and that the ideal rate was 1.8% of the labour force. The average rate in the 1960s was 1.9%, and this was mildly inflationary in itself. But the other effect was a creeping price rise, in which unions and others became increasingly concerned by the erosion between wage rounds of real earnings, so that the wage–price spiral was strengthened. In retrospect, it seems possible that the troubles of the 1970s would have been less serious if the critical rate had been adhered to in earlier years.

---

[1]   R.C.O.Matthews, 'Why has Britain had Full Employment Since the War?', *EJ*, September 1968.
[2]   Dow, *op. cit.*, Ch. XVI, and F.W.Paish, *Studies in an Inflationary Economy* (Macmillan, 1962).

5.3   Economic Policy and Inflation

Inflation does not in itself reduce the average level of real income, although, of course, policies to counter it may have this consequence. Its main effect is the achievement of an arbitrary transfer of real incomes from some groups to others: from members of weak trade unions to members of stronger unions, from the old to the able-bodied, from non-indexed retirement incomes to the incomes of those at work.

Fast inflation produces sharp declines in real income between one annual wage settlement and the next, and this can cause unrest. It acts as a 'tax' on cash holdings, reducing their purchasing power; and if nominal interest rates are sticky, it reduces the real value of certain types of asset – thus leading to transfers of wealth between different groups of people. Finally, the prospect of inflation creates the fear that living standards will drop, and destroys confidence in the government's management of the economy.

In the period when inflation was merely creeping it may have been possible to regard it as a small price to pay for high employment. A gently sloping trade-off between inflation and unemployment made the problem of political compromise minimal compared with the situation in the 1970s and 1980s. The advocacy of an incomes policy in the 1960s was associated either with those who hoped to be able to run the economy at a still higher pressure of demand, or else with those who sought to use it as an instrument of income redistribution.

The arrival of fast inflation in the 1970s transformed the policy problem. It meant that real incomes were rapidly eroded between wage settlements, and it transformed economic behaviour. Economic units learned how to live with inflation and sought to defend their real wages either by insisting on a full compensation for past increases in the cost of living or, perhaps, by bargaining on the basis of price forecasts. This meant that there were two main methods of bringing inflation under control. One was to deflate domestic demand to such a low pressure that the downwards effect of unemployment and low demand was large enough to offset that of prior price increases. Given that prices in some years were increasing at rates of over 15 or 20%, this would have necessitated either intolerably high unemployment or an unbearably long period of correction. The other alternative was an incomes policy under which the rate of wage increase was subjected to statutory or firm quasi-statutory control.

A statutory incomes policy was tried by the Conservative government in 1972–4 after its attempt to secure a voluntary policy had failed. The policy coincided with a major rise in import prices, and the provision in stage III of the policy for the effective indexation of wages to the cost of living had the unfortunate further effect of linking wages to import prices. The policy collapsed, despite its statutory powers, chiefly because one strong trade union, the National Union of Mineworkers was prepared to go slow and finally strike rather than accept the terms of the policy. It was this which led to the early election of February 1974, and, it is argued, to the defeat of the Conservative Party.[1]

The incoming Labour government continued the indexation provisions under the 'Social Contract' but little further was done to prevent inflation until July 1975, when a voluntary incomes policy was introduced in three stages, starting with a maximum increase of £6 per week.

This was certainly the first time that an incomes policy can be said to have made a significant impact upon the rate of wage inflation. The equation reported in section 4 suggests that the effect of the policy was to reduce wages below what they would otherwise have been by about 3% per annum for three years. But in the 'catch-up' that followed, the estimates suggest that these effects were partly eliminated.[2] Other work has suggested still less effect, but whatever the numerical effects of the incomes policies, few governments would be prepared to accept a repetition of the spate of industrial disputes during the 'winter of discontent' period in 1978/79. The government was unable to obtain union agreement to a continuation of incomes policy in 1978, and was unwilling to enforce a statutory policy.

5.4   Counter-inflationary Policy Since 1979: The MTFS and After

The Conservative government which was returned in May 1979 was determined to reduce inflation without recourse to incomes policy. The government was also pledged to reduce income tax, and in the Budget of June 1979, the standard rate was lowered from 33 to 30p in the £. The revenue effects were counterbalanced by an increase in VAT from 8 to 15%, an act of policy which was itself inflationary – adding an estimated 4% to the RPI directly and still more via the wage–price spiral.

The chosen method for dealing with inflation was the Medium Term Financial Strategy (or MTFS) which was introduced with the budget of March 1980. The strategy set target rates for the growth of the broad money stock (£M3) over a four-year period together with a planned reduction in the PSBR (the combined deficit of the central government, local authorities and public corporations):

Financial Year	*1980/81*	*1981/82*	*1982/83*	*1983/84*
Target growth of £M3 (%)	7–11	6–10	5–9	4–8
Projected PSBR as % of GDP	3.75	3.0	2.25	1.5
Actuals: growth of £M3 (%)	19.4	12.8	11.2	9.4
PSBR as % of GDP	5.6	3.4	3.2	3.2

---

[1]   For an account of this period see M.J.Stewart, *Politics and Economic Policy in the UK since 1964* (Pergamon, 1978).

[2]   S.G.B.Henry, 'Income Policy and Aggregate Pay', in J.L.Fallick and R.F.Elliott (eds.), *Incomes Policies, Inflation and Relative Pay* (Allen and Unwin, 1981); see also K.Mayhew, 'Traditional Incomes Policies', *Oxford Bulletin of Economics and Statistics*, February 1983. The effects of wage-reduction are, of course, multiplied via effects on prices and back, via the spiral, to wages.

The ideas behind the MTFS reflected a variety of views and attitudes. A prominent element was the crude 'monetarist' belief that inflation is caused by prior increases in the stock of money. On this assumption, a progressive reduction in the money stock was a necessary condition for a gradual fall in the inflation rate. But given that the budget deficit (and PSBR) were financed by a mix of money creation and debt issue, the fall in money creation would mean that new issues of debt would be increasing over time. The effect would be to raise interest rates and 'crowd out' private sector investment – something which the government did not wish to happen. Hence the solution chosen by the government was to enforce a decline in the PSBR itself, and projections to this effect were included in the FSBR.

A second idea behind the MTFS was the belief that expectations were of key significance in the inflationary process, and that these in turn were determined by the expected growth of the money stock. In some quarters, it was even believed that this would affect wage demands. Thus the 1980 FSBR stated that 'the speed with which inflation falls will depend crucially upon expectations both in the United Kingdom and overseas'. The MTFS also gained support from those who believed it would act as a discipline for budgetary policy, ensuring that the recession would not be countered and would thus, on Phillips curve lines, bring down the rate of wage inflation by creating unemployment. Finally, it appealed to those who thought that public expenditure was too high.

In the first two years of the MTFS, the projected PSBR was treated as an inflexible target, and this meant that when unemployment rose by more than had been allowed for in the FSBR projection, the government felt impelled to look either for cuts in expenditure (which made the recession worse) or for increases in nationalized industry prices (which made inflation worse). In this latter sense the policy was counter-productive.

The MTFS also failed to achieve its monetary targets, which were exceeded by 8% in 1980/81 and 3% in 1981/82, a result which put in question the Bank of England's ability to control the stock of money at all precisely.[1] The renewal of the MTFS in 1981, when unemployment was well over two million and the policy was under attack from inside the government as well as outside, had the effect of making the recession worse than it need have been. This was at a time when the rise in the exchange rate (due mainly to North Sea oil and high interest rates) had severely damaged the export and manufacturing sectors. The combined effect was to induce a state of extreme slack in the labour market, such that wage increases abated, and the inflation rate, which had been 18% in 1980 (after the VAT increase) fell to 5% in 1983 and 3% in 1986 (table 1.10). The MFTS can, perhaps, take credit for this achievement, although

---

[1] See J. C. R. Dow and I. D. Saville, *A Critique of Monetary Policy* (Oxford, 1988).

its success was due not so much to the monetary strategy as to the recession which it helped to bring about. There is no way of knowing whether it had significant effects through the medium of price expectations.[1]

After 1983, the MTFS was retained in name but no longer in substance. The term figured annually in the Financial Statement and Budget Report, but its character changed. Increases in the money stock, which had been seen as pre-cursors of the inflation rate, were now regarded as related to 'nominal income' (GDP in money terms). The crude monetarist belief that monetary growth precedes and causes inflation gave way to more technical considerations such as the proposition that – given the right definition of money – there is a stable demand for money or a stable velocity of circulation. The broad monetary aggregates, including £M3, were found to have unstable velocities of circulation, and in 1986 MO replaced £M3 as the target variable on the grounds of its more stable velocity. For this reason, it could be seen as a forward indicator of nominal GDP – forward in the sense of being available well in advance of quarterly GDP figures. But, in substance, MO consists solely of notes, coin and bankers balances at the Bank of England. It does not include current account deposits, and, at only 7% the size of M3, it can hardly rank as an important monetary aggregate – even if it is controllable. It is difficult to believe that its 'targeting' is of any real significance. But the retention of something that could be called a 'monetary target' helped to preserve the illusion that the MTFS was still in business.

Meanwhile, ministerial discussion of inflation has moved away from concern with the monetary growth rate to concern with import prices, wage demands, and the pressure of demand in the economy – in short, all the factors which the Treasury used to believe in before the 'monetarist revolution' (and which were discussed in section 4 of this chapter).

5.5   The Inflation–Unemployment Dilemma

The dependence of the rate of increase in wage rates (or earnings) upon the pressure of demand for labour has for many years been taken to signify an important and serious dilemma between the two main policy objectives. According to the original Phillips relationship, the *critical rate of unemployment* was some $2\frac{1}{4}\%$ of the labour force, this being the position at which money wage rates increase at the same rate as productivity – thus holding unit labour costs constant. Under the expectations-augmented Phillips curve – in which the rate of wage change is assumed to be dependent upon both the unemployment rate and the expected price change – the

---

[1]   For a further discussion, see C. Allsopp, 'Monetary and Fiscal Policy in the 1980s', *OREP*, Spring, 1985 and the books by Browning, Gardner, Kaldor, Keegan, Maynard and Riddell cited at the end of this chapter.

term NAIRU (or 'non-accelerating inflation rate of unemployment') has been used in place of the old critical rate. The two rates are numerically equal, but whereas the critical rate signified a zero rate of inflation, the NAIRU holds for any *constant* rate of inflation – zero or otherwise. It is the rate of unemployment at which the inflation rate will remain steady if there are no demand disturbances. In the simplest terms (and ignoring open economy repercussions), if inflation is initially x% per annum, then price expectations will rise also at x%; wage rates will increase by x% if the economy is at the NAIRU; and prices will follow the course of wages. If, however, the initial inflation rate is zero and the economy is again at NAIRU, then inflation too will be zero. (The usual analysis ignores the exchange-rate–import price linkage, but this works to ensure a one-to-one relationship between costs and prices.)

The term 'natural rate' is sometimes used in place of the critical rate or NAIRU, although the latter is not equivalent to Friedman's use of the term *natural rate of unemployment*.[1] His natural rate was a full employment rate of unemployment. It was 'ground out by Walrasian equilibrium equations', and represents general equilibrium throughout the labour market. Supply and demand are equal in each subsector, and there is, therefore, a complete absence of involuntary unemployment. Friedman and his followers believe that there is a natural tendency for the economy to return to the natural rate of unemployment, i.e. to full employment or a state of no involuntary unemployment. This, however, is a long-term and highly speculative view, dependent upon a belief in market forces and on the eventual downwards flexibility of money wage rates.

The economy in the 1980s may, at times, have been not far from its *critical* rate of unemployment. But it has never been at its natural rate on Friedman's original definition because this implied a complete absence of involuntary unemployment. The unemployed, for the most part, and with only minor qualifications, are actively seeking work at going wage rates. Their unemployment is essentially involuntary and it is misleading to call it 'natural'.

During the period from 1983 to 1987, the rate of inflation was fairly constant, varying between 3 and 6% per annum, and, although there was some increase in import prices, this may signify that the pressure of demand in this period was roughly at its critical rate. Unemployment averaged 10–11% on the official definition and the vacancy rate 0.6%.[2] The implication must be that a reasonably acceptable level of unemployment is no longer attainable – with present institutions and attitudes – without increas-

---

[1]   M. Friedman, 'The Role of Monetary Policy', *AER*, Vol. 58(1), pp. 1–17, and M. Friedman and D. Laidler, 'Unemployment *versus* Inflation', IEA, 1975, Occasional Paper 44.
[2]   Regression equations must be treated with caution, but the earnings relationship in section 4 implies that unit labour costs will remain constant for vacancy rates of 0.36 and 0.49% for productivity growth rates of 2.0 and 3.0% per annum respectively. These critical vacancy rates correspond to the situation in 1981–2 (the recession) and 1985.

ing inflation: or, conversely, that an acceptable rate of inflation implies an unacceptable number of unemployed. Thus the need for an incomes policy that really works is more serious today than it has ever been before.

6   ECONOMIC PROSPECTS AND POLICIES

Early in 1989 the economy appeared to be just past its cyclical peak, with the prospect of some slowdown to come. Since 1985 real GDP had grown at an average rate of about 4% per annum. This rate of expansion, being faster than the growth of potential, had helped to bring about a decline in unemployment and a rise in vacancies, with consequential inflationary pressures. At the same time a large balance of payments deficit had developed.

The expansion of total demand had been led by a strong growth of fixed investment, which rose by over 20% in a two-year period. Consumer spending also rose rapidly, helped by tax reductions in the budgets of 1986–88, and by the huge growth of consumer credit. The growth of consumption was 12% between the first halves of 1986 and 1988, and the Treasury was estimating a $4\frac{1}{2}$% increase from then to the first half of 1989. Meanwhile the growth of imports by volume was more than twice as fast as that of exports, with the result that the balance of payments, which had been in very substantial surplus throughout the 1980–85 period, moved into deficit in 1987. By 1988 the current account deficit amounted to 3.0% of market price GDP.

Unemployment fell below two million in March 1989, having declined steadily for $2\frac{1}{2}$ years from a peak of 3.1 million in 1986. The decline was partly statistical, reflecting new definitions and new conditions for claimants, but a substantial part of the fall was a genuine improvement. Vacancies reached their peak levels in 1987 and 1988 (when they were not far short of the 1979 level). The tighter labour market helped towards a build-up of inflation, with earnings rising at some $9\frac{1}{2}$% a year in the first few months of 1989 – about 2% faster than two years earlier. With help from rising profit margins, the rate of retail price inflation went up from only 3% in early 1988 to nearly 8% in March 1989. Part of the rise (about $1\frac{1}{2}$%) reflected higher mortgage interest rates, following a series of increases in bank base rate – from 8.5% in January 1988 to 13% in November 1988.

The economic outlook as seen by the Treasury in March 1989 is summarised in Table 1.12. The rise in investment was expected to slacken in 1989 and 1990, and consumption was predicted to grow at half its previous rate. Thus the annual rate of growth of real GDP was put at $2\frac{1}{2}$% for the two years up to the first half of 1989 – roughly the growth rate of productive potential. Most outside forecasters were predicting not much further decline in unemployment. As for inflation, the Treasury was predicting that the rate of retail price increase would fall to $5\frac{1}{2}$% by the fourth quarter of 1989 and $4\frac{1}{2}$% by the second quarter of 1989. The National Institute

TABLE 1.12
Economic Trends and Prospects, UK, 1986–90

	Level, 1st half 1988 (£bn, 1985 prices, s.a.)	*Changes over 2 years:*	
		1st half 1986 to 1st half 1988 (%)	1st half 1988 to 1st half 1990 (%)
Consumers' expenditure	125.9	12	6
Government consumption	38.2	2	2
Fixed investment	36.6	23	8
Exports	55.9	7	9
Stockbuilding (changes as % of GDP)	0.6	0	−1
Imports	61.2	20	11
Factor cost adjustment	27.9	9	6
GDP (average estimate)	169.7	9	5

Source: FSBR, 1989–90.

(*Economic Review*, February 1989) was expecting slightly more than this – a 5.8% rise for the fourth quarter of 1989 and 5.9% from then until the fourth quarter of 1990. Increased oil prices in April suggested that both these forecasts might have to be revised upwards.

The resurgence of inflation was blamed in some quarters on the budget of 1988 which had reduced the standard rate of income tax by 2p to 25p, and the higher rates of tax to 40p (with a revenue effect of about £5 billion). Both monetary and fiscal policy had been expansionary after the stock market crash of October 1987 because of fears of a world recession, and the budget judgement was misled by the Treasury's forecast for 1988, which turned out to be too low (by 1.5% for the second half-year). The 1989 budget was broadly neutral, with no tax changes of macroeconomic significance.

The main economic policy objective continued to be the containment of inflation. The ultimate aim was said to be price stability, although the MTFS in 1989 was still projecting a rise in the GDP deflator of $2\frac{1}{2}\%$ in 1992–93. The reduction of unemployment was seen as fortunate if it occurred but not as an explicit goal of macroeconomic policy. The other main objective was the reduction of tax rates – although in 1989 this was not allowed to conflict with that of price stability. A balance of payments surplus was *not* an aim of policy, but the large current account deficit carried implications for other objectives. Any depreciation of the exchange rate to accommodate the deficit threatened to add to inflation by raising import prices. To prevent this from happening, policy in 1988 and 1989 was striving to maintain higher interest rates in London than in other financial centres, thus attracting short-term capital from abroad. The main drawback to the policy – especially when maintained over long periods of time – is that it discourages domestic fixed investment, thus retarding the long-term growth rate with a threat to future living standards.

REFERENCES AND FURTHER READING

C.J.Allsopp, 'Monetary and Fiscal Policies in the 1980s', *OREP*, Spring, 1985.

F.T.Blackaby (ed.), *British Economic Policy 1960–74* (NIESR and Cambridge University Press, 1979).

P.Browning, *The Treasury and Economic Policy 1964–1985* (Longman, 1986).

Central Statistical Office, *United Kingdom National Accounts* (1988 Edition, HMSO). The CSO Blue Book.

Charter for Jobs, *We Can Cut Unemployment* (London, 1985).

J.C.R.Dow and I.D.Saville, *A Critique of Monetary Policy* (Oxford University Press, 1988).

C.H.Feinstein, *National Income, Expenditure and Output of the United Kingdom 1855–1965* (Cambridge University Press, 1972).

N.Gardner, *Decade of Discontent: The Changing British Economy since 1973* (Blackwell, 1987).

Sir Bryan Hopkin, M.Miller and B.Reddaway, 'An Alternative Economic Strategy – a Message of Hope', *Cambridge Journal of Economics*, March, 1982.

C. Johnson, *Measuring the Economy* (Penguin Books, 1988).

Lord Kaldor, *The Scourge of Monetarism* (Oxford University Press, 2nd edition, 1986).

W.Keegan, *Mrs Thatcher's Economic Experiment* (Penguin Books, 1984).

R.Layard, *How to Beat Unemployment* (Oxford University Press, 1986).

G.Maynard, *The Economy under Mrs Thatcher* (Blackwell, 1988).

R.C.O.Matthews, C.H.Feinstein and J.C.Odling-Smee, *British Economic Growth 1856–1973* (Stanford University Press, 1982).

National Institute Economic Review.

P.Riddell, *The Thatcher Government* (Martin Robertson, 1983).

P.Rowlatt, 'An Analysis of the Recent Path of UK Inflation', *Oxford Bulletin of Economics and Statistics*, November 1988.

M.Stewart, *Politics and Economic Policy in the UK since 1964* (Pergamon, 1978).

Treasury, *Financial Statement and Budget Report 1989–90*.

2

Money and finance: public expenditure and taxation

R.L.Harrington

1 INTRODUCTION

Chapter 1 considered the UK economy from the macroeconomic point of view. As well as examining the main categories of expenditure and considering some of the main macroeconomic problems, the chapter also dealt with government policies for managing aggregate demand. Such policies involve adjusting the levels of public expenditure and of taxation (budgetary policy), and varying the cost of funds in the financial markets, so as to increase or decrease the amounts of money and credit available to the economy (monetary policy).

These policies are likely to have many repercussions on the economy over and above their effects on aggregate demand. Further, how well any particular policy works is likely to depend on the structure of the economy at any one time. That is to say, macroeconomic policy, like other policies, does not operate in a vacuum. In planning and in assessing policy, governments must take into account potential side-effects of policy actions; equally they have to consider the influence of changes in the structure of the economy on the effectiveness of policy.

Consider first budgetary policy. The prime purpose of public expenditure is not as a means of regulating aggregate demand. We have public expenditure because we want the things it buys: hospitals and people to work in them, schools and school-teachers, fighter aeroplanes and pilots, etc. The many services provided collectively and paid for out of taxation are of importance in their own right. Demand management should, therefore, be conducted in ways which do not adversely affect the efficiency of publicly provided services. One way that budgetary policy can work adversely in this manner is when policies are changed too frequently. If, in attempts to adjust finely the level of demand in the economy, governments continually alter their expenditure plans, it becomes difficult for those responsible for providing public services to plan ahead and efficiency is likely to suffer.

So attempts to use public expenditure as a means of influencing the level of aggregate demand are constrained by the need not to chop and change spending plans too frequently. For this reason, budgetary policy has tended to rely more on tax changes. But here also, policy is constrained by concerns other than demand management. Taxes have many side effects. Changes in the taxation of company profits may affect the ability or willingness of firms to undertake new investment. High marginal rates of taxation on persons may diminish productive effort and increase the amount of time and resources devoted to tax avoidance. And frequent changes of tax regime will be justly unpopular with companies trying to predict their cash flow and with the Inland Revenue, responsible for collecting direct taxes such as income tax and corporation tax.

The effectiveness of taxes can vary over time as economic circumstances change. An example is the stamp duty imposed on transactions in ordinary shares. For many years this tax produced modest sums of revenue and there was little scope for it to be avoided. But in recent years, there has been a rapid internationalization of finance, and many transactions in shares, including shares of large UK companies, can now be carried out equally well outside the United Kingdom as within it. There is increasing scope for the tax to be avoided by switching share-dealing abroad. To lessen the incentive for this, the government first reduced the tax from 2% to ½% in two stages in 1984 and 1986.

Consider now monetary policy. The problems are the same in principle, but in practice they have become more acute. During the 1950s and 1960s the authorities could think in terms of a national financial system and could impose a variety of constraints on financial intermediaries in order to influence the availability and/or the cost of finance. But the process of internationalization of finance has gone so far, that by the mid-1980s, it makes more sense to view the British financial system as part of a world financial system. And it is a world financial system in which much business is mobile and in which different centres, e.g. London, New York, Tokyo, Zurich, are in competition with each other. The UK authorities, not unnaturally, wish to see London maintain its position as a key financial centre, with all the earnings and the jobs that go with it, and so they have had to adjust policy accordingly. Constraints imposed on financial institutions which reduce their ability to compete with foreign institutions, or which create incentives for business to be done abroad, have been dropped. The authorities have had to completely rethink their methods of implementing monetary policy.

Enough has been said to show that one cannot properly understand macroeconomic policy unless one understands the context and the institutional environment in which it takes place. This requires both an understanding of the working of the financial system and of that important subset of it which is the monetary system, and also an understanding of the size and composition of public expenditure and of how it is financed. Of course, knowledge of private finance and of public finance is not only necessary in order to comprehend policy. Both are crucial for all aspects of economic life. It is the purpose of the rest of this chapter to explain first private finance, then public finance in the UK. We consider first the financial system and the many important changes that have occurred in it in recent years and then we turn our attention to the composition of government spending and the sources of government revenue.

2   THE FINANCIAL SYSTEM
2.1   Nature and Functions

A financial system is composed of institutions and markets which fulfil a variety of economic functions. Central to all is arranging or facilitating the lending of funds from one economic agent to another. Most other financial services are ancillary to, or derived from, this one. The lending of funds from one economic agent to another – from lender to borrower – can be accomplished in many different ways; but all of these can be classified into just two distinct approaches.

Firstly, the lender can lend direct to the borrower, albeit perhaps with the assistance of brokers who act in an agency capacity. This is what happens when a person subscribes to a new issue of government stock, deposits money with a local authority or buys a share in a public company. In each case, the person is lending direct to the borrower and is incurring all the risks that such lending involves. This may be called direct finance.

The second approach, which may be called indirect finance, involves a financial intermediary standing between borrower and lender. The lender lends his funds to the intermediary, e.g. a bank or a building society. The intermediary collects funds from many lenders and decides to whom it will lend. Borrowers approach the intermediary and, if credit-worthy, they receive loans. There is no direct contact between lender and borrower. Each deals with the intermediary, each has his contract with the intermediary; instead of one transaction, there are two.

This form of finance seems at first sight to be more roundabout, and to involve the use of more real resources of capital and labour than direct finance. But financial intermediaries are numerous and indirect finance more common than direct finance. What, then, are its advantages? They are many, and they derive from the ability of financial institutions to use their size and their expertise to transform financial claims, so that they can offer to savers a wider choice of assets than ultimate borrowers are able to do. At the same time, they can offer to borrowers a more varied choice of credit terms than ultimate lenders are able to do. To fully appreciate this, consider the most important financial intermediary: the general-purpose bank.

Such a bank accepts deposits of all sizes and on a variety of terms. In the United Kingdom, the largest banks each have many millions of individual deposits, which in the aggregate sum to more than £30 bn. Such banks know that, every day, many depositors will withdraw money, but that many others will make new deposits. The law of averages will, in normal circumstances, ensure that the total sum of money deposited with them does not vary greatly. In consequence, they can allow each individual lender of money the freedom to withdraw his funds with little or no notice, whilst at the same time making loans to borrowers which last for many years. The banks are said to engage in *maturity transformation*, that is, they borrow short and lend long. It is not only banks that do this. Building Societies lend money on mortgages for periods up to thirty years, whilst still allowing most depositors freedom to withdraw their money on demand or at short notice.

Financial intermediaries not only transform maturities, they also transform risk. With direct finance, the ultimate lender bears the risk of default by the borrower, e.g. a person who buys a share in company X is likely to lose money if company X goes into liquidation. The retail banks, who between them have millions of loans outstanding, also stand to lose when borrowers default. But because they are large institutions and employ trained staff who are able to judge to whom it is safe to lend and to whom it is not, they are usually able to keep loan losses to a small proportion of total sums advanced. And as past experience enables them to estimate the likely amount of bad debts, they can allow for this by adding a risk premium to the interest they charge borrowers. In this way banks, like other intermediaries, can bear risks and absorb losses, whilst their depositors, in normal times, can know that their deposits are virtually riskless.

Financial intermediaries provide other services. Retail banks not only offer deposits withdrawable on demand, they also provide facilities for deposits to be transferred from one account to another, and thereby provide a money-transfer system. Sight deposits in banks have become a superior form of money to notes and coin for most purposes, other than small day-to-day transactions. Life assurance companies, whose main business nowadays is accepting regular payments from lenders of funds, over a number of years, and then providing either a lump sum payment or an annuity, combine this business with insurance against death. Thus, while the lender expects to receive a certain sum of money in, say, 20 years' time, he knows that should he die prematurely, the same or another guaranteed sum will be paid to his dependents.

So financial intermediaries perform many functions. And for this reason, many lenders and borrowers find it preferable to deal with intermediaries, rather than to deal direct with each other. This is especially true of small lenders and borrowers, for whom the time-and-trouble costs of direct dealing would normally far outweigh any gain in terms of a more favourable interest rate. But there is still need for direct finance. Many wealthy persons are prepared to incur risk by lending direct to private enterprises in the hope of earning extra returns. If the enterprises fail, they lose money, but if the enterprises prosper, they will receive increased returns in the form both of higher dividends and of capital gains. Further, many persons, rich and poor alike, are happy to lend direct to the government as, here, the risk of default is considered negligible. Those with large sums to lend can buy gilt-edged stock (marketable government bonds) but small savers can also lend direct to the government by purchasing such assets as savings certificates and premium bonds.

During the last 20 years, the financial system, both in the United Kingdom and elsewhere, has been changing rapidly. Banks have introduced new financial instruments; they have developed new techniques of raising funds and of making loans; new financial markets have been created. This process – known as financial innovation – has already had a profound impact on the ways in which financial services are provided, what costs are involved, and where financial services are provided. For all these reasons, it is important to understand what is going on and why.

2.2   Internationalization

The world is shrinking rapidly. Advances in technology have made communications of all sorts easier and faster. People can travel rapidly by air between different parts of the globe and they can communicate easily and cheaply by telephone and telex between different parts of the globe. Computer networks can be operated on a worldwide basis and information made instantly available to people in many different countries. For many economic purposes, national frontiers are of less and less significance, and it is now possible for large firms to run their operations on a global basis. Of course, multinational firms are not new in themselves. But, in earlier times, such firms could not easily integrate their worldwide operations, as communications between head office and foreign subsidiaries were slow and costly. Subsidiaries tended to operate with a considerable degree of autonomy. Now, it is possible for head office to be in almost continuous contact with foreign subsidiaries and branches and to co-ordinate operations in one worldwide strategy.

These changes have been particularly in evidence in banking and in other areas of finance. Large banks have established networks of offices around the world. These offices can deal actively in the financial markets where they are situated and still report, promptly to head office, full details of all business done. In consequence, senior officials in head office can monitor closely the worldwide position of the bank in many different financial markets. And if they wish, they can undertake new business, designed to offset or to complement the activities of offices abroad, so as to keep the bank's global balance-sheet in line with what is desired.

At the same time, new international markets have grown in short-term financial assets, in bank loans and in securities. These markets are worldwide, although they tend to be dominated by trading in a limited number of major financial centres. London, with over 700 banks, is the largest, but other centres are important as well; and since much business is potentially mobile, international financial centres are, inevitably, in competition with each other. International bank loans arranged in New York could be arranged in Paris or Amsterdam: international securities issued in London could be issued in Brussels or Zurich. Success in this competition depends upon things such as good telecommunications facilities, the availability of skilled labour, the tax regime, reserve requirements imposed on banks, the time zone in which a centre finds itself, and many others. This, in turn, means that governments and central banks, if they are concerned about the size of their financial industry (and most of them are) now have to consider carefully how policy actions may affect their national share of what has become an international business.

2.3   Technological Change

Developments in micro-electronic technology have been a crucial factor in the internationalization of banking, but they have also had other effects on banking, as well as on other areas of finance. This is a complex topic, about which books have been written, so what follows should only be seen as a brief summary.[1]

The initial uses of computers in financial institutions were in keeping records and in automating labour-intensive activities such as cheque clearing. As computers became more sophisticated and computing power cheaper, it became possible for records to be updated with increasing frequency and for the information to be accessed more easily. This was of great importance: decisions in banking depend on information. Decisions about new business depend on what existing loans are outstanding, to which industrial sectors, in which geographical areas, to which large firms; what is the banks' position in the short-term financial markets; what are the maturity structures of assets and liabilities; what is the currency-composition of assets and liabilities, and on many other aspects of the existing portfolio. Banks which have such information readily available will be able to take quicker decisions about new transactions than banks which do not. In modern banking, keeping track of one's position is not just for purposes of record, it is a key input into new business decisions.

Computers have also made it possible for financial institutions to cope with a much wider range of business. This is one reason for the fading of traditional demarcations between different types of financial institutions. When calculations were done manually, it was cost-efficient for intermediaries to keep operations simple and this meant undertaking only a restricted range of business. But now that all sorts of complex calculations can be performed instantaneously, banks and other intermediaries can introduce a more varied range of assets and liabilities, they can deal easily in assets and liabilities denominated in many different currencies (including composite currencies such as the ECU) and they can more readily envisage competing for new types of business. And however complex the balance sheet, however variegated are assets and liabilities, if a bank has access to appropriate computer hardware and software, its managers can still keep track

---

[1]   A recent authoritative survey of developments in this area is provided by J.R.S.Revell, *Banking and Electronic Fund Transfers* (OECD, 1983).

of credit exposures to firms or to industries, of mismatches between the maturities of assets and of liabilities, of risks due to financing fixed-interest loans on the basis of variable-rate deposits and so on.

New technology has changed dealing rooms out of all recognition. Dealers, whether in foreign exchange, in short-term financial assets or in securities, now use the latest micro-electronic equipment. They have access to video screens on which any one of a number of pages of information on interest rates, exchange rates, etc., can be displayed at the touch of a button. Telephone contact with money brokers, with foreign-exchange brokers and with other leading banks is also instantaneous and deals once struck can be automatically recorded in seconds. This considerable mechanization of dealing has both permitted and encouraged the surge in money-market activity that has occurred during the last two decades, both in London and elsewhere.

The foregoing can be described as back-office technology; it is not seen by most bank clients. But the use of new technology has spread to the front office, to the point of direct contact between banks and clients. The most obvious manifestation to date is the growth in usage of automatic teller machines (ATMs) which permit depositors to withdraw cash or carry out other simple transactions automatically and outside normal banking hours. But experiments have been taking place, both in the UK and abroad, on what is known as electronic funds transfer at point of sale (EFT/POS). This is a system, already technologically feasible, which is expected, in time, to replace many payments in cash or by cheque. It requires retailers to have specially designed computer terminals at check-outs or cash desks, and it requires banks' customers to have their own personal debit card. When the card is inserted in the retailer's terminal and when, at the same time, the card-holder registers his personal identification number, then payment for purchases is made automatically by the instantaneous debit to the buyer's account and credit to the retailer's account of the sum due.

During 1988, the first banks began offering debit cards to their clients. As yet, there are no widespread direct computer links between retailers and banks so for each transaction a voucher has to be submitted to the bank just as with transactions involving credit cards. But this will only mean a delay of some four days before the sum involved is deducted from the client's bank account, unlike credit card transactions where payment may be delayed, at no cost to the customer, for up to seven weeks. Given this difference, the banks may find that not all of their clients are as enthusiastic about the new debit cards as they themselves are.

It is common for newspaper accounts of EFT/POS to claim that it heralds the advent of the cashless society. This is clearly a gross exaggeration. For inter-personal transactions and for many small purchases, e.g. bus fares, newspapers or packets of chewing gum, cash is likely to remain the cheapest and most efficient means of payment. But EFT/POS may, in time, substantially reduce the number of payments by cash and by cheque, with consequent savings in costs for both banks and retailers. It may also mean new changes in the demand for different types of media of exchange and new difficulties in interpreting movements in statistics of the money supply.

Another way in which new technology is directly affecting relations between banks and their customers is through what is called office banking. In essence, what this means is that corporate clients, provided they have basic computing facilities, can communicate directly with their bank's computer to obtain details of their accounts or to initiate any of a number of transactions. Thus, the finance director can send instructions to the bank to make payments, to move money between accounts, to buy or sell foreign exchange or to buy any of a number of short-term financial assets, simply by tapping at a keyboard in his own office. For important clients, banks guarantee fulfilment of the instructions within agreed limits as to amount. In some cases, involving large clients and large banks, such direct computer links can be international.

A number of banks and one building society are offering analogous facilities to personal clients under the name of home banking. This enables anyone with a home computer and a telephone to call up details of his bank account and to initiate a number of transactions.

2.4   The Bank of England

The Bank of England was established as a joint-stock company by Act of Parliament in 1694. In return for a large loan to the then government, it was granted important monopoly rights. Over the years, while still a privately-owned institution, it came to exercise a number of important public functions, notably holding the nation's stock of gold and (later) foreign-currency reserves. The Bank (as it is known in financial circles) was nationalized in 1946 and made subject to the authority of the Chancellor of the Exchequer. It is now unambiguously an arm of government and its main purpose is to carry out a number of important public functions; although it continues to provide banking services for a number of private clients, comprised chiefly of members of its staff, a number of banks, and a small number of old-established clients who have had accounts with the Bank from the days when it was still a joint-stock company.

Of the many functions of the Bank of England, the following are the most important:

(a) banker to the government;
(b) banker to the clearing banks;
(c) holder of the nation's stock of gold and foreign-exchange reserves;
(d) manager of the issue of notes and coins;
(e) implementation of government monetary policy;
(f) supervision of banks and of certain other financial institutions.

The Bank of England is banker to Her Majesty's Government; that is to say, it keeps all the main government accounts, receives tax revenues and makes payments in respect of government expenditures. When necessary, the Bank also arranges borrowing for the government through the issue of new gilt-edge stock. In most years since World War II, this was necessary and the Bank of England was regularly engaged in selling bonds on behalf of the government; but in 1987 and 1988 the government accounts were in surplus and appeared set to remain so for a number of years. Rather than selling new stock, the Bank has used the public-sector surplus to buy back previously issued government bonds.

Notwithstanding this, there remains a large amount of outstanding government stock and this is actively traded by investors, brokers and gilt-edged market makers. The Bank of England is in a position to exert an influence over this trading and can thereby have some impact upon market expectations of future interest rates. However, in recent years, the Bank has tended to sell or to buy stock at rates in line with prevailing market interest rates and has chosen to exert its main influence on interest rates by means of its operations in short-term bill markets.

The Bank of England is also banker to the clearing banks, i.e. those retail banks which operate the system through which cheques are cleared and monies transferred from one bank account to another. Although the gross sums transferred through clearing, each day, are very large, payments due from one bank to another are normally offset, to a great extent, by payments due in the reverse direction, and it is only necessary to settle a relatively small net balance. This is done, each working day, by transfers between bankers' accounts at the Bank of England.

The Bank of England holds, on behalf of Her Majesty's Government, the nation's stock of gold and foreign-exchange reserves. It can use this stock to intervene on the foreign-exchange market. If it is government policy to support the international value of the pound, the Bank will sell chosen foreign currencies in exchange for sterling. If it is government policy to prevent the pound from rising in value, the Bank will sell pounds and buy chosen foreign currencies.

The Bank of England acts as the note-issuing authority and (on behalf of the government) manages the minting and the issue of new coins. This is a large task: notes wear out and old notes have to be continually withdrawn from circulation and new ones printed and distributed to the banks. Also, as the economy expands and as inflation erodes the value of money, there is a need for more notes and coins, so the Bank has to see that the supply is continually augmented. There are also seasonal fluctuations, with demands for extra notes and coin at Christmas and over bank-holiday weekends.

The Bank implements government monetary policy. In some accounts of monetary policy, there has been confusion about the division of responsibility between the Bank and the Treasury; but the position is, in principle, quite clear. It is the government, acting through the Treasury, which is responsible for monetary policy, and it is the Chancellor of the Exchequer who has to defend to Parliament the government's exercise of policy. The

Bank can give advice, and given its knowledge and experience of financial markets, its advice will often be influential, but ultimate responsibility lies with the government.

Once the broad outlines of policy have been decided, it is the task of the Bank of England to implement policy. In order to do this, the Bank is allowed a considerable degree of autonomy. This is quite usual: central banks in other developed countries are also granted autonomy in their day-to-day operations. The reason is readily apparent. Monetary policy is conducted largely through operations in financial markets where conditions change from hour to hour, or even minute to minute. Thus, while the objectives of policy may be clear, the Bank must still use discretion in how best to pursue these objectives. For instance, if it were policy to support the international value of the pound, the Bank still has to decide when, and by how much, to intervene on the foreign-exchange market. If there were heavy selling of sterling, the Bank might judge that immediate intervention would be futile. On the other hand, if there were signs that market traders were hesitating and were unsure of official intentions, even modest intervention by the Bank might be effective in halting a decline. Similarly, in dealing in the domestic markets in government bonds and in short-term bills, the Bank has to exercise discretion in the timing of its actions and in the amount which it buys or sells.

The supervision of the financial system has become of increasing importance. Many modern financial institutions are of such size that were they to fail there would be serious consequences for thousands, or even millions, of persons and firms, with obvious secondary effects on the economy as a whole. Further, many institutions, especially the banks, borrow and lend amongst themselves, so there is a degree of inter-dependence between institutions. The failure of one could provoke the failure of others and, in the worst case, there could be a chain reaction with a succession of financial institutions becoming insolvent. One only has to imagine what would be the consequences of the failure of even one large bank, let alone several, to see that there is a clear public interest in ensuring the efficient and prudent management of banks, as well as of other financial intermediaries.

The 1979 and 1987 Banking Acts provide legal backing to the role of the Bank of England as supervisor of the banking system. In order to carry on a banking business, all institutions, apart from a limited number of specific exceptions, now require to be authorized by the Bank of England. Further, all authorized banks are expected to supply the Bank of England with information about their business on a regular basis, and they are required to respond to directives given to them by the Bank. For instance, the Bank has laid down criteria for the capital adequacy of banks, and how these should apply to each bank is one of the matters discussed at the regular meetings that officials of the Bank hold with senior staff at each bank. In the last resort, should the Bank of England be seriously concerned about the conduct or the performance of any bank, it can withdraw its authorization.

2.5   The Retail Banks

The retail banks, as their name suggests, are banks which offer retail banking services to business and personal clients, both small and large, through a network of branches. Such services traditionally cover the taking of deposits at sight and at short notice, the provision of cheque books and the clearing of cheques, the making of short- and medium-term loans, sale and purchase of foreign currency and travellers' cheques, dealing with international remittances, safe-deposit facilities, financial advice and maybe insurance broking. In recent years, banks have been actively seeking to increase business and a number of other services have been introduced, of which the most notable are cheque-guarantee cards, networks of automated teller machines, eurocheques (cheques which may be written in any one of a number of foreign currencies), long-term mortgage lending for house purchase, and opportunities for mutual investment in equity shares and other securities through bank-managed unit trusts. In addition, the larger banks either own or have established links with firms of security traders, so also offer facilities for buying and selling securities.

Retail banking is nowadays contrasted with wholesale banking which involves dealing in large sums of money (one million dollars and over) at fixed term, in sterling and in foreign currencies. A large part of such business is undertaken in organized short-term financial markets and it is concentrated in a limited number of international centres such as London, New York, Tokyo and Paris. The distinction is conceptual rather than legal and most of the banks classified as retail banks are, in reality, mixed banks which undertake both retail and wholesale banking. Other banks specialize largely or entirely in wholesale banking.

The published balance sheets of the different groups of banks are drawn up in the same way, so it will only be necessary to discuss these once. Accordingly, we shall discuss in detail the combined balance sheet of the retail banks, and will then confine ourselves to noting the main differences when we look at the other groups of banks.

The banks classified by the Bank of England as retail banks are (at 19 February 1989) as follows:

> Allied Irish Banks plc
> Bank of England, Banking Department
> Bank of Ireland
> Bank of Scotland
> Barclays Bank plc
> Clydesdale Bank plc
> Co-operative Bank plc
> Coutts & Co.
> Girobank plc
> Lloyds Bank plc
> Midland Bank plc
> National Westminster Bank plc
> Northern Bank Ltd
> The Royal Bank of Scotland plc
> TSB England & Wales plc
> TSB Northern Ireland plc

TSB Scotland plc
Ulster Bank Ltd
Yorkshire Bank plc

Of these banks, Barclays, Lloyds, Midland and National Westminster are the main retail banks of England and Wales; Bank of Scotland, Clydesdale Bank and Royal Bank of Scotland are the main retail banks in Scotland, although the last named also has a number of branches in England and Wales; and Allied Irish Banks, Bank of Ireland, Northern Bank and Ulster Bank are the main retail banks in both Northern Ireland and in the Republic of Ireland.

The combined balance sheet of the retail banks as at 30 December 1988 is given in table 2.1. This table covers all business of the retail banks (including wholesale business) on the books of their UK offices on that date.

Both liabilities and assets are classified according to whether they are denominated in sterling or in foreign currencies. In recent years, foreign-currency business has grown rapidly as a share of total business. On the liabilities side of the balance sheet, it will be noticed that most sterling deposits are from the UK private sector, although significant amounts are also received from other banks and from abroad. Most foreign-currency deposits come from abroad, although again there are also important sums derived from other banks as well as from non-bank domestic residents. The items labelled 'certificates of deposit' refer to term deposits taken against the issue of a certificate. Such certificates of deposits (CDs) are negotiable and hence allow lenders of money to make a deposit for a fixed period of, say, three or six months, whilst having the option of selling the CD, should they wish to get their money back before the end of the fixed period. Since CD prices fluctuate in value, an early sale may involve a capital gain or loss.

The small item 'notes issued' refers to private banknotes issued by Scottish and by Northern Ireland banks. These banks alone retain the historic right to issue their own notes, although apart from a small fiduciary issue, they have to be backed by holdings of Bank of England notes. The last items on the liabilities side covers items held in suspense for whatever reason (e.g. uncertainty as to who is the rightful owner of a deposit); items in transmission between accounts; and banks' long-term liabilities to shareholders and to bondholders.

Retail bank assets have become very diverse, as table 2.1 shows. Of the sterling assets, firstly there are holdings of notes and coin (till money), together with balances at the Bank of England. The former are necessary for retail banks on account of their large volume of sight deposits, and the need to be able to convert these into currency, on demand. It will be seen below that the other banks, whose main business is wholesale banking and who have few deposits subject to cheque, keep only negligible amounts of notes and coin in their tills. Balances with the Bank of England are composed of obligatory cash ratio deposits and of other deposits, which are those deposits that banks choose to keep with the Bank for their own convenience.

TABLE 2.1

Retail Banks: Balance Sheet, 30 December 1988 (£m)

Sterling Liabilities	
Notes issued	1,407
Deposits: UK monetary sector	20,165
UK public sector	4,080
UK private sector	13,467
overseas	17,609
certificates of deposit & other short-term paper	11,965
Other Currency Liabilities	
Deposits: UK monetary sector	6,373
other United Kingdom	6,883
overseas	26,211
certificates of deposit & other short-term paper	3,549
Items in suspense and transmission, capital and other funds (sterling and other currencies)	46,863
Total Liabilities	282,573
Sterling Assets	
Notes and coins	3,375
Balances with Bank of England (including cash-ratio deposits)	749
Market loans: secured money with the discount market	5,220
other UK monetary sector	17,639
UK monetary sector CDs	4,201
UK local authorities	738
overseas	3,573
Bills: Treasury bills	1,502
eligible local authority bills	388
eligible bank bills	6,060
other	137
Advances: UK public sector	715
UK private sector	147,907
overseas	5,284
Banking Department lending to central government (net)	956
Investments: UK government stocks	3,547
others	5,123
Other Currency Assets	
Market loans and advances: UK monetary sector	10,007
UK monetary sector CDs	234
UK public sector	33
UK private sector	7,616
overseas	30,165
Bills	436
Investments	6,143
Miscellaneous (sterling and other currencies)	20,824
Total Assets	282,573
Acceptances outstanding	6,456
Eligible liabilities	160,312

Source: BEQB, February 1989.

Sterling market loans are sums of money lent in one of several short-term money markets. Secured money with the discount market represents loans against the security of bills or bonds made to the eight discount houses which comprise the London Discount Market Association. Loans to 'other UK monetary sector' represent short-term interbank lending. The sterling interbank market is a very active over-the-telephone market in which banks borrow and lend large sums of money of £1m and above. It is used for many purposes. Banks temporarily short of funds can borrow there; banks temporarily with excess funds can lend there; those who wish to, can improve liquidity by, say, borrowing for two months and lending for two weeks; and those prepared to take risks, in the hope of earning extra profit, can anticipate future interest-rate movements by borrowing short and lending long (if rates are expected to fall) or by lending short and borrowing long (if rates are expected to rise).

Holdings of UK monetary sector CDs represent another form of inter-bank lending: lending to another bank by purchasing its certificate of deposit. This has the same advantage to a bank as it does to a non-bank purchaser of a CD; the loan is more liquid in that the CD can always be sold prior to maturity.

Loans to UK local authorities are short-term loans of periods ranging from a few days up to one year. Loans made to overseas residents include many loans to banks abroad. Banks also make many loans by discounting bills. Bills are short-term IOUs which may be issued by the government (Treasury bills), local authorities (local-authority bills) or private companies (commercial bills). They are usually issued for three months, although other terms are possible, and are sold to banks, discount houses or other purchasers, at a discount from their value on redemption. The discount is calculated so as to give the purchaser a rate of interest in line with current market rates of interest for similar types of lending. For instance, if a bank buys a 91 day commercial bill worth £1,000,000 at a 2% discount, it pays £980,000. That is to say, it is lending, for 91 days, a sum of £980,000 in the expectation of earning interest of £20,000. It is easy to calculate that this represents a rate of interest of 2.04% over the 91 days, or 8.19% when expressed at an annual rate.

Bills are highly marketable, and a bank having made a loan in exchange for a bill is free to rediscount it (i.e. sell it) if it wishes to do so. The Bank of England uses the bill market as a means of influencing the liquidity of the banking system. When it wishes to take money out of the system (and hence raise interest rates), it sells bills. When it wishes to put money into the system (and hence lower interest rates), it buys bills. All Treasury bills are eligible for rediscount with the Bank of England, but only certain 'eligible' local authority bills and only those commercial bills which bear the acceptance of a bank which has fulfilled certain conditions laid down by the Bank of England are. Such commercial bills are described as eligible bank bills.

Advances represent the main form of sterling lending to non-bank customers. It will be seen that the greater part of such lending is to the UK private sector – persons and firms – with a relatively small amount being lent to customers abroad, and an even smaller amount being lent to the UK public sector. But this does not, of course, represent total bank lending to the public sector. We have already seen that banks lend to local authorities via money market loans and by discounting their bills. And banks lend to central government in a number of ways, including discounting Treasury bills and buying government bonds.

For statistical purposes, the Banking Department of the Bank of England is included within the retail-banking sector. This may seem anomalous, but it will be recalled that the Bank of England as well as being banker to the government and to the banks also has a number of private accounts. Lending by the Banking Department to central government is shown net, and can be either positive or negative, but since April 1986, it has remained positive.

Sterling investments cover bank holdings of securities, chiefly British government bonds, but also a number of other securities, including sterling-denominated bonds issued by foreign borrowers.

Assets denominated in currencies other than sterling are dominated by interbank lending (within the UK) and by lending overseas, much of which is to banks abroad, but significant sums have also been used for lending to the UK private sector.

Acceptances outstanding and eligible liabilities do not constitute additional actual liabilities. Acceptances relate to bank acceptances of commercial bills. A bank accepts a commercial bill when it puts its own name on the bill as a guarantee that, if the company due to redeem the bill should default, the bank itself will pay all monies due. For this service the bank is paid a fee. As it is only in the case of a prior default by another party that the bank becomes liable, acceptances outstanding represent contingent liabilities rather than actual liabilities.

Eligible liabilities are a subset of all bank liabilities and are defined, broadly speaking, so as to represent, for each bank, its total sterling resources. More formally, eligible liabilities comprise the following:

(1) all sterling deposits from non-bank sources with an original maturity of two years or less;
(2) net sterling interbank borrowing;
(3) sterling CDs issued less sterling CDs held;
(4) any net deposit liabilities in sterling to overseas offices;
(5) any net liability in currencies other than sterling *less*
(6) 60% of the net value of transit items.[1]

This magnitude is of importance, as it is the volume of its eligible liabilities that determines for each bank the amount of 'cash ratio deposits' that

---

[1]   These components of eligible liabilities are described in detail in 'Reserve Ratios: Further Definitions', *BEQB*, December 1971.

it must make with the Bank of England. Since August 1981, all banks with eligible liabilities in excess of £10m have been required to deposit a percentage of these eligible liabilities in a non-interest-bearing account with the Bank. Initially, this was set at 0.5%, but since October 1986, it has been 0.45%. Cash ratio deposits are not, at present, of significance for monetary policy, but are used as a means of providing resources and income to the Bank of England to enable it to carry out its general central banking functions.

2.6   Merchant Banks and Other British Banks

In Bank of England statistics, the domestically-owned banks which are not retail banks are divided into two groups: British merchant banks and other British banks. The distinction is less one of function than of status. The former group is comprised of long-established City institutions which hitherto constituted the membership of the prestigious Accepting Houses Committee. Currently, 16 independent banks plus a number of subsidiaries are included within this group: they include such well-known names as Warburg, Rothschild and Morgan Grenfell.

The banking business of the British merchant banks is composed largely of wholesale banking   dealing in large sums of money in the short-term money markets. Their retail business is small and only a minority of such banks have offices in mainland Britain outside London. An abridged balance sheet for the British merchant banks is given in table 2.2. It can be seen that approximately one-third of deposits are in currencies other than sterling. Over 20% of all deposits originate abroad and a further 23% of all deposits is derived from the interbank markets. Correspondingly, on the assets side of the balance sheet, much lending is through the various money markets. Large sums are lent on the domestic interbank market and a large amount is lent abroad, much of it to banks abroad. Direct advances to non-bank customers represent a much smaller proportion of total assets than in the case of the retail banks. Eligible liabilities are relatively low.

These banks also undertake a number of other financial activities. They act as issuing houses; that is to say, they act for companies wishing to offer shares to the public and make all arrangements necessary including drawing up the prospectus, receiving applications for shares and making the initial allotment. They also act as fund managers and manage the investments of wealthy individuals, companies, pension funds, etc. Many run unit trusts, and a number are prominent as financial advisers, notably in the field of corporate mergers and take-overs.

The category of other British banks comprises a large number of banks of varying origins. Some are specialized subsidiaries of large retail banks, a few are long-established institutions with historical connections with particular areas abroad, but many are relatively small institutions providing

TABLE 2.2

British Merchant Banks: Abridged Balance Sheet, 30 December 1988 (£m)

Sterling Liabilities	
Deposits: UK monetary sector	6,203
other United Kingdom	13,732
overseas	1,756
certificates of deposit & other short-term paper	2,443
Other Currency Liabilities	
Deposits: UK monetary sector	3,564
other United Kingdom	2,095
overseas	7,194
certificates of deposit & other short-term paper	422
Items in suspense and transmission, capital and other funds (sterling and other currencies)	4,798
Total Liabilities	42,209
Sterling Assets	
Notes and coins	3
Balances with Bank of England (including cash-ratio deposits)	48
Market loans: UK monetary sector	10,425
UK monetary sector CDs	2,173
UK local authorities	84
overseas	2,508
Bills	283
Advances: United Kingdom	7,777
overseas	1,191
Investments	1,663
Other Currency Assets	
Market loans and advances: UK monetary sector	3,357
UK monetary sector CDs	364
other United Kingdom	1,277
overseas	8,075
Bills	59
Investments	1,155
Miscellaneous (sterling and other currencies)	1,767
Total Assets	42,209
Acceptances outstanding	3,417
Eligible liabilities	11,736

Source: BEQB, February 1989.

only a limited range of financial services. A number regard themselves as merchant banks and, as well as undertaking wholesale banking activities, compete with the officially classified merchant banks for the business of arranging new issues, fund management, and advising on mergers and take-overs. But for many of these banks, the main business is that of a finance house: raising money in the wholesale markets and lending both to industry, for the purchase of capital equipment, and to persons, for the purchase of consumer durables.

An abridged balance sheet of the other British banks is given in table 2.3. It can be seen that, as with the accepting houses, foreign-currency

TABLE 2.3

Other British Banks: Abridged Balance Sheet, 30 December 1988 (£m)

Sterling Liabilities	
Deposits: UK monetary sector	14,016
other United Kingdom	18,187
overseas	5,418
certificates of deposit & other short-term paper	4,020
Other Currency Liabilities	
Deposits: UK monetary sector	7,471
other United Kingdom	1,808
overseas	11,787
certificates of deposit & other short-term paper	1,654
Items in suspense and transmission, capital and other funds (sterling and other currencies)	12,657
Total Liabilities	77,017
Sterling Assets	
Notes and coins	3
Balances with Bank of England (including cash-ratio deposits)	115
Market loans: UK monetary sector	13,892
UK monetary sector CDs	2,321
UK local authorities	211
overseas	1,574
Bills	407
Advances: United Kingdom	26,735
overseas	838
Investments	2,504
Other Currency Assets	
Market loans and advances: UK monetary sector	6,374
UK monetary sector CDs	164
other United Kingdom	2,236
overseas	17,049
Bills	75
Investments	725
Miscellaneous (sterling and other currencies)	1,793
Total Assets	77,017
Acceptances outstanding	532
Eligible liabilities	23,538

Source: BEQB, December 1988.

deposits exceed sterling deposits and that a large amount of business is accounted for by transactions on the interbank market and with overseas clients. But there is also a large amount of sterling lending to domestic borrowers, of which all bar a small amount is to the private sector. Eligible liabilities account for nearly 30% of total liabilities.

2.7 Foreign Banks and Consortium Banks

On 6 January 1989 there were 364 different foreign banks operating in the UK, of which 46 were American and 29 were Japanese. Most had

only the one office in, or close to, the City of London. A small number
of North American and Western European banks have had a London office
since the days before World War II, in some cases since the nineteenth
century, but for the most part these foreign banks are comparative newcomers. Most arrived during the 1960s and 1970s.

It was during these decades that a new international banking system
was developing. This system, often referred to as the eurodollar market
or, more accurately, the euro-currency markets, proved a magnet to banks
worldwide. All large banks, as well as many medium-sized banks, wished
to become involved. And while the euro-currency markets were truly international, with active dealing in many centres in Western Europe and elsewhere, London was, and still remains, the most important single centre.
So it was to London that most foreign banks went, when they decided
to compete for a share of the new international banking business; although,
naturally, the large banks also established offices in the other important
centres of the market as well.

The growth and the functioning of the euro-currency markets are discussed below. For present purposes it is sufficient to note that virtually
all of the foreign banks have as their main business wholesale banking
in foreign currencies, notably the US dollar, and that much of this business
is conducted with companies, persons and banks outside the UK. This
is evident from inspection of the abridged balance sheet for foreign banks
in table 2.4.

In the Bank of England statistics, a separate balance sheet is given for
the American banks, the Japanese banks, and for all other overseas banks.
So as not to overburden the reader with statistics, we give here just one
combined balance sheet for all foreign banks. Those readers who require
more detail are referred to the *Bank of England Quarterly Bulletin*.

Table 2.4 shows all assets and liabilities on the books of UK offices
of foreign-owned banks on 30 December 1988. It will be seen that the
total of assets and liabilities is far greater than the total assets and liabilities
held by all British-owned banks. The business of the foreign-owned banks
is primarily in dollars and other non-sterling currencies, and sterling
deposits account for less than 20% of total deposits. Of the foreign-currency
deposits, two-thirds come from abroad (much of it from banks abroad)
and approximately a further 12% is accounted for by borrowing in the
London interbank market. On the assets side of the balance sheet it will
be seen that much lending is to foreign residents, of which a large proportion
goes to banks abroad. There is also substantial domestic interbank lending.

Although sterling business of the foreign banks only represents a small
proportion of total business, it is far from negligible. Eligible liabilities,
which give a good indication of sterling business with the domestic sector
after netting out interbank transactions, amounted to £78,365m, or nearly
49% of the eligible liabilities of the UK retail banks. Having come to
London primarily to do international banking, many of the foreign banks
have, nonetheless, been very ready to compete for domestic business as

TABLE 2.4

Foreign Banks: Abridged Balance Sheet, 30 December 1988 (£m)

Sterling Liabilities	
Deposits: UK monetary sector	33,290
other United Kingdom	25,666
overseas	34,543
certificates of deposit & other short-term paper	19,348
Other Currency Liabilities	
Deposits: UK monetary sector	67,289
other United Kingdom	22,330
overseas	328,822
certificates of deposit & other short-term paper	72,352
Items in suspense and transmission, capital and other funds (sterling and other currencies)	15,089
Total Liabilities	618,727
Sterling Assets	
Notes and coins	23
Balances with Bank of England (including cash-ratio deposits)	365
Market loans: UK monetary sector	29,492
UK monetary sector CDs	3,943
UK local authorities	421
overseas	16,708
Bills	702
Advances: United Kingdom	54,502
overseas	6,279
Investments	7,051
Other Currency Assets	
Market loans and advances: UK monetary sector	59,429
UK monetary sector CDs	6,757
other United Kingdom	43,825
overseas	349,950
Bills	3,266
Investments	28,307
Miscellaneous (sterling and other currencies)	7,707
Total Assets	618,727
Acceptances outstanding	11,846
Eligible liabilities	78,365

Source: BEQB, February 1989.

well. In a small number of cases, foreign banks have opened offices in provincial centres, such as Birmingham or Manchester.

2.8 Measures of Money

Given the number of different banks in the UK and the variety of types of deposit and other bank liabilities, it is clear that there can be no unambiguous definition of what constitutes money. Indeed the notion of *the* money supply is almost as much an abstraction as is the economist's concept of *the* rate of interest. All one can do is to aggregate different sets of assets and derive different measures of money. And this is what is now done in all developed economies, with central banks publishing data for a number of definitions of money. In the UK, the Bank of England publishes information on no less than seven different measures of money. These are briefly discussed below, while the relationships between the different measures are shown in figure 2.1.

The narrowest definition, **M0** covers just notes and coin in circulation plus banks' operational balances at the Bank of England. Operational balances exclude required cash-ratio deposits that banks have to maintain. This is not really a measure of money in the conventional sense, more a measure of the potential cash reserves available to support further bank expansion of credit. But, nowadays, there is no attempt to control bank deposits by limiting the availability of cash reserves, so M0 is a somewhat artificial construct. However, it tends to be dominated by the component notes and coin, and holdings of these tend to move in line with spending, with the result that M0 is a good coincident indicator of the state of aggregate demand in the economy. Since the 1984 budget, the government has set annual targets for the growth of M0.

M1 is defined as notes and coin in circulation plus all sterling sight deposits. Here, as in all other definitions, the deposits are those of the private sector only and the modest balances of government are excluded. M1 is a narrow measure of those forms of money which are available for instant use. For a number of years, the next broadest measures of money were **M3**, which covered notes and coin and all sterling bank deposits, both sight and time deposits, and certificates of deposit, and **M3c**, which included the same sterling items but also included foreign currency deposits. But whilst these definitions which show the extent of bank intermediation were and are useful, a number of developments, inside and outside the banking sector, suggested that other definitions might also be helpful.

There was a growth of interest-bearing sight deposits, offered by banks to large corporate customers. These deposits, it was felt, were probably held for different motives than were the traditional non-interest-bearing sight deposits, used predominantly as transactions balances. Secondly, building society deposits were being used increasingly as close substitutes to bank deposits. So a new measure of **M2** was defined, aimed at capturing all retail liquid assets but excluding 'wholesale assets'; those traded in financial markets and limited to very large transactors. In addition to notes and coin, M2 covers non-interest-bearing sight deposits and interest-bearing retail deposits at banks, plus the retail shares and deposits of building societies and balances held in the ordinary account of the National Savings Bank.

Finally, the increasing bank-like nature of much of the deposits of the building societies and the widespread availability of other short-term financial assets suggested that new all-embracing measures were needed. **M4** was defined to cover all the assets included in M3 plus holdings of building society shares and deposits, and **M5**, the widest of all measures, added,

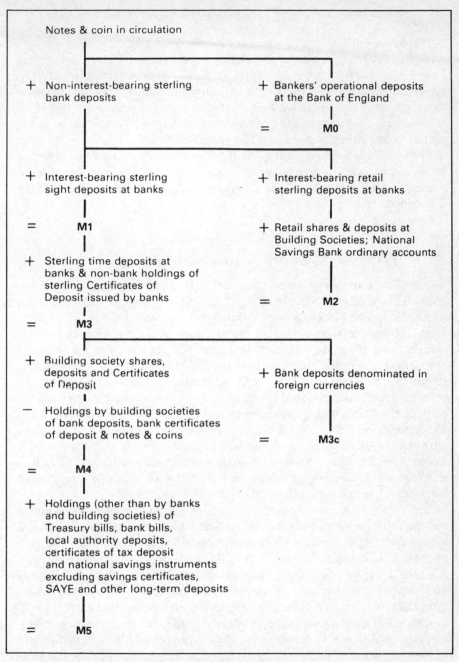

Notes & coin in circulation

+ Non-interest-bearing sterling
bank deposits

+ Bankers' operational deposits
at the Bank of England

= **M0**

+ Interest-bearing sterling
sight deposits at banks

+ Interest-bearing retail
sterling deposits at banks

= **M1**

+ Retail shares & deposits at
Building Societies; National
Savings Bank ordinary accounts

+ Sterling time deposits at
banks & non-bank holdings of
sterling Certificates of
Deposit issued by banks

= **M2**

= **M3**

+ Building society shares,
deposits and Certificates
of Deposit

+ Bank deposits denominated in
foreign currencies

− Holdings by building societies
of bank deposits, bank certificates
of deposit & notes & coins

= **M3c**

= **M4**

+ Holdings (other than by banks
and building societies) of
Treasury bills, bank bills,
local authority deposits,
certificates of tax deposit
and national savings instruments
excluding savings certificates,
SAYE and other long-term deposits

= **M5**

Figure 2.1   Relationships between the Monetary Aggregates
(*Source:* Adapted from 'Measures of Broad Money', *BEQB*, May 1987.)

in addition, holdings of certain very liquid short-term financial assets. To
avoid double counting, both of these measures deduct the building societies'
own holdings of notes and coin, bank deposits and certificates of deposit,
and M5 does not include liquid assets that are held by banks and building
societies themselves.

This whole collection of measures of money goes from very narrow definitions to very broad. All the measures are monitored by the authorities as well as by outside commentators. Often the different measures will exhibit widely differing rates of growth and, in consequence, they will not provide any unambiguous indication of the state of the economy. But if all or nearly all are moving in the same direction, this would usually be interpreted as indicating movements in aggregate demand. This was the case in 1987 and 1988, when all the definitions showed rapid growth. During these years, demand grew rapidly and by late 1988 the rate of inflation was increasing rapidly and the balance of payments had moved sharply into deficit.

2.9   The Sterling Money Market (Discount Market)

The sterling money market or discount market involves a number of discount houses, other traders in bills, a large number of banks and the Bank of England. The market plays a central role within the monetary system. Discount houses borrow money, mainly from banks but also from other sources, and invest this in short-term financial assets, notably bills and certificates of deposit. The funds they borrow are almost wholly short-term, either overnight or at call (i.e. can be recalled without notice) and are secured against the financial assets they hold. Thus, the discount houses provide the banks with a convenient form of liquidity which can be added to, or subtracted from, on a day-to-day basis. Banks finding themselves with temporarily surplus funds can add to their deposits with the discount market; banks with a shortage of funds can call back monies already lent to the market. Deposits with discount houses earn a competitive rate of interest and, as they are fully secured, any risk is slight.

The discount market's role in providing liquidity does not end here, for the discount houses also act as market makers in Treasury bills, local authority bills, commercial bills and in certificates of deposit. The role of market maker is an important one. For financial assets to be negotiable (i.e. readily tradeable), there have to be dealers who stand ready to buy and sell on a regular basis. Assets that are not negotiable are not liquid. And efficient financial markets need liquid assets in order that market participants can quickly respond to changes in cash flow by buying or selling assets. The discount houses stand ready to buy or sell bills and certificates of deposit and in so doing, they guarantee the negotiability of these instruments, thus making them that much more useful as liquid assets, both for banks and for other market participants.

It is not only the commercial banks who benefit from an active market in bills. The Bank of England uses the bill market for purposes of monetary policy, in order to put money into, or take money out of, the banking system. The operations of the Bank can be summarized as follows. Each day, there are very large flows of funds between the commercial banks and the Bank of England. Since the Bank acts as banker to the government, all payments to the government involve money flowing out of the commercial banks into the Bank. Similarly, all payments by the government involve money flowing from the Bank toward the commercial banks. And the Bank of England will also be making and receiving other payments as well, e.g. on account of foreign-exchange transactions, or due to payments by banking clients of the Bank other than the government. These movements of money both ways will only exactly cancel out by accident; usually there will be a net balance either way. This will normally mean that the banking system will find itself with either a surplus or a shortage of cash. Whichever is the position, it will quickly be communicated to the discount market, as banks either offer new deposits or call for the repayment of existing ones. When the market is in surplus, the Bank of England will sell bills in order to absorb the surplus. When the market is short of funds, the Bank will announce its willingness to buy eligible bills, but will leave the discount houses individually to decide at what price to offer these. If the Bank is happy with the level of short-term interest rates implied by the offers from the discount houses, it will then buy the bills, thereby relieving the shortage of cash. On the other hand, if the Bank is not happy with the interest rates implied by the offers of any discount houses, it can reject those offers. The discount houses will then have to seek a 'lender-of-last-resort' loan from the Bank and will pay a penal rate for it.

In this way, the Bank of England uses the bill market and the discount houses to smooth out shortages or surpluses of cash in the banking system. Its tactics are designed so as to avoid always imposing a pattern of interest rates on the market, whilst still leaving itself free to influence such rates when it deems this desirable.[1]

Although the Bank of England does, at times, make loans direct to a number of financial institutions, e.g. stock jobbers, money brokers, it is traditionally through the discount market that the Bank deals with the banking system. And whilst, on occasions, the Bank will deal direct with one or more clearing banks, it is still the case that only the discount houses are formally entitled to request loans from the Bank of England as lender of last resort.

Given that the Bank of England has chosen to operate in the sterling money market in the way and for the purposes described, it is important that the market should remain a large and active one. But over the years, the number of discount houses committed to making markets in bills and to taking short-term deposits from banks has dwindled due to mergers among houses. By 1988, the number was down to eight. To try to reverse

---

[1] This description of Bank of England operations in the money market is, necessarily, a brief one. For a detailed account, the reader should refer to, 'The role of the Bank of England in the Money Market', *BEQB*, March 1982, and to 'Bank of England Operations in the Sterling Money Market', Annex 3, 'Bank of England Dealings in the Sterling Money Market: Operational Arrangements', *BEQB*, August 1988.

this trend, in Autumn 1988, the Bank of England invited other financial institutions with experience in dealing in bills to apply to become formal market makers – on a par with the discount houses – with the responsibilities and privileges that this entails, including the privilege of formal borrowing rights at the Bank of England.[1] In January 1989, it was announced that two new firms had been admitted as full market makers.

2.10   Other Domestic Short-Term Markets

The sterling money market is the traditional money market in London. For a long time it was the only significant short-term financial market in Britain but, since the mid-1960s, a number of new and important markets have been created where short-term financial assets are actively traded. This is a development of great significance and one that has occurred in virtually all developed countries. In this section, we look briefly at the more important of the new domestic markets in short-term financial assets: in the next section we describe the equivalent short-term international markets.

In London, the main markets for short-term funds for immediate delivery are the interbank market, the market in large time deposits from non-bank sources and the market in certificates of deposit. All of these include deals in sterling, in dollars and in a number of other currencies. There are also markets for deposits with local authorities and with finance houses (in sterling) and, since the mid-1980s, markets have also existed for short-term deposits denominated in European Currency Units (ECUs) and Special Drawing Rights (SDRs). Transactions in these markets are in large round sums ($1m and upwards) and are agreed over the telephone, often through specialist money brokers but also, on occasion, direct between the contracting parties.

The existence of active markets in a number of different currencies means that banks and other dealers will frequently wish to buy or sell particular currencies, so a foreign-exchange market is a necessary complement to these short-term markets. In fact, such is the importance of London as a financial centre, that its foreign-exchange market is, in terms of turnover, the largest in the world. A survey conducted by the Bank of England in March 1986[2] produced estimates of turnover of $90bn a day: of this sum, nearly one-third was accounted for by trading between sterling and the US dollar and only slightly less by trading between the Deutsche Mark and the US dollar. Most trading is between banks and about half of it is conducted through the intermediation of specialist foreign-exchange brokers. Parallel surveys conducted in New York and in Tokyo during

[1]   See 'Bank of England Operations in the Sterling Money Market', *BEQB*, February 1989.
[2]   Details of the results of the survey are given in 'The Market in Foreign Exchange in London', *BEQB*, September 1986.

the same year showed turnover in those markets to be substantially lower than in London.

There are also a growing number of markets in financial futures and in traded options. A financial future is a financial asset, e.g. a three-month bank deposit or a long-term government bond, which is traded today for delivery in the future. A traded option contract is a saleable right to buy or sell a standard quantity of a given financial asset at a fixed price within a given period of time. Both futures and options markets include contracts to buy or sell currencies, as well as contracts to buy or sell a number of financial assets denominated in sterling or in dollars. It may seem surprising that people should wish to deal, now, in contracts that only come into force (or may be exercised) in the future. But such contracts can be used to manage risk. For instance, a bank makes a six-month, fixed-interest loan on the basis of a three-month deposit. It runs the risk that in three months' time, when it replaces the maturing deposit, rates of interest will have risen and it will lose money on the deal. It can hedge the risk by negotiating, now, a three-month deposit, at an agreed rate of interest, for delivery three months hence.

The growth of short-term money markets where rates of interest are determined by supply and demand for funds is something new. Traditionally, most banks in the UK had their interest rates tied to the Bank of England's discount rate (bank rate), which meant that rates were administered rather than being competitively determined. It also meant there was little scope for price competition between banks and, apart from some elements of non-price competition, most banks were in the position of just accepting passively such deposits as were offered. Lending was restricted in accordance with funds available as well as by frequent official credit-control measures. Credit rationing was an entrenched feature of the UK financial system.

All this started to change when banks began to compete with each other on price and to bid for new deposits. It started with the growth, in the 1960s, of the market in dollar deposits. The market was international and not subject to the many traditional restraints on domestic sterling business. It was a new development and there was no established customer loyalty among depositors. It involved sufficient numbers of banks from many different countries that agreements on rates of interest were unlikely. The market began as a highly competitive market and has remained so.

The growth of an international market in dollar deposits, centred in London, precipitated an influx of foreign banks, which banks, being newcomers to the United Kingdom, were outside all traditional agreements on interest rates. In addition, they had no existing stock of sterling deposits. If they were to do any business in sterling they would have to compete for deposits by offering a competitive rate of interest. And since they were already competing actively for dollar deposits, this was not a difficult step to take. The process snowballed as domestic banks sought, where possible, to match the rates being offered elsewhere. In 1971, the Bank of England introduced new monetary measures, known as Competition and Credit Control which, significantly, abolished all the old controls and agreements on rates of interest. Thenceforth, all banks were free to set their own rates of interest and to compete for funds.

For many banks, it soon became the case that virtually all deposits were taken at market-determined or market-influenced rates of interest. And even for the large retail banks, who for many years had had large volumes of modestly remunerated deposits, the position was changing as competition spread downwards with better terms being offered, even on comparatively small deposits. In 1989, these banks, in the face of competition from smaller banks and some building societies, began to offer interest-bearing chequing accounts. This trend, inevitably, meant a higher average cost of funds and, in turn, greater pressure on banks to maximize the return on assets. Non-obligatory reserve assets and especially unproductive cash holdings were cut to a minimum. This could be done without increasing the risk of illiquidity, as banks were able to use the new markets, and especially the interbank market, as a means of lending funds short-term. In this way, they could maintain liquidity at little sacrifice of interest.

So, the short-term financial markets served the dual function of providing funds for those banks that needed them and providing remunerative short-term assets for banks with surplus funds. Both functions were a source of liquidity. Banks can regard their short-term assets as being a source of liquidity, in the traditional manner, but they can also, quite legitimately, regard their ability to borrow new funds at short notice as an additional source of liquidity.

As markets grew, both in number and in depth, so banks became more confident of being able to borrow and lend as they wished. 'Liability management' – the continual adjusting of short-term liabilities – became accepted as a part of modern banking and as a necessary complement to the more traditional asset management. Non-bank borrowers and lenders also adjusted their behaviour. Cash management became the order of the day with finance departments of large companies devoting considerable resources to monitoring market trends and ensuring that their own borrowing and lending were on the best terms.

By 1989, the process of marketization of banking appears irreversible. The short-term markets have become an integral part of the financial system, and much business is premised on their continued existence. And for many banks, their standing in the short-term markets and their ability to deal quickly and in large amounts is an important weapon in the competitive struggle for business. We saw above that many banks, as part of their office-banking packages were ready to guarantee, within limits, the fulfilment of clients' orders for foreign exchange or for the purchase or sale of short-term assets. Such guarantees can only be given by banks confident of their own ability to deal instantly in the relevant financial markets.

2.11 Euro-Currency Markets

Of the short-term markets, the largest are the Euro-currency markets. In broad terms, these markets can be defined as international markets for short-term time deposits and for bank loans (not necessarily short-term) in currencies other than that of the country where the transaction takes place. That is to say, the Euro-dollar market is a market in dollar deposits and loans outside of the United States of America; the Euro-Deutsche Mark market is a market in Deutsche Mark deposits and loans outside of Federal Germany, etc. And for completeness, it should be added that, in addition to loans and deposits, the markets now trade certificates of deposit and other short-term financial instruments.

This raises the obvious question: what is so important about location? Why is a dollar deposit held at a bank in London different from a dollar deposit held with a bank in Chicago? After all, apart from location, there is no difference whatsoever in the actual dollars themselves; the holder of either deposit could use them to acquire goods and services in America in the normal way. The answer, essentially, is that dollar deposits held in the USA are subject to all the rules and regulations of the Federal Reserve Board and the other American regulatory agencies; dollar deposits held outside the USA are not. It is a question of jurisdiction. The position of other monies is analogous, but to explain this point more fully we shall remain with the US dollar and with the Euro-dollar market.

Dollar deposits held outside the USA are not normally subject to reserve requirements. This is so with dollar deposits in most European countries, including the UK. Since reserve requirements in the USA, as in most other countries, earn no interest, they are a significant cost to banks. In their absence, banks can operate on narrower margins and hence can offer better interest rates to both lenders and borrowers of money. Other costs are lower too. The Euro-dollar market is a wholesale market dealing almost entirely in sums equal to or in excess of $1m. Deposits and loans are for a fixed term and there are virtually no retail deposits. So the first advantage of the non-resident dollar market is low costs which enable banks to offer more favourable rates of interest.

A second advantage is freedom from exchange controls. This was illustrated in the 1960s when the American authorities introduced a range of measures designed to curb the high level of capital exports from the USA. These included restraints on resident US banks lending dollars abroad. But, the demand for dollars in the rest of the world remained high and this demand was channelled into the Euro-dollar market, where rates of interest rose above the level of rates in the USA. This led non-American residents, who were not subject to US regulations, to switch holdings of dollars from American to European banks, including European branches of American-owned banks. Also, those who received dollars in the normal way of business (e.g. exporters to the USA) and wished to hold on to them, rather than sell them for another money, naturally chose to keep the dollars in Europe rather than in America. Even central banks switched some of their dollar holdings to commercial banks in Europe. In general, the American measures were a failure and were abolished in January 1974, but not before most of the internationally-mobile dollar funds had shifted to Europe.

The Euro-dollar market is not subject to national restrictions on interest rates. This was also an important influence on developments in the 1960s. Twice during that decade, the US authorities put an effective ceiling on the interest rates that resident American banks could pay on time deposits. The ceiling did not apply outside the USA, so again there was scope and reason for higher rates of interest to be paid on dollar deposits in Europe than in the USA. Analogous situations have occurred with other monies. On occasions, the German authorities, in attempts to curb speculative buying of Deutsche Marks, have ordered domestic banks to pay zero or very low rates of interest on new mark deposits by non-residents. The chief result was not to discourage non-residents from holding mark deposits, but to ensure that they held them with banks in Luxemburg or Zurich not subject to the German controls.

During the 1960s and 1970s, the Euro-dollar market and the parallel markets in other currencies grew rapidly. During much of the 1980s, due, *inter alia*, to the international debt problem, growth was more subdued. But the markets remain large, unfettered, competitive markets for both time deposits and for term loans. Their very size is an attraction in itself, as loans can be arranged of much larger amounts than would be possible in the domestic markets of many European countries. Large loans are usually syndicated, i.e. shared by a group of banks.

A key element in Euro-dollar trading is the active interbank market. This market fulfils the functions described in section 2.9 above, and in the process, effectively knits together the many hundreds of different and disparate banks into one coherent market. General shortages or surpluses of funds are quickly reflected in demands for borrowing or in offers of funds in the interbank market and have prompt effects on interest rates there.

Such rates are a barometer of market conditions and are widely used as a basis for determining the rates charged on loans to non-bank customers. The most important rate is the London interbank offered rate for dollar deposits, or LIBOR. It is the rate at which the larger banks are prepared to lend dollars. The key term is for three-month loans although there are also LIBORs for six-month dollar loans, for one-month loans, etc. There are also LIBORs for a number of other currencies widely traded in London. But since the dollar remains the dominant currency in international banking, it is LIBOR for dollar deposits which is of most significance.

Most Euro-currency deposits are short-term, but lending to non-bank borrowers is often for a period of years. In order to make such medium-term (1–5 years) and long-term (over 5 years) loans, banks have to regularly replace or renegotiate maturing short-term deposits. But they cannot know in advance what interest rates they will have to pay in the future. It follows that it would be highly risky to offer loans stretching over a number of years at fixed rates of interest. The solution adopted has been to make loans on a variable-rate basis, where the interest rate is expressed as LIBOR plus a percentage and is recalculated every three or six months. The percentage depends on the borrower's credit standing. In this way, banks avoid a direct interest-rate risk, although they only do so by passing the risk to the borrower, which is not always a satisfactory solution.

2.12   The International Debt Problem

During the 1970s, banks active in the Euro-currency markets increased substantially their lending to a number of developing countries. These loans were directed towards a number of actual or future oil producers (Indonesia, Mexico, Nigeria, Venezuela) and to a number of middle-income oil importers (Argentina, Brazil, and other Latin American countries). The loans were of varying terms, but all or virtually all were at rates of interest pegged to LIBOR, or other reference rates, and adjustable regularly.

In the early 1980s, a sharp recession in the developed world coincided with a period of exceptionally high rates of interest. Developing countries found their exports stagnating and their debt-service charges rising. For the oil importers, this was on top of the jump in import bills after the 1979 oil-price rise. The result was that in 1982 and 1983 a succession of countries announced they were unable to meet their obligations to the banks as well as to other official creditors. Thus began what has become known as the international debt problem.

A discussion of this episode and of the subsequent negotiations between the IMF, the banks and the debtor nations, which resulted in the widespread rescheduling of bank debts, can be found in section 3 of chapter 3 below. It need not be repeated here. What we are concerned with are the consequences of this problem for banks and for the wider financial system.

Many banks found themselves faced with a sudden and, to all intents and purposes, forced conversion of short-term loans into what were long-term and effectively frozen assets. This was preferable to having the debtor countries default outright, but it was, nevertheless, undesirable in itself. Firstly, there was the obvious question mark over the value of the rescheduled assets – whether all interest payments and amortization would, in practice, be forthcoming. Secondly, there was a substantial increase in the gap between maturities of assets and of liabilities. While banks operating in the Euro-currency markets have always granted loans of terms longer than those of deposits, they have been careful to control the extent of the maturity mismatch between assets and liabilities. Some mismatching was seen as acceptable, even inevitable; too much was seen as dangerous. Now, all of a sudden, many banks found themselves with a greater maturity mismatch than could be considered prudent.

There have been two main responses to this situation. Firstly, the banks, under pressure from national supervisory authorities (the Bank of England, in the UK) have built up their capital resources by issuing new equity shares, in some cases new long-term bonds, and by diverting large amounts of annual profits into reserve funds against possible future losses. This was an obviously sensible measure to take and will enable banks to withstand greater loan losses, should they occur, without their solvency being called into question.

The second response has been to try to compensate for the large volumes of frozen loans by increasing the liquidity of other bank assets. One way to do this is for banks to make new international loans against the security of marketable assets. Previously, although large Euro-currency loans were syndicated among a number of banks, each bank retained its portion of the loan. Loans and participations in loans were not normally re-saleable. Now, in the wake of the international debt problem, large loans are often arranged in ways which involve the borrower issuing a succession of short-term negotiable notes. For instance, a five-year loan may involve the borrower in issuing a succession of three-month notes at three-monthly intervals throughout the five years. Individual banks bid for the notes, at each time of issue, as they choose. If they wish to make a long-term loan, they can do so, by purchasing and repurchasing the borrower's notes. If they wish to curtail their involvement in the loan, they can decline to bid for new notes at the next issue date. In this way, banks have more flexibility in managing their assets.

It should be noted, however, that many borrowers, sensitive to the risk of not being able to sell notes at some time in the future, ask for guarantees of stand-by funds in such an eventuality. Certain banks choose to provide such guarantees in exchange for a fee, thereby incurring long-term contingent (and off-balance-sheet) liabilities, instead of long-term actual (and on-balance-sheet) liabilities. Not all banks choose to avoid all long-term commitments, but the system of loans via renewable notes does allow many banks scope to adjust their loan portfolio more quickly than was hitherto possible.

This development is likely to prove of considerable significance for the whole financial industry. For, once bank loans are commonly made against the issue of negotiable paper, the gap between direct and indirect finance is diminished. The same issue of paper can be sold partly to banks (indirect finance) and partly to final investors (direct finance). This already happens with international issues of notes. Along with the banks who bid for notes to hold in their own name, are international security houses (usually of American or Japanese origin) who purchase notes with the intention of re-selling them to their clients. And a number of banks have created, or are creating, their own security dealing capacity and are seeking to expand their client base among mutual funds and wealthy personal investors, with whom they can place notes and other securities. In the end, the economic difference between an institution that first borrows funds from lenders and then subscribes, in its own name, for the notes of borrowers, and an institution that arranges for lenders to subscribe direct, may not be very great.

2.13   The Determination of Short-Term Interest Rates

It was pointed out in the section on the sterling money market, that the Bank of England exercises a key role in that market and remains in a position to influence short-term rates of interest therein. Due to the many payments being made each day between the government and the private sector, it will frequently be the case that the net balance is in favour of the government. This will mean a net loss of funds to the banking system which will be translated quickly into a shortage of money deposited with the discount houses. Only the Bank of England is in a position to relieve this shortage and it is able to decide the price it will charge for so doing and thereby to influence short-term rates of interest in the market.

Subsequently, in discussion of other short-term domestic markets, it was pointed out that these were free competitive markets where interest rates were set in accordance with supply of and demand for funds. It was partly due to the growing importance of these markets that official controls over many rates of interest paid and charged by retail banks were abolished. Since 1971, all banks in Britain have been free to set their own rates and nowadays most rates, even in retail banking, follow the trend of rates in the wholesale markets.

This sometimes gives rise to confusion: is it the case that the authorities set the rates, or is it the case that rates are determined by supply and demand? The position, in reality, is quite clear. The authorities no longer impose specific rates of interest on particular financial institutions. Nor, at present, do they seek to control long-term rates of interest. Therefore, they do not directly influence the pattern or structure of *relative interest rates*. Supply of and demand for funds is free to exert its influence and those intermediaries or groups of intermediaries which are more efficient are free to quote better rates than their rivals.

But the Bank of England, through its own market operations, can alter the supply of funds and hence can push the *general level of interest rates* up or down as it sees fit. And whilst the Bank normally only operates in the one market, arbitrage ensures that changes in short-term rates there will promptly be mirrored elsewhere. In fact, the Bank's powers are so well understood that it only needs a sign that the Bank is ready to see rates move one way or another for the banks to move their rates into line.

So the position is that it is the authorities, operating through the Bank of England, who effectively determine the general level of short-term sterling rates of interest. It is then up to market forces to determine the pattern of different relative rates of interest.

The position is similar in most other developed countries. Thus in the

USA, the Federal Reserve Board has the power to determine the level of short-term interest rates. Given this level, it is up to each and every market participant to decide how to react: what rates it is prepared to pay; what rates it can afford to charge.

None of this says that the authorities, in the UK or in other countries, will exercise their power over short-term rates of interest regardless of the consequences. For instance, very low short-term sterling rates of interest might encourage foreign-exchange traders to sell sterling. If the British authorities do not wish sterling to depreciate, then they cannot, at the same time, operate so as to bring about very low short-term rates of interest.

2.14   The Capital Market: (1) The Traditional Market

The capital market is a general term which covers the markets in which securities – equity shares, preference shares and bonds – are bought and sold. Essentially, there are two related markets: the new issue market, where new securities are offered to the public by borrowers wishing to raise new funds; and the secondary market, where existing securities are bought and sold. In principle, the capital market is an example of what we earlier termed direct finance: lenders of funds lending direct to the ultimate borrower, without the intervention of a financial intermediary. In some cases this is so, as for instance when many individuals subscribed to the issue of shares by British Telecom. But, it is by no means always the case. The majority of the securities listed on the British Stock Exchange are now held by institutional investors such as insurance companies, super-annuation funds, unit trusts and investment trusts. Over the years, many personal holders of securities have chosen to sell out and to entrust their financial wealth to intermediaries; so indirect finance has increased. This has been encouraged by a tax system which has favoured saving via superannuation funds and (until 1984) life assurance. The Conservative government of the 1980s has tried to reverse the trend and to encourage more personal share-owning. It has met with some initial success, but it is too early to say whether this will be durable.

The new issue market is the market where private companies, the government, local authorities and some foreign borrowers seek money from the general public against the issue of securities. Not all securities are offered to the general public. There are many small companies, termed private companies, which have shares held by a limited number of owners (sometimes all from the same family) and where there is no formal means of trading these. But the new issue market is concerned with securities that are offered to the general public. Such offers are governed by legislation, notably by the Financial Services Act of 1986 and, if it is proposed to have the securities listed on the Stock Exchange, by the rules of that institution also. The two most frequent types of issue of new securities are issues of equity shares by firms going public (i.e. a hitherto private company offering its shares to the public) and issues of bonds on behalf of companies, public undertakings and foreign governments. The UK government was a regular issuer of bonds until 1987 but, since then, it has run a budget surplus and so has had no need to borrow.

In the case of equity shares, the issue will normally be managed by one of the larger security dealers. Much legal and administrative work has to be done and a detailed prospectus has to be prepared giving full information on the existing owners and managers of the firm, on its history, its past and present trading performance and giving audited profit figures for a number of years. This prospectus will be distributed to other security dealers, banks, investment managers and financial advisers in the United Kingdom and (for large issues) abroad as well. It must also be advertised in a number of national newspapers. The issue will probably be underwritten, that is to say, a number of institutional investors will, for a fee, agree to take up any shares which remain unsold. The managers of the issue have to arrange for applications for shares to be received and checked and shares allocated among would-be purchasers. If applications for shares exceed the quantity offered for sale, some form of rationing becomes necessary: all investors may be allotted the same proportion of the shares for which they applied, or a preference may be given to certain types of applicant, e.g. those applying for small amounts.

In the case of an issue of UK government bonds, the procedure is somewhat simpler. The issue is managed by the Bank of England. A prospectus is issued and published but it is much shorter than a company prospectus because (a) the government is a regular borrower and (b) the affairs of the government are already public knowledge in a way that those of a company are not. But, it may be noted that, if a foreign government wishes to raise money in Britain, it does have to produce a lengthy prospectus including information on the recent political and economic history of its country. For UK government bonds, issues are usually made in large amounts – anything from £100m to £1,000m – and applications are invited at a minimum price. In most cases, total applications fall short of the amount of stock on offer so applicants receive the amount applied for. The unsold stock is taken on to the books of the Bank of England and is sold on the Stock Exchange over a period of time, as demand materializes. When the government was borrowing regularly, the Bank normally expected to have at least one such stock on its books at any time, so that it could always make new sales of stock, whenever the demand was there. But, as noted above, the government has not needed to issue new stock since 1987.

There is no legal requirement on issuers of new shares or bonds to seek a listing on the Stock Exchange, but many do so and those that do not, make other arrangements to ensure the securities offered for sale are easily negotiable. People are more likely to buy securities if they know they can sell them again. Neither persons nor corporate bodies can reliably predict their financial circumstances far into the future and know what needs for money may arise. They will not wish to be locked into investments for many years ahead; so assets that can easily be resold will be more attractive than those which cannot. This is the importance of secondary financial markets.

Complying with the requirements for a full listing on the Stock Exchange is expensive. But, so as not to discourage smaller companies from making a public offering of shares, the Exchange permits trading in what are called unlisted securities, i.e. securities not admitted to the official list. The conditions to be fulfilled before a company can have its shares traded on the unlisted securities market are not negligible, but they are less onerous and less costly than for a full listing. A number of companies have gone public through this route.

Further, in January 1987, a Third Market was started where the requirements for shares to be traded were reduced still further. Shares could be issued in a company that had been trading for only one year and there was no minimum set on the percentage of the equity which was offered for sale. In January 1989, two years after its launch, the Third Market had attracted 58 companies.

The London Stock Exchange was traditionally the dominant secondary market where securities issued in the United Kingdom were traded. Prior to 1973, there had been a number of other small exchanges operating in provincial cities but in that year they merged, along with exchanges in Cork and Dublin, to form a single Stock Exchange for the entire British Isles. Subsequently, whilst many brokers continued to operate from provincial bases in Britain and in Ireland, the trading of securities soon became confined to London (for UK securities) and Dublin (for Irish securities).

Trading on The Stock Exchange (as the combined exchange was called) followed essentially the rules of the former London Stock Exchange and involved a sharp distinction between the roles of stockbroker and stockjobber. The broker was the person in contact with the public and all persons and firms wishing to buy or sell securities had first to approach a stockbroker. The broker acted as agent for his client and for this he charged a commission. In order to execute his client's instructions, the broker had to deal with a stockjobber or market maker who held portfolios of securities and who stood ready to buy and sell for his own account. There were a number of competitive jobbers, each specializing in a range of securities and brokers were free to shop around and do business with whoever quoted the most favourable price. Stockjobbers were restricted to dealing only with stockbrokers and did not deal direct with the public. All trading was conducted on the floors of the Exchange, apart from some after-hours business conducted over the telephone.

This system imposed what was called 'single capacity', that is to say a firm that was a member of the Stock Exchange either dealt as agent for non-members or it traded for its own account, in which case it did not deal directly with non-members. The system had a number of advantages, notably in avoiding conflicts of interest among practitioners and it had long been defended by many member firms of the Exchange. But whether it was a good system or not, it was not the way the rest of the world operated. In national markets abroad and in international security dealing, there was dual capacity: large firms combined the roles of broker and jobber and held portfolios of securities in their own name, while still dealing direct with investors. And trading in securities, like other financial activity, was becoming increasingly international. During the 1960s and 1970s, a large new international market in bonds – the Eurobond market – had grown up with many of its leading traders based in London. It clearly represented a threat to the traditional British way of dealing in securities.

2.15 The Capital Market: (2) The Eurobond Market

The Eurobond market is an international capital market in which securities – predominantly fixed-interest securities but also including some variable or floating rate notes (FRNs) – are issued and sold worldwide. The market is dominated by a number of international security houses and international banks which act both as issuing houses and as market makers. The main borrowers of funds are international organizations, public corporations and large internationally-known companies. Securities are issued in a range of currencies, but the US dollar is the dominant one. There is no physical market place and the market functions as a worldwide over-the-telephone market. London is the single most important centre.

The issue of new securities involves a lead manager or managers and a syndicate of subscribing banks and security houses. The lead managers arrange the details of the issue: size, currency, duration, interest terms, etc. and then assemble the syndicate of subscribers. Members of the syndicate will intend to place the securities with clients and will subscribe for that amount of securities they feel they can re-sell. The syndicate will normally be international, and in this way, the securities will end up spread among a wide range of investors in a number of different countries.

The securities are not normally traded on a recognized Stock Exchange. Instead, for each security, a number of banks and security houses act as market maker and stand ready to buy or sell. They will usually be comprised of the original lead managers and a number of the original syndicate members. Competition between them ensures that the prices quoted to would-be buyers or sellers of the security remain in line with prevailing market conditions.

Several features of the market are noteworthy. Firstly, it is a market which is subject to minimal official regulation; for while dealers are subject to laws against fraud and malpractice in the countries where they operate, they are not subject to long lists of rules such as apply to those wishing to have securities listed on the London or New York Stock Exchanges. No lengthy prospectus is prepared for a new issue and there is no requirement to advertise a proposed new issue in national newspapers. This is justified by market practitioners on the grounds that Eurobonds are not offered for sale to the general public; they are traded by professional dealers and only sold to a relatively narrow range of professional investors. This argument seems to have been accepted by the UK authorities when framing the 1986 Financial Services Act. The result is that issue costs are low and considerably less than for a public offering of securities in most domestic markets. But, at the same time, the scope for worldwide distribution of Eurobonds means that large sums of money – often in excess of $100m – can be raised.

The market represents an internationalization of security dealing in the same way that the Euro-currency markets represent an internationalization of banking. It also represents a diversification of business for a number of banks who through this market have become actively involved in the issuing and trading of securities. In many cases, banks are doing business in the international capital market that they would not be allowed to do in their own domestic market. In Japan and the USA, national laws still impose a separation of banking and security trading.

In the Eurobond market, there is no separation of stockbrokers and stockjobbers as was the case on the UK Stock Exchange. The dealers are the security houses and the banks who buy and sell shares on their own behalf and who combine the functions of jobber and broker. For this reason, British stockbrokers and stockjobbers had been unable to participate in what was a fast-growing market; the jobbers because the regulations of the Stock Exchange prevented them from dealing direct with the general public; the brokers because the regulations prevented them from dealing in securities as principals. And the newer markets were taking away business from the Stock Exchange: a number of large UK firms having chosen to issue international bonds rather than raise new funds on the domestic market.

2.16   The Capital Market: (3) The 1986 Reforms and After

By the early 1980s it had become apparent to the more far-sighted that the Stock Exchange in Britain would have to change. In effect, members' firms, the jobbers and the brokers, faced a stark choice: they could continue with their traditional ways of doing business and lose the chance of becoming involved in the expanding international business in securities and probably also lose an increasing share of trading in bonds of large UK companies, or they could change their practices to bring them more into line with what happened elsewhere. But it so happened that, at the time, the Stock Exchange authorities were preoccupied with preparing a defence of their rule book subsequent to a hearing before the Restrictive Practices Court. The rules of the Exchange had been referred by the Office of Fair Trading (OFT) to the Court under the previous Labour government and, given the complexities of the Exchange rule-book, it was taking time for both the OFT and the Stock Exchange to prepare their respective arguments. But with a growing awareness that this hearing was proving a distraction from the real issues and that other reforms were urgent, the Department of Trade and Industry reached an agreement with the Stock Exchange authorities in July 1983 to drop the case before the Restrictive Practices Court on condition that the Exchange abandon the fixing of commissions for all share and bond dealing. Competitively negotiated commission rates could be expected to be lower than the hitherto fixed rates, and it was soon decided that they would not be adequate to support the expensive system of dual capacity. So it was decided that, along with the move to negotiated commissions, the Exchange would permit dual capacity: the combining within one firm of the roles of market maker and broker.[1]

By now, it was a question of the total reform of the Stock Exchange: and one thing led to another. The new market makers would need sufficient capital resources, for market makers necessarily hold blocks of securities so as to be able to sell as well as buy on demand; and whilst they hope to make profits over the long run, no market maker can always avoid capital losses in the short run on the occasions when security prices are falling. To be able to absorb such short-term losses, it is necessary to hold large capital reserves. This was the experience of the large American and Japanese security houses, but previously the London stockjobbers had had only modest capital resources and the brokers, whose function had only been that of agent, had had virtually none. So it was necessary for the would be new market makers to acquire new capital – and fast – and this meant outside shareholders. The only really likely candidates with sufficient funds to spare were banks, both British and foreign, and certain foreign security dealers.

And there was the question of new technology. Security prices could be displayed on VDU screens, transactions could be arranged over the telephone; this was how the Eurobond market worked already; so was a trading floor necessary any longer? It was decided to create the infrastructure for a computerized trading system but to leave firms the choice of whether to deal over the telephone or to deal between representatives on the floor of the Exchange.

After some discussion of whether the reforms should be introduced piecemeal or altogether, it was decided to go for the latter option with most of the changes occurring in one 'big bang' on Monday 27 October 1986.

Big Bang, as it became known, saw the greatest reform of security trading in Britain this century. Large new market makers were created, usually by mergers of broking firms and/or jobbing firms and bank interests. Many were owned by large banks or overseas security houses who saw this as a unique opportunity to become established in the London security markets

---

[1]   The details of the negotiations between the Stock Exchange and the Department of Trade and Industry and their political background are admirably described in Chapter 2 of Margaret Reid, *All Change in the City* (Macmillan, 1988).

and who were prepared to pay considerable sums of money for the privilege. It was soon found to be more convenient to deal over the telephone and trading on the floor of the London Exchange soon ceased. Following agreements between the governing body of the Exchange and a similar body representing Eurobond dealers, the Exchange was reconstituted as the International Stock Exchange of the United Kingdom and the Republic of Ireland, although, for brevity, the shorter name 'The Stock Exchange' is still widely used. The new Exchange is a Recognised Investment Exchange (RIE) within the terms of the Financial Services Act of 1986.

Under the new system, those firms which opt to be market makers in specified securities agree to display their prices by means of the Stock Exchange Automated Quotations (SEAQ) and this makes them instantly accessible on VDU screens to all other traders. Market makers are committed to dealing, up to published maximum amounts, at the prices displayed. As one would expect, the selling price will be slightly above the buying price and market makers will earn income from this difference. They are also at liberty to charge a commission on all transactions, but at times competition has driven this commission to low levels or even to zero. Many brokers, notably the smaller firms of brokers and provincial brokers, did not become market makers, and have continued to act in an agency capacity, buying and selling securities in transactions with market makers on behalf of their clients. But, in contrast to what went before, clients, at least the larger ones, are free to deal direct with market makers: they are not obliged to use the services of a broker.

The new system did attract new capital into the market and it resulted in a more competitive system with more firms of market makers competing for business in all the regularly traded securities. Commission rates have tended to fall for large transactions and there has been some tendency for the 'market touch', the gap between best buying and best selling price, to narrow as well. Also, London has significantly increased its trade in foreign securities. This said, however, it must be noted that the initial success of Big Bang owed much to the fact that, at the time, share prices were rising strongly and had been rising for a number of years. It is always much easier for dealers to make money in a rising market. But in October 1987, share prices fell dramatically and subsequently turnover in equity shares was much reduced. A number of security firms lost large amounts of money and a few have withdrawn from market making, either in equities or in bonds or both. At the time of writing (April 1989), it is clear that there can be no going back on the reforms entailed in Big Bang, but it is equally clear that all its ramifications will not be fully clear for some years yet.

Some indication of the importance of the capital market can be gained by looking at the sums of money raised on the new issue market, and also by looking at turnover of securities on the secondary market. During the three years 1986–88, new issues of all securities, excluding UK government bonds, averaged £11,935m a year. Of this total, over 60% was accounted for by rights issues, i.e. issues of additional shares by existing public companies and offered, in priority, to existing shareholders. A certain amount of outstanding fixed-interest stock was redeemed each year, both by public companies and by local authorities, so the net amount of new money raised was less than the gross figure given above. For public companies and all overseas borrowers, total net new money raised, in 1983–85, averaged £10,684m a year.

Although this is a large amount, it is not large relative to net new lending by banks or by building societies. But it should be borne in mind that equity capital is a strategic form of fund raising in that it is risk-bearing. All firms require risk-bearing capital in order that small or temporary losses can be sustained without the existence of the firm being called into question. This is as true of banks as it is of industrial and commercial companies, and many banks have figured among the companies raising new capital in recent years. The capital market is not the largest source of funds to domestic enterprises, but it remains a crucial one.

Throughout most of the period since World War II, long-term funds raised by the government were usually in excess of those raised on behalf of the private sector and foreign borrowers. But, as has already been noted, in recent years the government accounts have moved into surplus. During 1986, the government raised over £2,400m through the sale of bonds but, in 1987 and 1988, the government raised no new funds: rather it was paying back existing loans.

Turnover on the Stock Exchange during the years 1986–88 averaged slightly over £1,335bn a year, or nearly £5,300m per working day. Of the annual average, just over £900bn was accounted for by transactions in UK government stock and over £360bn was accounted for by transactions in ordinary shares, of which a growing proportion was in foreign shares.

2.17 Building Societies

The building societies began as part of the self-help movement among skilled workers during the Industrial Revolution. Early societies pooled the savings of members to build houses for them. Often, lotteries were used to decide in what order members had access to the houses as they were finished. When all members were housed, the society was wound up. But, over time, the societies ceased to do their own building and evolved into purely financial institutions. They also largely ceased to be terminating societies and the word 'permanent' entered the name of many societies.

The building societies have grown rapidly in the period since World War II, playing the dominant role in the finance of the great growth of owner-occupancy. Their traditional business is simple to describe. They are mutual societies which collect money from many millions of savers in the form of shares and deposits. The word 'share' is a misnomer and shareholders do not participate in profits. The difference between shares and deposits is that shareholders are members of the society and are entitled to vote at annual general meetings. They receive a slightly higher rate of interest but rank below depositors, as creditors, in the event of a dissolution of the society. But since the risks of investing with building societies are low, most investors opt for the higher interest offered by shares and the amount of money held as deposits has dwindled.

The societies devote approximately 80% of their funds to making loans on the security of first mortgages on residential property. The remaining 20% finances modest amounts of other lending to clients but is used mainly as a reserve of liquidity and is invested chiefly in British government bonds and such money market assets as term deposits with banks and certificates of deposits.

But whilst the traditional business of collecting savings and providing mortgages to owner-occupiers remains central to their activities, the building societies, like other parts of the financial system, are going through a period of great change. The Building Societies Act of 1986 and subsequent Orders in Council laid before Parliament in 1988, have considerably widened the powers of the societies. On the liabilities side of their account, they now offer a wide range of 'shares' at differing rates of interest and they have also moved into money transmission with many societies offering accounts subject to cash withdrawal through automatic teller machines and a number offering accounts subject to cheque. The building societies have also become large borrowers in the wholesale money markets, borrowing from banks, selling certificates of deposit and selling short-term and medium-term bonds. On the assets side, the societies are now permitted to lend limited amounts of money on second mortgages and also provide unsecured personal loans up to a maximum of £10,000.

The building societies have also been empowered to undertake a range of other financial services including estate agency, insurance broking, fund management, and financial advice: societies may, if they wish, take an equity stake in both life and general insurance companies and in stockbrokers. The two largest societies have already established large estate agent businesses with widespread networks of offices.

These new functions represent a considerable extension of building society activities and are another example of the despecialization that is taking place in finance and of the growth of conglomerates providing a wide range of financial services. Many observers see these changes as the thin end of the wedge and predict that many of the building societies will in time evolve into all-purpose banks. Significantly, the 1986 Act permits building societies to shed their mutual status and to convert to that of a limited company whereon they may seek authorization as banks. One society, the Abbey National, has already balloted its members (both investors and borrowers) and received the support of a large majority for the switch to limited liability status. Other societies are now expected to follow this route. It may be noted that in Australia and in South Africa where building societies have recently been given the freedom to turn themselves

TABLE 2.5

Building Societies: Balance Sheet, 31 December 1988 (£m)

Liabilities	
Retail shares and deposits	150,779
Wholesale deposits and commercial paper	8,968
Certificates of deposits	4,437
Bonds	9,222
Syndicated borrowing	1,629
Other liabilities and reserves	16,968
Assets	
Liquid assets	
Bank deposits in sterling, including CDs	19,473
British government bonds	8,779
Other	3,899
Commercial assets	
First mortgages on owner-occupied property	153,996
Other advances secured on property	2,118
Other lending	951
Other assets	2,787
Total assets = total liabilities	192,003

Source: BEQB, February 1989.

into banks with limited liability status, most large societies, in both countries, have already made the change.

With the probable conversion of large societies into banks and the continuing trend to merger among smaller societies, it is likely that the number of independent societies will continue to fall. In 1960, there were over 700 societies, by 1985 the number had fallen below 170 and it has fallen since then to less than 140. There is a high degree of concentration of business with the five largest societies accounting for nearly 60% of the assets of all the societies.

Table 2.5 shows the assets and liabilities of building societies at end-December 1988.

2.18 Life Assurance Companies and Superannuation Funds

Both life assurance companies and pension funds must be classed as financial intermediaries in terms of the description given of financial intermediaries in the introduction to this section. Both take funds from savers and lend these to borrowers. The big difference between them and most of the institutions previously considered is that they do not provide liquid financial assets. Both offer savers long-term investment possibilities.

The most popular form of life assurance contract nowadays is the endowment policy, although this can come in a number of forms. The essential feature of an endowment policy is that the assured agrees to pay, to the insurance company, regular premiums over a fixed number of years, e.g. 20 or 25. At the end of this time, the insurance company guarantees to pay a lump sum. If the policy is without profits, this will be a known amount (the sum assured) agreed at the outset. If the policy is with profits, it will be a basic sum assured plus bonuses, as with-profits policies share in the profits of the assurer and earn regular bonuses.

Should the policyholder die before expiry of the policy, his dependants will receive the sum assured plus bonuses (if any). Thus, an endowment policy is a mixed financial instrument. It is largely a straightforward long-term financial contract, in which what is returned reflects what has been paid in plus accrued interest and, maybe, a share in profits, but it also includes insurance cover against death within the currency of the policy.

There are a number of other forms of life assurance contract, but almost all involve regular payments by the assured over a number of years, or possibly a single large payment, in exchange for a guarantee of an eventual lump sum payment to the assured, or to his dependants.

Life assurance has been a popular form of saving in the United Kingdom and was, until the 1984 Budget, encouraged by tax relief on premiums paid. The life assurance companies comprise a number of specialist life companies as well as the large general insurance companies who also offer marine, fire and accident insurance. The latter categories of insurance do not represent financial contracts, as we are here using the term, as there is no lending or borrowing involved. The person who insures his house or his car buys a service (indemnity in the event of loss) for which he pays a price. His payment represents consumption expenditure, not saving. The law recognizes the fundamental difference between the two forms of insurance by requiring all general insurance companies to keep separate the funds accumulated to pay for claims under marine, fire, and accident policies and the funds accumulated in order to meet liabilities to holders of life policies.

Total accumulated funds held by all life assurers (specialist and general insurance companies) amounted, at end-1987, to £173,370m. Apart from a number of short-term assets, this money was largely invested in three different ways: in ordinary shares of UK companies, in British government securities, and in land, property and ground rents in the United Kingdom. Although, it should be added, that since the abolition of exchange control in 1980, life companies have begun to build up their foreign assets.

Superannuation funds are set up to provide pensions for members of a particular occupational group, or for employees of a particular firm or public-sector body. The principle is simple: those covered by the fund make regular contributions over a number of years and, upon retirement, are entitled to an annual pension until death. This pension may be of a fixed amount or it may allow for adjustments to compensate for inflation.

The number and size of pension funds have grown rapidly during recent decades as more and more firms have set up funds to cover their employees. In some cases of large firms or public corporations, the pension funds now administer considerable sums of money and are numbered among the largest discretionary managers of funds in the country. At end-1987, total net assets of superannuation funds amounted to £196,282m of which nearly

£26,000m was accounted for by local authority pension funds, over £40,000m by other public-sector pension funds and nearly £130,000m by private-sector pension funds.

Slightly over one-half of total assets are invested in the ordinary shares of UK companies, and most of the rest is spread over investments in British government securities, in ordinary shares of foreign companies, in land, property and ground rents in the UK and in short-term assets.

Life assurance companies also provide pensions both for individuals (notably the self-employed) and for groups. For many small firms, it is easier to make pension provision for staff through a life assurance company, than to set up one's own fund. All pension funds, whether administered by independent superannuation funds or by life assurance companies, have a favourable tax status and do not pay tax on interest and dividends received on their investments.

2.19   Other Financial Intermediaries

Unit trusts and investment trusts: There are two forms of mutual investment that are common in the United Kingdom: unit trusts and investment trusts. The intention of mutual investment is to enable small investors to pool resources in order to gain the benefits of diversification which would not be available to each one individually. There are high fixed costs of dealing in negotiable securities and a small investor with, say, £5,000 to invest would not be able to spread this over a number of different companies. He would, most likely, have to put all his eggs in one basket and invest all the money in one company. That would be a risky strategy. But if 1,000 investors, each with £5,000 to invest, were to come together and put their money in a common pool, they would have £5m to invest. This could be diversified over many companies, so reducing risk. This is the principle of mutual investment.

Unit trusts are legally constituted as trusts with a trust deed and a trustee. The trustee, which is usually a bank or an insurance company, holds all the assets of the unit trust on behalf of the beneficial owners – the unit-holders. The trust is managed by a professional manager who is responsible for decisions about investment policy, subject to the provisions of his trust deed. Units can be sold at any time and the sums raised added to the pool of investible resources. Similarly, units can be sold back to the manager, who is then obliged to sell some investments to repay the unit-holder. Unitholders are each entitled to a *pro-rata* share of the value of the invested funds of the trust and the Department of Trade and Industry lays down precise rules for calculating the value of individual units.

Investment trusts are not, in fact, trusts in the legal sense. They are limited companies which issue their own shares and which use the proceeds to invest in other companies. Thus, anyone who buys shares in an investment trust automatically buys a diversified investment. Investment trusts have their shares listed on the Stock Exchange and they are bought and sold like other equity shares.

At end-1988, funds managed by units trusts amounted to over £41bn of which the greater part was invested in ordinary shares of companies, both in the United Kingdom and abroad. The total assets of investment trusts are somewhat smaller and, at end 1987, amounted to something over £15bn and again most was invested in ordinary shares.

Finance houses: There are a number of finance houses and consumer credit companies active in the UK. They tend to be small as most of the larger institutions have now taken the status of bank and are included within the category 'other British banks', discussed above. Many are specialized institutions set up to finance the products of particular manufacturers or retailers. Funds are raised largely by issuing bills and by borrowing from banks. At end 1988, such companies had assets outstanding of £7,867m, of which nearly £6bn was accounted for by loans to persons and to industrial and commercial companies.

3   REGULATING THE FINANCIAL SYSTEM

Financial activity is a large and important part of modern economic activity. In Britain, in 1988, financial services accounted for approximately 10% of gross national product. And finance is not a separate activity from others: all firms and all individuals depend directly and indirectly on the efficiency and the probity of financial institutions. There is, therefore, a clear public interest in both the competence and the integrity of financial practitioners and this has resulted in increased official involvement in the regulation of the financial system.

Traditionally, financial institutions were governed by a number of different Acts of Parliament, each relating to different aspects of their business but, more recently, Parliament has sought to provide comprehensive regulation within the framework of a small number of Acts covering specific financial behaviour. The 1979 and 1987 Banking Acts cover the activities of all banks; the 1986 Building Societies Act regulates the building societies and the 1986 Financial Services Act seeks to regulate all trading of securities, of life assurance and of a wide range of ancillary activity.

The provisions of the 1979 and 1987 Banking Acts have already been discussed in section 2.4 above. These stipulate that all firms undertaking banking business must be authorized by the Bank of England and lay down detailed conditions for authorization. These include the requirements to supply the Bank regularly with statistical information, to open one's books for inspection upon request from the Bank and to respond to any directives given by the Bank. It is apparent that the Acts give considerable power to the Bank of England although there is provision for any bank refused authorization to appeal to the Treasury. The regulations cover all engaged in banking within the United Kingdom, both British-owned and foreign-owned banks.

The main public efforts of the Bank, to date, have been in the areas of capital adequacy and of liquidity. It has laid down, for all banks, minimum standards of capital (i.e. equity capital, reserves and other irredeemable or long-term funds) dependent on both the size and composition of their assets. The published standards, which stem from an international agreement between bank supervisors in the leading industrial countries, are minimum standards and the Bank reserves the right to treat each bank individually and to impose stricter standards where it feels these to be appropriate. The Bank also imposes requirements on each bank as to its liquidity, meaning both its short-term borrowing ability and its holdings of liquid assets.

The provisions of the Building Societies Act of 1986 have already been touched on in section 2.17 above. As well as laying down many detailed rules about what activities building societies could and could not engage in, this Act also created a Building Societies Commission with powers over the societies analogous to those of the Bank of England over the banks.

The Financial Services Act of 1986 was a very wide-ranging measure designed to regulate in some detail the activities of security traders, brokers, agents and advisers. For all of these it is now necessary to be authorized in order to carry out business and authorization requires compliance with an extensive set of rules of conduct.

The Act established a Securities & Investment Board (SIB) with powers of supervision over all firms engaged in financial investment but with powers to delegate this supervision to approved regulatory organizations. It was intended that such organizations should be set up for different sections of the industry and that they would include representatives of the firms being regulated, i.e. there would be an element of self-regulation. This was seen as desirable as much of modern financial activity is complex and the only people with a detailed understanding of it are those who are actually engaged in the business.

Five self-regulatory organizations (SROs) have been set up. They are:

(1) the Securities Association (TSA), covering all traders and brokers in securities;
(2) the Association of Futures Brokers and Dealers (AFBD), covering all traders and brokers in futures and options;
(3) the Life Assurance & Unit Trust Regulatory Organisation (LAUTRO), covering all life assurance companies and unit trusts;
(4) the Investment Managers Regulatory Organisation (IMRO), covering all fund managers; and
(5) the Financial Intermediaries, Managers & Brokers Regulatory Association (FIMBRA), covering all agents, brokers and other intermediaries not already covered by one of the other SROs.

Each of these self-regulatory organizations establishes and publishes its own rules of conduct but these rules have to be approved by the Securities & Investment Board. Thus it is not correct to say that the system is wholly one of self-regulation: it is a mixed system in which self-regulation is permitted but subject to the ultimate authority of a statutory body. It was the government's hope that this would produce an effective system of regulation but without the bureaucracy and the legalistic approach believed to be inherent in the American model with a single powerful statutory body: the Securities & Exchange Commission.

The Act also established the idea of a recognized investment exchange (RIE). The SIB will recognize an exchange where it is satisfied that it provides an efficient and well-run market with adequate financial resources to safeguard investors. Where firms transact business on an RIE, the requirements on them will be less onerous than where transactions are carried out on unrecognized exchanges.

The Act also provides for certain professional bodies (e.g. solicitors, accountants) to be recognized by the SIB so as to enable their members to continue with traditional financial activities without having to join one of the SROs. But recognition does require the professional bodies to have adequate rules to ensure investor protection.

In the aftermath of the coming into force of the Act, there have been widespread complaints about the length and detail of rule books with accusations of regulatory overkill and concern about the costs of compliance. At the time of writing (April 1989), the SIB has embarked on an attempt to simplify its rule book (which serves as a model for the rule books of the SROs) and is trying to establish a set of principles of good conduct as a substitute for many specific rules.

4   GOVERNMENT SPENDING AND TAXATION
4.1   The Volume and Composition of Government Spending

Government expenditure accounts for a large part of national income. In the financial year to end-March 1988, total expenditure of general government (i.e. central and local government combined) amounted to £177bn, or 41.5% of gross domestic product. But not all of this represented purchases of goods and services by the public sector; nearly one-half was accounted for by transfer payments such as pensions, unemployment benefits and sickness payments. For many purposes, it is important to distinguish these two categories of expenditure. General government expenditure on goods and services represents a claim on the resources of the country: government hires the services of schoolteachers, policemen, etc., it purchases warships from shipbuilders, ambulances from car manufacturers, etc. Transfer payments, on the other hand, involve no direct claim on resources. Government collects the money in the form of taxes and national insurance contributions and promptly redistributes it as cash payments to pensioners, social-security claimants and others. Transfer payments represent a redistribution of income and it is only when the recipients of the pensions, benefits, etc., spend the money that there is an actual claim on resources.

Government expenditure has grown over time. This is true of expenditure on goods and services and of total expenditure inclusive of transfer payments, both of which have risen in absolute amount and both of which, for many years, were rising as a share of national income. These trends,

TABLE 2.6

General Government Expenditure as a Percentage of GDP, 1946–87

	Expenditure on goods and services	All expenditure including transfer payments
1946	23.9	45.6
1950	19.8	34.6
1955	20.3	33.4
1960	19.7	34.7
1965	20.9	37.1
1970	22.3	40.5
1975	26.4	48.5
1980	23.6	45.1
1981	23.5	45.9
1982	23.4	46.4
1983	23.7	45.6
1984	23.7	45.5
1985	22.9	44.5
1986	22.9	42.8
1987	22.3	40.9

Note: All expenditure includes net lending by government less any privatization receipts. GDP is GDP at market prices.
Source: Economic Trends, annual supplements, 1986, 1989.

which are of long standing and date back to the nineteenth century, continued for much of the period since World War II. This is illustrated in appendix table A.5 which shows general government current expenditure over the years 1975–1987 and in table 2.6, which shows general government expenditure on goods and services and total government expenditure, both expressed as percentages of GDP, over the period 1946–1987.

It can be seen that both series, after dropping back from high war-time levels, showed a tendency to rise subsequently. By the mid-1970s, both expenditure on goods and services and total expenditure accounted for higher shares of national income than they had done in the immediate post-war year of 1946. But, during the 1970s, the size of public expenditure and the level of taxation became major political issues. First, the Labour government, with Denis Healey as Chancellor of the Exchequer, made some efforts to curb the growth of government expenditure and then, in 1979, a Conservative government was elected on a programme which gave priority to controlling public expenditure and reducing the 'burden of taxation'. Attempts to implement this programme had mixed results: for some years, total government expenditure continued to absorb an increasing share of GDP, but by the mid-1980s, a definite downward trend had been established. By the financial year 1988–89, total government expenditure was below 40% of GDP for the first time in over 20 years and further declines are predicted.[1]

British experience with public expenditure is not out of line with what has happened abroad. This is evident from table 2.7 which shows, for seven

TABLE 2.7

Total Government Expenditure: Seven Industrial Countries (% of GDP, average figures)

	1960–67	*1968–73*	*1974–79*	*1980–85*
United States	28.3	31.0	32.6	35.6
Japan	19.1	20.2	28.4	33.3
Federal Germany	35.7	39.8	47.5	48.4
France	37.4	39.0	43.7	50.6
United Kingdom	34.7	39.9	44.4	47.0
Italy	31.9	36.0	42.9	54.2
Canada	29.4	34.7	39.2	44.9

Source: OECD, *Historical Statistics 1960–1985*, Table 6.5.

industrial countries, the average share of total government expenditure in GDP, in four different time periods between the years 1960 and 1985. The figures have been standardized, as far as possible, to make them comparable. It will be seen that the trend increase in the share of government expenditure was common to all seven nations. The share of government expenditure in the UK is close to that in France, West Germany and Italy in all four periods. The relative size of the public sector is larger in these European countries than in the USA and Japan.

The composition of government spending is shown in table 2.8. This table gives a breakdown of all expenditure by general government into fourteen separate categories. It covers the years 1979, 1985, 1986 and 1987. In addition to the three latest years for which comprehensive data were available, 1979 has been included as this was the year in which the present Conservative government came into office. In view of the considerable public discussion about cuts in government expenditure, it seemed of interest to show what has happened to spending in all the different spheres of government activity under Mrs Thatcher's administration. The percentage change in nominal spending, over the years 1979–84, is shown, for each category, in the last column of the table. During this eight-year period, prices rose by an estimated 81.3%; therefore, increases greater than this can be seen as a rise in real expenditure, increases of less than this can be seen as a decline in real expenditure.

But comparisons of this sort involve a number of difficulties, so it is important to be clear what is involved. The stated increase in prices of

---

[1] See the *Financial Statement & Budget Report 1988–89* (H.M. Treasury, March 1989).

81.3% is an approximation, but it is the best indicator available of the movement of all prices within the economy. It is derived from the so-called

TABLE 2.8

General Government Expenditure by Category (£m)

	1979	1985	1986	1987	% change 1979–1987
General public services	3,706	5,675	6,218	6,455	74.2
Defence	8,969	18,256	19,108	18,912	110.9
Public order and safety	2,893	6,191	6,712	7,676	165.3
Education	10,310	17,401	19,349	21,204	105.7
Health	9,082	17,889	19,448	21,265	134.1
Social security	20,998	46,496	49,775	51,852	146.9
Housing & Community Amenities	7,250	6,998	8,079	8,503	17.3
Recreational & Cultural Affairs	1,138	2,196	2,302	2,637	131.7
Fuel & Energy	1,218	1,480	−943	−3,002	—
Agriculture, Forestry & Fishing	1,163	2,704	2,342	2,150	84.9
Mining & Mineral Resources, Manufacturing & Construction	2,463	2,260	1,845	1,348	−45.3
Transport & Communication	3,216	3,847	3,409	3,664	13.9
Other Economic Affairs & Services	1,876	4,257	3,941	3,420	82.3
Other expenditure	11,414	21,729	20,249	21,966	92.4
Total	85,696	157,379	161,834	168,050	96.1

Source: BB, 1988.

Memorandum Item: Increase in prices (GDP deflator) 1979–1987 = 81.3%

GDP deflator, which in turn is derived from a comparison of index numbers of nominal output and real output across the whole economy. As such, it is an attempt to capture the change in all prices, including those of exports, capital goods and publicly-provided services, not just those of consumer goods. It shows that expenditure on a representative basket of goods and services produced in the UK would have had to rise by 81.3% over the years in question in order to purchase the same volume of output. In this sense we can talk about a constant level of real expenditure.

But not all expenditure is on a representative basket of goods and services. Some prices rose more than average, some less. Constant real expenditure on goods whose prices were in the former category would be insufficient to maintain a constant volume of output; constant real expenditure on goods whose prices were in the latter category would be more than sufficient to do so. The cost of providing government services is normally estimated to rise faster than prices generally, although there are severe problems in making any estimate at all due to the near-impossibility of deriving measures of real output for much of government activity. For instance, due to technological development, the cost of military equipment tends to rise faster than the average level of prices: as new equipment is purchased, should we view this as an increase in the efficiency of the military services and, therefore, an increase in output of defence provision, or should we view it as an increase in the cost of providing the same level of output? There is no space to discuss this issue here, but the point to bear in mind is that constant real expenditure does not mean a constant volume of any particular type of output. This is as true at the national level as it is at the personal level. In what follows, we are concerned with expenditure.

It is clear from table 2.8 that the largest categories of spending are social security, health, education, defence and the final 'other expenditure' category. Social security expenditure, which in the years 1985–7 accounted for over 30% of all government expenditure, is largely composed of transfer payments: grants and allowances paid direct to beneficiaries. Expenditure has been increasing steadily for many years. The largest single item is the retirement pension and as the number of pensioners has risen steadily, so, inevitably, has the cost of pensions. This cost, at £19bn in 1987, was approximately double the real cost of pensions twenty years earlier. Other large items of expenditure are income support (supplementary benefits) which amounted to over £8bn in 1987, family benefits which were of £5bn in 1987 and unemployment and incapacity benefits which had risen to nearly £5bn by 1987.

Expenditure on health, most of which is accounted for by the cost of the National Health Service, has been rising rapidly since 1950 and has accounted for a steadily increasing share of public expenditure. Current government plans allow for further sharp increases in 1989 and 1990.

Real expenditure on education (which includes expenditure on the research councils) has grown only slowly since the early 1970s; but this is unsurprising when it is recalled that the number of children of school age has declined for much of this period. Expenditure on primary and secondary schools accounts for 60% of this item.

Defence expenditure has also risen in real terms but, in most periods since 1950, its growth has been slow and, until 1979, it represented a declining share of total public expenditure. During the early 1980s, there was a reversal of this trend when defence spending rose sharply but this has subsequently fallen back and current plans for the years to 1991 are for only modest growth.

The category of 'other expenditure' is dominated by interest payments on the national debt. Growth, in recent years, has been largely due to the high level of interest rates; but as the government is now making large net repayments of debt, this item of expenditure can be expected to decline in future years.

The category 'housing and community amenities' includes – as well as housing – water, sanitation, street lighting and other community services. Expenditure on housing, which usually accounts for over one-half of the total, is a mixture of capital expenditure, subsidies and grants. This category has been cut heavily since 1979. The figures shown are for expenditure net of receipts from sales of council houses. If we count such receipts as income, and not as negative expenditure, then the reduction in expenditure is somewhat less, but it is still substantial. Even on this basis, real expenditure on housing etc. has fallen, in the eight years, by approximately 20%.

Public order and safety covers expenditure on police and fire services, law courts and prisons. Here, real expenditure has increased by 16%, since 1979, and this increase has been spread evenly over all four sub-categories.

General public services include the costs of running the apparatus of government, i.e. expenditure on the home and foreign civil service, local government administration, Parliament and tax collection, as well as the UK contribution to the EEC and foreign aid. In real terms, expenditure under this heading has been reduced, since 1979, by about 4%. Much of this is accounted for by a reduction in civil service manpower of over 100,000.[1]

Expenditure on transport and communication covers government expenditure on road, rail, air and water transport, pipelines and communications. In real terms, it appears to have been cut drastically during the 1980s, but this is misleading. The government figures show expenditure net of receipts from sales of public assets (privatization) and in recent years, such receipts have been large, due mainly to the privatization of British Telecom and British Airways. Without this deduction, total expenditure in 1987 would have been £5,387m and growth over the years 1979–87 was approximately 68%: the real decline in expenditure over the period was approximately 8%.

There is a similar problem in interpreting the statistics for the category 'fuel and energy' which covers government expenditure on coal mining, petroleum and natural gas, nuclear fuel and electricity. Whilst there were receipts from sales of assets in all years covered by table 2.8, these were particularly large in 1986 and 1987 and, in addition, there were net repayments of debt to the government by public corporations. Without these negative items, total expenditure in 1987 would have been £1,469m and the fall in real terms since 1979 would be approximately 25%.

The heading 'mining and mineral resources, manufacturing and construction' is self-explanatory, except to add that it excludes expenditure on fuel resources, dealt with elsewhere, and that it includes expenditure on consumer protection. The bulk of expenditure is accounted for by transfer payments, notably capital grants to the private sector and the provision of capital for public corporations. There has been a reduction in expenditure on the latter of these items since 1979 and this more than accounts for the fall in total spending.

The remaining two specific categories of expenditure – 'agriculture, forestry and fishing' and 'recreational and cultural affairs' – are largely self-explanatory. Real expenditure under the former heading rose sharply between 1979 and 1985 but has fallen back since. Expenditure under the latter heading has tended to grow steadily year by year. The final category – 'other economic affairs and services' – covers government expenditure

---

[1]   See *Economic Progress Report* (H.M. Treasury, June 1984).

on the distributive trades, hotels and restaurants, tourism, multipurpose development projects, other economic and commercial affairs and general labour services. About 60% of expenditure is accounted for by subsidies and by grants to the personal sector. Total expenditure, in real terms, increased considerably in the years to 1985 but has fallen back subsequently.

This discussion of public spending has been in terms of aggregate expenditure by general government, i.e. central and local government combined. The share of local government is slightly less than 30%. In 1987, total expenditure by all local authorities amounted to nearly £49bn, of which education alone accounted for over £16.5bn. Other large claims on local authority resources are public order and safety, social security, housing, and debt interest.

4.2   The Budget

The Budget is presented by the Chancellor of the Exchequer to the House of Commons each Spring, in March or April. It is the most public of the several occasions on which the government sets before Parliament its economic forecasts and its policy proposals. The Budget serves several purposes. Firstly, it is the normal occasion for the government to propose changes in taxation. These changes may include the introduction of new taxes or the abolition of existing taxes, they may include changes in tax rates, and they almost certainly will include changes in the law concerning what persons or what activities are liable to tax. Proposed changes in the law include both substantive changes, i.e. where the government is introducing a new policy, and changes designed to block loop-holes in existing laws that are being exploited to avoid paying tax. The government's proposals become effective either on Budget Day itself, or on an announced date shortly thereafter; but they still require the subsequent approval of the House of Commons. After debate and possible modification, the Budget proposals are presented to the House of Commons in the form of a Finance Bill. When passed by the House, this becomes the Finance Act and is the definitive legal statement of the changes in taxation.

A summary statement of the proposed tax changes and of their effect on Exchequer revenues is given in the *Financial Statement and Budget Report* (*FSBR*), published immediately after the Chancellor's statement to the House of Commons. This document also gives details of estimated tax receipts for the past financial year and forecasts of tax receipts for the forthcoming one. Table 2.9 reproduces the figures given in the *FSBR*, 1989–90. Appendix table A.5 shows government receipts over a period of years 1975–1987.

It can be seen that the greater part of tax receipts is accounted for by the collections of the Inland Revenue (broadly speaking, direct taxes) and the Customs & Excise (broadly speaking, indirect taxes). In addition, there are a number of other receipts of which the most important is provided by local authority rates and the community charge (in force in Scotland from 1 April 1989 and due to come into force in England and Wales on 1 April 1990). National insurance contributions are not officially classed as taxation although, from the point of view of those who pay them, they are virtually indistinguishable from other taxes. But, however they are classified, it can be seen that they produce substantial amounts of revenue to the government.

The Budget is frequently the occasion for announcing some changes in government expenditures. It is also the time when the Supply Estimates, i.e. the estimates for the coming year of tax-financed public expenditure, are presented to the House of Commons. But the expenditure changes announced in the Budget are usually small in size and the Estimates only repeat what has already been made public. The main discussion of public

TABLE 2.9

Receipts of General Government (£m)

	1988–89 Latest Estimate	1989–90 Forecast
Inland Revenue		
Income tax	43.8	46.9
Corporation tax	18.4	22.4
Petroleum revenue tax	1.3	1.4
Capital gains tax	2.4	2.1
Inheritance tax	1.1	1.1
Stamp duties	2.3	2.4
Total Inland Revenue	69.3	76.3
Customs & Excise		
Value Added Tax	27.5	30.0
Petrol, derve duties, etc.	8.7	8.8
Tobacco duties	5.0	5.1
Alcohol duties	4.6	4.7
Betting and gaming duties	0.9	1.0
Car tax	1.4	1.4
(EEC own resources)		
customs duties	1.7	1.8
agricultural levies	0.2	0.1
Total Customs & Excise	49.9	52.9
Vehicle excise duties	2.8	2.9
Local authority rates and community charge	18.9	20.6
Other taxes and royalties	3.7	4.3
Total taxes and royalties	144.6	156.9
National insurance and other contributions	32.8	34.0
Interest and dividends	6.6	7.0
Gross trading surpluses and rent	3.0	3.3
Other receipts	3.9	5.2
General government receipts	190.9	206.4

Source: Financial Statement and Budget Report, 1989–90.

expenditure is when the government produces its annual Public Expenditure White Paper, usually well before the Budget, either in late Autumn or early in the New Year. This White Paper gives firm projections of government expenditure for the financial years ahead and more tentative projections for the two following years. The figures are broken down into the main categories of expenditure and within each category there is a further breakdown, giving a detailed picture, item-by-item, of public expenditure.

Until recently, it was a frequent criticism of the annual Budget procedures that tax changes were presented separately from public expenditure changes. In addition, there was the problem that the Budget only concentrates on the tax revenue of central government and does not consider national insurance contributions and local authority revenues. Similarly, the annual Supply Estimates presented with the Budget proposals cover only expenditures financed by these tax revenues. For many years, there was no attempt to give an overall picture of total public spending and total public receipts.

But in 1980 the Conservative government introduced, as part of its economic policy, a medium-term financial strategy (MFTS) in which total public expenditure and total public resources are central elements. This somewhat flexible strategy has been reconfirmed in subsequent years, and it is now the case that considerable attention is paid to the total spending and the total receipts of general government, both in the Chancellor's Budget speech and in the FSBR. The government's need to borrow/ability to repay debt is seen as a crucial policy variable.

4.3   The PSBR and the PSDR

In most years since the end of World War II, general government revenues from taxation, national insurance, royalties, etc., as well as from sales of publicly owned assets, have been insufficient to finance total expenditure. In consequence, government has had to borrow. Central government has financed most or all of the borrowing needs of local government and it has also loaned funds to public corporations. In this way the bulk of the borrowing of the public sector has been centralized and managed by the central government. The total need to borrow each year – the public-sector borrowing requirement or PSBR – was given a prominent role under the government's Medium Term Financial Strategy.

The importance of the PSBR, it was argued, had to do with how it was financed. The authorities had a basic choice: they could borrow from the banking system (including, for this purpose, the Bank of England), in which case the money supply would rise; or they could borrow from the non-bank private sector, in which case there would be no effect on the money supply. As it was a central objective of the MTFS to limit the growth of the money supply, there was a clear preference for the latter. But, other things being equal, the more the authorities borrow from the non-bank private sector, the more they will bid up rates of interest. And high rates of interest were seen as undesirable in that, other things being equal, they would be expected to act as a disincentive to capital investment. So we had the situation that the government wished to control the money supply, and wished to do this without pushing up rates of interest any more than necessary. The implication was that the government should limit its own borrowing; hence the importance of the PSBR.

In its immediate objective, the government has been remarkably successful. The PSBR which, during the years 1979–84, had averaged over £10bn per annum, was greatly reduced in 1985 and 1986 and became a government surplus in 1987. In 1988, the surplus was of the order of £14bn or 3% of GDP and further large surpluses are predicted for 1989 and 1990. These surpluses are used to repay outstanding government debt, hence the term public-sector debt repayment or PSDR.

However, notwithstanding this switch from public-sector deficit to surplus, virtually all measures of money showed rapid growth during the years 1985–88, the balance of payments deteriorated and, by 1988, inflation had again become a serious problem. The result was that interest rates had to be raised to high levels (clearing banks' base rates at 13%) in order both to curb bank lending and to encourage an inflow of foreign capital to finance the deficit on the current account of the balance of payments.

At present, there is no obvious link between the PSDR and the level of rates of interest and the combination of tight monetary policy and tight fiscal policy, confirmed by the 1989 budget, seems more explicable in terms of demand management measures designed to reduce inflationary pressures, than by reference to the MTFS.

4.4 Income Tax

Income tax is the single most important tax in terms of revenue produced. It can be seen from table 2.9 that, in financial years 1988–89, it yielded nearly £44bn, or nearly one quarter of total government receipts. Income tax is also one of the oldest of taxes, having been first introduced by William Pitt in 1799. It is straightforward in principle, but is complex in practice. All personal incomes are assessable to tax, but each taxpayer is allowed to earn up to a certain amount before starting to pay tax. This amount is known as the personal allowance. There are a number of other possible allowances. For instance, expenses necessarily incurred in earning income are not taxable and constitute an additional tax allowance. The sum of all allowances is deducted from total income and what is left is taxable income. It is this that is subject to tax.

There are different personal allowances for the single and for the married. The single person's allowance in financial year 1989–90 is £2,785, which means that a single man or woman, without other allowances, can earn £232 a month or nearly £54 a week before starting to pay tax. For married couples, one spouse can claim a higher married allowance, which in 1989–90 amounts to £4,375. Therefore, a married man, claiming the higher allowance, but with no other allowances, can earn almost £365 a month or £84 a week before starting to pay tax.

Income tax in Britain, as in most other countries, is a progressive tax, that is to say, the share of income that is taken in tax rises as income rises. Those with higher taxable incomes pay a larger proportion of their income in tax. This is justifiable on the principle of ability to pay: those with higher taxable incomes are presumed to be able to afford to contribute a larger proportion of their income in tax. It is also justifiable if one accepts that the taxation system should serve as a means of income redistribution. Progressivity is achieved by having different tax rates apply to different levels of taxable income. For many years, there were as many as six different tax rates, each applicable to different levels of income. But, in 1988, most of these were abolished and the system was reduced to one of just two rates: a basic rate and a higher rate. For 1989–90 the rates are as follows:

Tax rate (%)	Taxable income (£)
25	20,700
40	over 20,700

Personal allowances, rates of tax and the tax bands to which they apply are announced each year in the Budget speech. The Chancellor is free to vary these, although he is now under a requirement to state what upward variation would be required to compensate for inflation. This means that proposed tax changes can be promptly judged by their real not just their monetary effects. Clearly, if annual inflation were 10% and personal allowances were only raised by 5%, then people would start to pay tax at lower levels of real income than before. Similarly, if the higher rate threshold was raised by less than 10%, people would find themselves moving into the higher tax band at lower levels of real income than before. If such changes are deliberately sought, the Chancellor can alter allowances and thresholds accordingly, but he now has to do so openly and compare the changes he is making with neutral (i.e. inflation-adjusted) changes.

There are a number of problems with the present system of income tax. It must be accepted that some problems are inevitable, and one should not look for perfection in a system which involves several hundred tax offices assessing the incomes of over 20 million people, all of whom have their own unique circumstances. However, it is desirable to improve equity and efficiency as far as is possible. One source of general dissatisfaction for many years was the taxation of husbands and wives. Traditionally, their incomes have always been aggregated and treated as one. Not only did this mean that wives had no privacy in their tax affairs, it also meant that a married couple where both were earning would move more quickly into higher tax brackets than would a couple who were living together but unmarried. There was a possible taxation penalty on marriage.

There was also an apparent lack of equity as between married couples where both worked and married couples where the husband was the sole earner. This stemmed from the system of personal allowances (income which was not taxable) which included both a single person's allowance and a married allowance. This latter had been introduced as the married man's allowance at a time when fewer married women took paid employment. It was reasoned that the married man's income was supporting two people (at least) and therefore, on the principle of ability to pay, he should be required to pay less tax than a single person. So a married man's allowance was set at approximately 1.6 times that of a single person. But the allowance remained, even when both spouses were working; and as a working wife had an earned income-allowance equal to that of a single person, it meant that a married couple, when both were earning, received tax allowances equal to 2.6 times that of a single person.

In 1988, it was announced that there would be a reform of personal taxation with effect from April 1990. Husbands and wives are to be taxed separately both for income tax and for capital gains tax. This will give financial privacy to wives and will remove the potential tax penalty on married couples. In fact, the position will be reversed as the married allowance has been retained. A married couple where both work will continue to have combined personal allowances equal to 2.6 times the single allowance but will no longer have the risk of their two incomes getting into a higher tax bracket due to their being aggregated: their financial position will be better than that of two unmarried persons living together. And given that it is generally accepted that the cost of living of a single person is more than half that of a couple, it seems inequitable that a married couple should enjoy two allowances 2.6 times that of a single person. The proposed 1990 reforms are, in themselves, to be welcomed but they do not go far enough. Where both spouses are working and entitled to their own allowances, an additional married allowance seems overly generous.

4.5   Corporation Tax and Oil Taxation

Corporation tax is levied on company profits. As with persons, companies can take advantage of a number of allowances against earnings, and it is the total of profits less allowances which is subject to tax. For many years, the rate of tax was relatively high at 52% but, at the same time, there were generous provisions whereby much capital expenditure constituted an allowance against income and served to reduce taxable profits. The result was that the yield from corporation tax was low: many companies, in spite of earning subtantial profits, paid little in tax.[1] In 1984, the government initiated a major reform of the tax which involved the progressive reduction of the rate of tax and the simultaneous phasing out of some of the more generous tax allowances. From March 1986, the stan-

---

[1]   See J. A. Kay and M. A. King, *The British Tax System*, fourth edition (Oxford University Press, 1986).

dard rate of corporation tax has been 35%. For companies with profits below £150,000 a reduced rate of 25% applies.

The tax payable by a company depends directly on the size of taxable profits and is unaffected by whether profits are distributed to shareholders or are retained in the business. But the tax is paid in two parts: advanced corporation tax (ACT) and mainstream corporation tax, and the division between these two parts does depend on how much is paid to shareholders in the form of dividends. For when dividends are paid, these are treated as net-of-tax payments and the company has to pay tax on behalf of the shareholders at the basic rate of income tax. It is these payments which constitute ACT. The system is best explained by an example.

Assume a company with taxable profits of £100m. Its total liability for corporation tax is £35m. That is fixed. Now, suppose the company pays to shareholders, dividends of £20m. Since these payments are regarded as being net-of-tax, they have to be grossed-up in order to determine the shareholders' gross income and the company's liability to ACT. The principle of grossing-up is straightforward. If a taxpayer with a marginal tax rate of 50% receives a net-of-tax payment of £500, it can easily be seen that the gross payment must have been £1,000: the taxpayer needed to earn £1,000 in order to be left with a net £500 after tax. If the marginal rate of tax had been 25% (the basic rate in 1989–90), a net-of-tax payment of £500 would have corresponded to a gross payment of $100/75 \times £500$ = £666.7. On the same basis, shareholders who have received £20m net of tax are deemed to have received a gross income of $100/75 \times £20m$ = £26.7m, of which £6.7m is tax due. And this is the amount that the company has to pay in ACT. Subsequently, it will pay mainstream corporation tax of £35m less the £6.7m already paid.

For shareholders liable to tax at the basic rate of income tax, there is no further tax liability. They are deemed to have received a gross income equal to $100/75$ of dividends received and to have had tax paid on their behalf by the company. For shareholders whose marginal tax rate exceeds 25%, additional tax is due on the deemed gross payment. Conversely, shareholders such as pension funds, who do not pay tax, can claim a refund of the tax paid on their behalf.

Of the allowances which companies can set against income, the most important are in respect of depreciation. In order to produce, and to generate profits, all companies require some capital. But capital depreciates in value due to use and due to age. If a company is to remain in business, it has to set aside sufficient funds to be able to replace worn-out plant and machinery. So not all corporate earnings can be viewed as profit, in the sense that they could be distributed and spent by shareholders: some earnings have to be set aside in order to maintain intact the capital stock. This is recognized by the tax authorities and corporation tax is levied on profits after provision for depreciation. To avoid the trouble and expense of trying to assess physical depreciation for each company separately, general rules are laid down. Physical depreciation is translated into accounting depreciation and standard percentage allowances are granted in respect of plant and equipment and in respect of industrial holdings.

There are two common methods that accountants use to calculate depreciation. These can be explained by the following example. Assume a depreciation allowance of 20% a year applied to a machine costing £1,000. We could assume that, each year, the machine loses 20% of its existing value. So, in year 1, it loses £200 in value and is then worth £800. In year 2, it loses 20% of £800, i.e. £160 and is then worth £640. In year 3, it loses 20% of £640, i.e. £128 and so on. This is the declining balance method and it results in depreciation allowances being greater in the early period of life of capital equipment. Alternatively, we could assume that, each year, the machine loses 20% of its initial value. This would mean that depreciation was a constant £200 a year, and that the machine was fully depreciated after five years. This is the straight line method. Both methods are used at times by the Inland Revenue.

Depreciation allowances have been widely used in the years since World War II as a means to try to stimulate investment. Governments have increased the permitted rate of depreciation so that firms installing new equipment could get the tax relief earlier, and they have also granted initial allowances or first-year allowances whereby a large part of new investment became tax deductible in the year in which it was installed, regardless of any actual physical depreciation. This was carried to its logical conclusion in 1972, when all capital expenditure on plant and machinery, excluding passenger cars, was made subject to a first-year allowance of 100%. This meant that a company purchasing a machine worth £10,000 could immediately reduce taxable income by this amount and, at the then rate of corporation tax, save £5,200 in tax. Subsequently the initial allowance in respect of industrial buildings was raised to 75%.

These first-year and initial allowances were phased out between 1984 and 1986. After 1 April 1986, allowances were limited to 25% (on a reducing balance basis) in respect of plant and machinery and to 4% (on a straight line basis) in respect of industrial buildings, agricultural buildings and hotels.[1] These are the standard allowances, but additional allowances, as part of regional policy, are given on certain categories of expenditure in development areas, special development areas and in Northern Ireland. (There is a discussion of regional policy in Chapter 4 below.)

Oil taxation: Oil taxation involves three separate elements: royalties, petroleum revenue tax (PRT), and corporation tax. Royalties, which are now charged only on certain oil and gas fields, are a direct levy on the value of all production. PRT is a tax levied on the receipts from the sale

---

[1]   For a discussion of investment allowances in general and of the specific changes introduced in the 1984 Budget, see J.R.Sargent and M.F.G.Scott, 'Investment and the Tax System in the UK', *MBR*, Spring 1986.

of oil and gas – above an exempt initial amount – less operating costs and royalties. Both royalties and PRT are imposed on oil and gas fields individually. Corporation tax is applied normally to the profits of oil and gas producers, but after deduction of royalties and PRT.

This range of taxes, which, at first sight, appears unduly complicated, was designed to ensure a high yield to the Exchequer from the profitable large fields whilst, at the same time, not overtaxing smaller or more costly fields. To further ensure that taxation should not deter the extraction of oil and gas from marginal fields, the Secretary of State for Energy is given the power to refund royalties and to cancel PRT in cases where the profitability of a field is low.

In the early 1980s, there was concern that the most promising geological areas had already been exploited and that companies were increasingly unwilling to look for oil in other offshore areas, many of which were in less congenial situations and involved drilling at great depths below sea level. To provide additional incentive, the government announced, in the 1982 Budget, the abolition of royalties on newly-developed oil and gas fields, apart from onshore fields and those in the relatively shallow waters of the Southern Basin of the North Sea (between 52°N and 55°N). In 1984, it was officially estimated that this change and the subsequent changes in corporation tax and in investment allowances would have the result of reducing the marginal rate of taxation of new offshore oil fields, outside the Southern Basin, from 88% to 83.75%.

Total revenues from all royalties and taxes on oil and gas production depend closely on the sterling price of oil and gas. These depend on changes in world prices expressed in dollars, and on the pound–dollar exchange rate. Receipts were at a peak during financial years 1984–5 and 1985–6 when they averaged some £12bn per annum but due, *inter alia*, to a fall in world oil prices, they have fallen back considerably since then. In financial year 1987–8, receipts from all royalties and taxes were less than £5bn.

4.6   Capital Gains Tax

Tax is levied on capital gains: for persons it is levied at a rate equal to that which would apply if the gain were treated as additional income; for companies it is levied at the corporation-tax rate. The case for such a tax is partly one of equity: why should a person who receives £1,000, in the form of a capital gain, pay no tax, when a person who receives the same sum, in the form of income, does have to pay tax? But there is also a case for such a tax on the grounds of efficiency: without it, much energy will be spent on seeking ways to convert income into capital gains, in order to avoid tax. The case for capital gains tax (CGT) is strong.

But there are inherent difficulties in implementing fairly such a tax and, in consequence, the present tax represents something of a compromise between what is desirable in theory, and what is convenient in practice.

Many assets are exempt entirely from the tax. These include a person's principal private residence, agricultural property, motorcars, most life assurance policies, assets donated to charities, winnings from gambling, National Savings instruments and, if held for more than twelve months, gilt-edged stock and most corporate fixed-interest securities. There are provisions for allowing losses on assets subject to CGT to be offset against gains; and to avoid the high cost of collecting many small amounts of tax, there is an annual personal allowance, whereby gains below a certain amount are exempt from taxation. Since 1987, this allowance has been fixed at £5,000.

A complication of capital gains tax is that gains usually accrue over time and hence it is desirable to distinguish between real and monetary gains. A person who bought a share in company X in 1979 for £1,000 and sold it in 1989 for £2,000 has made a gain on paper; but since the general level of prices approximately doubled over the same period, it is clear there has been no real gain. Since March 1982, CGT has been on an indexed basis and only real gains have been subject to tax.

4.7　Inheritance Tax

There is a good case on grounds of equity for a tax on wealth. If two people earn the same income, but one also owns a large personal fortune whereas the other has no capital, it would normally be presumed that the former had a greater ability to pay than the latter. But, there are a number of severe practical problems that arise in attempts to tax wealth directly. While income usually accrues in the form of money, which means there is no special problem in making a money payment of taxes, much wealth is in illiquid form and may be indivisible. Thus, a person who owns a stately home, but who has little other wealth, may find himself unable to pay even a modest rate of wealth tax, without selling the home. Similarly many farmers and many small businessmen (who often have more debt than liquid assets) would find themselves unable to pay a wealth tax without selling part of the farm or the business. But governments usually wish to encourage both an efficient agriculture and a productive small business sector, and this is one main reason why they have shied away from direct wealth taxes which would make difficult the accumulation and productive use of wealth.

A common fall-back position has been to tax wealth when it changes hands at death. This was the approach in Britain between 1894 and 1974. But, in practice, estate duty, as it was known, yielded only modest amounts of revenue. There were a number of exemptions from the reductions in duty in respect of certain assets (e.g. agricultural land), and, in any case, those with large estates could transfer them to their heirs during their lifetime. Provisions were introduced to levy estate duty on property disposed of within a specified period prior to death, and this period was progressively extended to seven years. But, in spite of this, it was still commonly alleged that estate duty was an avoidable tax.

In 1974, the new Labour government replaced estate duty by a capital transfer tax (CTT), under which disposals of property were made subject to tax, whether made during life or at death. Tax was levied, at a progressive rate, on the cumulative value of all gifts over a period of ten years. That is to say, in calculating tax due, gifts in any one year were aggregated with the cumulative total of gifts in the preceding nine years. It was the total of all gifts over the ten-year period which determined which rate of tax should apply.

There were a number of exemptions. Transfers of property between husbands and wives, in life and at death, were free of all tax, as were outright gifts and bequests to charities. Gifts, during any one year, to one individual, up to the value of £250 were exempt from duty, and so also were total gifts, during any one year, up to the value of £3,000. After allowing for exemptions, all transfers of property were cumulated. Of the cumulative total, an initial amount (£67,000 in 1985–6) was free of duty and then tax rates increased as total transfers increased. In financial year 1985–6, the maximum rate was 30% for lifetime gifts and 60% for bequests, and was reached when cumulative transfers of property reached £300,000.

In 1986, the government abolished the tax on lifetime gifts between persons. Gifts into, or out of, trusts and gifts involving companies remain subject to tax. Gifts, at death, are taxed as before and provisions to tax gifts made within seven years of death have been reintroduced. The reason given for this change was that CTT deterred lifetime giving, had the effect of freezing the ownership of assets, especially the ownership of family businesses and that this was often detrimental to such businesses. The tax now applies mainly to transfers of property at death and has been renamed the inheritance tax. Since 1988, a flat rate of 40% has been levied on all taxable transfers in excess of an initial exempt amount. This amount, in recent years, has been raised annually in line (at least) with the increase in retail prices. For the financial year 1989–90, it stands at £118,000.

4.8   Value Added Tax

Value added tax (VAT) is, after income tax and national insurance, the largest producer of revenue to the government. It is intended as a broadly based expenditure tax and was introduced, in 1973, following the accession of the United Kingdom to the EEC. VAT had, by then, become part of the process of fiscal harmonization within the Community, although, since for many years there was no attempt to harmonize *rates* of tax, it remained, at best, only a partial harmonization. The tax is intended to be non-discriminatory and is levied on producers of intermediate goods as well as on producers of final goods. This raises considerably the costs of collection which fall both on the revenue authorities – the Customs

& Excise – and on the taxpayer themselves. But since complete non-discrimination would have undesirable redistributive effects, there are different rates of VAT, so the objective is not achieved in practice.

The tax is levied at all stages of production and is imposed on the value added by each producer. How it works in practice can be illustrated by the following simple example. We assume a VAT of 15% which is the standard rate in force in the United Kingdom since 1979. A manufacturer purchases raw materials at a price of £115 inclusive of VAT, i.e. the cost of the raw materials is £100 and tax is £15. This latter is known as the input tax. The manufacturer then uses capital and labour to produce a finished article which he sells to a retailer for £230 including VAT. £30 is the output tax, and the manufacturer has to pay to the Customs & Excise the difference between output and input taxes, namely £15. So the cost of the product, net of tax, is £200 and tax, at the rate of 15% has been paid. The initial suppliers of raw materials added value of £100 and so paid £15 in tax; the manufacturer also added value of £100 and so paid the same amount in tax. If, now, we assume that the retailer will earn £20 net on each product he sells, then this sum is the value added at the retail stage, and tax is due thereon. The retailer will sell the product at a price of £253; his output tax will be £33, his input tax was £30, so he is liable to pay VAT of £3. The total amount of tax paid (£33) is equal to 15% of the total net-of-tax sale value of the product. It has been collected, at each stage of the production process, by taxing each producer according to his value added.

It may be asked at this stage, why not levy the 15% tax at the retail stage and save bothering all manufacturers and suppliers with calculations of input and output taxes? This was essentially the procedure adopted with the purchase tax in force prior to 1973. The only answer to this question would appear to be that we have VAT because it is an EEC requirement. It is not obviously superior to alternatives and it is costly to collect for the authorities and complex, and therefore costly, for many of those who pay it. Large firms with sophisticated accounting systems cope without difficulty but, for many small businesses, the costs of calculating VAT are high. It may be noted that the change from purchase tax to VAT raised the number of taxpayers from 74,000 to 1.2 million and the number of collectors from 2,000 to 13,000.[1]

If the standard rate of VAT of 15% were levied on all items, it would bear heavily on the poor: unlike income tax, where no tax is payable on very low incomes, the full tax would be levied on very low expenditures. To prevent this and to introduce some progressivity into the tax, certain items, which form a large proportion of the expenditure of those on low incomes, are zero-rated. Not only is no VAT levied on the production and sale of these commodities, but producers can also reclaim VAT paid

[1]   See Parr and Day, 'Value Added Tax in the United Kingdom', *NWBQR*, 1977, and the discussion in Kay and King, *op. cit.*

by suppliers of intermediate goods. Such items include food, fuel and power, transport and children's clothing. There is a third category of goods, those that are exempt from VAT. Exemption is not the same as zero rating: producers of exempt goods pay no VAT themselves, but cannot reclaim what has already been paid on inputs supplied to them. Exempt goods and services include health care, education, insurance and financial services, postal services and land. Very small firms with turnover less than prescribed amounts are also exempt from VAT. In financial year 1989–90, the amounts are £23,600 per annum and £8,000 per quarter.

In 1987, with the supposed creation of a single European market in mind, the EEC Commission proposed a move towards greater standardization of VAT rates throughout the Community. Specifically, it was proposed that there should be just two rates for all member countries: a normal rate fixed between 14–20% for standard items and a reduced rate between 4–9% for items judged to be basic personal necessities. The proposal provoked considerable hostility from a number of quarters, not least from the British and Irish governments which wish to retain their zero rate, and it seems unlikely that it will be implemented without modification.

The EEC Commission has also been seeking to narrow down the range of items which are subject to existing lower rates of tax and has taken a number of cases to the European Court of Justice. As a consequence, the UK government has had to levy the standard rate of VAT on items previously zero-rated, such as non-residential construction (subject to VAT from April 1989) and fuel and power supplied to business and water and sewerage services supplied to industry (all subject to VAT from April 1990).

4.9   Excise Duties and Customs Duties

Excise duties are duties levied on goods, whether produced domestically or imported, and which have as their prime objective the raising of revenue. Customs duties are duties levied specifically on imported goods and where the objective may be to protect domestic producers, to raise revenue, or both. Following the entry of the United Kingdom into the EEC, and after an initial transitional phase, customs duties have no longer been levied on imports from other member states of the EEC; and those that are levied on imports from non-member countries are now determined jointly for all EEC members in order to maintain a common external tariff. Receipts of customs duties are regarded as part of the 'own resources' of the Community and are paid over to Brussels.

The most significant excise duties, in terms of revenue raised, are clearly those on oil, tobacco and alcohol. As can be seen from table 2.9, these three duties raised, in financial year 1989–90, a total of £17.3bn. It could be asked why one should single out for tax, in what is a highly discriminatory way, these three commodities? The first answer is that all three have inelastic demands, i.e. increases in price have only a small effect on demand, so they are eminently suitable as a means of raising revenue. This, and the fact that the duties are all of long standing and have become accepted (albeit grudgingly), are probably sufficient reasons for most Chancellors of the Exchequer. But other good economic reasons can be advanced. The consumption of tobacco, as a widely accepted cause of cancer, has a very high human cost in terms of suffering and premature death. Alcohol abuse, which is widespread, has both a high human cost and a high social cost. Motoring has high social costs in terms of congestion, pollution and the expense of policing, while the large numbers of accidents to which it gives rise have both high human and social costs.

The duties on oil, tobacco and alcohol are all stated as fixed monetary amounts. So, unlike VAT – defined as a percentage rate – they are not automatically indexed for inflation. Increases in the duties are regularly made at the time of the Budget, but for many years during the 1960s and 1970s there was a tendency for increases to fall short of the rate of inflation, with the result that the real value of the duties fell. Increases in excise taxes inevitably raise prices, and so themselves contribute to measured inflation, and this appeared, on occasions, to have dissuaded Chancellors from making sizeable increases. During the early 1980s, duties were raised more systematically and tended to maintain or even to increase their real value with the tax on cigarettes rising considerably; but in both the 1987 and 1989 budgets, excise rates were largely unchanged.

The question of harmonizing excise taxes throughout the EEC, previously discussed in a somewhat academic manner, has acquired greater importance with the approach of 1992 and the 'single European market'. If, as is foreseen, customs checks at borders are substantially reduced or even abolished altogether, then one may expect goods subject to excise taxes to be purchased where rates are low and imported into those countries where rates are high. But if this means there is a strong case for some harmonization, the problems remain formidable. Rates differ greatly between EEC member states and, in those countries where rates are high, there would be difficulties about making significant reductions both on grounds of loss of revenue and from political concerns about matters such as health and the environment; in those countries where rates are low, there would frequently be political difficulties about making significant increases. To date, the EEC Commission has not produced any definite proposals.

4.10   Local Taxation

Local taxation is currently undergoing a complete upheaval. The system of levying rates on immovable property, which has existed for centuries, is being abolished for residential properties and is being brought under central control for non-residential properties. A brand new tax – the community charge – which replaces rates on residential properties, came into force in Scotland in April 1989 and is due to come into force in England and Wales in April 1990.

The rating system worked as follows. Rates were charged on all immovable property: residential houses, industrial and commercial properties, but not farms, which remained exempt from rating. The rates charged depended both upon the value of the property and upon the levy imposed. The value of property was defined as its rental value and rates were then levied on the basis of so many pence per pound; i.e. if the assessed rental value (termed the rateable value) of a property was £400 and the local authority rate set at 80p in the pound, then the sum payable was £320.

A good economic case could be made out for a tax on property in the manner of rates but the tax, as it was levied, had become widely disliked. The case for a tax on all immovable property is that the incidence of such a tax will fall largely on economic rent and will not, in the long run, affect the cost of the property. For the purchase price of private houses, just like office blocks, does not usually depend wholly, or even mainly, on cost of production but on scarcity and location. If people pay £500,000 for luxury houses in exclusive parts of Berkshire, this is not because such houses cost that amount to build – many were built many years ago at a fraction of such a sum – but because wealthy people wish to live there and because suitable properties are scarce. Similarly, office blocks in the City of London can be worth over a hundred million pounds, not because they cost such sums to produce but because, for many businesses, a City office is worth a great deal and office space is limited. In both cases, high demand and an inelastic supply combine to raise prices and primarily they raise the price of the scarce factor, i.e. land.

It is well known and explained in most economics textbooks[1] that high demand for land will raise its value – the supply of land cannot be increased in the way that, say, the supply of consumer durables can be – and will, in the process, create Ricardian rent. The returns accruing to the land-owners are rent precisely because they are not a cost of production but are a return to scarcity of a specific factor, in this case, land. And rising rents do not increase the supply of land because the supply to the economy as a whole is fixed. So why not levy a tax on the rent which is what a property tax is?

If a house sells for £500,000 because that is what people are prepared to pay for it, i.e. price is determined by demand, then levying a tax will not raise that price. If a tax of, say, £100,000 were levied upon sale, then the price would be expected to remain the same but the vendor would receive only £400,000. The same principle would apply for a house of £50,000 and a tax of £10,000. Rates were not a lump sum tax but an annual

---

[1]   See, for instance, R.G.Lipsey, *An Introduction to Positive Economics* (7th edition, Weidenfeld & Nicolson, 1989).

tax, but the principle is the same: an annual tax has an equivalent capital value and will affect the price people are prepared to pay for property.

The position is analogous with commercial property. If firms are prepared to pay £60 a square foot as an annual rental for good London office accommodation, a tax of, say, £10 per square foot will just reduce the net return to the lessor by that amount.

In short, a tax on immovable property meant that its price was reduced in line with the tax. Rates did not add to the cost of housing in the long run because, in their absence, house prices would have been higher. And economists would predict that, in the long run, the abolition of domestic rates will lead to a higher level of house prices. What people save on rate payments they will spend on the extra interest on a higher mortgage. Of course, in the short run, these influences may be hidden by changes in any of the other factors which exert an influence on house prices, notably rates of interest.

But if economists could make out a good case for rates, they were nonetheless an exceedingly unpopular form of taxation. Partly, this was because they were a tax on wealth and had the practical disadvantages associated with such a tax that were mentioned earlier, in the discussion of CTT. Many people, and especially the elderly, live in houses which reflect past rather than present income. They resented paying high rate demands, but equally, and not unnaturally, did not wish to sell a home that they spent many years saving to buy. And the problem was not limited to domestic rates. In the early 1980s, there were substantial increases in rate levies at a time when the economy was experiencing its worst depression since the 1930s. Many firms found their rate demands rising steeply, precisely at a time when revenues and profits were falling.

There was an additional reason for the general dislike of domestic rates: they are widely believed to be inequitable between one property-owner and another. There was much justice in this complaint. The problem stemmed from the valuation of properties in terms of their rental value; something which was justifiable when most private residences were rented from landlords, but which was no longer so in an age when the vast majority of houses and flats were either in owner-occupancy or were in the council-housing sector. In modern times, there has been no broadly-based free market for rented accommodation and so rental values had to be estimated and periodically re-estimated. Revaluations of domestic properties were carried out in 1963 and in 1973, and both led to much discontent. Such a response seems inevitable, as the resentment (usually directed against the government of the day) of those who saw their rateable value increased invariably outweighed any gratitude of those who saw their rateable value reduced. In consequence, rating revaluations were not an attractive prospect for any government and the one due in 1983 was cancelled. The idea of basing rates on sale values rather than rental values had been widely canvassed and had much to commend it; but, the initial effect of such a change would have been large shifts in liability to tax, and so, again, it was a politically unattractive measure for any government. So rates continued to be levied on out-of-date assessments of rental values which became increasingly arbitrary as time passed.

Resentment against rates was one reason why so much of the expenditure of local government has been financed by grants from central government. For many years, such grants were regularly increased in order to avoid significant rises in rates and by the mid-1970s they accounted for over 60% of all local authority expenditure. Subsequently, the percentage was reduced, and in consequence both domestic and non-domestic rates rose appreciably; but, in the late 1980s, the contribution of central government to local authority finance is still in the region of 50%. And since non-domestic rates and other sources of income account for well over half of what remains, it meant that domestic ratepayers contribute, directly, less than one-fifth of local authority revenues. This contribution had been declining over a number of years, as can be seen from table 2.10. This raises the obvious problem of accountability: local electors have every incentive to vote for more and more services if they know they will only pay a small part of the cost of providing them. In principle, such a situation can be avoided – if central government grants are for a known amount, fixed in advance, then local ratepayers will know that marginal additions to expenditure will be largely reflected in their own rate bills. But prior to the mid-1970s, there were frequent changes in central government support for local authorities and this tended to respond to the size of local government expenditure and to political pressure and lobbying on behalf of ratepayers. So local government expenditure continued to rise rapidly and those voting for it paid only a fraction of its cost. But, after 1976, central government support was less readily forthcoming and did not increase in real terms. And, not altogether by coincidence, local government expenditure also ceased to grow.

TABLE 2.10
Proportion of Local Authority Revenue Expenditure Financed by Domestic Ratepayers (%)

1948–49	31*
1958–59	28*
1968–69	15.1
1978–79	14.2
1982–83	13.8
1983–84	12*

Source: Hepworth.[1]
* Approximate percentages.

[1]   N.Hepworth, *The Reform of Local Government Finance*, Transactions of the Manchester Statistical Society, 1985–86.

However, the situation remained unsatisfactory. Domestic rates were highly unpopular and business rates increasingly contested. Many commentators and an official committee of enquiry (the Layfield Committee[1]) argued the case for the supplementation of rates by a local income tax. But the government decided to abolish domestic rates altogether and to replace them by the Community Charge.

This new tax will be levied at a flat rate on all adults subject to a limited number of exemptions. It is not a property tax, nor is it an income tax: it is levied on each person regardless of their property and, above a certain minimum level, regardless of their income. Supporters claim that since the new tax will widen the number of people who pay local taxation directly, it will give more people an incentive to scrutinize the behaviour of their local authority and to demand value for money. Opponents have stressed the flat rate nature of the tax and its not being related to ability to pay, a criticism which is only partially met by exempting certain categories of persons from all payment and by reducing the liability of others. Those exempt include children under 18 and all persons still at school, the severely mentally handicapped, long-term hospital patients and those living in nursing homes or hostels, prison inmates and certain members of religious communities. Foreign diplomats are also exempt but other foreign nationals resident in Britain are liable for the tax. Those who will benefit from a reduced liability to the Community Charge include full-time students (who will pay only 20%) and those on low incomes (who can apply for a rebate of up to 80% dependent upon their economic circumstances).

Apart from these categories of persons, everyone will pay the full Community Charge. The actual charge will vary from authority to authority depending upon the level of spending of the council in each area.

Business rates are to be retained, but are to be set nationally. Instead of each local authority setting its own rates, the government will set a uniform rate which will apply to all business premises across the country. Here, there may be some distinct economic gains. In the past, high rate levies have been imposed in what are generally poorer areas and this has had the long-run effect of encouraging business to move to areas where rates were lower. A uniform national rate will not only end this but it will ensure that where commercial property prices are higher, the amount of tax levied will be proportionately higher. Once the system is fully in force, it can be expected that commercial rates will be higher in the more affluent areas of the country such as London and the South East and lower in less affluent places such as many of the older industrial towns in the North. Thus local taxation of business will be providing the right incentives for firms to relocate in poorer areas rather than encouraging them to move away.

---

[1] *Local Government Finance*, Report of the Committee of Enquiry (Chairman F. Layfield), Cmnd. 6543 (HMSO, 1976).

4.11   Taxation and the EEC

Membership of the European Economic Community impinges on taxation within the UK in two main ways: some tax revenue has to be paid to the Community, and the structure and rates of certain taxes are influenced by Community requirements.

Tax paid to the EEC is comprised of all customs duties, certain agricultural levies, and a proportion of the proceeds of a flat rate of VAT imposed on a standardized range of goods and services. The amount actually paid depends upon the size of the EEC budget but is subject to a maximum, due to the proportion of VAT paid over being subject to a maximum. This was originally 1%, was raised to 1.4% and subsequently, in 1988, to 1.6%.

For various reasons, these rules, which apply to all member countries, result in the UK making a net contribution to the EEC far in excess of its relative resources. To offset this, a rebate is paid annually to the UK amounting to 66% of the difference, in the previous year, between its share in the Community's VAT receipts and its share in expenditures from the 'allocated' Community budget. The allocated budget accounts for over 90% of Community expenditure, the main 'unallocated' item being foreign aid.

The EEC is concerned to harmonize certain indirect taxes levied by member states. This has been touched on already in the section on value added tax, where Commission proposals for maximum and minimum rates of VAT were discussed, and in the section on excise taxes where potential pressures for some harmonization were foreseen. A third area where there has been some talk of the need for minimum common standards is the taxation of interest and dividends. The traditional exchange controls which restricted capital movements between nations have already been eased or abolished in most EEC member states and remaining restrictions are due to go as part of the progress towards the 'single European market'. A number of national governments fear that the ability of persons to invest freely abroad will lead to significant tax avoidance and are pressing for a community-wide withholding tax, i.e. a tax at source on all payments of interest and dividends. This pressure from a number of governments has found an echo in Brussels but it is being resisted by Luxemburg and the UK, both concerned at the potential effects of a withholding tax on their international financial business.

Apart from concerns to harmonize tax rates or to promote common taxation arrangements, the EEC authorities are concerned to see that member countries should not use excise duties so as to discriminate in favour of domestic produce and against the produce of other member states. In 1983, the European Court of Justice decided that British excise duties on alcoholic beverages were discriminatory in that beer, largely home produced, was less heavily taxed than wine, most of which was imported from other EEC countries. As a result, in the 1984 UK Budget, tax on beer was raised more than was necessary to keep pace with inflation, while tax on wine was reduced.

More recently, the European Court has ruled that the reduced rate bands of VAT (zero in the case of Ireland and the UK) should only apply to items which can be seen as necessary personal consumption and not to items which are bought for commercial use. As a result of a judgement on 21 June 1988, the UK has imposed VAT on non-residential construction and property development with effect from April 1989 and is planning to impose VAT on fuel and power supplied to business and on water and sewerage services supplied to industry, both with effect from 1 July 1990.

FURTHER READING

A.D.Bain, *The Economics of the Financial System* (Martin Robertson, 1981).

Bank of England Quarterly Bulletin.

M.Hall, *The City Revolution: Causes and Consequences* (Macmillan, 1987).

J.A.Kay and M.A.King, *The British Tax System* (4th edition, Oxford University Press, 1986).

B.Kettell, *Monetary Economics* (Graham & Trotman, 1985).

A.R.Prest and N.A.Barr, *Public Finance in Theory and Practice* (7th edition, Weidenfeld & Nicolson, 1985).

M.Reid, *All Change in the City: The Revolution in Britain's Financial Sector* (Macmillan, 1988).

3

The balance of payments

C. J. Green

1 THE OVERALL BALANCE OF PAYMENTS
1.1 Introduction

The importance to the UK of the balance of payments, foreign trade and foreign investment will be obvious to anyone who has followed the course of events during any period since 1945. The growth of the UK economy, the level of employment, and the standard of living have been, and will continue to be, greatly influenced by external economic events. The purpose of this chapter is to outline the main features of the external relationships of the UK and to discuss economic policies adopted to influence these external relationships, with the primary focus of attention being on the years since 1972.[1]

It is often said that the UK is a highly 'open' economy and an indication of the meaning of this is given by the fact that in 1987, exports of goods and services were 25.5% of GNP (at market prices) and imports of goods and services were 26.6% of GNP. These percentages are substantially larger than the comparable figures for the mid-1960s and for 1946, with the most rapid increase coming about since the UK joined the EEC in 1973.[2] A high degree of openness implies that the structure of production and employment is greatly influenced by international specialization. For the UK it also means that over 30% of the foodstuffs consumed and the bulk of raw materials necessary to maintain inputs for industry have to be imported. In the sense defined, the UK is a more open economy than many industrial nations, for example West Germany and France, but less open than some others such as Belgium.

1.2 Basic Concepts

The balance of payments accounts: The concept of the balance of payments is central to a study of the external economic relationships of a country but, as with any unifying concept, it is not free from ambiguities. Such ambiguities stem from at least two sources, viz. the different uses to which the concept may be put and the different ways in which we may

---

[1] 1972 coincides with the floating of the sterling exchange rate. Earlier editions of this volume contain a discussion of external developments between 1945 and 1972. See, in particular, the 5th edition (1974) and the 11th edition (1986).
[2] The export–GNP ratio stood at 14.1% in 1946 and at 18.2% in 1965. The import–GNP ratio stood at 18.0% in 1946 and at 19.2% in 1965.

approach the concept – either as a system of accounts or as a measure of transactions in the foreign-exchange market.

From an accounting viewpoint, we may define the balance of payments as a systematic record, over a given period of time, of all transactions between domestic residents and residents of foreign nations. In this context, residents are defined as those individuals living in the UK, and UK government agencies and military forces located abroad. Ideally, the transactions involved should be recorded at the time of the change of ownership of commodities and assets, or at the time specific services are performed. In practice, trade flows are recorded on a shipment basis, at the time when the export documents are lodged with the Customs and Excise, and at the time when imports are cleared through Customs. As the time of shipment need bear no close or stable relationship to the time of payment for the goods concerned, this method gives rise to errors in the recording of the accounts. All transactions are recorded as sterling money flows, and when transactions are invoiced in foreign currencies, their values are converted into sterling at the appropriate exchange rate. Because sterling is a 'key' or 'vehicle' currency, and is used as an international medium of exchange, it transpires that around 76% of UK exports and 38% of UK imports are invoiced directly in sterling.[1]

Like all systems of income and expenditure accounts, the balance-of-payments accounts are an *ex post* record, constructed on the principle of double-entry book-keeping. Thus, each external transaction is in principle entered twice, once to indicate the original transaction and again to indicate the manner in which that transaction was financed. The convention is that credit items, which give rise to a flow of funds into the UK (e.g. exports of goods and services and foreign investment in the UK), are entered with a positive sign, and that debit items, which give rise to a flow of funds out of the UK (e.g. imports of goods and services and investments by UK residents overseas), are entered with a negative sign. It follows that, by definition, the balance-of-payments accounts always balance – the total of credit items must equal the total of debit items. The interpretation to be read into the accounts therefore depends on dividing the accounts up in particular ways. As there are many such ways of dividing up the accounts, they cannot be used to present a single, unique picture of a country's external economic relationships.

The structure of the balance of payments: In common with most other countries, the UK balance-of-payments accounts are itemized in a manner which generally follows the recommendations laid down by international agreement through the offices of the International Monetary Fund (IMF). However, the grouping and aggregation of individual items in official UK

---

[1] S.A.Page, 'The Choice of Invoicing Currency in Merchandise Trade', *NIER*, No. 98, 1981. End-1988 exchange rates for the pound and the US dollar, in terms of SDRs and ECUs, are given at the end of this chapter on page 226.

balance-of-payments statistics, particularly within the capital account, have changed over the years, the most recent changes becoming effective in 1985. Changes in the UK's presentation of its balance of payments have not always enhanced the analytical value of the statistics, whereas the IMF has recommended a standard and useful presentation which has not changed markedly over many years. For these reasons, the summary statement of the UK's balance of payments for 1984–88, contained in table 3.1, follows, with one exception, the IMF's presentation rather than that in official UK sources.[1]

The first major feature of the IMF presentation is the distinction between current and capital accounts and, for many purposes, this is the most convenient summary division of the accounts. The current account records all trade in goods and services including current transfers (table 3.1: lines A1–A5); whereas the capital account records all transactions in assets and liabilities including capital transfers (table 3.1: lines A6–A13).

First in the current account are the so-called 'visible' trade items consisting of the exports (A1) and imports (A2) of commodities. These are shown separately in table 3.1, whereas all subsequent items are shown on a net basis, i.e. receipts less payments. Full details of separate debit and credit items are given in the official sources. Exports are recorded 'free on board' (f.o.b.), that is, at their value at the port of exit excluding the cost of international shipping and insurance. Import statistics are more usually collected c.i.f. (cost, insurance, freight), that is, at their value inclusive of international shipping and insurance. As shipping and insurance are not part of the producer cost of a product, it has become conventional to adjust import data to their f.o.b. basis for reporting in the balance of payments.

The remaining items in the current account are the so-called 'invisibles'. Services (A3) include receipts and payments arising from charges for the insurance and shipping services associated with the international exchange of goods. When imports are adjusted from a c.i.f. to an f.o.b. basis, the bulk of the adjustment is imputed back into the accounts as part of the debit items in respect of services purchased. Other services arise independently of the exchange of goods, notably the expenditures of tourists when abroad, and the burgeoning activity of consultancy services. Remittances on account of interest, and profits and dividends (IPD)(A4) arise when, for example, British firms pay dividends to foreign shareholders (a debit) or vice-versa (a credit). Shareholders and holders of other assets perform a service in lending capital funds to firms and governments; the dividend or interest payments are their rewards for performing this service. Note therefore that, whereas interest and dividend income from assets appear in the current account, revenues from the purchase or sale of an asset appear (by definition)

---

[1]   It should be emphasized that the individual items in the accounts emanate directly from UK official statistics; it is their aggregation and grouping in table 3.1 which follow the IMF presentation. For a readable summary of the IMF presentation see 'Guide to Analytic Presentation of the Balance of Payments', *IMF Survey*, 6 February 1978. UK balance of payments statistics are published annually in the CSO, *United Kingdom Balance of Payments*, HMSO; also known by its cover as 'The Pink Book'.

TABLE 3.1

UK Summary Balance of Payments 1984–88 (£m : credits+/debits−)

	1984	1985	1986	1987	1988
Current Account					
A1. Exports (fob)	70,263	77,988	72,678	79,422	80,157
A2. Imports (fob)	−74,843	−80,334	−81,394	−89,584	−100,714
B1. Balance of Visible Trade					
A1 + A2	−4,580	−2,346	−8,716	−10,162	−20,557
A3. Services	3,941	5,962	5,618	5,638	3,473
A4. Interest Profits and Dividends	4,433	2,800	5,079	5,523	6,001
A5. Transfers	−1,772	−3,079	−2;180	−3,503	−3,582
B2. Balance of Invisible Trade					
A4 + A5 + A6	6,602	5,683	8,517	7,658	5,892
B3. Balance on Current Account					
B1 + B2	2,022	3,337	−199	−2,504	−14,665
Capital Account					
A6. Capital Transfers	—	—	—	—	—
A7. Direct Investment	−6,184	−4,440	−7,349	−9,419	−7,823
A8. Portfolio Investment	−8,635	−13,801	−17,074	15,946	−6,738
A9. Other Capital nie					
A9.1 + A9.2 + A9.3	4,940	9,348	13,086	128	16,760
A9.1 Government	(−881)	(−652)	(−364)	(−589)	(−403)
A9.2 UK Banks	(9,485)	(7,340)	(10,029)	(844)	(14,446)
A9.3 Other	(−3,664)	(2,660)	(3,421)	(−127)	(2,717)
A10. Foreign Authorities' Sterling Reserves	1,308	1,577	27	4,318	na[1]
B4. Balance on Capital Flows					
A6 + A7 + A8 + A9 + A10	8,571	−7,316	−11,310	10,973	2,199
A11. Balancing Item	5,641	5,737	14,400	3,543	15,227
B5. Balance for Official Financing					
B3 + B4 + A11	−908	1,758	2,891	12,012	2,761
A12. Allocation of SDRs and IMF Reserve Tranche Position	—	—	—	—	—
A13. Official Financing A13.1 + A13.2					
= −(B5 + A12)	908	−1,758	−2,891	−12,012	−2,761
A13.1 Official Reserves (Increase−)	(908)	(−1,758)	(−2,891)	(−12,012)	(−2,761)
A13.2 Change in Net IMF position	(—)	(—)	(—)	(—)	(—)

Source: *Pink Book* and *ET*.
[1] Not available separately. Included under A9.1 and A9.2.

in the capital account. Current transfers (A5) are so-called 'unrequited' in nature as they do not directly arise from the sale of goods and services or of assets. Remittances home by immigrant workers, payments to and from the EC, and foreign aid payments or receipts are the main examples.

Turning to the capital account, capital transfers (A6) are difficult in practice to distinguish from current transfers and, apart from certain exceptional governmental transfers of assets, identifiable transfers are all typically recorded in the current account. Direct investment (A7) consists of transactions undertaken to acquire or extend control over a foreign enterprise; portfolio investment (A8) consists of transactions aimed at securing investment income or capital gains. The distinction between these two classes is clearer in practice than it might appear. In general, direct investment abroad by the UK involves the construction and equipping of factories abroad or the acquisition or sale of foreign subsidiaries by British firms. Thus, direct investment, whether by UK firms abroad, or by foreign firms in the UK, is carried out mainly for the purpose of undertaking production of goods or services in a foreign country. In contrast, agents undertaking portfolio investment act 'at arms length' and have no direct managerial interest in the activity in which the investment is made. Portfolio investment involves the purchase or sale of securities of overseas companies or governments. Such securities are typically held by financial institutions, such as pension funds, as part of their overall investment operations.

Other capital not included elsewhere (n.i.e.) is, as its name implies, relatively heterogeneous. In principle, the IMF presentation calls for a distinction between 'long-term' and 'short-term' capital. In practice, this distinction is difficult to sustain and is not generally used in the UK accounts. A high proportion of recognizably long-term capital transactions are already included under portfolio and direct investment. Government transactions recorded in this section (A9.1) include various long-term intergovernmental transactions, for example subscriptions to international bodies such as the World Bank, and all short-term borrowings apart from two items recorded specifically elsewhere. The latter consist of borrowings which are counted by overseas monetary authorities as part of their reserves (A10) and loans from the IMF which, along with government liquid asset transactions, are shown in official financing (A13). Transactions by UK banks (A9.2) consist of the vast majority of their sterling and foreign-currency transactions with overseas residents, including all their loans and deposits but excluding their transactions in long-term bonds which are recorded under A8. Finally in this group, 'Other' (A9.3) consists of the identified transactions of other sectors. Items of note here include overseas borrowings by Public Corporations, and transactions in respect of trade credit. The immediate counterpart of a high proportion of export and import payments is the trade credit, usually of between one and six months, granted by the supplier to the purchaser. The amount of such credit outstanding at any one time is very large, although it obviously has a rapid turnover. However, the balance-of-payments accounts record only the net transactions and hence the net change in trade credit outstanding during the year, and these amounts are usually relatively small.

We will defer consideration of line A10 until later and come next to the balancing item (A11) which is calculated as the residual in the accounts, and which is required to compensate for the total of measurement errors and omissions. These can arise from a variety of sources. In general, the two sides of any given transaction cannot be recorded simultaneously. For example the value of commodity exports is recorded mainly by the Customs and Excise Department, but the proceeds from these exports are recorded only indirectly using statistics provided by banks and other financial institutions. Although, in principle, the accounts should balance, in practice numerous discrepancies in recording procedures generally give rise to a positive or negative balancing item. A positive balancing item reflects unrecorded receipts and a negative balancing item reflects unrecorded payments. The major source of errors and discrepancies in the accounts arises when data are collected mainly by sample surveys, especially if respondents have an incentive to under- or over-report. These circumstances occur particularly in the recording of trade in services and in capital account items other than those reported by government or financial institutions. Particular problem areas include revenues and expenditures associated with tourism, and trade credit flows. As discussed in section 1.4, the size of the balancing item has been a source of increasing concern in the UK's accounts in recent years.

Line A12 relates to the UK's membership of the IMF. Allocations of Special Drawing Rights (SDRs) to the UK are treated as a credit item, even though they do not correspond to any actual transactions, because an allocation effectively increases the UK's reserves (A13). Likewise, when the UK's quota in the IMF is increased, the UK is required to subscribe 25% (the so-called 'reserve tranche') of the increase to the IMF in the form of SDRs or other 'convertible' foreign currencies,[1] and the official reserves fall by the corresponding amount.

The remaining lines of the balance of payments constitute official financing. The sum of lines A13.1 and A13.2 gives the amount by which the country's official foreign-exchange reserves increased ($-$) or decreased over the year. Foreign-exchange reserves consist of the immediately liquid foreign-currency assets of the central bank, together with its automatic drawing rights at the IMF. These play a specific role in balance-of-payments and exchange-rate policy. The transactions which make up the balance of payments involve a myriad of individual decisions to make transactions with other countries, many of which involve a purchase or sale of foreign currency. There is no guarantee that, in aggregate, demands by domestic residents to purchase foreign currency in exchange for pounds will exactly match sales of foreign currency for pounds. Given the price of foreign currency, an excess demand or supply of foreign currency has to be met from some source. It is the central bank in a country (in the UK, the Bank of England) which acts as the last line of defence in supplying foreign currency if there is excess demand for it, or in acquiring it if there is excess supply. Of course, excess demand or supply could lead to a change in price – of the foreign-exchange rate – but this is a large subject in its own right and is deferred to Section 2. In reckoning a country's official foreign-exchange reserves, only assets are included as these are immediately available. In a crisis, central banks can find it difficult to borrow without the attachment of conditions. Indeed, the inclusion of a country's automatic drawing rights in the IMF in this reckoning acknowledges that the only guaranteed source of foreign-currency borrowing for a central bank resides in these rights. An amount equal to 25% of a country's quota (the reserve

---

[1] A currency is said to be 'convertible' if it can be freely exchanged into other currencies by domestic and foreign residents. Many countries impose tight restrictions on the convertibility of their currencies.

tranche position) may be used automatically. Along with other IMF member countries, the UK has further access to four credit tranches, each of which corresponds to 25% of quota, but access is dependent on the country concerned adopting economic policies which meet with the approval of the IMF, this being particularly so for drawings beyond the first credit tranche. The maximum amount the UK could borrow at end-1988 (excluding the reserve tranche position) amounted to SDR 6.2bn (£4.6bn). Borrowings in the credit tranches are recorded separately under official financing in line A13.2. The main point of IMF borrowing is that it is the only form of unsecured foreign assistance for a central bank which is always certainly available, subject to the conditionality required by the IMF.

We return finally to line A10, which consists of movements of funds arising from transactions made by overseas monetary authorities (mainly central banks) who hold sterling assets as part of their own official reserves. These assets include ordinary deposits with UK banks and with the Bank of England as well as holdings of government bonds and Treasury Bills. The IMF recommends the recording of this item as part of official financing on grounds of symmetry so as to ensure that the sum of all countries' official financing surpluses world-wide is, in principle, equal to the sum of official financing deficits. This procedure has never been followed precisely by the UK and a number of other countries, because movements in these funds are largely outside the control of the domestic monetary authority and they can therefore equally well be seen as generating a requirement for official financing as much as they can be seen as contributing to that financing. Indeed, in the sixties, movements in these funds, on occasion, caused considerable problems of reserve management for the UK authorities. These funds correspond to what were formerly called 'the sterling balances'. They arose originally from the role of sterling as a key settlement currency in international trade and their level reached a peak at the end of World War II. During the late sixties and early seventies the amounts outstanding were gradually reduced, and the guarantees which holders of these funds had enjoyed were correspondingly discontinued.[1] However, this item continues to play an identifiable role in the UK's balance of payments. With currency exchange rates floating, central banks around the world have found it prudent to hold relatively diversified portfolios of major currencies in their official reserves, and this includes sterling, holdings of which for official reserves purposes amounted to £13.8bn at end-1987, up from £4.6bn at end-1980. In this chapter, we take the view that movements in these funds are best thought of as generating a requirement for official financing and we therefore depart from the IMF presentation and show them separately as contributing to the balance on capital flows. It should be emphasized, however, that this is just one of many occasions when the appropriate classification is a matter of judgement and no one view can be regarded as unambiguously 'right' or 'wrong'.

---

[1]   For a full account of the sterling balances see the 11th edition of this book.

Main balances in the balance of payments: As we have seen, in an accounting sense it can be said that the balance of payments always balances. The interpretation of the accounts therefore depends on their being divided up in particular ways. It is customary to select a number of main 'balances' in the accounts which give a summary picture of different aspects of a country's overall balance of payments (table 3.1, lines B1–B5). Two major balances are those on current account (B3) and on the capital account excluding the balancing item and official financing (B4). These two balances give respectively the net receipts or payments on account of all identified transactions in goods, services and transfers (the current account), and in assets and liabilities other than official financing (the balance on capital flows). The balance for official financing (B5) is also regarded as important for the reasons given above – it shows the amount of 'last resort' activity undertaken by the central bank in buying or selling foreign-currency reserves. The balance for official financing is often called the 'overall balance'. Within the current account itself, a distinction is made between the balance of visible trade (B1) and the invisible balance (B2). To some extent, this is because statistics on the visible trade balance become available more rapidly than other items in the accounts apart from official financing, and therefore provide a leading indicator of possible trends in the accounts. Finally, reference may be made to the basic balance which may be found in older treatments of the balance of payments, and which is defined as the sum of the current account and the net flow of long-term capital. The argument for including these items together is that they were thought to be largely 'autonomous' in nature, whereas the remaining short-term capital flows, including official financing, were thought to be more 'accommodating', being carried out mainly in order to finance trade and long-term capital flows. The basic balance is currently less widely used, in large part because it is extremely difficult in practice to distinguish 'long-term' and 'short-term' capital flows and to determine, other than arbitrarily, which are autonomous and which accommodating.

The balance of international indebtedness: The balance of international indebtedness is a reckoning of the net external assets and liabilities of a country. It therefore gives the value of all assets held abroad and borrowings from abroad by UK residents as well as all assets held in the UK and borrowings from the UK by overseas residents. Whereas the balance of payments gives a record of transactions and therefore of flows of funds during some particular time-period, the balance of international indebtedness gives the stocks of assets and liabilities at a particular point in time. Thus, the total balance of international indebtedness on any given date is equivalent to the UK's total net overseas assets. As far as possible, the stocks of assets and liabilities in this balance are valued at current market prices.

Table 3.2 gives the balance of international indebtedness for the UK over the 1983–87 period. It can be seen that the classification of this account

The balance of payments

TABLE 3.2

UK: Net External Assets and Liabilities* 1983–87 (£bn, end of period)

	1983	1984	1985	1986	1987
1. Direct Investment	20.6	39.0	30.9	39.8	38.0
2. Portfolio Investment	40.2	60.0	69.5	101.6	65.6
3. Other Capital nie	−19.4	−32.0	−33.2	−45.6	−41.1
3.1 Government nie	(2.7)	(3.5)	(4.4)	(4.7)	(3.4)
3.2 UK Banks	(26.7)	(−47.6)	(−46.2)	(−55.1)	(−48.8)
3.3 Other	(4.6)	(12.1)	(8.6)	(4.8)	(4.3)
4. Reserves	12.8	13.2	13.2	17.4	27.0
4.1 Official Reserves	(12.8)	(13.2)	(13.2)	(17.4)	(27.0)
4.2 Net IMF Position	(—)	(—)	(—)	(—)	(—)
5. Net UK Assets	54.3	80.3	80.3	113.2	89.5
6. Change from Previous Year	12.3	26.0	—	31.9	−23.7
7. Current Account Balance (Calendar Year)	3.8	2.0	3.3	−0.2	−2.5
8. GNP at Market Prices (Calendar Year)	305.8	328.2	357.1	384.4	421.0
9. Net UK Assets in per cent of GNP (%)	17.8	24.5	22.5	29.4	21.3

Source: Pink Book.
* *Net Liabilities are shown with a negative sign.*

is similar to that of the capital account of the balance of payments. Indeed this should not cause surprise as the capital account shows transactions in the same assets and liabilities whose outstanding stocks are given in the balance of international indebtedness. However, it is important to appreciate that the capital account over any particular year is not simply equal to the change in the corresponding items in the balance of international indebtedness over that year. The differences are due in part to errors and omissions in the different procedures for estimating the stocks of assets and liabilities and for recording the net transactions which make up the balance-of-payments account. However, the differences also arise more particularly because the value of a nation's assets and liabilities can change for two reasons: first, net new lending or borrowing may take place: this is recorded in the capital account. Second, the price of an asset or liability may change and this is not recorded in the capital account because it does not correspond to any transaction but only a valuation change. A major cause of changes in international asset values is exchange-rate movements. Thus, when the price of sterling in terms of foreign currencies falls, the pound is said to depreciate.[1] Each unit of foreign currency will exchange for more pounds than before. Hence UK residents holding assets overseas whose values are denominated in foreign currencies will experience an

---

[1]   The terminology should be kept clear. When the price of sterling in terms of foreign currency falls, the pound is said to *depreciate*; when the price of sterling rises, the pound *appreciates*. Thus a move from £1 = US$1.40 to £1 = US$1.30 represents a depreciation of the pound *vis-à-vis* the dollar, and a move in the other direction represents an appreciation.

increase in the sterling value of their assets – they will make capital gains. UK residents who have loans denominated in foreign currencies will experience an increase in the sterling value of their liabilities – they will make capital losses as increased sterling amounts will be required to repay the loan. The reverse is true when the pound appreciates. However, it should be emphasized that not all overseas assets and liabilities are denominated in foreign currencies; many are denominated in sterling, as, for example, when the British Government sells sterling gilt-edged securities (bonds) to overseas residents. The sterling values of such assets and liabilities are not directly affected by movements in the exchange rate. In general, therefore, the relation between the capital account of the balance of payments and the balance of international indebtedness is not a simple one. Moreover, when the exchange rate of sterling changes, overseas residents who hold sterling-denominated assets or liabilities will make capital gains or losses in terms of their own currencies. Clearly, exchange-rate movements have complex effects on international asset and liability holdings and thus on individual decisions to adjust these holdings. These effects are considered in more detail in section 2.

1.3 Equilibrium and Disequilibrium in the Balance of Payments

It is obviously important both for purposes of economic policy and historical analysis, to have clear notions of balance-of-payments equilibrium and disequilibrium. It would simplify matters if we could calculate easily the 'deficit' or 'surplus' in the balance of payments, and thus refer to the balance of payments as being 'out of equilibrium', or 'in equilibrium' if the deficit or surplus were thought to be sufficiently small in magnitude. However, the formulation of such concepts is not easy and depends to a large extent on the purposes for which they are to be used. The time-span over which equilibrium is defined is obviously important. A daily or even monthly time-span would be of little value and it is generally accepted that a sufficient span of years should be allowed so that the effects of cyclical fluctuations in income will have no appreciable net impact on external transactions. The exchange-rate regime in force and the degree of intervention by the authorities are also important. The concept of equilibrium is often defined with reference solely to the private sector. However, if the authorities are intervening in the external accounts in a variety of ways, it becomes necessary to consider which interventions are intended either to restore or perturb an equilibrium and which are carried out for other purposes largely incidental to the balance of payments. Thus, sales of foreign-currency bonds to augment the official reserves on the one hand, and the granting of foreign aid on the other, both have an impact on the external accounts but decisions about the latter would not normally be thought of primarily as constituting 'balance-of-payments policy'. In practice, equilibrium in the balance of payments is usually defined with reference to one of the various balances introduced in section 1.2. Which of the balances is utilized depends on the purpose at hand.

Balance for Official Financing (overall balance): This is the most commonly used concept of equilibrium and the Balance for Official Financing (BOF) is often simply referred to as 'the balance of payments surplus' (or deficit). Its rationale arises from the role of the central bank in the foreign-exchange market. If the exchange rate is allowed to float freely to equate the supply and demand for foreign exchange, including central government foreign transactions incidental to balance-of-payments policy, then equilibrium in the market is always attained automatically and this coincides with the fact that the BOF will, under these circumstances, always be identically zero.

Since 1972, successive UK governments have allowed sterling to float but this float, like that of other currencies, has never been completely free. The authorities have intervened in the foreign-exchange market in a variety of ways and, as shown in table 3.1, the BOF has never been identically zero but has often been quite large in magnitude. When the exchange rate is managed by the authorities to any degree, a key role is assigned to the central bank as the last-resort provider of foreign currency, although this is by no means the only instrument which can be used to influence the exchange rate. Thus, the BOF does provide an appropriate indicator of the balance of pressures on the exchange rate. If the BOF is positive (in surplus), the Bank of England has been able to increase its reserves at the prevailing sterling exchange rate, suggesting an excess supply of foreign currencies at this rate and consequent upward pressure on the exchange rate; whereas the existence of a deficit on the BOF suggests an excess demand for foreign currencies and consequent downward pressure on the exchange rate.[1]

A further advantage of the BOF is that it shows the potential increase (decrease) in the (UK) money supply as a result of a surplus (deficit) in the balance of payments, and hence gives an estimate of at least the general direction of expansionary (contractionary) forces in the economy emanating from the external accounts. The link between the BOF and the supply of money arises through the central-bank balance sheet. As a matter of necessity, an increase (decrease) in central-bank foreign assets must be exactly balanced by an increase (decrease) in its liabilities. In general, the counterpart of a purchase (sale) of foreign exchange by the central bank is an increase (decrease) in its sterling deposit liabilities to the commercial bank from which it purchased the currency. Such deposits are included in a commercial bank's 'operational deposits' and an increase (decrease) in these deposits therefore allows an expansion (contraction) in the commer-

---

[1] This and succeeding arguments must all be subject to the caveat noted earlier that there is not necessarily universal agreement about the appropriate definition of the BOF.

cial bank's loans and hence in its deposit liabilities, thus leading to an increase (decrease) in the money supply. The central bank can offset this effect by carrying out what is commonly called 'sterilization'. A sale (purchase) of Treasury bills or bonds to the commercial bank in question will sterilize the monetary implications of the surplus on the BOF by drawing down (increasing) the commercial bank's operational deposits to their original level. Thus, while the link between the BOF and the potential change in the money supply is a direct one, the link between the BOF and the actual change in the money supply is a good deal more tenuous, depending as it does on the sterilization policy of the authorities and the exact responses of commercial banks to changes in the levels of their operational deposits.[1]

A final argument for focusing on the BOF is that most other definitions of surplus or deficit involve some element of arbitrariness in classifying the accounts. In particular, all other definitions do not take into account the balancing item which, by its very nature, cannot be allocated among the identified items in the accounts. Such definitions are therefore inherently subject to some degree of mismeasurement and hence of misinterpretation.

There are, however, arguments for not focusing exclusively on the BOF, the main one having to do with the role of the authorities. Acquisition or use of reserves is not the only nor even the most common method for the authorities to influence the balance of payments and the exchange rate. The level of interest rates in the economy has a direct influence on the exchange rate, as discussed in section 2. More generally, the level of income is a powerful determinant of many of the transactions which make up the balance of payments and few policy measures exist which do not have at least some effect on the level of incomes in the economy. Thus, the authorities may pursue policies which produce equilibrium in the BOF but which result in unacceptable levels of interest rates, unemployment, or inflation in the economy. This implies that the authorities have to keep in mind other policy objectives as well as equilibrium in the BOF and, in designing policies, must recognize the interactions between the balance of payments and the rest of the economy.

The current account balance: This is of interest because it marks the division between trade in goods and services and transactions in assets. Examination of the current account balance also brings out the relationship between the balance of payments and the national income and expenditure accounts. In discussing this relationship it is helpful to use some notation. Let: Y = GDP at market prices; C = consumers' expenditure; G = government expenditure; I = private investment; X = exports of goods and services; Z = imports of goods and services; S = private savings;

---

[1] For useful accounts of the links between external transactions and the domestic money supply, see 'External and Foreign Currency Flows and the Money Supply', *BEQB*, December 1978; 'External Flows and Broad Money', *BEQB*, December 1983; and 'Measures of Broad Money', *BEQB*, May 1987.

T = tax revenues; F = net transfers abroad. Using this notation, the GDP calculated from the expenditure side can be written:

$$Y = C + I + G + X - Z \qquad (1)$$

In this identity, we see that the balance on goods and services ($X - Z$: equal to the current account balance exclusive of transfers) is arithmetically identical to the excess of domestic income (Y) over domestic expenditures ($C + I + G$). This fact often leads to a statement that a deficit in the goods and services balance is *caused* by an excess of domestic expenditure over domestic incomes. Since one is simply identical to the other, attribution of causation is incorrect; it is necessary to look more deeply for the causes of the excess of domestic expenditures over income. However, it is true that, if it were thought desirable to reduce a deficit on goods and services, this would of necessity involve a cut in domestic expenditures *relative* to domestic incomes. More generally, any policy which influences the balance between domestic incomes and expenditures (and few policies will not do this in some measure) will also necessarily affect the current account.

It is also illuminating to write the disposition of the GDP by income recipients as

$$Y = C + S + T + F \qquad (2)$$

Deducting (2) from (1) and rearranging the resultant identity gives the following:

$$(X - Z - F) = (T - G) + (S - I) \qquad (3)$$

Current Account = Government Budget + Private Sector
Surplus/Deficit   Surplus/Deficit   Surplus/Deficit

In other words, the current account surplus (deficit) is arithmetically identical to the sum of the government budget surplus (deficit) and the private sector's surplus (deficit) of savings over investment. Since (3) is an identity, we still cannot describe either side of the identity as causing the other, but we can again state that policies which influence private saving and investment and the government budget balance will, unless they are exactly offsetting, of necessity affect the current account balance.

The current account balance is also related in an important way to the balance of international indebtedness. The private-sector surplus (deficit) is equivalent to its net acquisition of financial assets (liabilities); likewise the government budget surplus (deficit) is equivalent to net government lending (borrowing). By analogy, the current account surplus (deficit), which is identical to the capital account deficit (surplus), is equivalent to the net acquisition (sales) of overseas assets by UK residents. As we have seen, the value of the UK's net external assets may change either because of net new lending or borrowing, or because of changes in the prices of existing holdings of assets and liabilities. Net new lending or borrowing in total is equivalent to the current account surplus or deficit. Hence, the

UK can only acquire net new overseas assets (liabilities) to the extent that it runs a current account surplus (deficit). In table 3.2, the current account balance is shown together with the change in UK net overseas assets, the difference between the two being attributable to valuation effects and net errors and omissions.

The concepts of equilibrium compared: It should be clear that whereas the BOF focuses in particular on the role of the authorities, the current account position draws attention to the interaction between the balance of payments and the economy as a whole. A reasonable summary of their relative uses would emphasize that the BOF is a relatively short-run equilibrium concept while the current account balance is of more interest in the longer run. Thus a substantial deficit on the BOF generally requires some immediate action on the part of the authorities. Indeed, in the era of relatively fixed exchange rates between 1945 and 1972, the IMF defined a 'fundamental disequilibrium' in the balance of payments as a deficit on the BOF which could not be financed or rectified by the authorities without a change in the exchange rate. On the other hand, a deficit on the current account can be financed for relatively long periods by capital inflows, but at a cost of steadily increasing international indebtedness. It should be emphasized that no single concept can be universally applicable. Different items in the balance of payments are interlinked. One obvious linkage is that while an outflow of capital may produce a once-for-all deficit on the capital account, the return flows of IPD in later periods will lead to a smaller but continuing inflow which improves the current account. Other less obvious linkages are too numerous to mention. Thus, the most firm guidance available is that whatever concept of equilibrium is used, it should be justified as being appropriate for the purpose to which it is applied.

1.4   Trends in the Balance of Payments and External Assets

The historic position: We turn now to considering more specifically the balance-of-payments performance of the United Kingdom. For this purpose we examine first table 3.3, which contains average annual figures for the main items in the balance of payments covering selected periods since 1952, together with movements in the GNP and outstanding net external assets over the same periods. The first sub-period covers the 1950s, a time which in retrospect appears relatively tranquil. The second sub-period leads up to the devaluation of the pound in 1967. The end of the third sub-period is marked by the floating of sterling in June 1972. The end of the next sub-period coincides with the access to power of the first Thatcher government in 1979, but more particularly also with the beginning of the major boost to export revenues from North Sea oil. The 1986–87 sub-period is marked out as the time when revenues from North Sea oil dropped sharply. Finally, 1988 is shown separately for purposes of comparison with table 3.1. The averaging process hides substantial variations in the accounts from year to year, but this very averaging also helps uncover any longer-term trends in the accounts.

A useful starting point is with the characterization of the UK balance of payments given by Cooper in 1968.[1] This runs in terms of four main propositions: (1) the UK normally has a deficit on visible trade which is more than offset by a surplus on invisibles. (ii) This implies a surplus on current account. In addition the UK is normally a net exporter (i.e. experiences net outflows) of long-term capital. (iii) The role of the UK as an international banking centre, with the focus particularly on London, tends to produce volatile short-term capital flows which have an important influence on the overall balance of payments. (iv) These activities are all carried out with a very inadequate underpinning of official exchange reserves.

By and large, this was the picture throughout the 1950s and 1960s. Through 1962, the UK generally experienced a modest current account surplus and was able to add to its reserves at an average rate of £24m per year. In 1963–67, the broad features remained unchanged but the visible-trade balance worsened sufficiently to produce a deficit on current account. This precipitated a devaluation of the pound in 1967 and this was followed by an improvement in the current account although, as table 3.3 shows, this improvement took place in large part because of the strong performance of invisible exports. The visible balance improved in 1968–71 but deteriorated substantially in 1972. Table 3.3 also confirms the picture of the UK as a net exporter of long-term capital (portfolio and direct investment). As far as reserves and short-term capital are concerned, Cooper's summary is again broadly accurate for the 1950s and 1960s. A convenient reckoning of the strength of a country's official international reserve position is in terms of the number of months' imports which outstanding reserves could be used to finance. In the period 1952–62 the UK's official reserves were broadly stable at about 3 months' imports. The position deteriorated sharply in the sixties to 2.1 months' average over 1963–67, recovering slightly to 2.4 months' average in 1968–72. This was considerably less than virtually any other Western European country. Industrial Europe as a whole (excluding the UK) maintained reserve levels averaging about 6 months' imports throughout the fifties and sixties.

The UK's reserve position might have been more tenable were it not for the large swings in short-term capital to which Cooper refers. When the UK balance of payments deteriorated, short-term capital flowed out of London as its holders feared a possible devaluation of the currency. However, this very outflow often turned a barely manageable position into a crisis and such crises were a recurrent theme of the UK balance of payments in the fifties and sixties. That these crises were, to some extent, 'unnecessary' can be brought out by noting that the magnitude of both

---

[1]   R. E. Caves (ed.), *Britain's Economic Prospects* (Allen and Unwin, 1968), Chapter 3.

TABLE 3.3

Trends in the UK Balance of Payments, Annual Averages for Selected Periods (£m)

	1952–62	1963–67	1968–72	1973–79	1980–85	1986–87	1988
1. Balance on visible Trade	−158	−326	−303	−3,190	−180	−9,439	−20,557
o/w North Sea Oil (Net)	—	—	—	—	(5,010)	(4,120)	(2,345)
2. Balance on Invisibles[1]	269	249	762	2,286	4,169	8,088	5,892
Government	(−277)	(−589)	(−733)	(−1,676)	(−3,474)	(−5,239)	(−4,470)
Private	(546)	(838)	(1,495)	(3,962)	(7,643)	(13,327)	(10,362)
3. Current Account Balance	111	−77	459	−904	3,989	−1,351	−14,665
4. Portfolio and Direct Investment	145	−136	−99	−154	−9,445	−8,148	−14,561
5. Capital Account nie		171	10	765	3,258	7,980	16,760
6. Balancing Item	58	15	−65	1,121	1,728	8,971	15,227
7. Balance for Official Financing	24	−27	305	828	−470	7,452	2,761
8. Official Reserves and Net IMF (− increase)	−24	27	−305	−828	470	−7,452	−2,761
GNP at Market Prices (£bn)	22.3	36.1	53.4	129.8	290.8	402.7	463.9[3]
Net External Assets (£bn; end of period[2])	1.5	2.3	6.4	12.1	80.3	89.5	na[4]

Sources: Pink Book and ET.

1. The Government/Private split for 1952–62 is partly estimated.
2. Amount outstanding at end-1962, end-1967 (etc.).
3. Estimated.
4. Not available.

the current balance and the BOF during the fifties and the sixties tended to decline in relation to GNP and also in relation to the UK's overall net overseas assets position. It was shortage of international liquidity in relation to short-term capital flows which was a major cause of the periodic crises.

Developments since 1972:   After 1972, the UK balance-of-payments position underwent important changes, most of which can be traced back to three major factors. First, the floating of sterling in 1972 presaged a more general international move towards floating exchange rates by the major industrial countries. This, in turn, changed considerably the rules and constraints associated with balance-of-payments management. The second major factor was the UK's accession to the EC in January 1973 which, it is estimated, resulted in the UK running a larger balance-of-payments deficit or smaller surplus than would otherwise have been the case.[1] Third and probably of most immediate importance for the UK, was the discovery and subsequent exploitation of North Sea oil. Accompanying these developments were dramatic changes in the world price of oil: sharp increases in 1973 and 1979, followed by a precipitate slump in 1985–86. We discuss these factors in more detail below. Here we continue to concentrate on the basic facts of the UK's balance-of-payments performance.

The period immediately following the floating of sterling (1973–79) saw a sustained worsening of the visible-trade balance and consequently a succession of current account deficits of unprecedented magnitude. The deficit on long-term capital also persisted over this period despite a substantial inflow of private capital in connection with North Sea oil exploration. That the current account deficit was permitted to persist over this period was in part a deliberate act of policy. Successive governments accommodated the current account deficit by a substantial programme of official long-term borrowing, with repayments effectively guaranteed by a portion of future North Sea oil revenues. The UK also borrowed from the IMF during this period as part of a process of balance-of-payments adjustment. Overall, however, the UK was able to absorb a sequence of large current account deficits without having to undertake such a major adjustment programme as would otherwise have been required in the absence of North Sea oil. In this connection, the recorded increase in net external assets during 1973–79 reflects in part a valuation effect resulting from the depreciation of sterling over this period, but also to some extent an improvement in the coverage of the official statistics, and it therefore disguises the scale of the sustained programme of official foreign borrowing. Outstanding official short- and medium-term foreign debt, incurred mainly for balance-of-payments

---

[1]   See: M.H.Miller, 'Estimates of the Static Balance of Payments and Welfare Costs Compared,' Ch. 6 in J.Pinder (ed.), *The Economics of Europe* (Charles Knight, 1971).

financing, increased from US$0.4bn at end-1972 to a peak of US$18.0bn at end-1977, a rate of borrowing which considerably exceeded the cumulative current account deficit over the same period. The amount outstanding levelled off and began to decline gradually after 1978 as North Sea oil revenues accelerated and net repayments were made. By end-1979, outstanding official foreign debt amounted to US$14.6bn.

The turnround in the balance of payments was even more dramatic than its earlier deterioration. The oil price rise of 1979 coincided with the coming on stream of major North Sea oil fields. Oil exports doubled between 1979 and 1981, even as the non-oil visible balance deteriorated further. The net result was a shrinking of the overall deficit on visible trade which, together with the continued strengthening of the invisibles balance, combined to produce a sequence of record current account surpluses. On the capital account, the abolition of exchange controls in 1979 accentuated the traditional pattern, and record outflows of long-term capital were experienced. The net result of these developments was a massive increase in the net external assets of the UK from $12.1bn at end-1979 to £80.3bn at end-1985. However, the existence of a deficit on average in the BOF during this period illustrates the hazards of placing too much emphasis on one particular measure of the balance-of-payments deficit or surplus. Despite the underlying strength of the balance of payments, official reserves fell, as the UK continued its programme of repayments of official foreign debt.

The most recent period has been marked by further dramatic shifts in the accounts. The fall in the price of oil in 1985–86 coincided with a levelling-off of output from the North Sea and resulted in a fall in the net oil contribution to the visible balance. This was felt most severely in 1986. In 1987 the net oil contribution remained at about the same level, but it fell further in 1988. The increase in non-oil exports could not prevent the visible balance from lurching into a deep deficit, a deficit that was accentuated by a particularly sharp rise in imports in 1987. In 1986–88, therefore, the UK has returned to the situation of the mid-seventies in experiencing significant current account deficits despite having substantial reserves of North Sea oil. On the capital account there have also been substantial swings in the net flows. The UK's position as a net exporter of capital was dramatically reversed in 1987 as UK residents repatriated substantial sums in respect of earlier portfolio investments. Meanwhile, the UK authorities sold sterling as part of an active policy of exchange-rate management aimed at preventing an excessive appreciation of the currency. The result was a record current account deficit combined with a record surplus on the BOF in 1987. The net effect of these developments, including a partial appreciation of sterling, particularly against the dollar, was a relatively sharp decline in the UK's net external assets to £89.5bn at end-1987. Finally, in 1988 the capital account returned to its more familiar pattern but the BOF remained in surplus despite a further deterioration in the current account balance.

Appraisal: The main concern about the recent balance-of-payments performance has been the slide into substantial current account deficit even
while North Sea oil production is high. This appears to hold out a difficult
future as oil production declines. To some extent, however, as we discuss
in section 2, the relatively poor performance of the non-oil trade account
in recent years is simply the obverse of the high level of oil exports, and
it is to be expected that the non-oil visible balance should worsen along
with the expansion of oil activities. Moreover, the swings in the visible
balance have been overlaid by a seeming inexorable expansion in the surplus
on invisibles. It is sometimes remarked that, as a trading nation, the UK
cannot survive solely by producing services, and as a literal statement this
is true. However, the gloomy emphasis in such statements does overlook
the UK's historic position as a major net exporter of services, many of
which are essential to the flow of trade. The invisible balance is likely
to continue to improve in future, especially as a result of increased IPD
flows resulting from the expansion of the UK's overseas investment activities in recent years. Even at a modest annual yield of 5%, the UK's current
net external assets are capable of returning an IPD surplus of over £4.5bn
per annum which would represent a significant contribution to the current
account.

   A more general difficulty in interpreting recent balance-of-payments performance stems from the quality of the data themselves, reflected in the
persistent exceptionally large and positive balancing item (table 3.1). Apart
from 1987, the balancing item alone has more than covered the visible-trade
deficit in recent years. In general, the balancing item is thought to relate
to unrecorded capital flows, especially of trade credit, and the increase
in its size is attributed to the abolition of exchange controls in 1979. The
control procedure provided a relatively accurate source of capital account
data. These are now gathered through a variety of survey sources, some
of which are voluntary and inevitably less reliable than before. However,
the sheer size, sign, and persistence of the balancing item must invoke
caution in attributing it to any one source. If it did reflect entirely unrecorded capital inflows, then we would expect to see some impact on the
invisibles account in the return outflows of IPD, and there is no discernable
impact of this kind in any of the detailed items which make up this account.
It is possible, therefore, that the balancing item may include substantial
unrecorded current account items, particularly services. Moreover, the
recording of current account flows is likely to prove increasingly difficult,
with the removal of trade barriers within the EC in the run-up to the
creation of a Single European Market in 1992. (See section 5.2 for more
details.)

   In summary, it is clear that the position of the UK's non-oil visible trade
is a source of considerable concern. However, until more is known about
the disposition of the large positive balancing item, the UK balance of
payments seems likely to end the 1980s on a note of very cautious optimism:
with unprecedented strength in the net overseas asset and official reserve

positions being combined with a seemingly inexorable increase in the invisible surplus, and the prospect of a continued but declining flow of production from North Sea oil-wells.

1.5   North Sea Oil and Gas

The North Sea oil and gas discoveries constitute the single most important set of influences on the UK economy since World War II. Exploration began in 1960; the first gas production came on stream in 1964 and the first oil in 1975. However, most of the early production went to domestic consumption, effectively replacing imports, and net oil exports only began in 1980 when the UK became fully self-sufficient in energy.[1] The impact of the North Sea on the economy has been lopsided. Thus, oil and gas production and processing contributed some 14.2% of the output of UK production industries but only 5.3% of total GDP in 1980. These percentages rose to peaks of 20.9% and 7.2% respectively in 1984, since when they have levelled off and begun to decline. However, the major effects of the North Sea fall disproportionately on the balance of payments and the government budget. It has also altered the overall environment in which economic and financial policy is made. These policy implications are discussed in section 2. We have already noted above the size of the contribution of North Sea oil to the visible balance in recent years. Here, we look in more detail at the impact of North Sea oil and gas on the balance of payments as a whole and at some of the difficulties involved in forecasting its impact in the future.

When calculating the overall direct impact of North Sea oil and gas on the UK balance of payments, account has to be taken of several factors. First, is the net effect on the balance of trade in oil and gas as home output is exported or substituted for imports. Second, is the net trade in equipment and technical services to discover and extract oil and gas. This is a particularly slippery concept in that one could argue that, as UK-based oil-equipment industries developed and began exporting their output, these exports could be regarded as contributing to North Sea oil-related revenues. In practice, such exports are rather indirectly related to North Sea oil and most calculations of balance-of-payments effects only cover imports of equipment which can be easily identified as intended for North Sea exploration and extraction purposes. The third main item consists of the inflows of foreign capital required to help finance the extraction and development of oil; and fourth are the net IPD outflows remitted overseas by foreign

---

[1]   Throughout the period the UK has been both an exporter and an importer of crude oil. Refineries are built to utilize a particular 'balance' of crude oil and UK refineries require a mix of domestic and foreign crude. Clearly it is the net balance of these transactions which is relevant for balance of payments purposes, and the term 'energy self-sufficiency' implies that the economy can sustain net exports of energy production.

firms operating in the North Sea, and reflecting the earnings on their invested capital.

As shown in table 3.4, the effects of North Sea oil were felt well before the UK became a net exporter of crude oil. Prior to 1976 the net effects were relatively small, as direct investment in the North Sea was, to a large extent, offset by imports of equipment and services. After 1976, the build-up in production generated substantial net benefits. As should be clear from table 3.4, the major part of the benefits from North Sea oil and gas arise not so much in the form of direct exports but in import substitution: domestic production replaces energy sources which would otherwise have to be imported. Through 1985, the cumulative balance-of-payments saving totalled approximately £115bn or more than one-third of the GDP in that year.[1] It should be emphasized that these calculations only estimate the proximate effects of the North Sea, they are not an estimate of the overall effects, nor indeed can they be used to predict what would have happened in the absence of North Sea oil. Developments in the North Sea also influenced the exchange rate and many other variables in the economy, which in turn affected production and consumption in all sectors. Thus far, all we can say is that the North Sea provided an unexpected windfall which substantially increased the wealth of the United Kingdom. A deeper analysis is required to ascertain more fully the ramifications which this increased wealth has implied for the economy, and this is deferred to section 2.

TABLE 3.4
North Sea Oil and Gas: Proximate Balance-of-Payments Effects

	1976–79	*1980–83*	*1984–85*
	Cumulative Flows (£bn, 1985 Prices)		
1. Net Exports of Oil and Gas	−24.5	10.4	16.2
2. Direct Investment Less Imports			
Destined for North Sea	0.8	1.4	−1.0
3. IPD Remittances	−5.1	−11.6	−6.8
4. Direct Balance of Payments Effect (1 + 2 + 3)	−28.8	0.2	8.4
5. Domestic Consumption of Oil and Gas	49.5	57.4	28.4
6. Total Balance of Payments Saving (4 + 5)	20.7	57.6	36.8
7. Annual Average Saving (6/No. of years)	5.2	14.4	18.4

Source: BEQB, March 1982, December 1986.

Forecasts of the future development of the North Sea are evidently extremely important but, like all forecasts, they are subject to considerable uncertainty. Clearly it can be difficult to forecast trends in exploration and production costs and in domestic demand. However, the two major

---

[1]   For further details, see 'North Sea Oil and Gas: Costs and Benefits', *BEQB*, March 1982; and 'North Sea Oil and Gas', *BEQB*, December 1986.

elements of uncertainty concern the size of recoverable reserves and the sterling price of crude oil. Recoverable reserves depend both on the size of existing oil and gas reserves as well as on new discoveries and the state of technology. As technology evolves over time, it typically makes possible the recovery of an increasing proportion of the reserves which are known to exist, as well as making exploration possible in increasingly inhospitable sectors. Above all, however, the size of recoverable reserves depends on the price of oil, as this determines which segments can be profitably re-covered and which not.

The major uncertainties surrounding the future price of oil concern the balance of world energy supply and demand, the role of OPEC in setting the world dollar price of crude oil, and the future course of the sterling–dollar exchange rate. OPEC was able to act as a cartel and enforce a substantial increase in world oil prices in 1973 and again in 1979–80. How-ever, partly as a result of programmes of energy-saving in the major indus-trial countries, the balance of world supply and demand moved to such an extent that in late 1985 and early 1986 there was a collapse in the world oil price from US$29 a barrel to US$10 within the space of a few months. By comparison, average North Sea oil production costs in 1985 were esti-mated to be about US$10 a barrel and these will rise over time as more marginal fields are brought into operation. Although the price of oil has risen since early 1986 to a level of US$19 a barrel[1] by April 1989, any further substantial increases in oil prices are likely to depend on the reconsti-tution of the OPEC cartel. As far as the exchange rate is concerned, the more sterling is appreciated against the dollar, the smaller will be the net oil export revenues and the smaller will be the government's tax revenues from the North Sea. Other aspects of government policy will also be import-ant – in particular, the production and depletion policy adopted, and the levels of royalty and petroleum revenue tax charged, which will determine the proportion of profits left to the oil-producing firms.

Bearing in mind these uncertainties, it is nevertheless interesting to cite one set of calculations of future North Sea oil and gas benefits.[2] Adopting the assumption of a constant average price in real terms of US$20 a barrel, it transpires that oil production would peak in the mid-1990s and gradually decline to zero around the year 2025. Using the same assumption, the present value of the economic rents to be earned from North Sea production beginning in 1986, amount to about twice the rents already earned through end-1985. In short, nearly two-thirds of the total benefits of North Sea oil production have still to materialize, and should do so during the course of the next 35 years. It seems fair to assume therefore that the North Sea will continue to exert a significant influence on the balance of payments for some time to come.

---

[1] This is the spot market price of Brent crude, the main price for North Sea oil.
[2] For further details of these calculations see 'North Sea Oil and Gas', *BEQB*, December 1986.

2   ECONOMIC POLICY, THE EXCHANGE RATE, AND THE BALANCE OF PAYMENTS

2.1   Introduction

The coverage of this section is limited in two ways. First, the concept of economic policy is limited mainly to government intervention where the prime concern is to influence the balance of payments and the exchange rate. In principle, *all* economic policy affects the balance of payments, since any non-trivial intervention in the economy is likely to produce at least minor alterations in the balance of forces affecting trade and payments flows and the exchange rate. Thus, policies to control inflation or to stimulate growth are likely to have substantial impacts on trade and capital flows, but these problems are discussed elsewhere in this book and are of interest for reasons other than those concerned with the balance of payments. For present purposes, such policies are not regarded as balance-of-payments policies. On the other hand, policies which are directed explicitly at trade and capital flows may have effects on other sectors of the economy. However, in this section we will concentrate primarily on the exchange and payments implications of such policies. Second, this section is confined largely to the domestic aspects of exchange and payments policies. The numerous international aspects of economic policy-making in the UK are considered separately in sections 3 and 5.

2.2   The Exchange Market Framework

Modern industrial economies have evolved by means of a progressive specialization of labour and capital, and one important pre-condition for this is the adoption of a single internal currency, to act as an intermediary in all economic transactions. At the international level, specialization has so far proceeded without this advantage. Since nations continue to maintain separate currencies for internal use, it follows that, in general, international transactions must proceed with the simultaneous exchange of national currencies. This exchange of currencies takes place in the foreign-exchange market and it is there that the relative prices of different national currencies – exchange rates – are established. An important policy issue which faces the government of any country is, therefore, that of the degree of restraint which it wishes to place on the exchange of its own currency with the currencies of other nations. Not only may the chosen restraints limit the type and geographical direction of transactions which domestic residents may make with foreigners, but they will also have an important bearing upon the conduct of policy to achieve internal objectives such as full employment and price stability. Successive UK governments have exercised their options in two ways: by adopting particular forms of exchange-rate policy, and by placing restrictions upon the currencies against which sterling may be exchanged for the purpose of specified transactions, i.e. by exchange control.

Fixed and flexible exchange rates: Between 1945 and June 1972, exchange-rate policy in the UK was operated in accordance with the rules of the par-value system.[1] This required the adoption of a fixed spot-market exchange rate for sterling ('the par-value'),[2] which was maintained by the authorities buying or selling sterling whenever the exchange rate threatened to move outside a permitted band of fluctuation about the par-value.[3] A country with a 'fundamental disequilibrium' in its balance of payments, and after consultation with the IMF, was expected to change its par-value, as did the UK government in 1949 and 1967. In the market for forward exchange, the par-value system imposed no formal restrictions. There are, in fact, good reasons to believe that spot and forward exchange rates will necessarily be fairly closely related. The *Covered* Interest Parity Theorem states that, provided arbitrage funds are in perfectly elastic supply, the percentage difference between the spot and a forward exchange rate in any pair of currencies will equal the interest differential on assets of the corresponding maturity denominated in those currencies.[4] With arbitrage funds not in infinitely elastic supply, the forward rate will deviate from its covered interest parity value. Evidence for the 1960s and 1970s is consistent with the view that forward exchange rates up to three months mostly approximated their interest parity values quite closely.[5] The implication of covered interest parity is that, if spot exchange rates are fixed, similar restrictions on forward exchange rates will either be unnecessary or, in circumstances in which different countries' interest rates diverge very sharply, will probably be unenforceable.

A major change in policy took place in June 1972 when the UK abandoned its commitment to maintain a fixed (though adjustable) exchange rate, and instead allowed sterling to take whatever values the balance of demand and supply for foreign exchange might dictate. This policy of allowing sterling to float does not mean that the exchange market ceases to be an object of concern. The government still has to decide to what extent sterling will float freely without official intervention in the exchange

---

[1]   This is the name given to the exchange-rate system adopted by the majority of Western nations after the Second World War. The central body of the system is the IMF. The treaty establishing the IMF was signed at Bretton Woods in the USA, and the par-value system is often called the Bretton Woods system. The par-value system was suspended in December 1971 and its rules relaxed; the system was never restored. A fuller discussion of the rules of the par-value system may be found in the tenth and earlier editions of this volume.

[2]   A distinction must be made between the spot market and the forward-market exchange rates for a currency. The spot exchange-rate is the price of foreign currency for immediate delivery, that is, at the time the rate for the transaction is agreed (or, strictly, within two working days). A forward exchange-rate is the price of foreign currency for delivery at a specified date in the future. The most widely traded forward contract in practice is that for delivery in three months.

[3]   The permitted band of fluctuation was 1% either side of par. Under the Smithsonian Agreement of December 1971, this band was widened to 2.25% either side of par.

[4]   For a more detailed discussion see, for example, V. Argy, *The Post War Money Crisis: An Analysis* (Allen and Unwin, 1981), ch. 19.

[5]   See the evidence in J. A. Frenkel and R. Levitch, 'Covered Interest Arbitrage: Unexploited Profits?', *JPE*, Vol. 83, No. 2, 1975.

market by the authorities' buying or selling foreign currency. Moreover, even in the absence of official intervention, the authorities have considerable scope for influencing the exchange rate by less direct means relating particularly to the determinants of capital flows and their influence on the exchange rate. Capital flows are motivated primarily by the relative rates of return on domestic and foreign assets after due allowance is made for the effects of risk and taxation. These rates of return are affected by variations in domestic and foreign interest rates, but they are also affected by anticipated exchange-rate changes which would result in capital gains or losses for holders of foreign-currency assets. If a sterling depreciation is anticipated, for example, this will provide an incentive for wealth-holders to switch any sterling-denominated assets they hold into foreign-currency-denominated assets in order to avoid the expected capital loss on holdings of sterling assets. As it is relatively difficult to obtain forward cover for periods of much over 6 months, judgements about the expected future course of the exchange rate are a key ingredient in most foreign investment decisions.[1] Variations in the relative rates of return on domestic and foreign-currency assets will affect capital flows and hence the demand and supply of sterling and therefore, under a floating rate regime, will affect the spot exchange rate of sterling. It follows that any policy measure which affects domestic interest rates or the market's expectations of the future spot exchange rate will, given foreign interest rates, influence the current spot exchange rate and the forward rate. When the exchange rate is floating, spot and forward rates as well as exchange-rate expectations may all be influenced in differing degrees by an interest-rate change. It follows that the whole range of monetary policy actions which affect interest rates will also, to some extent, influence the exchange rate, and can therefore be used more explicitly for this purpose.

It should, however, be emphasized that the effects of monetary policy on the exchange rate depend, *inter alia*, on the interest elasticity of arbitrage and speculative funds and on the elasticity of expectations of the future exchange rate with respect to movements in current interest rates and exchange rates. Thus, while the qualitative effect of monetary policy on the exchange rate may be relatively straightforward to work out, its exact quantitative effect is, in general, subject to a very high degree of uncertainty.

Exchange controls: Exchange control constitutes the other main aspect of exchange-rate policy.[2] Through 1979, various direct controls were placed on the freedom of UK residents to carry out transactions in the

---

[1] Reference may be made here to *uncovered* interest parity which is said to hold if the interest differential on assets of a given maturity denominated in different currencies is equal to the *expected* percentage change in the spot exchange rate between now and the maturity date of the assets. Uncovered interest parity holds when speculative funds are in infinitely elastic supply, but available evidence suggests that, in general, this is not the case.

[2] An account of UK exchange control regulations can be found in the tenth and earlier editions of this volume. See also B.Tew, *International Monetary Co-operation 1945–1970*, Hutchinson, 1971; and the IMF *Annual Reports on Exchange Restrictions*.

foreign-exchange market. However, floating exchange rates remove one of the principal justifications for exchange controls; that is, the restriction of exchange-market transactions so as to help maintain the exchange rate of a currency at a particular level. In practice, this usually meant restricting private sales of sterling to defend an over-valuation of the currency. Following the floating of sterling in 1972, exchange controls were administered in an increasingly liberal way, and the anomaly of combining exchange controls and a floating exchange rate was finally recognized when, in October 1979, they were abolished altogether. The main direct implications of the abolition of exchange controls relate to capital account transactions, which are discussed in section 4.

The evolution of the exchange rate: The floating of sterling in June 1972 marked a watershed in postwar British external economic policy and, as it transpired, for the world as a whole. By the middle of 1973, sterling had been joined in floating by all other major currencies. For the advanced industrial nations as a whole, the par-value system was effectively abandoned. With sterling only one of many currencies engaged in a simultaneous float, there is no simple index of movements in the international value of sterling. Sterling may appreciate in terms of some currencies while, at the same time, it depreciates in terms of others. Current practice is to rely upon the 'effective exchange rate' index, which is a weighted average of the bilateral exchange rates between sterling and 16 other currencies, the weights being given by the relative importance of the countries concerned in the UK's trade in manufactured goods.[1] The evolution of the effective exchange rate index since 1972 is shown in figure 3.1.

The broad trends in the movement of the effective exchange rate since 1972 can be divided conveniently into three phases. The first, to November 1976, was a period of steady and, at times, rapid depreciation culminating in a sharp fall in value after February 1976. In the last quarter of that year, the effective rate (with 1975 = 100) averaged 76.6, compared to an average of 92.5 in the first quarter and an average of 125.1 in 1972. In the second phase, between the end of 1976 and January 1981, the effective rate generally appreciated in value, particularly in 1979 and 1980, so that by January 1981 it had reached a value of 105.2. The final stage after January 1981, was one in which the effective rate has once again trended downwards. It reached a low of 68.1 in November 1986, since when it has recovered somewhat to reach 77.8 by the end of 1988. Although the trend since 1981 has been downwards, it is evident from figure 3.1 that there has been considerable movement about that trend, with spells of depreciation followed by a partial appreciation and this cycle repeated, though not with any degree of regularity.

---

[1]   For details of the current method of calculating the effective exchange-rate, see 'Revisions to the Calculation of Effective Exchange-rates', *BEQB*, November 1988, pp. 528–9. Reference to earlier methods of calculating the effective rate may also be found in this article.

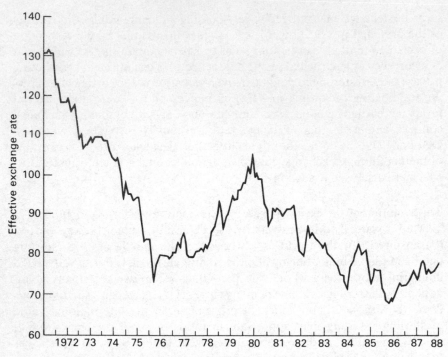

Figure 3.1   Sterling's Effective Exchange Rate, 1972–88

The movement of sterling relative to individual currencies, particularly the dollar, has been more volatile although, until 1981, the broad trends were very similar to that of the effective rate. Between 1981 and 1985, however, the movement in the effective rate concealed important changes in the pattern of sterling's behaviour *vis-à-vis* the US dollar on the one hand, and the Japanese and European currencies on the other. The predominant feature of international currency markets over that period was the appreciation of the US dollar from an effective rate of 95.0 (1975 = 100) in January 1981 to a high of 155.4 in March 1985, a remarkable 64% rise. This was followed by a yet more precipitate depreciation to an effective rate of 90.5 by end-December 1987. The fall and subsequent partial recovery of the pound over the same period mirrored, to a large extent, the movement in the dollar; sterling's movement against other European currencies and the Yen was much less marked and, until mid-1985, was generally one of steady depreciation.

2.3   Economic Policy with a Floating Exchange Rate

The exchange rate and the adjustment process: Before we consider the likely causes of the movements in the pound since 1972, it will prove useful to outline some of the main economic implications of floating exchange rates. The exchange rate plays an important role in the balance-of-payments adjustment process and an exchange-rate depreciation (appreciation) is generally thought to be a necessary component of any policy measures taken to eliminate a balance-of-payments deficit (surplus). However, the exact mechanisms by which an exchange-rate change influences the balance of payments are by no means universally agreed.

The so-called 'elasticities approach' lays emphasis on the effect of an exchange-rate change in altering the relative prices of domestic and foreign goods and services, and thus altering the demands and supplies of these goods and services, thereby changing the current account balance. Thus, a depreciation raises the domestic price of imported goods, depressing the demand for imports and lowers the foreign price or increases the domestic profitability of export goods, thus tending to stimulate the export effort, and by these means improving the current account. The 'absorption approach' also focuses on the current account but lays stress on the fact, noted in section 1.3, that a current account deficit (surplus) is associated with an excess (deficiency) of domestic expenditure in relation to income. On this view, a depreciation improves the current account by stimulating incomes through the expansion in exports. Expenditures will typically rise by less than incomes as a part of the increase is saved, and so the current account improves. A depreciation may also depress expenditures by increasing domestic prices which may reduce demand directly, as well as indirectly, through a rise in the rate of interest, if the quantity of money is being tightly controlled. Finally, the 'monetary approach' concentrates on the BOF, noting that a deficit implies that there is a net outflow of reserves and can thus be interpreted as corresponding to an excess supply of money in the domestic economy relative to demand, with the excess being 'worked-off' through the balance-of-payments deficit. In this approach, a depreciation works primarily through the money market by increasing the price level and thus reducing the real supply of money in the economy, with the central bank being required to maintain relatively tight control over the nominal money supply. A reduction in the supply of money in its turn has a familiar deflationary impact on the economy as a whole.

It should be evident that these different approaches are interlinked.[1] Different aspects of the adjustment process are important at different times but, in practice, exchange-rate changes work, at least to some extent, through all the channels listed above. However, different circumstances are likely to call for different sets of supporting policies to accompany an exchange-rate change. For example, at full employment, a depreciation will only increase domestic money incomes rather than real incomes, and emphasis has to be placed on deflating the economy to some extent while switching domestic expenditures away from import goods.

---

[1] For an entertaining account of these different approaches and their deficiencies see A.P. Thirwall, 'What is wrong with Balance of Payments Adjustment Theory?', *RBSR*, March 1988, No. 157.

The case for floating exchange rates: In its simplest form, the case for floating exchange rates rests upon the efficiency and automaticity of the free-market mechanism in reallocating resources in response to changing circumstances. In a dynamic world in which comparative advantages change over time and national inflation rates differ, changes in exchange rates are necessary if widespread misallocation of productive resources is to be avoided. The advantage of floating rates, it is argued, is that the amount and timing of the necessary changes can occur progressively at a pace dictated by the costs and profitability of resource allocation, and not, as with the par-value system, by periodic, discrete jumps dictated by speculative pressures and political expediency.

Floating exchange rates also have important implications for macroeconomic policy. Under a floating-rate regime, the government is under less pressure to decide precisely what constitutes an equilibrium exchange rate, as this will be decided automatically within the foreign-exchange market. This does not, however, imply that the conduct of domestic economic policy, particularly demand management, can proceed independently of developments in the foreign-exchange market. Balance-of-payments problems do not disappear with the adoption of a floating exchange rate, they simply appear in different forms. Developments that would lead to a loss of reserves with a fixed exchange rate, lead to a depreciation in the foreign-exchange value of the currency if the exchange rate is allowed to float. In the first case, a continuing loss of reserves will result in a policy-induced contraction in domestic income; while with a floating rate, the loss in real domestic purchasing power occurs as the prices of tradeable commodities rise and the real value of the money stock declines with the currency depreciation.

The main advantage of a floating exchange rate was traditionally thought to be that it allowed greater independence in domestic macroeconomic policy-making. As there is some value of the exchange rate which will give exactly a zero BOF at any level of employment, the objective of full employment may be more consistently pursued. Likewise, a floating rate tends to isolate the level of demand for domestic goods from changes in foreign incomes and preferences. An increase in foreign demand which, under a fixed rate, would generate a multiple expansion in UK output and employment, now generates an appreciation of the sterling exchange rate until the final increase in the value of UK exports is exactly matched by an appreciation-induced increase in the value of UK imports. The total demand for UK goods, and therefore UK output, will remain unchanged.

The experience of the 1970s, however, suggests that this case for floating exchange rates may have been misstated. Although the substantial external disturbances which occurred in that era would have generated insoluble policy problems if the UK had adhered to the par-value system, floating rates did not fully insulate the UK economy from these disturbances, and floating itself posed new policy problems for the authorities. The traditional arguments for floating rates overlook the fact that, in a relatively free international capital market, the exchange rate affects not just the prices of internationally traded products but also the prices of internationally traded assets. The exchange rate which is determined in a free market depends on the demand and supply of foreign currency, emanating from both trade in products and in assets. There is no reason to expect any immediate relationship between day-to-day transactions in foreign currency generated by product markets and those generated by asset markets, and the equilibrium exchange rate implied by product-market considerations may be very different from that implied by asset-market considerations. The volume of international transactions in financial assets has mushroomed in the last fifteen years[1] and it is now generally recognized that, in the short run, exchange rates in the industrial world are determined mainly by asset-market considerations, particularly by relative international interest rates and expectations of future economic trends. Product-market factors may reassert themselves in the longer term. But it is unclear just what 'longer term' means in calendar time. Certainly, the four-year appreciation of the US dollar to March 1985 must have been caused to a large extent by a worldwide portfolio shift in favour of US dollars. The current account of the US balance of payments worsened continuously from a surplus of $6.9bn in 1981 to a deficit of $107.1bn in 1984, but this appeared to have little effect in checking the simultaneous rise of the dollar.

Floating exchange rates, asset markets and 'overshooting': It was recognized for many years that floating rates might be volatile because of speculation in financial markets. If the markets for foreign exchange are to be cleared continuously without the intervention of the monetary authorities and without undue fluctuations in the exchange rate, it is essential that speculators take over the role of the authorities and operate in a stabilizing manner, selling sterling when the rate is temporarily 'too high' and buying sterling when the rate is temporarily 'too low'. Proponents of floating rates argued that speculative activity will be stabilizing because destabilizing speculation (buying when the rate is 'high' and selling when it is 'low') is unprofitable.[2] However, this presumes that speculators can predict the 'true' equilibrium value of the exchange rate. Opponents fear that the exchange market will be dominated by too much uncertainty for speculators to recognize the equilibrium rate. Waves of optimism and pessimism will follow the frequent revision of expectations and will generate substantial movements in exchange rates, which are unrelated to 'fundamental' economic considerations.

---

[1] A precise estimate of the volume of international transactions in financial assets is impossible to obtain. A rough measure is provided by the size of commercial banks' foreign currency liabilities. According to *IFS*, worldwide commercial bank foreign-currency liabilities increased from $176bn in 1970 to $1,838bn in 1980 and $4,911bn by mid-1988. This represents an increase of about 21% per annum sustained over nearly 18 years.

[2] See M. Friedman, 'The Case for Flexible Exchange-Rates', in *Essays in Positive Economics* (University of Chicago Press, 1953).

The difficulty with the above arguments is that we have little factual evidence to decide either way. Certainly the period with floating rates has witnessed some sudden, sharp movements in exchange rates. There is evidence, too, that exchange rates respond to the publication of new economic statistics, no matter how provisional the data. However, it is unclear whether movements of this kind can be regarded as excessive.

It must not be overlooked that destabilizing speculation can disrupt any exchange-rate framework, and clearly did so with the par-value system. One of the major drawbacks of the par-value system was that it gave a one-way option to currency speculators. A currency under pressure would be pushed to one edge of the permitted band of fluctuation. This immediately signalled the possibility of a change in par-value which could be in one direction only. This encouraged a large and cumulative movement of funds across the exchanges, which tended to precipitate the very par-value adjustment which speculators had predicted. An important advantage of floating exchange rates is that the problem of recurrent one-way speculative options at the expense of the authorities is eliminated.

It has also been argued that floating rates increase the uncertainty faced by international traders and investors to the detriment of the international division of labour. It is the volatility of exchange rates which may deter trade, and volatility will not be a serious problem in so far as speculation is able to stabilize floating exchange rates.[1] Moreover, many exchange risks involving trade in goods and services can be covered with simultaneous deals in spot and forward markets. For sterling transactions involving the major currencies, the forward exchange market currently provides active dealings for contracts up to one year in duration. Since over 90% of UK exports are financed on credit terms of less than six months' duration, with, no doubt, a similar proportion for imports, there should be no difficulty in traders covering their exchange risks. Longer-term trade contracts and international investment projects will face problems, but it is unlikely that the exchange risks are more severe than the other risks which such projects routinely incur. Moreover, new markets in futures and options considerably widen the range of possibilities for traders to hedge their exchange risks.[2]

A more subtle argument which has gained credibility in the light of experience is that exchange rates 'overshoot': thus if a disturbance requires an appreciation of the pound, it will tend to over-appreciate in the short run and subsequently depreciate to its equilibrium value. This is explained by the flexibility of the exchange rate relative to other prices in the economy, particularly money wage rates. If a general adjustment in wages and prices

---

[1] For a review of the impact of exchange-rate volatility on international trade flows, see 'The Variability of Exchange-Rates: Measurement and Effects', *BEQB*, September 1984, pp. 346–9.
[2] G. T. Gemmill, 'Financial Futures in London: Rational Market or New Casino?' *NWBQR*, February 1981.

is required, this will take time; in the meanwhile, asset prices, particularly the exchange rate, must 'over-adjust' to compensate for the sluggishness of wages and product prices.

In this connection, it is important to distinguish between the concept of *volatility* and that of *misalignment*. The exchange rate may be highly volatile on a day-to-day basis but nevertheless stay relatively close to its equilibrium value. When the exchange rate overshoots its equilibrium value for long periods, however, it can be said to be misaligned, and such misalignment may cause a systematic misallocation of resources in the economy. In this situation, a freely floating exchange rate may be detrimental rather than advantageous. As before, evidence is hard to find because of the difficulty of identifying the equilibrium exchange rate. However, as described below in sections 2.4 and 2.5, some of the broader movements in sterling during the seventies and eighties do appear consistent with the overshooting hypothesis.

Overall the balance of argument and evidence is that some flexibility in exchange rates is desirable as a means of promoting efficient resource allocation and reducing the vulnerability of the economy to external disturbances. However, there is still considerable room for debate about the optimum balance between flexibility and management by the authorities. Thus, if undue volatility and overshooting of the exchange rate prove serious, the authorities can engage in 'official' speculation or exchange-market intervention. This implies that, even with a floating exchange rate, the authorities must maintain a stock of exchange reserves. Widespread adoption of exchange-management practices also requires the institution of international co-ordination and surveillance of exchange-rate practices, and these are precisely the functions of the IMF under its revised Articles (see section 5.2 below).

2.4 The Exchange Rate and the Balance of Payments 1972–88

In section 1.4 we outlined the considerable changes in the UK's external position in the period since 1972, showing that from an initial surplus the current account moved into deficit during 1973–9 and then swung into substantial surplus between 1980 and 1985, followed by a sharp movement back into deficit from 1986 onwards. The purpose of this section is to outline some of the major factors leading to the changes in the current account and the exchange rate during the period, and their relation to domestic and international events. To conduct the analysis it is helpful to distinguish between those factors which are related to changes in national price levels, and those which are related to the forces of production, consumer preferences, productivity and thrift. It is to the former that we turn first. In interpreting the events of the period, it must also be emphasized that the exchange rate for sterling has not been allowed to float freely, rather it has been managed quite actively, and this policy has produced effects which

are a mixture of those occurring under the extremes of fixed and freely
floating rates. We return to this point subsequently.

Purchasing-power parity: A convenient place to begin is the theory which
relates the values taken by a currency's exchange rate to its purchasing-
power parity (PPP). Broadly speaking, this suggests that the equilibrium
exchange rate between the currencies of two countries is proportional to
the ratio of the price levels in the respective countries. Providing this factor
of proportionality remains constant, the proportionate rate of change of
the exchange rate will be approximately equal to the difference between
the inflation rates in the two countries.[1] With the exchange rate in equilibrium, the current account would be in balance. In this framework, the
proximate source of the rapid depreciation of sterling between 1972 and
1976 can be found in the excess of the UK rate of inflation over a suitably
weighted average of the inflation rates in our major trading partners; it
being a matter of indifference what the source of this inflation differential
may be, whether it be related to excessive monetary and fiscal expansion
in the UK or to excessive wage-push by UK trade unions. Similarly, the
rise in sterling after 1976 would be related to a lower UK inflation rate
in comparison to that of our major trading partners.

Figure 3.2 shows the monthly movements from 1974 to 1988 in an index

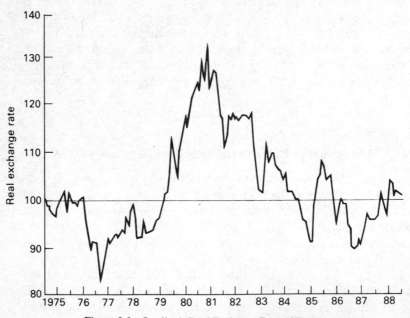

Figure 3.2   Sterling's Real Exchange Rate 1974–88

---

[1]   Probably the clearest statement of the purchasing-power parity theory is still contained
in J.M.Keynes, *A Tract on Monetary Reform* (Macmillan, 1923), pp. 70–93. A textbook
treatment of exchange rate theories can be found in R.MacDonald, *Floating Exchange Rates:
Theories and Evidence* (Unwin Hyman, 1988).

of the real exchange rate (REX), measured as the ratio of the effective exchange rate (EER) of sterling (in the computation of which the OECD countries have a weight of 100%), to the consumer price index (CPI) in the combined OECD countries relative to that in the UK. In symbols:

$$REX = \frac{EER}{OECD\ CPI/UK\ CPI}$$

The larger the value of this index, the more appreciated is the sterling exchange rate relative to its PPP value. Thus, movements in REX correspond to deviations from PPP. However, it should be emphasized that the index only measures *relative* movements. It is normalized to 1975 = 100 for convenience, but we cannot infer that sterling was at its equilibrium purchasing power value in that year.

From 1972–76, sterling depreciated more quickly than PPP would suggest. This was followed by a period of relative quiescence and then, during 1979 and 1980, a rapid appreciation, despite a simultaneous 7.4% decline in its purchasing power value. As a consequence, sterling stood well above PPP during 1980, a very sharp reversal from the position in 1976. Between 1980 and early 1984, UK prices rose by almost the same percentage as the OECD average of about 24%. Meanwhile, the effective exchange rate for sterling depreciated by some 19%, so that by early 1984 REX had approximately returned to the same level as in 1975. Since 1984 the real exchange rate of sterling has shown further fluctuations, but these have remained broadly centred about its 1975 purchasing power value. These are very approximate calculations but they indicate clearly that, even though PPP may capture the longer-term trend in the effective exchange rate, in the short term there have been substantial deviations from PPP.[1] The proximate sources of these deviations can be found by considering three main factors: capital movements, North Sea oil, and official intervention policy. As far as capital movements are concerned, a full analysis is contained in section 4; for the present the reader is reminded of the earlier discussion of the possible discrepancies between exchange-rate movements resulting from current account transactions and those resulting from capital flows.

Structural determinants of the exchange rate: On the question of economic structure, several factors are relevant. The first is the effect of UK membership of the EC and the associated longer-term trends in UK trade patterns, discussed in more detail in sections 3.2 and 5.1. *A priori*, it is impossible

---

[1] There is fairly considerable evidence that the major currencies (including sterling) have deviated substantially from PPP. Cf. G. Hacche and J. Townsend, 'A Broad Look at Exchange-Rate Movements for Eight Currencies, 1972–80', *BEQB*, December, 1981.

to say how these factors have affected the purchasing-power parity value of sterling. Certainly they are slow-moving, persistent forces which would be unlikely to explain relatively volatile movement in the exchange rate around PPP. Of much greater importance have been sharp changes in the terms of trade and the progression of the UK towards self-sufficiency in oil production. The most significant price changes involved those of crude oil. The posted price of oil was raised by the OPEC nations at the end of 1973, from $3.45 to $11.58 per barrel.[1] The implications of this development were considerable and worldwide, affecting not only individual economies but also the international monetary system as a whole. Between 1975 and 1978, the market price of oil remained within the range $12 to $14 per barrel but rose sharply again from June 1979, with a price at the beginning of 1981 of $36 per barrel.

Since 1982, however, a world oil glut has been created by a combination of slack energy demand, resulting from a world-wide recession and general conservation measures, and increased output on the part of non-OPEC countries, notably Mexico, Norway and the UK. Meanwhile, OPEC member countries have invariably failed to adhere to agreed limits on their own individual production levels. These factors created persistent downward pressures on oil prices between 1982 and 1985. The decline would have been more abrupt were it not for a substantial cut in output from Saudi Arabia, the world's largest oil-exporting country. Saudi output was reduced from an average of 9.8m barrels a day in 1981 to an average of about 4.1m barrels a day in 1985, in a deliberate effort to prevent an undue decline in prices. In December 1985, OPEC countries agreed to take steps, including an increase in production, to restore their share of the world oil market. Spot-market prices for Brent crude responded with a precipitate fall from $29 a barrel in early December 1985 to just $10 a barrel early in April 1986. Since then oil prices have recovered somewhat to trade broadly in the $12–16 range, rising to $19 per barrel in early 1989. However, this has been due mainly to a partial recovery in demand, together with a suspension of production in marginal fields, and hardly at all to the efforts of OPEC. The balance of world oil supply and demand is such that prices are unlikely to trade much above the $20 level for some time to come. OPEC's position in this balance is of diminished importance; OPEC oil contributed only 15% of the non-Communist world's energy in 1985, compared to $36\frac{1}{2}$% in 1973.[2]

As the short-run elasticity of demand for oil and associated products is extremely low, the impact effect of the first oil-price increase in 1973 was simultaneously to worsen the UK's trade balance and to generate defla-

---

[1] The posted price should not be confused with the market price of oil. The posted price is the administrative price from which the OPEC countries assess the royalty payments and tax payments from the oil-extracting companies.
[2] For further details on oil demand and supply prospects see P. R. Odell 'The Prospects for Oil Prices and The Energy Market', *LBR*, No. 165, July 1987.

tionary pressures on the economy, while also raising prices. This combination of circumstances produced the term 'stagflation' to describe the coexistence of falling demand and rising inflation. The UK government faced an unusual problem in 1973 in that it was already known that the North Sea contained oil reserves, though of an unknown quantity. If the UK had carried out the substantial adjustments needed to eliminate the current account deficit, it would have imposed possibly severe costs on the economy. With oil in the North Sea there was then every prospect that the UK would subsequently have to undertake further costly adjustments to accommodate a possibly substantial balance-of-payments contribution from domestic oil production. At the time, too, there was some uncertainty about the durability of the price rise initiated by the OPEC countries. In the context of these considerations, the government adopted a policy of substantial foreign borrowing, combined with a broadly neutral stance toward domestic aggregate demand. During the period 1974–77, total public-sector foreign-currency borrowing amounted to more than $14bn. Although this policy allowed the UK to accommodate its balance-of-payments deficit in anticipation of the benefits of North Sea oil, it also prevented the exchange rate from dropping even further below PPP than it otherwise would have done. The increased external debt also implied the need for a substantial UK current account surplus in the 1980s to service the interest and amortization payments, and, as discussed in section 1, such a surplus was indeed a feature of the early 1980s.

Turning now to the period after 1976, the most important fact to be explained is the rapid appreciation of sterling during 1979 and 1980. The major structural factor of relevance here is the growth in production from the North Sea oil fields, together with the second major OPEC oil price increase. The direct effect of this on the current account was reinforced by indirect effects on confidence and capital flows. From 1979 there was, in effect, a favourable reassessment of the long-term prospects for sterling and the associated exchange risks of holding sterling-denominated assets. A further structural influence on the exchange rate was the depth of the UK recession. Between 1978 and 1981, UK industrial output fell by 6.8% and unemployment rose sharply. The depth of the recession was associated with a decline in domestic demand and therefore an improvement in the current account. This in turn would have contributed to the buoyancy of sterling. A final factor was the rise in UK nominal interest rates, particularly short-term interest rates, relative to those in other OECD countries. Throughout 1979 and much of 1980, UK short-term rates were between 2% and 4% higher than comparable rates in the United States. This would tend to induce a capital inflow into the UK and hence raise the value of sterling. However, the 1979 abolition of exchange controls should, by facilitating a capital outflow, have moderated the rise in sterling to some extent.

Overall, there remains some disagreement both about the relative contribution of each factor to the appreciation of sterling and about whether, when put together, they provide a complete explanation of this appreciation.[1] It seems likely that increased confidence in sterling as a petrocurrency must have contributed to a substantial part of the appreciation, but this is to assert little more than that we cannot fully explain why the pound rose so strongly in 1979–80.

Since 1981, movements in the pound have, in part, reflected the larger movements in the value of the US dollar. The relative depreciation of the real exchange rate of the pound after 1981 is to be expected, given sterling's almost certain substantial over-valuation in that year. Moreover, a relative depreciation in the longer term is to be expected as North Sea oil is gradually depleted. In the short term, the value of the pound continues to be affected by changes in the world price of crude oil, and any significant rise in oil prices would almost certainly lead to a relative increase in the value of the pound.

Intervention and the exchange rate: So far we have looked at deviations from PPP in terms of shifts in various real factors impinging upon the exchange rate. Equal weight must also be given to government intervention in the foreign-exchange market. The next section deals with the theoretical pros and cons of intervention, so here we simply record that the float of sterling has been heavily managed since 1972. In addition to foreign-currency borrowing, the management of sterling has been effected in two main ways: by the use of reserves and by variations in interest rates. Between 1974 and 1976, annual reserve losses of $1.3bn were incurred to prevent an even more rapid slide of the exchange rate, while during 1977 the reserves were allowed to increase by the unprecedented sum of $16.4bn when the effective rate was stabilized. Further reserve gains of approximately $9bn during 1979 and 1980 also prevented an even greater appreciation above PPP. Since 1979, interest-rate policy has played an increasing role in exchange-rate management, with short-term interest rates being raised to generate an inflow of funds to prevent a depreciation of the pound and vice-versa. In October 1985, the authorities announced that they would use short-term interest rates more actively than previously and this would include adjustments required to help maintain the external value of the pound within a desired range. (This point is discussed further in section 2.5.) Despite this shift of emphasis, intervention still has a substantial role to play, as evidenced by the record $21.5bn increase in reserves during 1987 against a backcloth of the severe deterioration in the current account. Reserves were accumulated in an effort to stem the appreciation of the pound, particularly against the Deutsche Mark.

To sum up, it is clear that sterling has deviated very substantially from PPP for long periods. The reasons for these deviations can be catalogued in general terms, but on some occasions it is not easy to see precisely

---

[1]   For an appraisal of the causes of the rise in sterling see W.H.Buiter and M.H.Miller, 'Changing The Rules: Economic Consequences of the Thatcher Regime', *Brookings Papers*, 1983:2, pp. 305–65.

why the pound moved as strongly as it did. This puzzle is to some extent accentuated by the knowledge that the pound would, on occasion, have moved more strongly still were it not for various forms of intervention by the authorities.

2.5 Exchange-rate Policy

In the previous section we have indicated how the sterling exchange rate has been influenced by the activities of the authorities since 1972, their primary instruments being foreign-currency borrowing, domestic interest-rate policy, and changes in the stock of UK foreign-exchange reserves. We turn now to examine possible reasons why a government may wish to manage the exchange rate.

Industrial competitiveness and anti-inflation policy: It is sometimes argued that the UK should engineer a systematic *depreciation* of sterling to maintain or improve the international competitiveness of UK industrial products. The mechanism of a managed depreciation can be argued as follows. The impact effect will be a deterioration in the terms of trade, as sterling import prices rise relative to sterling export prices.[1] These changes induce substitutions in patterns of production and consumption, which grow in magnitude as contracts are renegotiated and as new plant and equipment is installed to take advantage of changed profit opportunities. In the long run, the trade balance will improve, provided domestic and foreign elasticities of demand for import goods and elasticities of supply of export goods are 'sufficiently' large.[2]

Available evidence suggests that these conditions are satisfied for the UK,[3] but there may be an initial deterioration as the immediate effects on relative prices precede the longer-term quantitative responses of trade flows. The deterioration and subsequent improvement in the trade balance is known as the 'J' curve effect. However, to the extent that the trade balance improves in terms of home currency, the aggregate demand for UK goods will be increased and, if the economy is near to full employment, this will be inflationary unless domestic expenditure is reduced to 'make room' for the improvement of the trade balance. Account must also be

---

[1] However, this depends in part on the pricing policies of domestic and foreign firms. For evidence on the pricing policies of UK firms following the 1967 devaluation, see P.B.Rosendale, 'The Short-run Pricing Policies of Some British Engineering Exporters', *NIER*, No. 65, 1973, and the valuable study by D.C.Hague, E.Oakeshott, and A.Strain, *Devaluation and Pricing Decisions* (Allen and Unwin, 1974).
[2] In the special case in which trade is initially balanced and supply elasticities of traded goods are infinite, then a depreciation improves the trade balance provided that the sum of foreign and domestic elasticities of demand for imported goods exceeds unity. For a more general statement, see Lindert and Kindleberger, *International Economics* (7th edition, Irwin 1982), chapter 15 and Appendix H.
[3] For a discussion of recent evidence on import and export elasticities, see J.Williamson, 'Is There an External Constraint?', *NIER*, August 1984, pp. 73–7.

taken of the import content of domestic production, and the effects of the devaluation in raising domestic costs and in creating pressure for higher money wages. Unless the depreciation is associated with a reduction in real wages, its effect may be to lower the long-run profitability of UK manufacturing industry. Moreover, if in addition, domestic firms follow pricing policies to maintain rates of return, then a *real* depreciation will be prevented, and the ultimate effect of the *nominal* depreciation will simply be to increase all prices and the level of official foreign-exchange reserves without any long-run effect on flows of exports and imports. The conclusion to be drawn from this is that powerful forces are at work to offset the possible benefits of a managed depreciation to the balance of trade. Recent calculations suggest that, in the UK, the 'J' curve effect is relatively strong and the benefits of a sustained real devaluation, if it can be achieved, take more than 5 years to accrue. These calculations also make clear that the effects of a devaluation depend on policies to control money incomes which should accompany the depreciation.[1]

In contrast, a second possible longer-term goal of exchange-rate management might be to engineer an *appreciation* of sterling to help combat domestic inflation. The main proposition here is that the rate of inflation is influenced by the pressure of demand in the labour market and by expectations of inflation, so that a currency appreciation reduces inflation in three ways: it directly lowers domestic production costs via the cost of imported inputs; it reduces the demand for labour by its adverse effects on total demand for UK output, and, since many of these effects take time to work, it also has the indirect effect of lowering the anticipated rate of inflation, thus moderating money wage demands. The effectiveness of such a policy must be questioned for similar reasons to those which cast doubt on the value of a managed depreciation. Moreover, even if an appreciation were to work in the way described, it is hard to see how a continuing reduction in inflation could be brought about by a *once-over* appreciation; a *continuing* appreciation would seem to be required. In addition, exchange-rate changes appear to have substantial real effects in the short term and an appreciation can prove a rather costly way (in terms of output forgone) of achieving a purely temporary fall in the inflation rate.

Exchange-rate target zones: The argument so far suggests that it is rather unlikely that the exchange rate can be managed to achieve permanent effects on the balance of payments, inflation, or employment. Other considerations support this view. First, in a world where all the major currencies

---

[1]   Cf. D.A.Currie and S.Hall, 'The Exchange Rate and The Balance of Payments', *NIER*, February 1986, pp. 74–82. It is particularly important that the money supply is not allowed to expand and negate the effects of depreciation in reducing real money balances and absorption.

are floating, governments may follow mutually inconsistent exchange-rate targets and find themselves in a situation of competitive exchange-rate management in which one country's policies are nullified by the actions of others. Second, the experience of the 1970s and 1980s suggests that there are limits to the ability of national authorities to set an exchange rate which is very different from that which would be set by the private market. When the authorities step outside these limits, the resulting flows of speculative short-term capital tend to force a change in policy. Third, any disequilibrium exchange rate will, in general, be associated with a non-zero BOF and thus with changes in the stock of foreign-exchange reserves and the domestic money supply. Changes in the domestic money supply will change domestic prices until the exchange rate returns to equilibrium. This must be so since, as long as the exchange rate is out of equilibrium, the money supply and therefore domestic prices will be changing; when the exchange rate is in equilibrium there are no forces impelling any further price or exchange-rate changes. It must be stressed that this is true only in the long run and that the links between reserve changes and the domestic money supply can, to some extent, be offset by sterilization, as explained in section 1.3. Nevertheless these arguments underline the point that the scope for exchange-rate management is confined mainly to the short run.

In the short run, however, there are several arguments to suggest that some degree of exchange-rate management might be desirable. First, the authorities may view changes in the demand and supply of foreign exchange as temporary and so act as a speculator to prevent such changes influencing the exchange rate and causing costly changes in trade flows. The difficulty with this argument is that it presumes that the authorities are substantially better informed than private investors as to what constitute 'permanent' and 'transitory' changes. On some occasions this presumption may be correct but it is certainly not true *in general*.[1]

A more complex argument for exchange-rate management in the short run is related to the interaction between interest rates, the exchange rate and monetary policy when international capital is highly mobile. In this environment it may be sensible for the authorities to pursue a target value or, more likely, a restricted 'zone' of values within which the exchange rate is allowed to fluctuate. This can be achieved by varying domestic interest rates to influence the flow of international capital. If the authorities were to attach overriding importance to the achievement of an exchange-rate target, they could not in general simultaneously expect to attain a target for the quantity of money, for it is by varying the quantity of money that the authorities can influence interest rates and thus accommodate shocks to the economy in such a way that they do not unduly affect the value of the exchange rate.

---

[1] The assessment of the effectiveness of official stabilization operations is fraught with difficulty. See 'Intervention, Stabilization and Profits', *BEQB*, September 1983, pp. 384–91.

The relative merits of monetary and exchange-rate targets are too complex to be debated in full here.[1] The choice of one or other should be determined by its ability to 'insulate' the economy from unwanted exogenous disturbances. Roughly, exchange-rate targets are likely to be preferable if the main disturbances to the economy originate in financial markets. An exchange-rate target helps prevent such disturbances from being transmitted to domestic production and prices.

Since 1976 the UK authorities have attached considerable importance to monetary targets. In the last few years, however, there have been numerous signs of a change in strategy towards greater emphasis on the relative stability of the exchange rate.[2] Notably, there were sharp increases in short-term interest rates in January 1985 and January 1986, which appeared to owe little to domestic monetary conditions but were implemented largely to arrest or attenuate a fall in sterling. Conversely, when interest rates were raised in successive steps during 1988, mainly because of adverse domestic monetary developments, the authorities were obliged to sell sterling on the foreign exchanges thus increasing official reserves, in order to avoid an appreciation of the currency which would have been deemed excessive given the backcloth of the worsening current account. The problem with this strategy is that if the target value of the exchange rate is chosen wrongly or too inflexibly, then maintaining the target will have adverse effects on either output or inflation which may persist for some time. This suggests the need for making the targets *conditional* on other aspects of the economic situation, including domestic monetary conditions and the level of demand. However, when, as in 1988, there is a potential conflict between the domestic and the external situation, it is far from clear which should be given priority.

In summary, exchange-rate management is fraught with problems, although it seems clear that some degree of management is desirable. It is not easy to judge the 'right' level of an exchange-rate target, or the priority which should be accorded that target. The difficulties are likely to continue to be particularly acute in the immediate future: innovations in financial markets make monetary targets difficult to judge, while turbulence in exchange markets makes it equally difficult to judge an exchange-rate target. One possible method of increasing exchange-rate stability would be for the UK to join the European Monetary System; this is discussed in section 5.1 below. As far back as 1973, the UK authorities set out their broad objectives of exchange-rate policy as being '. . . not to oppose any well-defined trend but merely to smooth excessive fluctuations'.[3] In the

---

[1] For a clear exposition of the issues involved see M.J.Artis, 'From Monetary to Exchange-Rate Targets', *Banca Nazionale del Lavoro Quarterly Review*, September 1981, pp. 339–58.

[2] See, for example, The Chancellor of The Exchequer's 1985 Mansion House Speech, reported in *The Financial Times*, 18 October 1985; and his speech to the House of Commons on 30 November 1988, when he stated, *inter alia*, that, 'The Government's anchor against inflation is its determination not to allow a devaluation of the pound.'

[3] Bank of England, *Annual Report and Accounts*, 1973, p. 21.

long-run, these relatively modest goals may be about the best that can reasonably be expected.

North Sea oil and exchange-rate policy: We have already described the direct effects on the balance of payments of the growing production of North Sea oil and gas since 1973, and argued that this was one of the key factors behind the appreciation of sterling between 1979 and 1980. The UK's benefit from North Sea oil amounts to a windfall gain resulting from the discovery and exploitation of oil reserves. The effects of oil price changes are more complex. On the one hand, the UK benefits from a rise in oil prices because of the improvement in its terms of trade. On the other hand, in so far as the rest of the world goes into recession as a result of higher oil prices, the total demand for UK goods and services falls and unemployment increases. On balance the UK is probably a net beneficiary from higher oil prices, and therefore a net loser as a result of the lower oil prices which have prevailed since 1986.

The policy implications of North Sea oil have been hotly contested.[1] Crude oil has certain specific uses, and therefore the benefits of oil resources can be spread across the whole community only if the oil is sold on the market and the government follows 'appropriate' monetary and fiscal policies to assure distribution of the benefits. Since all UK oil production represents an equivalent gross gain to the balance of visible trade, an increase in production will improve the current account and put upward pressure on the exchange rate. This depresses the production of non-oil tradeables in the UK and, since these are labour-intensive relative to oil, it has the effect of reducing the aggregate demand for labour at current levels of real wages. The non-oil tradeable sector consists largely of manufacturing industry and the adverse effects on manufacturing of a high exchange rate consequent on a resource discovery are known collectively as the 'Dutch disease', following the evolution of the Dutch economy after the discovery of natural gas in the sixties. The question is how far a sustained real appreciation of the currency, with its Dutch disease implications, is a necessary consequence of a resource discovery.

The Forsyth and Kay position is that a high real exchange rate is the principal, if not the only, mechanism by which the benefits of North Sea oil can be realized. Since oil has to be traded for consumer goods, the terms-of-trade improvement allows UK consumers to purchase foreign-manufactured goods more cheaply than would otherwise be the case. On this view, the real appreciation did not imply a general deterioration in UK competitiveness but rather reflected a change in the UK's comparative international advantage: from a manufacturing exporter to a resource

---

[1] The path-breaking contribution was P.J.Forsyth and J.A.Kay, 'The Economic Implications of North Sea Oil Revenues', *Fiscal Studies*, 1980, pp 1–28. For a rebuttal see T.Barker, *Energy, Industrialization and Economic Policy* (Academic Press, London, 1981). An official viewpoint is given in 'North Sea Oil and Gas: A Challenge for the Future', *BEQB*, Vol. 22, 1982.

exporter. It does not follow that the authorities should have allowed an unchecked appreciation of sterling. It does, however, follow that the correct way to limit the appreciation was for the UK government to invest the oil proceeds largely overseas, or to encourage the private sector to perform this task by, for example, abolishing exchange controls, as occurred in 1979. In effect, this policy implies the replacement (in part) of one national asset (oil) by others, such as overseas portfolio and direct investment assets.

The contrary argument is that the decline in UK manufacturing industry was caused by the real appreciation of sterling, was largely unnecessary and might be difficult to reverse, as it is more costly to open new factories than it is to close old ones. On this view, North Sea oil revenues should be invested by the UK government in the UK in a programme of industrial regeneration. In addition, the authorities should expand demand in a deliberate effort to depress sterling and reduce the unemployment rate.

In assessing these views it is difficult to resist the conclusion that some real appreciation must follow from North Sea oil. We have seen that the scope for a managed depreciation is inherently limited. Moreover, a demand-led expansion of the economy is constrained by the need of the UK to run balance-of-payments surpluses in the 1980s. These are required to generate overseas assets, in part so that future generations can benefit from the oil wealth, but also to repay foreign debt incurred in the mid-seventies. Indeed sterling's appreciation did not prevent such surpluses from appearing, which would suggest that the currency was not overvalued in the first half of the 1980s. The position in the late 1980s is less clear, given the large emergent current account deficit. However, as discussed in section 1.4, the interpretation of this deficit is clouded by the even larger balancing item in the accounts.

Turning to the utilization of oil resources, it is difficult not to be sceptical of a programme of industrial regeneration since this would involve investing in sectors rendered relatively unprofitable by the change in the UK's terms of trade. Investing in these sectors will not of itself make them more profitable nor will it reverse the terms-of-trade shift. More plausible is the argument that there should be investment in non-traded goods industries whose profitability would increase as a result of the appreciation of sterling. In the public sector this would include investment in roads and in health, education, and training. Through such investments, the North Sea oil benefit could be translated into physical and human capital assets, with positive effects on UK industrial competitiveness in the medium and long term when North Sea production declines.[1] These arguments should not be taken to imply that the 'Dutch disease' is of no concern. However, there is now a respectable body of evidence to suggest that the decline in UK manufacturing industry in the last decade cannot be attributed solely to North Sea oil or a high real exchange rate. Indeed, in a recent survey,

---

[1]   Cf. *The Challenge of North Sea Oil*, Cmnd. 7143 (HMSO, 1978).

many industrialists were concerned as much about the *stability* of the exchange rate as they were about its level.[1]

In summary, it seems clear that North Sea oil involves a higher sterling exchange rate than would otherwise prevail. Some structural change is certain to follow from this, with adverse consequences for employment in the production of tradeable goods. The pattern of comparative advantage has changed in a way which allows a higher average level of UK income than would otherwise prevail. The proper response is to devise policies aimed at accommodating North Sea resources with a minimum of transitional cost and a maximum of longer-term benefit.

3   THE CURRENT ACCOUNT
3.1   Long-Term Trends
The structure of trade: In this section we shall examine the major structural developments in the current account of the UK since 1950, concentrating in particular on the performance of merchandise trade and of services. IPD are considered with the capital account in section 4, while transfers are discussed in connection with the UK's membership of the EC in section 5.

Radical changes in the pattern of UK overseas trade have occurred in the last 40 years. Table 3.5 shows the major changes in the geographical composition of trade. Several general trends are immediately apparent. Compared to the 1950s, the following years show a decreased dependence on trade with developing countries, a trend which has been primarily at the expense of trade with the less developed members of the OSA, and the four major Commonwealth nations, Canada, Australia, New Zealand and South Africa. An interesting development since 1970 is the increased importance of the oil-exporting countries as a market for UK exports. The decline in their importance as a source of UK imports since 1980 is the direct result of the exploitation of the UK's North Sea oil resources. As far as trade with the developed nations is concerned, the most striking trend is the increasing importance of trade with the EC. In 1972, the year prior to entry, the current twelve EC members accounted for approximately 30% of UK exports and imports; by 1987 the export share had risen to 49.4% and the import share to 52.7%. The growing importance of Japan as a source of UK imports may also be noted.

The switch towards a greater trade dependence on the industrialized, high per capita income countries of Western Europe, Japan and North America has been matched by significant changes in the commodity structure of UK trade, particularly in respect of imports. The changing structure of UK import trade is shown in table 3.6. Most important here is the increase in the proportion of imports of manufactures and the decline in

---

[1]   House of Lords, *Report From The Select Committee on Overseas Trade* (HMSO, 30 July 1985).

TABLE 3.5

Area Composition of UK Merchandise Trade,[1] **1955–87**

	1955	1970	1980	1985	1987
	EXPORTS				
	(fob: in per cent of total)				
Western Europe	28.9	46.2	57.6	58.3	58.9
EC	(15.0)	(29.4)	(43.4)	(46.3)	(49.4)
North America	12.0	15.2	11.2	17.0	16.3
USA	(7.1)	(11.6)	(9.6)	(14.7)	(13.8)
Other Developed[2]	21.1	11.8	5.6	4.8	5.1
Japan	(0.6)	(1.8)	(1.3)	(1.3)	(1.9)
Total Developed Countries	62.0	73.2	74.5	80.0	80.3
Centrally planned economies	1.7	3.8	2.8	2.0	1.9
Oil exporting countries	5.1	5.8	10.1	7.6	6.5
Other developing countries	31.2	17.2	12.4	10.1	10.7
Total	100.0	100.0	100.0	100.0	100.0
	IMPORTS				
	(cif: in per cent of total)				
Western Europe	25.7	41.5	55.9	63.1	66.4
EC	(12.6)	(27.1)	(41.3)	(46.0)	(52.7)
North America	19.5	20.5	15.0	13.8	11.5
USA	(10.9)	(12.9)	(12.1)	(11.7)	(9.7)
Other Developed[2]	14.2	9.4	6.8	7.5	7.7
Japan	(0.6)	(1.5)	(3.4)	(4.9)	(5.8)
Total developed countries	59.4	71.4	77.7	84.3	85.6
Centrally planned economies	2.7	4.2	2.1	2.2	2.2
Oil exporting countries	9.2	9.1	8.6	3.3	1.8
Other developing countries	28.7	15.3	11.3	10.0	9.9
Total	100.0	100.0	100.0	100.0	100.0

Source: *AAS*, 1963, 1976, 1989.

[1] There are minor changes in definition over time of some of the classifications. The components do not sum exactly to 100% as items valued at less than £50 (1955, 1970); £200 (1980, 1985); or £475 (1987) are not classified by area.

[2] Australia, Japan, New Zealand, South Africa.

the proportion accounted for by foodstuffs, beverages and tobacco. Imports of manufactures (SITC Codes 5–8) now account for over 75% of total UK imports. This same trend has also been experienced by other EC countries, although it remains the case that the UK has a higher proportion of imports of non-manufactures than does, for example, France or West Germany.[1] On the export side, table 3.6 shows that changes in structure have been less marked. It is clear that North Sea oil has had an important influence on trade structure. This can be seen in the significant decline in the import share of fuels and lubricants, and a corresponding rise in the export share of these products, reflecting, respectively, the import-substitution and export-generating aspects of North Sea oil that we discussed in section 1.

---

[1] See M. Panic, 'Why the UK's Propensity to Import is High', *LBR*, No. 115, 1975, for an interesting study of these issues.

TABLE 3.6

Commodity Composition of UK Merchandise Trade and Services, 1955–87

SITC Code	Description	1955	1970	1980	1985	1987
		EXPORTS (fob: in per cent of total merchandise exports)				
	Merchandise					
0, 1	Food, Beverages, Tobacco	5.8	6.4	6.9	6.3	7.0
3	Fuel and Lubricants	4.8	2.6	13.6	21.4	11.0
2, 4	Basic Materials	3.9	3.4	3.1	2.7	2.7
5, 6	Semi-manufactures	38.9	34.3	29.6	25.3	28.0
7, 8	Manufactures	43.5	49.9	43.9	41.7	48.4
9	Unclassified	3.0	3.4	3.0	2.5	2.8
	Total Merchandise	100.0	100.0	100.0	100.0	100.0
	Private Services					
	Transport and Travel	22.4	25.8	19.0	15.0	16.1
	Financial & Related Services	11.6	15.0	13.7	16.0	18.4
		IMPORTS (cif: in per cent of total merchandise imports)				
	Merchandise					
0, 1	Food, Beverages, Tobacco	36.2	22.6	12.4	10.9	10.8
3	Fuel and Lubricants	10.4	10.4	13.8	12.4	6.5
2, 4	Basic Materials	28.7	15.1	8.1	6.3	6.0
5, 6	Semi-manufactures	19.2	27.7	27.1	25.0	26.9
7, 8	Manufactures	5.2	22.9	35.6	43.7	48.6
9	Unclassified	0.3	1.3	3.0	1.6	1.2
	Total Merchandise	100.0	100.0	100.0	100.0	100.0
	Private Services					
	Transport and Travel	19.0	23.1	16.6	14.4	16.5
	Financial & Related Services	4.8	5.7	4.8	5.5	5.2

Source: AAS, 1963, 1976, 1989; *Pink Book*.

For services, debits in proportion to total merchandise imports have remained relatively stable over four decades.[1] Service credits have shown a greater fluctuation. The positive balance on services in more recent years can be attributed largely to a rapid expansion in receipts from financial services (other than IPD) as receipts from travel and transport have increased more slowly. Interestingly, however, total revenues from service exports in proportion to merchandise exports are currently at about the same level as in the mid-1950s, and rather smaller than in 1970.

It will be apparent from this that UK trade is increasingly dominated by an exchange of manufactured goods and services for other manufactured goods and services with the advanced industrialized nations. These structural changes imply that British industry has experienced, and will continue to experience, greater foreign competition in home and export markets.

---

[1] This stability is, in part, due to the method of estimating certain invisibles, such as shipping and insurance, as a fixed percentage of the value of merchandise trade.

Competitive performance: The trend towards increased non-oil visible trade deficits has often been interpreted as evidence of a general lack of competitive edge in British industry relative to foreign industry. Related evidence is provided by the progressive decline of the UK's share of the total exports of manufactured goods of the major industrial countries,[1] and by the increased import penetration of the UK market by foreign products. These trends have prompted fears of the imminent 'de-industrialization' of the UK, with the manufacturing base so eroded by foreign competitors that full employment and balance-of-payments equilibrium cannot, in the long run, be achieved simultaneously.[2] As discussed above, these fears have been heightened rather than quelled by the development of North Sea oil and its implications for the adjustment of the economy. At the very least, the UK may begin to face a severe balance-of-payments constraint as North Sea oil is gradually depleted.[3] The statistics of the decline in the UK share of world exports of manufactures are dramatic and indicate that the share fell steadily from 20.4% in 1954 to a low of 8.8% in 1974. Since 1974, however, the UK's share of world trade in manufactures appears to have stabilized at around 9.0%. Of itself, the decline in export share need not give rise to concern, since it may simply reflect a decline in the UK share of world manufacturing production, the natural result of her early industrial start. (In 1899, the UK accounted for 32.5% of world exports of manufactures and 20% of world manufacturing production.) However, once it is recognized that during the 1960s and early seventies, the UK was alone among the major industrial countries in experiencing a drop in export share, there are grounds for disquiet. Furthermore, the decline in the UK's share in world manufacturing production may itself reflect the same factors which hinder UK trade performance.

On the import side, the evidence for loss of competitive edge is equally disturbing. Even though all the major industrialized nations, with the exception of Japan, have experienced a rising import share since 1955, the UK seems to be relatively more import-prone than her competitors and to have a relatively high income elasticity of demand for imports. A customary measure of import penetration is the ratio of imports to domestic consumption. For manufactured goods this ratio increased from 17% in 1968 to 26% in 1978, and again to 35% in 1987. This trend appears widespread across manufacturing industry and is not confined to any one sub-sector.[4] However, some care is required in interpreting these figures since, in part, they reflect the increasing division of labour in the international economy which has occurred since 1958. Thus, similar calculations on the export

---

[1] These consist of W. Germany, France, Italy, Netherlands, Belgium, Luxembourg, Canada, Japan, Sweden, Switzerland, USA and UK.
[2] See the various contributions to F. Blackaby (ed.), *Deindustrialization* (Heinemann, 1979).
[3] See J. Williamson, 'Is There An External Constraint?' *NIER*, August 1984, pp. 73–7.
[4] J.J. Hughes and A.P. Thirlwall, 'Trends in Cycles in Import Penetration in the UK', *BOUIES*, Vol. 39, 1977, pp. 301–17. See also *BB*, 19 June 1981, p. 348.

side show a corresponding, albeit less marked, trend increase in the proportion of UK output which is exported, with the average ratio of UK manufacturing exports to manufacturing production rising from 17.6% in 1968 to 26.1% in 1978 and 30.3% in 1987.[1]

To explain these developments in any precise sense is not easy; several interrelated factors are involved and the relative weight to be attached to each is difficult to establish and may vary over time. At the most general level, there would seem to be two potential sources of the poor UK trade performance: an increasing lack of price competitiveness; and a failure to produce and market commodities of the right quality, in the face of rapidly changing technologies and world demand structures. Unfortunately, the precise role of these factors has proved impossible, as yet, to determine, although it is interesting to note that similar explanations of poor British competitive performance were employed at the end of the nineteenth century.[2]

3.2 Explanations of Trade Performance

Some guidance on these matters may be provided by a brief consideration of theories of comparative advantage. Traditional trade theory explains patterns of international trade by reference to national differences in endowments of factors of production, a country exporting those commodities which use relatively intensively its abundant factors. While this may have some relevance to the explanation of exchanges of manufactured goods for raw materials between industrialized and developing countries, it is of less obvious relevance to the explanation of the dominant component of world trade, exchange of manufactures between industrialized nations. Indeed, the assumptions of traditional theory immediately invite a cautious interpretation of its content, for they specify homogeneous outputs of each industry, equal access to technical knowledge in all countries, and all factors of production of equal quality. *Prima facie*, they do not reflect the reality of modern industrial competition, i.e. conditions of imperfect competition with non-price factors being dominant in competitive performance.

A powerful indication of the weakness of traditional theory is provided by the phenomenon of intra-industry trade, the simultaneous importing and exporting of products of the same industry, which is estimated to com-

---

[1] It may be noted that the sectors experiencing the greatest improvement in export performance, e.g., chemicals, electrical engineering, mechanical engineering and scientific instruments, are also the sectors which perform two-thirds of the non-aerospace research and development carried out in UK manufacturing industry. See 'Manufacturing Industry in the Seventies: An Assessment of Import Penetration and Export Performance', *ET*, 1980. A useful account of some of the pitfalls of interpreting movements in these ratios, pitfalls which arise out of the foreign trade multiplier links between exports, imports and home output, is contained in C.Kennedy and A.P.Thirlwall, 'Import Penetration, Export Performance and Harrod's Trade Multiplier', *OEP*, July 1979, pp. 303–23.
[2] R.Hoffman, *Great Britain and the German Trade Rivalry 1875–1914* (Pennsylvania University Press, 1933), pp. 21–80.

prise some 60% of trade between developed countries.[1] In part, of course, this phenomenon is a statistical aberration, reflecting the lack of detail within even the finest classification of industrial statistics. For example, within the steel industry, there are many qualities of steel each of which is a poor substitute for the other in many applications but which are treated statistically as if they were perfect substitutes. More fundamentally, it reflects the role of intra-industry product-differentiation as a key element in the competitive process.[2] It is no puzzle that the UK should simultaneously import and export whisky or automobiles of different brands, given the many grades of product which exist within these commodity groups, each defined by a unique set of characteristics. Design, technical sophistication, after-sales service, durability and reliability are easily recognized as elements which successfully differentiate products in the minds of consumers.

The major determinants of intra-industry trade relate to product differences rather than cost differences, and may be outlined as follows. First, the existence of diversity of preferences for commodities of many different kinds within industrial countries. Second, the importance of a domestic market to the initial development of a new commodity, which implies that the types of commodities produced in an economy reflect the pattern of domestic preferences. The same industry within different countries will then produce different product designs. Third, the importance of economies of scale, including in this category the spreading of overhead marketing and R&D expenses, in inducing firms to specialize within particular product niches. In general, specialization will be directed to those products in which home demand is greatest. Economies of scale and diversity of preferences then create the basis for intra-industry trade between industries organized in an imperfectly competitive fashion. The conditions which generate intra-industry trade also make technological innovation an important element in trade performance. Economists have long recognized the connection between technical innovation, technology transfer and changes in the structure of foreign trade. Three factors are recognized as being of importance here: time-lags in the inter-country transfer of technology; differences in the national rate of diffusion of innovations; and differences in the rates of growth of national production capacity to exploit innovations.[3] From this perspective, a country's trade performance is determined by the rate at which it acquires and exploits new technologies relative to its major competitors. Moreover, as technologies mature, the inputs which are required for effective exploitation change significantly. A new technology

[1]   D.Greenaway and C.Milner, 'On the Measurement of Intra-Industry Trade', *EJ*, 1983, Vol. 93, pp. 900–8.
[2]   Intra-industry trade and other aspects of 'new' theories of trade patterns are discussed in the collection of readings on *Current Issues in International Trade, Theory and Policy*, ed. D.Greenaway (Macmillan, 1985).
[3]   The classic reference is M.V.Posner, 'International Trade and Technological Change', *OEP*, 1961, Vol. 13, pp. 323–41.

requires major scientific and technical manpower inputs to compete effectively. But as it matures, production processes become standardized and the emphasis shifts to the exploitation of economies of scale and access to cheap labour.

Although one can recognize the historical force of these arguments in the study of individual industries,[1] it has proved difficult to identify the role of innovation-related factors in UK trade performance as a whole. Some pieces of evidence may, however, be relevant. First, if one divides UK trade according to the R&D intensity of the underlying industries, one finds that throughout the 1970s, R&D intensive industries consistently experience a trade surplus, while other industries are in deficit.[2] Secondly, a variable which reflects the employment of professional and technically qualified manpower is statistically important in explaining UK trade performance.[3] These findings fit naturally with any explanation of trade in terms of human-capital inputs. More generally, there is also evidence to show that export success in the advanced industrialized nations is positively related to the resources devoted to R&D and to measures of inventive activity, e.g. patenting.[4]

These dynamic considerations can be reconciled with the factor-endowment theory of trade provided we interpret human-capital skills and the state of technology as part of the endowment. However, unlike raw material endowments, human-capital skills change over time, often rapidly as new knowledge is discovered and transmitted into the workforce by formal education and practical experience. Seen in this light it is clear that long-term trade trends will be profoundly influenced by the level of education and training of the labour force and its ability to innovate and adapt to new technologies. These qualities are exceedingly difficult to measure in practice and the exact ways in which they impinge on trade patterns are still not well understood.

Much of what we have said stresses the role of non-price factors in trade performance. It must not be read as implying that price factors are unimportant. The evidence suggests that price elasticities are an important influence on trade, even if they are not the overwhelming determining factor in trade performance. However, in addition to price, it is the relation of prices to costs that determines the financial base from which firms may engage

---

[1] Cotton textiles and the computer industry are excellent examples. On micro-electronic innovations and trade, see E.Braun and S.McDonald, *Revolution in Miniature* (Cambridge, 1978); E.Tilton, *International Diffusion of Technology: The Case of Semi Conductors* (Brookings Institution, 1971), and B.A.Majumdar, *Innovations, Product Developments and Technology Transfers* (University Press of America, 1982).
[2] Business Monitor, QAID. High-technology industries are those with a ratio of R&D expenditures to value added greater than 3%.
[3] S.R.Smith *et al.*, 'UK Trade in Manufacturing: The Pattern of Specialization During the 1970s', *GES Working Paper*, No. 56, June 1982.
[4] For a review, see the valuable paper by C.Freeman, 'Technical Innovation and British Trade Performance', in F.Blackaby (ed.), *op. cit.* See also the study by K.Pavitt and L.Soete, Ch. 3 of K.Pavitt (ed.), *Technological Innovation and British Export Performance* (Macmillan, 1980).

in R&D, investment and marketing. Thus profit margins are a key determinant of the resources available for innovation and the relative dynamic performance of different national industries.[1] Price elasticities are important, but they are only part of the picture. Nonetheless, indices of relative unit labour costs, adjusted for exchange-rate changes, do provide evidence of trends in competitive strength, depending as they do on the relationships between money wages and labour productivity in different countries.

The determinants of price competitiveness are complex, and include such factors as the structure of costs, the size and nature of different industries and the existence of economies of scale, labour productivity, the pricing policies of individual firms, and movements in wages and interest rates. Undoubtedly, a major influence is the level of the sterling exchange rate relative to domestic and international prices. Movements in measures of price competitiveness in the UK since 1972 reflect to a considerable extent movements in sterling, with the sharp appreciation of 1979 and 1980 associated with a severe loss of price competitiveness and the subsequent depreciation of the pound being accompanied by a recovery of price competitiveness. However, most indicators suggest that, throughout the eighties including the most recent years through 1988, UK prices were on average less internationally competitive even in comparison with the mid-sixties immediately before the 1967 devaluation of the pound. The latter comparison is particularly disturbing in that it was generally agreed that UK price competitiveness was inadequate prior to the 1967 devaluation which was, of course, implemented in large part to improve competitiveness. Moreover, it is likely that price competitiveness interacts with technological factors in determining trade performance with a deterioration in competitiveness resulting in a loss of markets, a slow rate of economic growth, and concomitant lack of resources to invest in new technologies. This, in turn, makes the UK less competitive in other markets, thus exacerbating the problem further in a form of vicious circle. A country such as the UK has no option but to maintain its technological level close to 'world best practice'. As technologies mature, the centre of comparative advantage moves to low real wage economies, so an advanced country such as the UK can only maintain its comparative advantage by continuously shifting resources into production at the frontiers of technological change. Only thus can the UK expect to maintain its historically high living standards.

Overlaying these forces since 1972 has been UK membership of the EC, which we discuss in detail in section 5.1. Here, however, it is worth recording that, geographically, the most severe deterioration in the UK's balance of trade in manufactured goods has been in trade with the EC countries. However, it would be simplistic to ascribe this deterioration to EC membership *per se*. As over 50% of the UK's visible trade is now

---

[1]   For a discussion of these issues see 'The Terms of Trade', *BEQB*, August 1987, pp. 371–9.

with other EC countries, it is inevitable that any fundamental deterioration in the UK's trade position would show up strongly in UK–EC trade, particularly as it is in this market that trade in manufactured goods is virtually free of restriction and therefore, in principle, most subject to forces of international competition. It is more likely that the deterioration in the UK's balance of manufactured trade with the EC is simply the most visible manifestation of the deeper-seated problems associated with price competiveness and innovation discussed above.[1]

3.3 Trade Policy

Arguments for free trade and protection: Trade policy is concerned, in the first instance, with the effects of tariffs and subsidies aimed at influencing the prices of exports and imports and thus the performance of exporting and import-competing industries. However, virtually any form of government intervention in the economy has some impact on the trading position. In this section we concentrate on policies which have as their primary purpose the influencing of international trade flows. Even thus defined, trade policy is by no means confined to tariffs and subsidies on exports and imports but includes also import quotas, taxes and subsidies on domestic production, and taxes and subsidies on the use of labour and capital in different industries. Moreover, in recent years, government intervention in this area has become increasingly complex and ingenious. Subsidized export credit, differential treatment of foreign firms in bidding procedures for government contracts, the establishment of product quality standards which favour particular firms, and voluntary export restraints are all examples of differing forms of trade intervention aimed at securing a competitive advantage for particular groups of firms or industries. In general, most of these kinds of trade policy involve, to differing degrees, some element of protection for domestic industries.

The principles of comparative advantage suggest that interventions in the flow of trade are generally harmful both to the country imposing the intervention and, if several countries act or 'retaliate' in this way, to the world as a whole. The case for free trade is largely analogous to the case for *laissez-faire*. It enables each country to produce the goods in which it has a comparative cost advantage and thus to export products which it can produce relatively cheaply and import products which can be produced relatively cheaply elsewhere. Each individual country, and thus the world as a whole, benefits from this international specialization.

Despite this argument, countries have intervened in trade over the years in a wide variety of ways, the most common being the imposition of tariffs on imports. Under certain assumptions, an import tariff can be expected to raise real wages in the tariff-imposing country, even though national

---

[1] For a detailed analysis of the impact of EEC membership on UK manufacturing trade see S.Deardon, 'EEC Membership and The United Kingdom's Trade in Manufactured Goods', *NWBQR*, February 1986.

income, and therefore overall welfare in that country, will fall as a result.[1] More recently, arguments have been devised to show that individual countries can benefit from certain forms of protection.[2] These arguments stem from a recognition that most industries do not correspond to the perfectly competitive paradigm of the theory of comparative advantage. There are numerous examples of 'natural' monopolies or industries where economies of scale are such as to keep the number of firms in the industry relatively few in number. In these cases, firms in the industry typically earn more than normal profit, i.e. they receive an economic rent. Intuition and theory suggest that it may pay an individual country to protect a firm in such an industry so as to help secure a share in the world-wide economic rents to be earned in the industry. A related argument is that certain industries create external economies in their operations, that is, their activities help reduce the costs of other firms. Knowledge-based high-technology industries are generally cited as examples of this phenomenon. 'Silicon Valley' and 'Route 128' computer firms are usually thought to benefit from their proximity to one another. Here, too, there is an argument for the protection of certain 'strategic' aspects of the activities of such industries which may be regarded as central to the operation of the industry as a whole but in which firms in the industry no longer enjoy a comparative advantage. Thus, local production of microchips is generally regarded as strategically important to American and European industry, even though other countries may well have a cost advantage in their production and thus, according to the theory of comparative advantage, should be the ones to specialize in their production. Such strategic aspects of protection have been at the forefront of recent international discussions of trade policy. However, it should be emphasized that these strategic arguments rest on the idea that an individual country can gain from protection. It must be questioned whether such protection produces any world-wide benefits or merely involves a transfer from one country to another.

Trade policy in practice: In the United Kingdom, tariff protection is circumscribed by UK membership of the EC and by membership of GATT. However, the influence of these bodies is different in that EC policy has concentrated on the removal of internal trade barriers to the extent that, by 1977 industrial tariffs on intra-EC trade and EC trade with EFTA had been completely removed, but has equally acted as a trading block to maintain and, in some cases, expand the degree of protection afforded to EC-based activities against comparable activities located elsewhere, the prime

---

[1]   This argument was originally set out by W.F.Stolper and P.A.Samuelson, 'Protection and Real wages', *Review of Economic Studies*, 9, 1941, 58–73. For a detailed study of arguments relating to the pros and cons of tariff protection, see W.M.Corden, *Trade Policy and Economic Welfare* (Oxford University Press, 1974).
[2]   For a comprehensive study of these arguments see P.R.Krugman (ed.), *Strategic Trade Policy and The New International Economics* (MIT Press, 1986).

example in this respect being the very high level of protection implicit in the Common Agricultural Policy (CAP).

In contrast, GATT is an international body founded in 1947 as a part of the international economic system which includes also the IMF and World Bank. By holding a succession of trade negotiations (called 'rounds'), GATT has succeeded over the years in bringing about an agreed, substantial world-wide reduction in the tariffs on industrial goods levied by all countries.[1] At the conclusion of the seventh (Tokyo) round of negotiations in 1979, the weighted average tariff on manufactured goods in the world's nine major industrial markets was reduced to about 4.7%. With the exception of some exemptions accorded to particular industries and, more generally, to developing country imports of certain kinds of industrial products, it can be said that the world is now relatively free of industrial tariffs.

This does not, however, mean that there is no protection. Agriculture remains highly protected, not just by the EC but also, in particular, by Japan and to some extent by the USA; and textiles have repeatedly been exempt from the provision of successive GATT agreements, exemptions which were formalized in 1974 with the Multifibre Arrangement (MFA) which in principle provided for the gradual liberalization of the textile trade but, in practice, ratified a relatively high level of protection and trade restraint for these industries, particularly in the industrial countries. Finally, as tariffs have come down, a very wide range of non-tariff barriers of the kind mentioned above have been erected in their place. The latest round of GATT – the Uruguay round – opened in 1986 with the specific aim of attacking these three problem areas. In principle, agreement on agriculture and textiles should not be difficult to achieve as the tax and subsidy arrangements in existence are relatively clearly defined. However, at the mid-point of the negotiations in December 1988, GATT was obliged to adjourn for 3 months precisely because of the inability of US and EC negotiators to agree on principles to be adopted in reducing agricultural protection. At the time of writing, such agreement was still proving elusive. This does not augur well for the second half of this round. In general, non-tariff barriers are easy to erect and defend as 'normal domestic practice' and, because each barrier is distinctive in certain ways, it will be exceedingly difficult to write an agreement which can cover any new devices which may be invented in the future.

A good example of this problem is provided by the enforcement of domestic product quality standards. Such standards often have the clear effect of protecting domestic industries to the exclusion of cheaper import-substitutes and thus to the detriment of local consumers. However, quality standards often constitute an 'externality' in the production of goods. Consumers are invariably not equipped nor can they reasonably be equipped to determine if a product is of a certain quality. This provides

---

[1] For a brief history of GATT and discussion of the current (Uruguay) round see S.J. Anjaria, 'A New Round of Global Trade Negotiations', *FD*, 23:2, June 1986, pp. 2–7.

a *prima facie* argument for official regulation in the provision and enforcement of quality standards. This means in practice that criticisms of one country's standards can easily appear arbitrary; it is not clear what basis can be used to assert that a particular standard is unjustifiably strict since it is put in place precisely to ensure that consumers obtain products of a particular quality. Clearly this calls for some degree of international agreement on quality standards, but this is a far more ambitious task than agreement on the level of a tariff. The problem for the GATT negotiators is compounded by the fact that many of these restrictions apply to trade in services which has so far not been subject to scrutiny by GATT. However, the Uruguay round also aims to look more generally at trade in services with a view to negotiating cuts in protection in this whole broad area.

In addition to recognizing these difficulties it must also be remembered that the actual tax or subsidy on a product does not, on its own, measure the full extent of the protection which that product enjoys. In particular, import-competing goods which use imported inputs and raw materials can be protected in (at least) two ways: first, by the imposition of a tariff on imports of the product itself, but second, by a cut in the tariff or the imposition of a subsidy on imports of the inputs and raw materials used in its manufacture. Thus a logical tariff system needs to take account of the industrial structure of the economy. Protection of products which are widely used as intermediate inputs can easily result in negative protection (or 'dis-protection') of the wide range of goods for which the intermediate inputs are required. The concept of 'effective protection' has been developed to measure the degree of protection afforded to an industry after allowing for tariffs and subsidies on intermediate inputs. Recognition of the industrial structure of an economy also gives rise to the principle of 'escalation', that is, that a rational tariff structure should involve increasing rates of tariff for goods which are relatively more highly processed, with the lowest tariff rates applying to commodities and raw materials.

Given our earlier discussion about the high degree of world-wide agricultural protection and relatively low degree of industrial protection, it will come as no surprise to learn that few countries have a rational tariff structure and the UK is no exception in this respect. A recent study[1] of the 1979 tariff structure of the UK found some evidence of escalation overall. However, in 99 industry groups only 44 had an effective tariff rate in excess of the nominal tariff, while 53 had an effective tariff rate less than the nominal rate; the remaining 2 had equal nominal and effective rates. This

---

[1]   See D. Greenaway, 'Effective Tariff Protection in The United Kingdom', *BOUIES*, 50:3, 1988, pp. 311–24. The concept of the effective rate of protection was devised by W. M. Corden and is discussed in detail in W. M. Corden, *The Theory of Protection* (Oxford University Press, 1971). A broader study of the impact of the whole range of domestic and international taxes and subsidies but on a relatively narrow range of commodities is contained in A. V. Deardorff and R. M. Stern, 'The Effects of Domestic Tax/Subsidies and Import Tariffs on the Structures of Protection in the United States, United Kingdom and Japan', Ch. 3 in J. Black and L. A. Winters (eds), *Policy and Performance in International Trade* (Macmillan, 1983).

means that for the 53 industries concerned, the nominal protection afforded by the tax on competing imports was partly or wholly offset by tariffs on intermediate inputs. The influence of agricultural protection was particularly marked. Thus agriculture itself enjoyed a nominal tariff of 16.3% but an effective tariff of 47.3%. However, food-processing industries such as milk and meat slaughtering, while nominally enjoying a tariff of 7.5% and 5.8% respectively, actually experienced substantial disprotection through the high cost of their agricultural raw materials, with effective tariff rates of −22.4% and −14.6% respectively, amounting to a net import subsidy. These and similar figures highlight the underlying absurdity of a good deal of protection. In practice, protection is often granted to an industry on an *ad hoc* basis as the result of an industrial lobby aimed at protecting real wages in that industry. The overall effects of this protection, both direct and indirect, are rarely taken into account. The result is a system in which consumers pay higher prices than necessary for some products while industries, often only distantly connected to the original protective measures, are unable to compete in world markets because they too have to pay higher prices than necessary for their raw materials and other inputs.

4   THE CAPITAL ACCOUNT
4.1   Portfolio and Direct Investment
Influences on overseas investment: Recent data as well as longer-term trends in the capital account as a whole have already been presented in tables 3.1 and 3.3. In this section, we examine in more detail the main influences on portfolio and direct investment and consider some of the possible costs and benefits of such investments. From the viewpoint of individual investors the main forces governing overseas portfolio and direct investment are not likely to be qualitatively very different from those governing domestic investment, with the overriding factor in decisions to invest being the anticipated rate of return on the project or security relative to the cost of any funds which have to be borrowed to finance the investment and relative to the perceived riskiness of the investment. In this calculation, investors will obviously be comparing the prospective risks and returns of overseas investments with those of alternative domestic investment opportunities. In practice, the calculation for overseas investment is more complex than that for domestic investment. Beginning with portfolio investment, investors not only have to evaluate the prospects of the company in which they are investing but also, to some extent, the overall prospects for the particular foreign economy in which the company operates, especially for interest rates, as these are likely to affect the performance of the stock market on which the shares of the company are quoted, and this in turn will have an impact on the share price of the individual company itself. Movements in the exchange rate also affect the return on overseas investment, with a depreciation of sterling increasing the sterling rate of

return of a foreign-currency investment and vice-versa. For direct investment the calculations are more complex still, as foreign countries typically
impose different rules and regulations on company investment activities
covering matters as diverse as taxation, quality control, employment standards, and information disclosure requirements. All these factors impose
both costs and benefits. Indeed, to a large extent, foreign direct investment
is just one mechanism by which modern corporations seek to gain competitive advantages over their rivals by siting their production, administration
and marketing activities in a combination of locations designed to take
maximum advantage of differential tariffs, investment incentives, wage
levels, and demand conditions for their products. Direct investment must
also be considered in relation to exporting and foreign licensing of its products as just one of several ways by which a firm can extract maximum
advantage from its knowledge and human capital base.[1]

Overseas investment may also be constrained by regulation, and UK
overseas investment was strictly regulated by exchange controls until their
abolition in 1979. For portfolio investment, exchange controls had the practical effect of largely deterring UK residents from investing overseas,
although it must be emphasized that many firms and individuals with a
substantial interest in the UK were nevertheless non-resident for exchange-
control purposes and thus permitted to purchase and sell foreign securities
freely. For direct investment, the aim of exchange controls was to ensure
that such investments were financed either from the retained profits of
foreign-currency operations or from foreign-currency borrowing.[2] Over
the period 1965 to 1978, roughly half of UK direct investment overseas
was financed out of retained profits and the remainder largely from foreign
borrowing.

The abolition of exchange controls produced a clear and relatively unambiguous effect on portfolio investment. Outward portfolio investment,
largely by financial institutions such as unit trusts and pension funds, rose
steeply from £0.8bn in 1979 to £4.3bn in 1980, followed by successive
increases of comparable magnitudes, so that the gross outflow in 1986
amounted to £25.2bn. However, many fund managers reported that their
activities corresponded to a once-for-all portfolio adjustment to bring overseas assets to the desired proportion in their portfolio following which
the outflow would level off.[3] In fact, there was no sign of any such levelling
off until 1987 when the gross outflow was dramatically reversed, with UK
residents repatriating a net $6.5bn of portfolio investment. However, to
the extent that the outflows did indeed reflect the abolition of exchange

---

[1]   Cf. R.E.Caves, 'International Corporations: The Industrial Economics of Foreign Investment', *Economica*, Vol. 38, 1971, pp. 1–27.
[2]   The 9th edition of this volume contains details of the capital controls on overseas direct
investment.
[3]   See the article 'The Effects of Exchange Control Abolition on Capital Flows', *BEQB*,
September 1981.

controls, then it is clear that this policy could be regarded as successful in helping to limit the oil effect on the sterling exchange rate and widening the ambit of profitable investment opportunities for UK residents.

The impact of exchange-control abolition on direct investment is harder to quantify because the practical effect of the controls in this area was less severe. The main implication of abolition is that firms face a wider range of financing options than before – they can either borrow from abroad or within the UK; or they can use retained earnings from abroad or from the UK. Direct investment actually fell from £5.9bn in 1979 to £4.9bn in 1980; it varied between £4.0bn and £9.0bn per annum between 1979 and 1985, before rising sharply in 1986 and 1987 to reach £15.3bn in 1987. It is probably reasonable to conclude that direct investment was stimulated by exchange-control abolition, but the exact magnitude of the stimulus must remain a matter for debate.

Other structural factors influencing the portfolio and direct investment position include North Sea oil, whose implications were considered in detail in section 1.5, and UK membership of the EC. The influence of EC membership on UK direct investment is again difficult to quantify with any precision. Of the total stock of UK direct investment assets in the mid-1970s, it has been estimated that 28% was located in Western Europe and 23% in North America, compared to 1962 figures of 13% in Western Europe and 23% in North America, suggesting a trend of increasing investment in Western Europe.[1] However, more recent balance-of-payments data show that during the ten years 1974–83 only 8% of total outward direct investment flows went to Western Europe with 51% going to North America. Between 1984 and 1987 the rate of direct investment in Western Europe was stepped up to 19.2% of the total outward flow. Over this period, too, there was a marked increase in European direct investment in the UK with a total of £8.5bn of other EC countries' direct investment in the UK, compared to £8.0bn of UK investment in the rest of the EC. Any explanation for these flows must be very tentative in nature. One possibility is that a major motive for outward investment is for large firms to avoid tariffs and other import restrictions imposed by the host country. On this interpretation, the dismantling of such barriers within the EC largely obviated the need for UK firms to invest in other EC countries, and provided incentives for them to concentrate their foreign investment activities instead in non-EC markets where barriers to imports may be more important. The more recent surge in investment in the EC and by the EC in the UK could, in turn, be associated with the forthcoming dismantling of internal barriers in the EC to form the Single European Market in 1992. However, these two explanations are, to some extent, in conflict with one another and the exact reasons must await more detailed analysis.

[1] For further details, see J.H.Dunning, 'The UK's International Direct Investment Position in the Mid-1970s', *LBR*, April 1978.

Costs and benefits of overseas investment: Historically, foreign investment
has been the subject of debate in the UK, one strand of thinking arguing
that investment overseas has an adverse effect on the UK economy because
it creates jobs in overseas countries rather than in the UK while at the
same time producing balance-of-payments pressures through the outflow
of funds associated with the investment activity. While it is obviously correct
that overseas investment helps create overseas jobs, it is far from being
the case that this is the only effect of such investments or, as a result,
that overseas investment harms the UK economy. In fact, to consider the
full costs and benefits of overseas investment, it is necessary to take account
of its overall effects both on the balance of payments and on the domestic
economy as well as of the opportunities open to domestic investors.

First, under a floating exchange rate, overseas investment by UK firms
tends to depress the sterling exchange rate because of the outflow of funds
which is implied. On the one hand, there are circumstances in which a
relative depreciation of the exchange rate is desirable and cannot easily
be brought about by other means. Indeed, as we saw in section 2.5, this
was exactly the situation in the early 1980s when North Sea oil production
and high oil prices were placing strong upward pressures on the currency.
At that time, the strong portfolio outflow of funds was desirable as a way
of relieving the upward pressure on the exchange rate. More generally,
it can be argued that a steady flow of net overseas investment is a sensible
method of keeping the exchange rate lower than would otherwise be the
case and thus helps to maintain the price competitiveness of British exports
and import-competing industries. Second, it is often argued that foreign
direct investment leads directly to a fall in exports and a rise in imports
because output which could have been produced in the UK is now produced
overseas. This argument presumes that the output could have been produced profitably in the UK. In many instances, the structure of costs, availability of raw materials and other factors mean that this is not the case.
If the project could not be carried out profitably in the UK, it is sensible
for British firms to undertake the investment overseas because the profit
will subsequently accrue to UK residents. Third, in practice, foreign investment may well be complementary to exports rather than competitive with
them. An overseas investment project may generate UK exports in the
form of the plant and equipment needed to set up the project or in the
form of exports of semi-finished goods required to run the plant. Clearly
these factors are complex and quantifying them is not easy. Available evidence does indicate that on balance UK overseas investment does not
adversely affect the UK economy.[1] More generally, the proposition that

---

[1]   The seminal study is by W.B. Reddaway, *Effects of UK Direct Investment Overseas* (Interviews and final report), Cambridge University Press 1968. This study has recently been partially
updated and the new results are summarized in D. Shepherd 'Assessing the Consequences
of Overseas Investment', *RBSR*, No. 152, December, 1986. See also E.J. Pentecost, 'A Model
of UK Non-Oil ICCs' Direct Investment', *Bank of England Discussion Paper* no. 30,
November 1987.

the UK should not invest overseas runs contrary to the principles of comparative advantage. If taken to extreme, the proposition could easily imply that the UK ought to attempt self-sufficiency in all areas of the economy – clearly an absurd and exceedingly wasteful proposal.

Ultimately, foreign investment should satisfy many of the same criteria as domestic investment, that is, it should be profitable. If UK firms cannot find profitable investment opportunities in the UK then, *prima facie*, if they can find such opportunities abroad they should exploit them. In this connection, an argument can reasonably be made that the restructuring associated with North Sea oil and oil-related industries combined with a high pound placed a severe squeeze on profit opportunities elsewhere in the UK and must have encouraged a relative outflow of funds. Rough calculations of rates of return on domestic and overseas investment as well as on overseas investment in the UK are given in table 3.7. We have already

TABLE 3.7

Rates of Return on Domestic and Overseas Assets, 1978–88

	1978	1981	1984	1987	1988
	Year average : % per annum				
Calculated Rates of Return[1]					
UK Direct Investment Overseas	13.18	16.32	13.54	12.14	13.54
UK Portfolio Investment Overseas	4.60	5.32	6.18	3.81	5.12
Overseas Direct Investment in the UK	14.22	17.81	16.88	11.92	12.68
Overseas Portfolio Investment in the UK	7.38	10.12	7.98	7.37	7.50
Market Rates of Return					
UK Equities: Earnings Yield	16.47	12.12	10.76	8.90	11.72
UK Equities: Dividend Yield	5.65	6.23	4.66	3.73	4.62
UK Government Bonds: Flat Yield on consols	11.92	12.99	10.15	9.31	9.12
	Year-end to year-end: % p.a.				
Depreciation (+)/Appreciation (−) of the pound	1.79	10.36	11.94	−9.54	−2.37

Sources: Pink Book, ET.
1 Calculated as the ratio of the current year flow of earnings (IPD account) to the stock of assets outstanding at the end of the previous year (Net External Assets Account).

emphasized the variable quality of capital account data and the change in recording procedures following exchange-control abolition which makes the pre-1979 figures conceptually different for the post-1979 figures. Thus the data in table 3.7 can be regarded as no more than indicative in nature. These data suggest that the return on UK direct investment has been of a comparable magnitude to and generally in excess of the domestic earning yield on UK equities, the appropriate benchmark for comparison. Likewise, portfolio investment has earned a rate broadly comparable to the UK dividend yield. For overseas investment in the UK, it is no surprise that portfolio investment earns a rather higher return than the dividend yield on equities, as a relatively high proportion of such investment is in UK government bonds. It is, however, more surprising that overseas direct investment in the UK has generally earned a rather higher return than UK investment overseas, although this could be due to the fact that a substantial part of such investment has been in the relatively profitable North Sea oil industries. It could also reflect a possible under-recording of inward direct investment in recent years. The overall trend in equity returns has been generally downwards in recent years with rising stock market prices around the world. This culminated in a dramatic crash in world equity markets in October 1987, and the rather higher equity rates of return in 1988 reflect the lower level of stock market prices which resulted from the crash. Exchange-rate changes also affect the return on overseas investment and the generally downward movement in sterling since 1981 has served to increase the realized rate of return on overseas investments because the sterling value of investments denominated in foreign currencies rises as the exchange rate depreciates, producing sterling gains for UK investors.

4.2 Other Capital Transactions

The remaining items in the capital account were formerly described as 'short term'. This description has now generally been discontinued as the distinction between 'short' and 'long' term is, to a large extent, arbitrary. Other capital transactions consist mainly of two components. First, those involving bank loans and deposits, representing either the business of UK residents with overseas banks or, more commonly, the business of overseas residents with UK banks, and second, transactions (some of which are included in banking transactions) which are related to the finance of foreign trade.

Short-term capital movements have traditionally played an important role in the overall UK balance-of-payments situation. Some short-term capital movements reflect changes in the sterling balances which foreign governments and individuals have acquired as matters of commercial and financial convenience. (These correspond to line A10 in table 3.1 on page 141: Foreign Authorities' Sterling Reserves.) The remainder reflect the role of London as the major centre for the Eurocurrency, Eurobond and other international financial markets, with banks in the UK lending and borrowing extensively in dollars and other currencies. The development of the Eurocurrency markets since 1958 has meant the increasing integration of European and American capital and money markets.[1] The net assets of the Eurocurrency market increased from \$85bn in 1971 to \$2,220bn in 1987. The volume of deposits and the ease with which they may be switched between currencies have important implications for the stability of exchange rates and the conduct of national monetary policies.

---

[1]   Eurocurrency deposits are bank deposits in currencies other than that of the country in which the banks in question are located. For the working and development of the Eurocurrency markets, consult R. B. Johnston, *The Economics of The Euro-Market* (Macmillan, 1983). See also 'Eurobanks and the Inter-Bank Market', *BEQB*, September 1981.

The significance of short-term capital flows for the conduct of UK policy arises from their magnitude relative to the official reserves and from their volatility. It is convenient, though artificial, to divide these flows into two broad classes; speculative and non-speculative. The motive behind speculative capital flows is one of making a capital gain from anticipated movements in spot exchange rates or interest rates. A risk-neutral currency speculator would be indifferent between holding sterling- or dollar-denominated assets, for example, if the interest rate on sterling assets equalled the interest rate on dollar assets plus the anticipated depreciation of sterling relative to the dollar. (This is equivalent to uncovered interest parity.) If the anticipated sterling devaluation exceeds the sterling interest advantage, holders of sterling assets will switch their assets into dollars while UK importers will accelerate (lead) dollar payments for imports and UK exporters will try to delay (lag) dollar payments due from foreigners. Non-speculative activities are undertaken to avoid the risk of capital gains or losses associated with exchange-rate movements, and typically involve simultaneous transactions in both spot and forward currency markets so that the risks associated with currency transactions may be shifted onto speculators.[1] In sum, short-term capital movements depend on a complex set of interactions between national interest rates, spot and forward exchange rates, and expectations of future changes in spot rates.

With floating exchange rates, the impact effect of a net capital flow falls directly upon the spot exchange rate:[2] a capital outflow will tend to depreciate sterling, and an inflow to appreciate sterling. Moreover, any such change in the exchange rate acts upon the current account in the same way as a policy-induced parity change. Hence, a capital inflow which generates an appreciation also has the effect of discouraging exports, encouraging imports, and depressing the inflation rate. It should be clear, therefore, that large sudden capital flows can provide difficult policy problems for economies operating with floating exchange rates and, in the light of this, it is relevant to enquire if the UK authorities can exert any substantial influence over short-term capital flows. In the first instance, some restraint on UK residents would be obtained via exchange-control provisions which, until 1979, were a major element in UK policy. Following the abolition of exchange controls in October 1979, the capital and money markets of the UK became fully integrated with those of the rest of the world, and the main weapon for influencing capital flows is now the manipulation of domestic interest rates. This has already been discussed in some detail in sections 2.3 and 2.5. However, it is worth emphasizing here that an additional argument for exchange-rate target zones is that they help minimize some of the adverse effects on the economy which may result from movements in the exchange rate which are prompted by short-term capital

---

[1]   For a more detailed treatment see *Lindert and Kindleberger, op. cit.* Ch. 13 and Appendix 9.
[2]   Under certain circumstances, capital flows may also affect the money supply, even under floating exchange-rates. See 'External Flows and Broad Money', *BEQB*, December 1983.

flows and are not related to the underlying 'fundamental' performance
of the economy.

By far the most significant structural element influencing short-term capital movements since 1973 has been the changes in the price of oil. The
price increases of 1973 and 1979 created a massive capacity to lend by
the OPEC nations and the second price increase enhanced the desirability
of depositing surplus funds in sterling as a 'petrocurrency'. The lower oil
prices since 1985 have, to some extent, had the opposite effect. Between
1978 and 1985 the outstanding sterling obligations of the UK monetary
sector and other financial institutions to the overseas sector increased more
than fivefold, from £7.9bn to £40.8bn. Since the balance-of-payments surpluses of OPEC countries have evaporated, the share of oil-exporting countries in the sterling balances has fallen sharply, from 26% in 1981 to 14%
in 1988. Meanwhile, the shares of other countries have risen, particularly
that of other EC countries which amounted to 29% in 1988.

5   INTERNATIONAL ECONOMIC RELATIONS
5.1   The UK and the European Community (EC)

The UK became a full member of the EC along with Denmark and Ireland
in January 1973. The Labour government of 1974 declared its intention
to renegotiate the original terms of entry,[1] completed the renegotiations
in March 1975[2] and then settled the question in favour of membership
with a referendum in July 1975. Since then, the EC has been enlarged
to twelve countries with the entry of Greece (in January 1981) and Portugal
and Spain (in January 1986). In this section we shall concentrate chiefly
on balance-of-payments and exchange-rate implications of UK membership
of the EC; other implications are treated in Chapters 2 and 4 of this volume.

 Calculation of the economic costs and benefits to the UK of EC membership can be made under two heads. First are the 'static' gains and losses,
which themselves arise from two sources: the formation of a customs union
between the UK and other EC members with a common external tariff;
and the inter-country transfers which result from aspects of the Common
Agricultural Policy (CAP) and the Community budget. The second head
includes 'dynamic' gains and losses which may result from selling in a larger
market: allowing, for example, the exploitation of economies of scale in
production and consequent improvement in competitiveness. If the combined static and dynamic effects led to a deterioration in the balance of
payments, the UK would have to restore external balance, typically by
a combination of a depreciation in the exchange rate and cuts in public
spending or tax increases. These policies would impose a measurable real

[1] *Renegotiation of the Terms of Entry into the European Economic Community*, Cmnd.
5593 (April 1974).
[2] *Membership of The European Community: Report on Renegotiation*, Cmnd. 6003 (March
1975).

resource cost on the UK. The reverse would be true if entry were to produce an improvement in the balance of payments.

Calculations made at the time of pre-entry negotiations were virtually unanimous in finding that entry would impose a static balance-of-payments cost, probably of around 1% of GDP in the long run.[1] Acceptable estimates of dynamic gains or losses have not so far been made. In fact, the UK's relative economic position in the EC has not changed markedly since entry. Since 1972, per capita GDP in the UK has fluctuated between about 93% and 104% of the EC average. This does not, however, answer the question: Would this performance have been better or worse if the UK had not been an EC member. In practice, of course, the benefits of UK membership of the EC are also concerned with the political gains to the UK of being a member of a larger grouping of nations which gives individual countries a greater say in world affairs through EC membership than they would have individually. However, such political gains have also proved elusive until recently as the EC has been mired for almost a decade in a series of internal debates which centre, not surprisingly, on issues concerning the extent of income redistribution between member countries. Moreover, with the enlargement of the EC, it is only to be expected that agreement on detailed matters of economic policy will continue to prove difficult. During 1987 and 1988, however, there were signs that the Community has found some new life with partial agreements being reached on the thorny agricultural and budgetary disputes but more particularly with the planning for the so-called 'Single European Market' in 1992.

Implications of EC membership for UK trade: The effects of EC membership on the UK balance of payments can be considered under three headings: changes in the pattern of trade, adoption of the CAP, and contributions to the Community budget. The main implications for trade in manufactures follow from the customs union aspects of the Community. All tariffs on trade between the UK and other members were reduced to zero in 1977 when the UK adopted the final stages of the common external tariff (CET) on trade with non-Community countries. The discrimination which is now imposed against former Commonwealth countries (excluding signatories of the Lomé Convention)[2] and the associated loss of UK export preferences in the same countries must also be taken into account. We have already shown, in section 3.1, that the direction of UK trade in the 1950s and 1960s swung progressively toward Western Europe and away from traditional markets in North America and the OSA. It

---

[1] The 1970 White Paper (*Britain and the European Communities: An Economic Assessment*, Cmnd. 4289 (February 1970)) suggested a balance-of-payments cost ranging between £100m and £1.1bn per annum.
[2] For additional details of the Lomé Convention, which grants tariff preferences on exports to the EC of industrial products and some agricultural products from signatory developing countries, see C.H.Kirkpatrick, 'The Renegotiation of the Lomé Convention', *NWBQR*, May 1979, pp. 23–33.

is clear that entry into the EC accelerated this trend. Over the years 1963 to 1973, UK exports of manufactures to the EC increased at an average annual rate of 10.7%, while imports from the EC increased by 16.6%. Between 1973 and 1983, these average annual growth rates of trade in manufactures increased dramatically, with exports to the EC increasing by 21.1% and imports from the EC increasing by 19.1%. By 1987, it could be said that the EC's share of UK merchandise trade was about the same as the EC average share for trade with other member countries at between 50% and 55%.

For services, the EC generally forms a much smaller share of the UK's trade, accounting for 20% of UK private-sector service credits and 44% of debits in 1987, the higher figure for debits being almost completely accounted for by UK residents' foreign travel within the EC. A major factor underlying the services position is the existence of various regulatory and other non-tariff barriers of the kind discussed in section 3.3. Such barriers are particularly evident in the financial services sector where the UK might be expected to have a comparative advantage over many of the other member countries. These barriers may in part also account for the relatively low share of the EC in UK outward and inward direct investment until recently, which we noted in section 4.1. A major part of the proposals for a Single European Market involves the elimination through harmonization of the multifarious regulatory and non-tariff barriers to trade. It is recognized that financial services pose special problems in this respect, and, in June 1988, the EC Council of Ministers issued a directive aimed at liberalizing all capital movements within the Community by June 1990, with special transitional arrangements for Greece, Ireland, Portugal and Spain. In principle the directive has the implication that a resident of one EC member country will have unrestricted access to banking services, stock exchanges, real estate and all financial services in other EC countries. However, the directive includes a safeguard clause similar to but more circumscribed than that in the original Treaty of Rome to allow individual countries to impose capital controls for up to six months to prevent disturbances to foreign-exchange markets and the balance of payments. It is recognized that harmonization of regulatory rules for financial services is required prior to full implementation of the directive. Nevertheless, its implementation is likely to have a major impact both on capital flows and on trade in financial services, and may well complicate the smooth operation of the European Monetary System.

The Common Agricultural Policy (CAP): The CAP system of agricultural price support has generally been reckoned to be the main source of costs imposed on the UK by entry to the EC. The original purpose of the CAP was to increase farm incomes with the twin aims of preserving family farms and promoting rural industrialization. These are laudable goals, but they can be achieved in different ways. Three are worth mentioning: direct income payments to farmers; producer price support through deficiency payments (the pre-entry UK system); and general price support by variable import and export taxes (the CAP). A detailed discussion of the relative merits of these schemes can be found elsewhere.[1] However, it is generally recognized that, on strict efficiency grounds, direct income payments are typically superior as they involve the smallest 'deadweight' loss. In practice, governments throughout the world have intervened in agriculture with a variety of price support schemes.

Under its pre-entry deficiency payments system, the UK imported and consumed foodstuffs at world prices and subsidized (less efficient) UK farmers out of general taxation. Under the CAP, a set of common EC farm prices are agreed annually. The prices of imports from non-EC countries are then brought up to EC prices by a system of variable import taxes. Likewise, EC food exports receive a variable subsidy. The main economic differences between deficiency payments and the CAP are two in number. First, CAP taxes and subsidies impose a cost on more efficient non-EC producers. Such producers affected by UK entry consisted mainly of Commonwealth countries. This was recognized in the 1974–5 renegotiations, which produced a guarantee of continued access to the Community for Commonwealth sugar and New Zealand dairy produce. Second, EC consumers suffer a loss under the CAP through having to pay higher-than-world prices for their foodstuffs. Thus, as compared with deficiency payments, the CAP shifts the cost of price support from general taxation onto foreign producers and domestic consumers of foodstuffs. Given that the UK has a much smaller and mostly more efficient farm sector than other EC countries, it is easy to see why the UK should prefer a system of deficiency payments.

The exact cost of the CAP to the UK balance of payments and to EC consumers in general depends largely on the gap between EC prices and world market prices for foodstuffs, which varies over time. Since EC farm prices are set by an annual round of bargaining, they are far more stable over time than world prices. Agricultural price stability has often been regarded as a desirable goal in its own right, but recent theoretical work casts doubt on this view.[2] Moreover, the EC bargaining process is such that it has proven much easier to raise intervention prices than to lower them. The fundamental fact is that, over nearly two decades, EC intervention prices have almost always been above world market prices and often

---

[1] See T. Josling, 'The Common Agricultural Policy of the European Economic Community', *Journal of Agricultural Economics*, May 1969, pp. 175–91.
[2] For a comprehensive but difficult analysis of price stabilization schemes, see D. M. G. Newbery and J. E. Stiglitz, *The Theory of Commodity Price Stabilization* (Oxford University Press, 1981).

far above these prices.[1] The result has been substantial over-production of many commodities, much of which has had to be stockpiled, forming the notorious 'food mountains', the management of which imposes a further substantial burden on the Community. Food stocks on this large scale are wasteful and absurd.

Substantial problems in the administration of the CAP have also arisen because EC food prices are set in terms of units of account and then translated into the respective member currencies at representative exchange rates, the so-called 'green currencies', fixed by administrative decision.[2] Since 1971, spot-market exchange rates for EC currencies have diverged substantially from the green-currency rates, undermining the principle of common Community-wide prices for foodstuffs and creating profitable opportunities for arbitrage. To prevent this, border taxes and subsidies have been levied on agricultural trade between EC countries, the total amounts of subsidy involved being known as monetary compensation amounts (MCAs). The MCA system began as a temporary measure following the collapse of the par-value system in 1972. But it continued in effect until March 1984, when the EC agreed to phase out MCAs. However, this agreement left unsolved the problem of managing the CAP when exchange rates are flexible. A stable currency area provided by a widened European Monetary System could resolve this problem. The objection to this argument is that it is the structure of the CAP which is deficient; it would be ironic if the EMS were broadened and strengthened for the sole object of shoring up the CAP.

The scale of intervention implied by the EC's farm policy has become such that it has had and is continuing to have a major global impact both on the EC's own budget and on the overall structure of world trade. Between 1980 and 1988 world food prices in US$ terms actually declined by 4%,[3] compared to an increase in average EC retail prices over the same period of 70%. Intervention prices also increased very substantially relative to world food prices. The result is that expenditures on agriculture have absorbed over 70% of the Community's total budget during the 1980s, and in 1987, Community expenditures were only kept within total revenues, thus avoiding a situation of technical bankruptcy, by postponing expenditures for price support until 1988. As far as world trade is concerned,

---

[1]   In 1979–80, EC farm prices varied from 31% above the world level (sugar) to a staggering 311% above the world level (butter). Since 1980 the EC Commission has stopped publishing the information necessary to facilitate such comparisons. As world food prices have fallen during the 1980s one can only assume that the comparisons would simply be too embarrassing for the Community to contemplate publication.

[2]   For further discussion, consult R. W. Irving and H. A. Fern, *Green Money and The Common Agricultural Policy* (Wye College, Occasional Paper No. 2, 1975), and C. Mackel, 'Green Money and the Common Agricultural Policy', *NWBR*, February 1978. The values for the green currencies are published monthly in *Bulletin of the European Communities* (Secretariat General, Brussels). An excellent account of the CAP and the green-currency system is given in A. E. Buckwell *et al.*, *The Costs of the Common Agricultural Policy* (Croom Helm, 1982).

[3]   According to *The Economist* US$ food price index.

the primary impact of EC food surpluses has been to depress world food prices, thus reducing production incentives and incomes in non-EC food-producing countries.[1] In large part, these are poor developing countries, many of whom are highly dependent on a few key export crops and have no resources to protect their own producers of these crops. Since 1980, the major industrial countries led by the EC have become substantial net food exporters, with both the socialist bloc and the developing countries as a whole becoming net food importers. The situation will be exacerbated further in the near future as EC prices have their full impact on the production of Mediterranean foodstuffs by Spain and Portugal. It is sometimes argued that the CAP has contributed to an improvement in global 'food security' by increasing and stabilizing world food production levels. This is completely incorrect. The CAP has created food self-sufficiency in the EC, a very different concept from global food security. The low world prices resulting from the CAP have done substantial damage to the agriculture of developing countries and thus have contributed significantly to a decrease in global food security, reflected in the recurrence of famine conditions and malnutrition problems in these countries during the 1980s. It is true that the United States and Japan have also pursued protectionist policies towards their respective agricultures. Only in the EC, however, has agricultural protection been pursued on such a scale with over 90% of farm output now covered by the CAP. Overall, the record of events constitutes a damning indictment of EC agriculture policy, particularly over the last decade.

As long as the basic principles of the CAP are adhered to, the only options for reform are a sharp cut in EC support prices together with rules to link them more closely to subsequent changes in world food prices, and the imposition of limits on the amount of farm production which will receive support. Very little progress has been made in either direction. In general, the Community has been unable to agree on meaningful price cuts and has preferred instead, beginning in 1984, to rely on production quotas for sectors in surplus. Such quotas are only effective if backed up by sanctions against over-production and, so far, few effective sanctions have been imposed. Since 1980, the annual farm price reviews have consistently failed to produce meaningful reforms.[2] Following the budgetary crisis of 1987 the Council of Ministers agreed to a new package of farm and budgetary measures at the Brussels summit in February 1988. As far as agriculture is concerned, an overall ceiling was imposed on the growth in agricultural spending relative to the growth in the Community's GNP.

---

[1] For further discussion see M.J.Roarty, 'The Impact of the Common Agricultural Policy on Agricultural Trade and Development', *NWBQR*, February 1987 and J.Rosenblatt, T.Mayer, K.Bartholdy, D.Demekas, S.Gupta and L.Lipschitz, 'The Common Agricultural Policy of the European Community: Principles and Consequences', *IMF Occasional Paper*, No. 62, February 1988.
[2] See the 11th and earlier editions of this volume for a discussion of successive farm price reviews.

However, it is not clear how the ceiling will be enforced. The 'Co-responsibility levy', a 3% tax on cereal production introduced in 1986, was extended to allow for a supplementary levy if production quotas are exceeded. For the first time, automatic price cuts were agreed for a range of products notably cereals, when quotas are exceeded. In addition, a 'land set-aside' scheme was introduced to compensate farmers for withdrawing land from agricultural production. Finally, in a typically cosmetic 'reform', the cost of depreciating surplus farm stocks was transferred from the agriculture budget to the general budget of the Community. While all but the last measure can be said to represent some progress on CAP reform, it is clear that until more vigorous action is taken, the CAP will continue to absorb a high volume of resources in an extremely wasteful and damaging manner.

The Community budget: Contributions to and receipts from the Community budget by the UK each involves transfers of funds across the foreign exchanges and may in turn require compensating exchange-rate adjustments. The EC budget is financed from the 'own resources' of the Community, which consist of all import duties and agricultural levies from non-EC sources (less 10% to cover costs of collection and administration) plus a VAT contribution which in January 1986 was raised from 1% to 1.4% of the proceeds of a VAT levied on a uniform basis in the Community. The contribution to own resources is known as the 'gross contribution', the 'net contribution' being the gross contribution less receipts from the budget in the form of regional aid, agricultural support and the like. Summary data on the UK's gross and net contributions are given in table 3.8. For the UK, the fundamental problem is that structural features of the

TABLE 3.8

UK Payments to and Receipts from European Community Institutions[1] 1984–90 (£bn cash basis; UK fiscal year: April–March)

	1984/85 Actual	1987/88 Actual	1988/89	1989/90
			Estimated	Budget
Gross Payments	3.6	4.9	5.2	5.8
Public Sector Receipts	−1.9	−2.0	−2.5	−2.4
Agriculture	(−1.2)	(1.1)	(−1.6)	(−1.5)
Other[2]	(−0.7)	(−0.9)	(−0.9)	(−0.9)
Negotiated Refunds[3]	−0.6	−1.1	−1.6	−1.3
Net Contribution to EC Budget	1.1	1.8	1.1	2.1
Other Net Payments (or Receipts−)[4]	−0.1	−0.1	−0.1	−0.1
Net Payments to EC Institutions Excluding Foreign Aid	1.0	1.7	1.0	2.0

Source: The Government's Expenditure Plans 1989/90–1991/92, Chapter 3: 'Net Payments to European Community Institutions', Cmnd 603, January 1989, HMSO.
[1] Payments +/Receipts−
[2] Regional and Social Funds and Miscellaneous.
[3] Agreed Refund 1984/85. From 1985/86 the refund represents an agreed abatement of VAT contributions; see text for details.
[4] Includes contributions to The European Investment Bank and Coal and Steel Community.

economy mean that its net budget contribution will be large and positive for the foreseeable future. The fact that the UK remains relatively dependent on food imports from (more efficient) non-EC producers enhances her gross contribution, while the small size and greater efficiency of her agricultural sector mean that receipts from the agricultural funds are relatively small. At the same time, because CAP expenditure is so large relative to other expenditures, the UK cannot expect to receive significant compensating benefits from these other programmes.

Between 1980 and 1984, negotiations took place aimed at securing for the UK a special system of rebates. These culminated in agreement at the June 1984 Fontainebleau summit, which confirmed a series of cash rebates to the UK for the years 1980 to 1984. From 1985 onwards, the UK will receive annual cash rebates equivalent to 66% of the gap between UK VAT payments to the Community and EC expenditures in the UK, and these rebates will continue at least until a further increase in EC revenues, to 1.6% of member states' VAT income, is agreed. The UK's rebates are financed by other member states according to their relative shares of the EC's VAT income although, exceptionally, West Germany contributes two-thirds of its share.

Although the Fontainebleau summit effectively settled the matter of the UK's budgetary contribution for the foreseeable future, the agreement to increase overall budgetary contributions was immediately overtaken by the inexorable rise in farm spending which produced the budgetary crisis of 1987. The February 1988 Brussels agreement called for the introduction of a 'fourth resource' for EC revenues, with national contributions based on GNPs of member states. At the same time, a ceiling was placed on the size of the base used to calculate a country's VAT-related budget contribution. However, the major budgetary proposal involved a new formula for determining Community expenditures; these will now be subject to an overall ceiling of 1.2% of EC GNP. This will permit the budget to rise to an estimated ECU 52.7bn at 1988 prices in 1992 (equivalent to £34.2bn) compared with ECU 44.1bn in 1988, representing a 19.5% increase over the four years. In addition, it was agreed that 'structural funds' for general economic assistance to poorer regions of the EC would be sharply increased over the same period. These measures do not give much encouragement for the future. As at Fontainebleau, the principal measure is a substantial increase in expenditures the revenue burden of which will be borne largely by the new 'fourth resource'. The main positive feature of these changes is a move towards the use of 'objective indicators' to guide the expenditure and revenue contributions of member states. In principle, such indicators are analogous to those used by the IMF and World Bank since their inception to determine national contributions to those bodies. On the debit side, there are still no real signs of effective expenditure control measures, and thus no clear mechanism, other than further tortuous ministerial meetings, to ensure that the new ceilings on expenditures, including that for agriculture, will not be breached. The CAP will continue to absorb about two-thirds of the Community budget for the forseeable future and, until its reform is squarely faced, the EC will remain in the midst of an unending sequence of budgetary problems.

The European Monetary System (EMS): The origins of the EMS can be traced to the 1970 Werner Report, which proposed the achievement of a full monetary union within the European Community by 1980. Monetary union would involve the establishment of a single Community-wide currency issued by a Community central bank with powers to determine monetary policy throughout the EC. Moreover, since any national government can issue currency as a means of financing its own budget deficit, acceptance of a single EC currency would necessarily require a considerable measure of Community-wide agreement on (though not necessarily harmonization of) national *fiscal* policies as well as on national *monetary* policies. The timetable proposed by the Werner Report was abandoned almost immediately, but renewed impetus for monetary union was given by the April 1989 report of the Delors Committee, composed mainly of EC central bank governors, which proposed that all EC currencies should be inside the EMS no later than 1 July 1990 as the next stage on the road to full monetary union.

The case for monetary union in the EC is often presented as analogous to the case for having a common market in commodities. Creation of a single currency reduces transactions costs and promotes exchange and the division of labour which, it could be argued, is necessary if the benefits of the EC are to be fully realized by member countries. Furthermore, it can be argued that as EC members develop intensive trade and investment links with one another, then adoption of a single currency is the only foreign-exchange-market policy consistent with price stability. However, the costs of complete monetary unification may also be considerable. With a single currency throughout the EC, each country becomes a region within a larger currency area. A country in balance-of-payments deficit to the rest of the EC would have to adjust in much the same way as a region of the UK in deficit to the rest of the UK currently has to adjust. Since an exchange-rate change is ruled out, adjustment must be by a combination of domestic deflation and changes in regional taxes and subsidies. Within the EC, of course, the latter are largely ruled out for balance-of-payments purposes by the CET. In practice, the process of balance-of-payments adjustment by a region within a single currency area depends to a large extent on the monetary effects of a balance-of-payments imbalance. A deficit for example will generate flows of money out of the region, depressing demand and, ultimately, prices and wages within the region. The effectiveness of this process in restoring regional balance-of-payments equilibrium without a sustained regional recession depends to a large extent on the flexibility of wages and prices, and on the mobility of labour and capital between occupations and regions in response to changed profit opportunities. There is no reason why the optimal areas for separate currencies should coincide with the jurisdictions of existing nation states. However, there is no general agreement as to what does constitute an optimal currency area. Clearly a high degree of wage and price flexibility and of labour and capital mobility within the currency area are likely to be necessary conditions, but they may not be sufficient conditions for optimality. Certainly, it would be wishful to assume that the entire EC with its evolving membership has ever constituted an optimal currency area, although it seems clear that stable exchange rates among certain sub-groups of EC members (notably Germany and the Netherlands) do appear desirable.

Following the collapse of the par-value system in 1971, the first steps towards monetary co-operation in the EC were taken in April 1972 with the establishment of 'the Snake in the Tunnel', the name commonly given to the agreement to limit the margins of fluctuation between EC currencies to one-half the permitted 'Smithsonian' limits.[1] However, it was not until 1978, at the Bremen conference of the European Council of Ministers, that proposals for the EMS were considered, and the system itself finally came into existence on 13 March 1979. The EMS has as its objective the creation of greater monetary stability in the EC, and is generally seen as a key element in plans to improve the harmonization of national economic policies. It consists of an exchange-rate structure, an intervention mechanism based on the European Currency Unit (ECU), and a system of credits for financing payments imbalances between members called the European Monetary Co-operation Fund (EMCF).[2] The exchange-rate structure consists of a 'currency grid' within which each member's currency is assigned a central rate against other EC currencies, together with a permitted band of fluctuation of 2.25% either side of this central rate.[3] The central rates are not irrevocably fixed, but may be adjusted, or 'realigned', after consultation among EMS members, although clearly one of the aims of the EMS mechanisms is to protect member currencies against speculative attack, and thus prevent 'unnecessary' exchange rate adjustments. To this end, central banks are obliged to keep their currencies within the margins of

---

[1]   The snake represented the set of closely linked EC currencies which under the pressure of market forces, was free to move up and down relative to the dollar in the 'tunnel' defined by the exchange-rate limits (see section 5.2). The 'tunnel' disappeared in March 1973 when the EC currencies engaged in a joint float against the dollar.
[2]   Full details of the EMS mechanisms are given in Commission of the European Communities, *European Economy*, July 1979. A useful exposition is given in: 'Intervention Arrangements in the European Monetary System', *BEQB*, June 1979. The arguments for monetary integration are set out by the then President of the European Commission, R.Jenkins, in 'European Monetary Union', *LBR*, No. 127, January 1978.
[3]   Exceptionally, the Italian Lira is permitted margins of 6% around its central rate.

fluctuation but, in practice, this can create an asymmetric burden of obligation. The weak-currency country loses reserves and is always under pressure to adjust its internal policies to a greater extent than is the strong-currency country.

To try and eliminate this asymmetry, the EMS includes an ingenious intervention mechanism, the key to which is the ECU, a basket of EC currencies which acts as numeraire for the exchange-rate mechanism. The ECU is a composite currency containing specific amounts of the currencies of EC member states which are reviewed every five years. The composition of the ECU and the implied currency weights following the last review are given in table 3.9. Between reviews, actual currency weights will change

TABLE 3.9
EMS Exchange Rates

| | ECU central rates (currency units per ECU) Effective 12 January 1987 | Composition of the ECU: | |
| | | Effective 17 September 1984 | |
		currency amounts	percentage currency weights
Belgian franc	42.4582	3.71	8.2
Danish krone	7.85212	0.219	2.7
Deutschmark	2.05853	0.719	32.1
French franc	6.90403	1.31	19.1
Irish punt	0.769411	0.00871	1.2
Italian lira	1,483.58	140.00	10.1
Luxembourg franc	42.4582	0.14	0.3
Netherlands guilder	2.31943	0.256	10.2
Greek drachma	150.792	1.15	1.3
UK pound	0.739615	0.0878	14.9

Source: EC Commission.

because of exchange-rate movements, particularly after realignments within the EMS. At present the ECU consists of ten currencies, although the UK pound and Greek Drachma do not participate in the EMS exchange-rate mechanism. At the next review in September 1989, the Spanish Peseta and Portuguese Escudo will be eligible for inclusion in the ECU.

The intervention mechanism is based on the currency grid exchange rates which constitute a set of central rates for each currency. When a currency reaches 2.25% above or below its central rate, the central banks of the strongest and weakest currencies are obliged to intervene and can call on financing from the EMCF for this purpose. However, other actions are triggered before intervention becomes obligatory. Around each country's central rate, a divergence threshold is defined whereby a currency may not diverge from its central ECU rate by more than three-quarters of its divergence rate.[1] The point of these restrictions is that, in general, a currency will reach its divergence threshold before it reaches any of the bilateral intervention limits defined by the currency grid, and, once this occurs, there is a presumption that consultation will be initiated with *all* Community members to decide upon intervention policy, possible changes in central parities and any necessary internal policy measures. These procedures were strengthened in September 1987 when, among other measures, it was agreed that non-mandatory intervention within the 2.25% limits could also be financed by drawings on the EMCF subject to the quota restrictions on individual countries' drawings from the fund. Although the onus is on the country whose currency is divergent to alter its policies, the divergent currency could be either depreciating or appreciating. Thus, it is hoped, burdens of adjustment will be more equally shared within the Community and the asymmetries of bilateral intervention avoided.

Table 3.9 shows EMS exchange rates as of 12 January 1987, the date of the last realignment of member currencies at the time of writing. From the establishment of the EMS to 12 January 1987, there have been 11 realignments of member currencies, involving a total of 38 changes in the exchange rates of individual EEC currencies *vis-à-vis* the ECU. Of these changes, 15 were devaluations and 23 revaluations. This is in sharp contrast to the experience of the world as a whole during the Bretton Woods era, when virtually all individual exchange-rate changes were devaluations, generally precipitated by the weight of external pressures. Thus, on the basis of this admittedly crude statistic, the EMS must be judged at least a partial success in initiating a more equitable sharing of the burden of adjustment between deficit and surplus countries.

Besides acting as numeraire in the EMS, the ECU has an important role as an instrument of settlement between Community central banks and ultimately as the planned reserve asset of the Community. Member countries deposit 20% of their gold and gross dollar reserves with the EMCF on a three-month renegotiable basis, and in return have access to a variety of credit facilities, to the total value of 25bn ECU, to finance payments

---

[1] The maximum range of divergence for each currency is determined by $\pm 2.25\,(1 - w_i)$ %, where w_i is the weight of that currency in the value of the ECU basket. When a currency diverges from its central rate it also pulls the value of the ECU with it to some extent. The adjustment $(1 - w_i)$ reflects this fact and ensures that the divergence range reflects deviations of a currency from other individual currencies in the ECU basket. An adjustment is also made for the wider margins specially applicable to Italy and for the fact that sterling and the drachma, while components of the ECU, are not participants in the EMS adjustment mechanism. Any divergence of these currencies in excess of 2.25% is excluded when the value of the ECU is calculated for the purposes of the divergence indicator. The notional weight of sterling in the ECU is currently 14.9%, giving a notional divergence range of $\pm 1.91\%$ for sterling against the ECU. The divergence threshold for sterling would be 75% of this, or $\pm 1.44\%$.

imbalances within the Community and to support the currency grid.[1] Of this total, 14bn ECU has been allocated to short-term monetary support and the remainder to medium-term credit facilities.

Although the UK participated fully in the setting up of the EMS, and contributes to the ECU credit arrangements, it has thus far declined to join the exchange-rate mechanism of the EMS. At the time of the establishment of the EMS, academic and government opinion in the UK was almost universally hostile to the idea.[2] Drawing on the apparent lessons from the collapse of the par-value system, it was widely agreed that the substantial disparities of economic performance within the EC made it unwise to fix exchange parities within the narrow limits set by the currency grid and the divergence indicators. Other factors which appeared to weigh specifically against UK membership included the possibility that oil-price changes would pose unacceptable strains on the EMS because of the divergence of interest between the UK as an oil exporter and other EEC countries as oil importers. In addition, there was a potential conflict between the Medium Term Financial Strategy (MTFS), which emphasized the money supply as an intermediate policy target, and the EMS, which emphasized the exchange rate as an intermediate target. To date, these and other arguments have mitigated against UK membership.

It now seems clear, however, that the actual experience of the EMS as well as other factors have forced a reappraisal of the position of many commentators *vis-à-vis* UK membership. First, there is some very tentative evidence that EMS membership may have contributed to greater stability of member countries' exchange rates and may therefore have promoted some convergence of economic policies and performance within the system. The obverse of this is that there has been considerable dissatisfaction in the UK at the relative volatility of the sterling exchange rate.[3] The two specific concerns of North Sea oil and the MTFS also seem less important. As oil production declines there is the prospect of a continued steady depreciation of sterling in the coming years. Likewise, and as noted in sections 2.4 and 2.5, the MTFS has increasingly become an exchange-rate

---

[1] The gold contribution is valued at the average London fixing price during the six months prior to valuation, and the dollar portion is valued at the market rate of the two working days prior to valuation.

[2] For a preliminary evaluation of the EMS, see 'The European Monetary System', *NIER*, February 1979, pp. 5–12. Official viewpoints are contained in HC (1978–79) 60: *First Report of the Expenditure Committee*, 1978–79, para. 15; and in *The European Monetary System*, Cmnd. 7405, November 1978. See also previous editions of this book.

[3] On all these issues see HC (1984–85), 57–IV, *Thirteenth Report from the Treasury and Civil Service Committee*, 1984–85. While the Select Committee came down against UK membership of the EMS, it clearly felt that the balance of argument had moved towards membership since the previous Select Committee report on the subject. A more recent appraisal of the EMS is given in M.J.Artis, 'The European Monetary System: An Evaluation', *University of Manchester Discussion Paper*, no. 57, 1988. See also, H.Ungerer, O.Evans, T.Mayer and P.Young, *The European Monetary System: Recent Developments*, IMF Occasional Paper No. 48, 1986. For an analysis of exchange-rate variability, see 'The Variability of Exchange-Rates: Measurement and Effects', *BEQB*, September 1984.

strategy as much as a money-supply strategy. The authorities are, in practice, already committed to a more active management of the exchange rate than was the case in the early 1980s.

Perhaps the most important factor is that it is now clear that there is a major difference between currency unification, the ostensible long-term aim of the EMS, and relative exchange-rate stability, which appears to be a practical short-term implication of the system as it is currently operated. Any move towards currency unification clearly requires far-reaching changes in the sovereignty of each nation's monetary and fiscal policies, which may be neither practicable nor desirable. As argued in section 2.5, however, there are some strong arguments for greater stability of exchange rates and there are equally powerful arguments suggesting small but useful gains from the co-ordination of international economic policy-making.[1] These considerations may suggest the desirability of UK membership of the EMS in the not-too-distant future, and as called for in the Delors Committee Report.[2]

The Single European Market (SEM): Probably the major concern of the EC over the next few years will be the programme aimed at creating the SEM by 1992. This programme has its origins in proposals made in 1985 by the now President of the European Commission, Jacques Delors, and subsequently set out in more detail in a Commission White Paper published in June 1985.[3] The creation of a single European market was, of course, one of the central aims of the EC embodied in the Treaty of Rome. Internal tariffs on industrial goods were largely eliminated by 1977, but there remain numerous obstacles to trade within the community. First, in the industrial sector, individual countries have adopted numerous special arrangements to protect their own industries, the Multifibre Arrangement being one example of a set of formal agreements. Second, the agricultural sector remains subject to internal restrictions because of the complexities of the CAP. The White Paper, however, focused on other restrictions, notably the kind of non-tariff barriers highlighted in section 3.3. Four in particular were singled out. First are inter-country differences in technical regulations and quality standards. Second are frontier delays and administrative burdens imposed on goods in transit. Third are restrictions on competition for public-sector contracts, which in practice favour home-country firms. Fourth are restrictions on trade in services, particularly financial services, which inhibit firms from setting up in other EC countries.

The White Paper sets out a comprehensive programme of liberalization

---

[1] For a non-technical exposition of the issues involved, see M.J.Artis and S.Ostry, 'International Economic Policy Co-ordination', *Chatham House Papers No. 30*, Royal Institute of International Affairs, 1986.

[2] For an analysis of the arguments for and against UK entry see M.J.Artis and M.H.Miller, 'On Joining The EMS', *MBR*, Winter 1986.

[3] 'Completing the Internal Market', White Paper from the Commission to the European Council, COM(85) 310 final, 28 and 29 June 1985.

measures (300 in all) which are required for completion of the SEM, with a timetable calling for full implementation by 1992, which in practice means that most of the proposed measures have to be in place well before 1992. The liberalization programme consists of three main components: the removal of physical barriers to movements of goods and people; the removal of technical barriers covering quality standards, public procurement, and regulation; and finally the removal of fiscal barriers. These proposals would, if implemented, involve major changes in the organization of the EC economies. Differential technical and quality standards are pervasive throughout the EC. The Commission's proposals imply, for example, that goods produced to a certain standard in one EC country could not be denied importation by another EC member on grounds of different standards. Likewise, the college degrees and other professional qualifications earned in one EC country would be accepted for all recognized purposes in other EC countries. Fiscal harmonization is implied by the free movement of goods and services. VAT rates, in particular, differ widely within the Community. At present EC countries impose border restrictions to prevent tax avoidance by limiting the importation of tax-paid goods purchased in other EC countries. If border checks are abolished, such restrictions cannot be enforced and in the absence of VAT harmonization, consumers will have an incentive to cross frontiers to purchase goods, especially high-value consumer durables, in the low-tax countries of the Community. An analogy is often drawn with the United States where different states maintain different sales tax rates but, to prevent tax avoidance, differences in rates between contiguous states have to be relatively small – no more than about 5%. This is in contrast to the EC where VAT rates vary from zero on selected items in the UK up to 38% on various consumer durables in Italy. The Commission proposed a set of uniform rates for 1992 with the standard rate between 14–20% and a reduced rate for an agreed list of basic items of 4–9%. Member states would be free to choose their VAT rates within these bands. Comparable proposals were made for excise duties. The changes proposed are relatively small in magnitude but they clearly raise more directly the question of the fiscal autonomy of individual states. Movement towards a single market logically implies some loss of national sovereignty which, in the final analysis, may not prove acceptable to individual EC members.

Nevertheless, progress towards the SEM has been more rapid than would have appeared possible in 1985. Several reasons can be advanced for this. First, the Single European Act (SEA) ratified by member governments in 1985 and coming into effect on 1 July 1987 represented the most significant amendment so far to the Treaty of Rome. The SEA not only codifies the main principles of the SEM in the form of legislation passed in all member countries, but it also makes some significant changes to the decision-making procedures within the Council of Ministers, involving a reduction in the blocking powers of individual members and a greater reliance on majority voting. Moreover, about two-thirds of the measures proposed by the Commission for the SEM are covered by these new arrangements. Second, in addition to the activities of the Commission in promoting the SEM, the 1988 Brussels agreement, despite its unsatisfactory nature, nevertheless represented a measure of progress on budgetary and agricultural matters and enabled member states to turn their attention to the SEM. Third, the Commission produced a major study of the costs and benefits of the creation of the SEM (the Cecchini Report).[1] This argued that considerable benefits would flow from the completion of the internal market: between ECU 70bn and ECU 190bn of static welfare gains, equivalent to between $2\frac{1}{2}\%$ and $6\frac{1}{2}\%$ of the EC's 1988 GDP; an increase in the potential growth rate of the Community by about 1% pa; the creation of some 2 million additional jobs in the Community; and a fall in consumer prices of as much as 6%.

These considerations have given a considerable impetus to the move towards the SEM and it seems clear that by 1992 the Community will enjoy a freer flow of goods, services, labour, and capital than before. However, it also seems likely that liberalization will be less than originally envisaged by the Commission. First, the economic arguments for liberalization are subject to a wide margin of error. In principle, it is clear that the standard arguments for freer trade are applicable to the SEM and benefits are likely to flow therefrom.[2] However, there are many areas in which unrestricted trade is recognized to be not the best option. Financial services are a case in point where some degree of regulation is desirable to ensure that consumers can make an informed choice among the services on offer and also to help prevent or to minimize the costs of bankruptcy if the management of a financial institution is either incompetent or incurs excessive risks in its investment policies. The costs of inappropriate liberalization in such areas are difficult to measure but are nevertheless real, and the Commission's calculations do not take them into account. The second factor likely to slow progress towards the SEM is that EC governments have so far been reluctant to give up any degree of sovereignty over their national affairs and it is clear that full implementation of the SEM will involve a greater loss of national sovereignty in certain key areas than has hitherto been conceded. As yet it is too early to say how complete will be the implementation of the SEM, but it is already clear that movement towards

[1] A version of the report intended for the general reader was published as P.Cecchini (ed.), *The European Challenge 1992: The Benefits of a Single Market* (Gower Press, 1988). A more technical report containing detailed economic analysis was published as 'The Economics of 1992: An Assessment of the Potential Economic Effects of Completing the Internal Market of the European Communities', in *European Economy*, No. 35, March 1988. Reports commissioned on individual sectors were published in a sixteen volume series by the EC entitled *Research on the Cost of Non-Europe*. Finally, the May 1988 (No. 36) issue of *European Economy*, is given over to a report on 'The Creation of a European Financial Area', which concentrates in particular on the implications of free movement of capital and financial services within the EC.
[2] A few independent studies have broadly confirmed the qualitative direction of the Cecchini report's findings but not necessarily its quantitative estimates. See for example L.A.Winters, *Completing The European Internal Market*, CEPR Discussion Paper No. 222.

the SEM has provided a major impetus to greater integration in the Community both in the private and the public sectors.

5.2   The International Monetary System

The International Monetary Fund: If the quarter-century from 1945 had one dominant characteristic in the international economic arena, it was the integration of national commodity and capital markets into a unified and rapidly growing system of world trade and investment. A key role in this process was played by the international financial rules established at the Bretton Woods conference of 1944, the supervisory institution of which is the International Monetary Fund (IMF). The principal features of the Bretton Woods system were its emphasis on international co-operation and its creation of a system of fixed but adjustable exchange rates, the Par Value System, together with the provision of temporary and conditional balance-of-payments finance by the IMF to assist the adjustment process. Under the Par Value System the world as a whole, and industrial countries in particular, enjoyed a period of unprecedented expansion in trade and prosperity. Nevertheless, the system itself was subject to increasing strain culminating in August 1971, when the US Government announced that the US dollar was no longer convertible into gold.[1] In June 1972 the pound sterling was floated and, by April 1973, the exchange rates of all the major currencies were floating independently of their par values. Since then, the world has been operating a system of relatively flexible exchange rates.

Throughout the post-war era the IMF has remained at the centre of the international monetary system with its role being progressively modified during the seventies and eighties following the abandonment of the par-value system. During this process, the IMF has acquired a number of the functions of a putative world central bank, but it would be a considerable exaggeration to claim that the IMF does actually act as a world central bank. Although the IMF's role of supervising par-value adjustments effectively disappeared after 1971, subsequent events proved that international co-operation on monetary and exchange-rate matters was, if anything, more important under flexible exchange rates than under the par-value system, and the IMF was able to act as the forum through which discussions furthering international monetary co-operation could take place. Thus, after a period of hiatus in the early seventies, the IMF has re-emerged as the central body in the international monetary system albeit with a modified role as compared with the Bretton Woods era.

As of end-1988, the IMF consisted of 151 member countries including all the industrialized and developing nations of the world and an increasing

---

[1]   For a detailed analysis of the par value system see, in particular, the tenth and eleventh editions of this volume.

number of socialist bloc countries, including China but excluding most notably the Soviet Union.[1] The basis for a good deal of Fund activity, including, in particular, country voting rights and amounts of IMF loans for which a country is eligible, is the quota of each country in the Fund. This is expressed in Special Drawing Rights (SDRs), a composite currency discussed more fully below, and it constitutes the country's subscription to the IMF, the total of all subscriptions being equivalent to the capital of the IMF. The relative size of each country's quota is determined largely by an objective formula based on indicators such as population, GNP, and role in world trade, but also to some extent by a process of bargaining among member countries. Quota sizes and formulae are reviewed every five years when the overall size of the IMF's capital is also reviewed. The last quinquennial review which was adopted in March 1983 called for an over-all 47.5% increase in quotas from SDR 61.1bn to SDR 90bn[2] and this was fully subscribed by 20 April 1984. Each country's quota must be subscribed 25% in SDRs and the remaining 75% in the member country's own currency.

There are three major aspects to the IMF's work namely: the provision of an international reserve currency, the SDR; the provision of a variety of lending facilities to assist countries in balance-of-payments difficulties; and the provision of a forum for debate on international monetary matters with its concomitant mechanisms for surveillance of the international monetary policies and practices pursued by member states.

Special Drawing Rights (SDRs):   SDRs are a composite international currency created in 1970, and analogous to but predating the ECU. The total allocation of SDRs is reviewed by the IMF on a regular but not a prescribed basis, and the allocation is increased as agreement is reached by IMF members on the need for an expansion in this particular source of supply of international liquidity. Thus far, there have been six SDR allocations totalling SDR 21.4bn, the most recent being in January 1981, since when a number of unsuccessful attempts have been made to reach agreement on a seventh allocation. Each country is assigned a net cumulative allocation of SDRs, in proportion to its allocation in the general account of the IMF, and can treat this allocation as 'owned reserves' to finance payments imbalances. A country in deficit, for example, may use its SDR quota to purchase needed foreign exchange from other countries. Use of SDRs was initially subject to several restrictions, of which the most important was the reconstitution requirement, that a country's average holding over a period of five years must not fall below 30% of its net cumulative allocation.

The fundamental question surrounding the SDR has always been that of whether SDRs simply co-exist with other reserve assets or whether they are destined to replace gold and foreign exchange, or both, as the reserve

---

[1]   For full details on the IMF the reader should consult the annual 'Supplement on the Fund' published each September in the *IMF Survey*.
[2]   SDR1 = £0.7395 at end-March 1983.

base of the system. In the initial arrangements, SDRs were effectively a gold substitute and carried a notional rate of interest on net holdings of 1.5%. Since the abandonment of the par-value system, however, the arrangements for SDRs have been progressively revised to extend the range of transactions for which they could be used. From 1981, the SDR interest rate was set at an average of short-term interest rates in the financial centres of the five countries with the largest SDR holdings, and its valuation was based on a basket of the currencies of the same five countries.[1] From 1 May 1981, the reconstitution requirement was eliminated, and with effect from the Seventh General Increase in Quotas in 1980, members now contribute 25% of their additional quota in SDRs. Finally, a multitude of developments have taken place, extending the right to hold SDRs to non-member organizations and legalizing the use of SDRs for currency swaps and forward transactions.[2]

Despite these developments aimed at enhancing the status of SDRs, the fact remains that SDRs only accounted for 4% of total world reserves (excluding gold) at end-1988. The main mechanism proposed for enhancing the role of the SDR is the introduction of a Substitution Account at the IMF, in which members would deposit currency reserves in return for SDRs. Thus far, however, little progress has been made with this idea.[3] Unless the Substitution Account or any similar idea is implemented, the SDR is likely to continue to play a relatively minor role in international monetary affairs, other than as a convenient international unit of account. Indeed, in the last two decades, the growth in reserves has generated periodic fears of there being excess liquidity rather than a shortage. Between end-1979 and end-1988 world international reserves (valued in SDRs and excluding gold) increased at an average rate of 9% per annum. In relation to world imports, however, the increase was much less. The reserves–imports ratio for the world as a whole has fluctuated about an average of around 23% since 1979, although it rose sharply in 1987 to 30%. Nevertheless, the failure of Fund members to agree on a new SDR allocation since 1981, despite the urgings of the IMF itself, indicates that fears of excess liquidity and its role as a possible cause of world inflation are still uppermost in the minds of national governments, particularly in the major industrial countries.

IMF lending facilities: Lending facilities provide the framework within which the IMF provides assistance to countries in balance-of-payments deficit. Underlying this assistance is the fundamental principle of conditionality, which simply means that in providing assistance the IMF must be assured that countries are pursuing policies consistent with the provisions

---

[1] For details, see the article, 'The New Method of Valuing Special Drawing Rights', *BEQB*, September 1974, and *IMF Annual Report*, 1981.
[2] IMF *Annual Report*, 1988. The total number of prescribed 'other holders' is currently 16.
[3] Cf. 'The Proposed Substitution Account in the IMF', *MBR*, Winter 1979, and P.B. Kenen, 'The Analytics of a Substitution Account', *Banca Nazionale del Lavoro*, Quarterly Review, December 1981.

of the Fund's Articles of Agreement. These policies have often provoked controversy in borrowing countries for being unduly restrictive. However, it must be remembered that IMF assistance is intended primarily to be relatively short term, repayable within three to five years except as discussed below, and the elimination of a balance-of-payments deficit within this or any other period necessarily involves a cut in national expenditures relative to national income and hence some fall in the domestic standard of living.

As well as involving conditionality, Fund lending is provided in tranches expressed as percentages of the size of a member's quota, which thus governs the amount of borrowing a country may have outstanding at any time. In the so-called reserve tranche, members are entitled to draw up to 25% of their quota automatically without incurring any conditionality. Further drawings incur different degrees of conditionality depending both on the amounts involved and the facility under which they are drawn. Under the Fund's credit tranche policies, members can borrow successive amounts in tranches of 25% of quota up to a cumulative maximum of 100% of quota. Countries may also borrow under the IMF's buffer stock facility, which helps finance contributions to an approved international buffer stock, and under its Compensatory and Contingency Financing Facility (CCFF), which was expanded in 1988 to provide special assistance to countries pursuing Fund-supported programmes in addition to its previous function of providing loans to countries in compensation for shortfalls in export revenues and/or excesses in the cost of cereal imports.

Until 1971, these four arrangements constituted the entire range of Fund lending facilities. The collapse of the Bretton Woods system and advent of world-wide floating exchange rates did not, however, alleviate the need for IMF lending facilities, as exchange rates have been actively managed by central banks around the world. During the seventies, the world economy was subject to a number of major shocks, notably the 1973 and 1979 oil price increases, which meant that balance-of-payments imbalances were larger and more prolonged in the seventies than in the sixties, with a concomitant need for additional temporary balance-of-payments financing. In response to these events as well as to intensive arguments on the part of developing countries, a range of additional lending facilities aimed at providing greater sums of money as well as making it available over a longer period than five years was developed. Arrangements which may be mentioned under this heading include the Oil Facility, set up to assist with adjustments after the 1973 oil price shock and since wound up; the Extended Fund Facility (EFF), and the Enlarged Access Policy (EAP), each of which has as its aim the provision of assistance for programmes of structural change with repayments being made over ten years (EFF) or seven years (EAP). In addition, the Structural Adjustment Facility and Enhanced Structural Adjustment Facility were created to provide, in conjunction with the World Bank, lending over a ten-year period to especially low-income countries to support programmes of balance-of-payments and structural adjustment, the distinguishing feature of these two facilities being that loans are made available on special concessional terms. Of equal importance has been the increased levels of Fund quotas, which raises the base on which assistance is given under the tranche policies and other facilities.

International monetary surveillance and co-operation: The collapse of the par-value system set in train a series of reviews of the international monetary system, the early results of which were largely overtaken by events following in particular on the 1973 oil price rise. Subsequently it was recognized that a return to the par-value system was infeasible and probably undesirable, and discussions were aimed at establishing 'orderly', but flexible, exchange-rate mechanisms. These culminated in the Second Amendment to the Articles of Agreement of the IMF in April 1978.

Without doubt, the most fundamental element in the Second Amendment is the amendment to Article 4 of the IMF Agreement. The main points of this Article are as follows:[1] (i) a general return to stable but adjustable par values can take place with the support of an 85% majority in the IMF; (ii) such par values may not be expressed in terms of gold or other currencies but can be expressed in terms of SDRs, the margins of fluctuation around par values remaining at ±2.25%; (iii) with the concurrence of the IMF, any country may abandon its par value and adopt a floating exchange rate; (iv) the exchange-rate management of a floating currency must be subject to IMF surveillance and must not be conducted so as to disadvantage other countries; (v) the agreed practices with respect to floating rates will operate until such time as a general return to par values is attained. In effect, these changes legitimize floating exchange rates within the framework of the IMF system and without any diminution of the powers of the IMF. A second aspect of the Second Amendment dealt with the relative positions of SDRs and gold. We have commented above on the attempts to enhance the reserve status of the SDR; the associated measures to demonetize gold were equally significant. In particular, the official price of gold was abolished and members were no longer allowed to use gold to make their general quota contributions. Furthermore, members were again allowed to trade in gold at free-market prices.

Although the reforms embodied in the Second Amendment constitute substantial progress in setting a framework for the orderly management of flexible exchange rates, they nevertheless left unresolved many of the practical issues concerned with exchange-rate management. Since 1978, there have been large swings in nominal exchange rates, well in excess of those which might be predicted by reference to purchasing-power parity, imperfect indicator though that may be. The volatility of capital flows at a time when capital restrictions in the UK and Japan were relaxed, the

---

[1] The text of Article IV is contained in the 19 January 1976 issue of *IMF Survey*, pp. 20–21. Full details of the Revised Articles of Agreement may be found in *The Second Amendment to the Articles of Agreement of the International Monetary Fund*, Cmnd. 6705 (HMSO, 1977).

differing success of governments in controlling inflation, the structural problems induced by the OPEC cartel, and nominal interest-rate structures which have not reflected inflationary expectations, no doubt have each played a role in the appreciation and subsequent decline in the US dollar since 1980. The IMF response to such volatility has been to emphasize the role of surveillance with the purpose of identifying unwelcome economic developments, including exchange-rate practices, which arise from inappropriate economic policies such as fiscal and monetary measures or exchange-market intervention. At the same time, under the auspices of the IMF, a number of ministerial committees have emerged to provide a basis for consultation and co-ordination at a more senior level than is possible at the regular meetings of the IMF's own executive board. Six such committees are now in existence, the oldest being the Group of Ten, formed in 1962 in connection with the establishment of the General Arrangements to Borrow (GAB) which provide a formal mechanism for the Fund to augment its resources through borrowing. The GAB have been used on nine occasions and were renewed most recently through December 1993. The Group of 24, formed in 1972, represents the developing countries in negotiations on international monetary matters. The interim and development committees were formed in 1974 to advise the Fund respectively on matters dealing with disturbances to the international monetary system, and on resource transfers to developing countries. However, of most importance in recent years have probably been the Group of 5 (G-5) and the Group of 7 (G-7). The G-5 consists of the countries whose currencies constitute the SDR: France, West Germany, Japan, the UK and the USA. Since an initial agreement in September 1985 (the so-called 'Plaza Agreement'), these countries' ministers have periodically agreed to engage in co-ordinated intervention, initially to reduce and subsequently to stabilize the value of the dollar. Of equal importance is the G-7, which consists of the G-5 together with Canada and Italy and whose heads of state have now evolved a regular pattern of annual 'economic summit' meetings. At the most recent of these, in June 1988, the G-7 agreed that stabilization of the dollar was desirable in the near term, implying neither an appreciation nor a depreciation, and periodic interventions have subsequently occurred with central banks aiming to prevent undue movements of the currency in the 'wrong' direction.

While it may be true that greater co-ordination is desirable, it remains unclear how effective co-ordination has thus far been, as it has largely been confined to intervention policy. As we have seen, exchange rates are more fundamentally determined by monetary and fiscal policy and any attempt to stabilize exchange rates at a level inconsistent with underlying policies is likely to prove expensive and futile for central banks. In this connection, it is clear that the US budget deficit has been a major cause of relatively high US interest rates which in turn have helped raise the value of the dollar. However, although the G-7 has had extensive discussions on national budgetary and interest-rate policy, very little positive action has yet emerged from these discussions.[1] In the near future, there seems to be little alternative to a regular round of consultations with the aim of minimizing excessive fluctuations in exchange rates. While the experience of the EMS has shown that greater stability of exchange rates is achievable, arguably this has been achieved as much through the relative 'similarity' of the economies concerned as through any great increase in co-ordination, and it is not clear that the lessons of the EMS could be applied on a global scale.

5.3 World Debt and Bank Lending

A considerable degree of concern has been expressed in recent years over a further consequence of the oil price shocks, namely the implications for the international debt structure of less developed countries (LDCs) and the associated risks of an international banking crisis. It should be remembered, at the outset, that the efficient allocation of resources on a world scale will generally require international lending and borrowing. Countries with a surplus of savings will find it advantageous to lend to countries with a savings deficiency through the medium of international capital flows. In the postwar world, the major savings-deficient nations have, of course, been the LDCs. The conditions for the international flow of capital to be sustainable are essentially twofold: the borrowing must be used to build up productive capacity in the debtor nation, with a gross rate of return on investment at least equal to the gross cost of borrowing; and the debtor country must be in a position to earn the foreign exchange required to service and repay the debt. Indeed, it is possible to identify for any country a set of circumstances which determines its capacity to accumulate external debt in a sustainable fashion. The simplest index of this capacity is measured by a ratio of foreign debt to gross domestic product. It may be shown that this sustainable ratio will be higher the greater the ratio of the trade surplus to national product, the greater the rate of growth of national product, and the lower the gross interest and amortization cost of borrowing. A country which is developing rapidly will enjoy a higher equilibrium debt-income ratio, and its total debt can increase over time at the rate of growth of income without any fear of insolvency.[2] The picture is complicated slightly by capital-market imperfections, which mean that the interest rate at which any country can borrow is likely to rise with the debt : income

---

[1] For an evaluation of how the effectiveness of policy co-ordination depends on the underlying structure of the economy see for example, R. van der Ploeg, 'International Interdependence and Policy Co-Ordination in Economics with Real and Nominal Wage Rigidity', Centre for Labour Economics Discussion Paper no. 986, September 1987.

[2] Thus, for example, a country exporting (net) 10% of its output, growing at 3% per annum and paying 10% gross on its foreign debt, would have a sustainable debt:income ratio of 2.85. Throughout the 1970s, the actual debt:income ratio of non-oil LDCs fluctuated between the values of one and five. The original statement of this condition is contained in E. Domar, *Essays on the Theory of Economic Growth* (Oxford, 1957), Chapter 6.

ratio, so that a country enjoying a higher elasticity of supply of finance will, *ceteris paribus*, enjoy a higher equilibrium debt : income ratio. It is important to remember that sustainable debt: income ratios will be as varied as the circumstances which determine the respective country's international credit rating, capacity to generate a net export surplus and rate of economic growth.

One final point concerning the foreign debt mechanism is worth noting before we turn to the events of the 1970s. This concerns the potential volatility of actual debt : income ratios. The problem is that when the actual debt : income ratio of a country diverges from the equilibrium value, a process of cumulative divergence is set in train, so driving the debt : income ratio further from the equilibrium level unless corrective action is taken. For example, a reduction in net exports below the level required to service the current debt : income ratio requires recourse to further foreign borrowing to meet the foreign-exchange shortfall.[1] The increase in borrowing adds to the servicing burden and creates the need for even greater borrowing, and so the process of cumulative divergence is reinforced. Conversely, the effects of an improvement in the net export position will permit a cumulative contraction of debt. Of course, in practice, such movements are likely to be halted by remedial structural changes but, nevertheless, debt : income ratios are likely to show significant short-term instability.

We turn now to the practical implications of this analysis. Throughout the postwar period to 1970, the LDCs had been net importers of foreign capital obtained primarily through direct foreign investment, official aid and official credits transferred through institutions such as the World Bank. The total foreign debt of LDCs increased against the backcloth of steadily expanding world trade and production, without servicing problems apart from those associated with export earnings instability in selected countries. The oil-price shocks of 1974 and 1979 changed this situation rather drastically, creating a rapid growth in LDC debt and simultaneously reducing their capacity to borrow in a sustainable fashion. For non-oil LDCs as a whole, the ratio of outstanding debt to exports rose from 1.15 in 1973 to 1.40 in 1982, with a particularly sharp rise occurring after 1979. However, the aggregate figures conceal the extent to which external debt is concentrated among a relatively small number of borrowers. Taking the twenty largest borrowers (accounting for 85% of total debt to private creditors in 1982 but only 50% of non-oil LDC exports), we find the ratio of debt to exports rising from 1.50 in 1973 to 2.00 in 1982.[2] The connection with the oil-price increase has both demand and supply aspects. On the demand

---

[1] We exclude here any temporary respite gained by drawing upon foreign-exchange reserves. For most LDCs, this option is of negligible importance. Instability depends upon the gross interest rate exceeding the growth rate of income in the LDCs. The average interest rate on total LDC debt averaged 6% in 1976–9 but rose to 10.25% in 1981. The median growth rates in non-oil LDCs are 5% and 3% for the same two periods. Cf. IMF, *World Economic Outlook* (1983), Appendix B, table 2.
[2] IMF, *Annual Report* (1983), p. 32.

side, the oil-price shock had two adverse effects on the LDCs: it directly increased oil import bills, and indirectly reduced export revenues as the effect of the oil-price-induced recession in the industrialized countries worked its way through to lower export volumes and worsening terms of trade. In these circumstances, rapid structural adjustment was not to be expected, and between 1979 and 1982 the non-oil LDCs accumulated trade deficits of $257bn and current-account deficits of $344bn. By contrast, the corresponding figures for the industrial countries were $136bn and $50bn respectively. The associated increase in demand to borrow was readily satisfied due to supply-side changes in international credit markets which involved an increasing role for commercial banks in the industrial countries. BIS figures show that the gross foreign liabilities of commercial banks within the reporting area increased sixty-fold between 1973 and 1979, and that an increasing proportion of the lending was in the form of short-term 'roll-over' credits often with a floating interest rate. In 1982, some 30% of non-oil LDC borrowing was of this nature. The pressures for commercial banks to lend to LDCs are not difficult to identify. The recession reduced the demand for credit within the industrial countries at the same time as their banking systems were receiving large flows of funds from the OPEC producers. Profit-seeking commercial banks were more than willing to lend to credit-worthy LDCs on competitive terms which appeared to minimize risks, for each bank taken by itself.

The denouement came in 1982, as the full effects of the decline in sustainable debt : income ratios became clear. The combination of world recession (world trade volume fell by 2.3% in 1982) and high interest rates on commercial loans put an increasing number of LDCs in a position in which they could not meet the repayment schedules on a debt burden which was increasingly sensitive to short-term changes in interest rates. In quick succession, a small number of major borrowers, such as Mexico and Brazil, and for different reasons, Poland, announced their inability to meet immediate obligations. This naturally raised questions that bankers, in general, would prefer not to be asked. Was default a possibility? If so, would any commercial bank find that bad debts exhausted its capital resources? Indeed so, for some banks found themselves with such debts amounting to 1.5 to 2 times their capital reserves. Would the appropriate national central bank act as lender of last resort in order to prevent a cumulative collapse in the credit structure, and what role might the IMF play in supporting this delicate situation?

At this stage it seems reasonable to report that the danger of a collapse in the international capital market has passed, although this has not resulted from any one major policy initiative. A variety of initiatives have been proposed, notably the Baker initiative in October 1985 and more recently in March 1989 an initiative by US Treasury Secretary Nicholas Brady. These and other proposals called for a variety of co-ordinated measures to ease the debt problems of LDCs concentrating in particular on improving policy-making mechanisms in these countries, to restore confidence, and on the joint use of IMF, World Bank, and private sources to increase the flow of resources to the LDCs. In practice, such initiatives have been less effective than the spur of imminent default on commercial bank thinking on the one hand, and the threat of exclusion from world capital markets on the thinking of LDC policy-makers on the other. The first has obliged the banks to consider more fully and more imaginatively a variety of re-scheduling arrangements. Such arrangements have included the extension of repayments, swaps of debt for equity, and the sale of claims in the open market at deep discounts, thus reducing the exposure of individual banks. Beginning in 1987, banks with large exposures to third-world debt substantially increased their contingency reserves, thus effectively writing off a part of the debt. As far as the LDCs themselves are concerned, there has been a greater recognition that external borrowings need to be associated with viable investment projects and not merely used to underpin a balance of payments deficit. Thus there has been a steady increase in the amount of borrowings from the IMF under Stand-by arrangements typically requiring some adjustments in economic policies, but also associated with a more substantial flow of resources from private and official lenders in the form of new lending and rescheduling of existing debt. Increasingly, such reschedulings have been characterized by the so-called 'menu' approach in which creditors and debtors are brought together under the auspices of the IMF or World Bank and offered a range of options for rescheduling.[1]

However, undoubtedly the major factor altering the overall debt picture was the sharp fall in oil prices during 1986 and their subsequent stabilization at lower levels than before. Overall this was a positive development, not least because it provided a spur to renewing economic growth in the world as a whole. Moreover, it considerably alleviated the position of the vast majority of LDCs with Brazil, for example, estimated to benefit to the extent of US$4bn per annum or 29% of imports from a $15 oil price.[2] However, the situation in certain oil-exporting countries, notably Nigeria, Mexico and Venezuela, was seriously exacerbated as a result of these developments. Even so, this could not be regarded as an unqualified disaster in that it soon became apparent that attention had to be focused on debt restructuring packages for such countries to avoid the adverse consequences of full default. Nevertheless, there is little room for complacency in the present situation. Net resource flows to LDCs dropped sharply after 1982 primarily because of a decline in private lending and a virtual secession of short-term export credit flows. The gap cannot be filled by the IMF which, despite almost trebling its outstanding lendings between 1981 and 1988 has, nevertheless, never during this time, accounted for more than 4% of the total reported external borrowings of LDCs. Although the situa-

---

[1]   See K.P. Regling, 'New Financing Approaches in the Debt Strategy', *FD*, March 1988.
[2]   For a more detailed discussion see G. Bird, 'Oil Prices and Debt', *RBSR*, No. 154, June 1987.

tion of the world banking system has eased, the overall position has if anything deteriorated, a significant indicator in this respect being a rapid growth in arrears of payments to the IMF which in the past has successfully established the position of being 'first-in-line' for repayment. It seems clear that a substantial increase in official lending is required to stave off a further deterioration in the position, as private banks have proved increasingly and perhaps understandably unwilling to increase or even renew their commitments to LDCs since 1982. In this respect, the recent Brady initiative may be useful as, for the first time in recent years, the USA indicated that it was willing to consider a substantial increase in IMF quotas, which is a necessary condition to allow the Fund to play a larger role in debt restructuring.

Nevertheless, the arithmetic is such that the IMF and World Bank can only act primarily as catalysts to provide a lending and a policy framework within which to exhort the governments of the industrial world to increase their own foreign assistance and, equally pertinently, to reform their trade practices which inhibit the expansion of many LDC economies. The comprehensive dismantling of the CAP would represent a significant contribution in this respect. In the absence of such measures, the medium-term outlook for many LDCs remains very bleak, with the prospect of continuing low economic growth and a seemingly endless struggle to reduce high debt-service ratios.

Exchange Rates, Last Working Day of December 1988

	£	$	DM	Yen	SDR	ECU
per £	–	1.80	3.20	225.91	1.33	1.54
per $	0.55	–	1.77	124.95	0.74	0.85

Source: BEQB, FS.

REFERENCES AND FURTHER READING

V. Argy, *The Post-War Money Crisis: An Analysis* (Allen and Unwin, 1981).

O. J. Blanchard, R. Dornbusch and R. Layard (eds), *Restoring Europe's Prosperity* (MIT Press, 1986).

Sir Alec Cairncross (ed.), *Britain's Economic Prospects Reconsidered* (Allen and Unwin, 1971).

R. E. Caves and Associates, *Britain's Economic Prospects* (Brookings Institution and Allen and Unwin, 1968).

R. E. Caves and L. B. Krause (eds), *Britain's Economic Performance* (Brookings Institution, 1980).

P. E. Cecchini (ed.), *The European Challenge 1992 – The Benefits of A Single Market* (Gower Press, 1988).

W.M.Corden, *The Theory of Protection* (Oxford University Press, 1971).

W.M.Corden, *Trade Policy and Economic Welfare* (Oxford University Press, 1974).

D.Greenaway (ed.), *Current Issues in International Trade: Theory and Policy* (Macmillan, 1986).

R.B.Johnston, *The Economics of The Euro-Market* (Macmillan, 1983).

P.R.Krugman (ed.), *Strategic Trade Policy and the New International Economics* (MIT Press, 1987).

P.H.Lindert and C.P.Kindleberger, *International Economics* (7th edition, Irwin, 1982).

R.MacDonald, *Floating Exchange Rates: Theories and Evidence* (Unwin Hyman, 1988).

R.L.Major, *Britain's Trade and Exchange Rate Policy* (Heinemann, 1979).

R.L.Miller and J.B.Wood, *Exchange Control For Ever?* (Institute of Economic Affairs, London, 1979).

J.Pinder (ed.), *The Economics of Europe* (Charles Knight, 1971).

B.Tew, *The Evolution of The International Monetary System 1945–77* (Hutchinson, 1977).

Official Publications

Bank of England Quarterly Bulletin

Central Statistical Office, *Economic Trends*, HMSO (regular analysis of balance of payments in March, June, September and December issues)

Central Statistical Office, *Monthly Digest of Statistics*, HMSO (especially for detailed up-to-date trade statistics)

Central Statistical Office, *The United Kingdom Balance of Payments* (The Pink Book), HMSO (indispensable annual reference for balance of payments data)

Commission of the European Communities, *European Economy*, Brussels (quarterly)

Department of Trade and Industry, *British Business* (weekly)

IMF *Annual Report*, and IMF *Survey* (twice monthly)

4

Industry

Malcolm Sawyer

1   INTRODUCTION

This chapter is concerned with the production of goods and services. It considers the role of different types of industry (i.e. primary, secondary and tertiary), the scale and operation of firms and then in the second part the type of policies which governments have adopted towards firms and industries.

The purpose of the first part of this chapter is to describe some important features of the industrial landscape. The descriptions are written to bring out features which are regarded as important for the perspective of theories on how industrialized economies work. The first section considers the composition of output and employment across different sectors of the economy. The reasons for this consideration include the view that different sectors display quite different productivity trends and make substantially different contributions to exports and to the balance of trade. Thus a changing composition of output and employment would have implications for the growth of productivity and for the balance of trade. The second section considers the size of firms, the extent to which industries are dominated by a few firms and the operation of multinational enterprises. Economic theory suggests that industries with a large number of small firms (atomistic competition) will perform in ways which are different as compared with industries with a few large firms (oligopoly and monopoly). The growth of multinational enterprises raises another range of issues from those of national sovereignty to the possible benefits of investment and technical innovation flowing from multinational enterprises.

2   COMPOSITION OF OUTPUT AND EMPLOYMENT

We begin by considering the composition of output and employment between different major sectors of the economy. Figure 4.1 provides some indication of the relative size of the three sectors (primary, secondary and tertiary) and some sub-sectors in 1967, 1977 and 1987.

The primary sector consists of industries which produce raw materials (e.g. minerals, crops), and encompasses agriculture, forestry and fishing (which for brevity will be hereafter referred to as agriculture), and the extraction of minerals and oil. The historic trend has been that of decline of the primary sector. For example, in Britain, agriculture accounted for

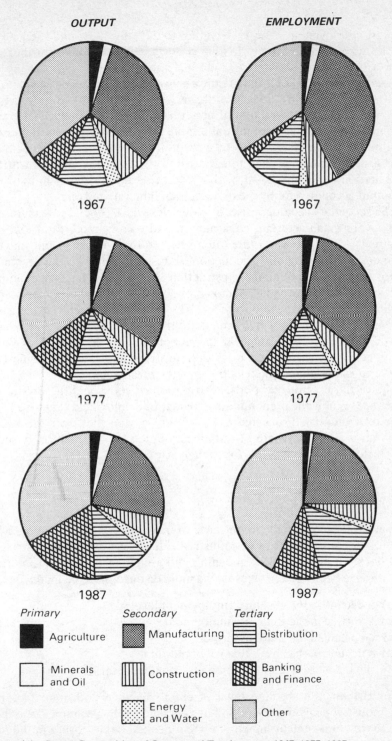

Figure 4.1   Sector Composition of Output and Employment, 1967, 1977, 1987.
(*Source:* Calculated from *United Kingdom National Income Accounts, DEG.*)

36% of employment in 1801, declining to 22% by 1851, and then to 9% by the turn of the century. In this century, there has been further and almost continuous decline to around 2% in the 1980s. This decline can be seen as still continuing in agriculture despite its already low share: from 1967 to 1987 the share of agriculture in total production was halved from 3.2% to 1.6%. The extraction of minerals and oils has similarly generally declined, with employment in coal mining falling from near three-quarters of a million in the late forties to well under 100,000 in the late eighties. This general trend has been temporarily reversed in the eighties with the exploitation of North Sea oil, with a slight rise in the eighties in the share of output accounted for by the extraction of minerals and oil.

The secondary sector consists of industries which process raw materials, and covers manufacturing, construction and energy production (gas and electricity). This sector is quite often referred to as industry, and statistics on industrial production ('production' industries) relate to the secondary sector plus mining but minus construction. In the early stages of economic development, the secondary sector grows rapidly, with the primary sector declining in relative importance. The secondary sector ('industry') accounted for 43% of employment in 1851, 46% by 1901, and peaked at 46% in 1966. The decline in the importance of the secondary sector has generally been referred to as de-industrialization, though sometimes that term is used to include only the manufacturing sector.

The tertiary sector covers the distribution of goods and the production of services is now the predominant provider of employment (and to a lesser degree of output). From figure 4.1 it can be seen that over the twenty years up to 1987 the share of output accounted for by the tertiary sector rose by ten percentage points to reach nearly 63½% by 1987.

2.1   De-industrialization

The general decline in the importance of manufacturing and the secondary sector is often described as de-industrialization. The term de-industrialization does not have a precise meaning and a number of different interpretations have been used. However, the main distinctions to be made are:

(a) a decline in the absolute employment level
(b) a decline in the share of employment
(c) a decline in the share of output
(d) a decline in the absolute level of output in
    the industrial sector (or often just in manufacturing).

For Britain, the absolute level of employment in both manufacturing and 'industry' peaked in 1966, and has been generally declining since then. The share of manufacturing employment peaked rather earlier in the mid-fifties at 36% in 1955, and stayed close to that level until 1966 (when it was 35%) but then declined significantly to reach 31% by 1979 and 23%

in 1988. The share of output accounted for by manufacturing has declined substantially in the past 20 years (cf. figure 4.1). And more remarkably, as will be seen below, there has been no upward trend in the level of manufacturing output since 1973.

These trends for British industry raise the question of whether they are of any significance. It could be (and is) argued by some that it is an inevitable accompaniment of economic development and growth. As the agricultural sector declined (especially in terms of employment) with the growth of the secondary sector, so now the secondary sector (especially manufacturing) declines as the composition of demand shifts away (in relative terms) from goods to services. In recent years, the advent of North Sea oil (and gas) would contribute to this trend (though as North Sea oil declines in importance this aspect would be expected to operate in reverse). North Sea oil affects the size of the secondary sector in two ways. First, it is obviously the case that if one sub-sector (here North Sea oil) grows rapidly then other sectors will thereby decline in relative importance. Second, North Sea oil tends to raise the sterling exchange rate (cf. chapter 3), which makes British exports more expensive (and imports cheaper). Since (as will be seen below) the secondary sector is much more heavily involved in international trade than the tertiary sector, the exchange rate is likely to have a greater impact on the secondary sector than on the tertiary sector.

The argument that the decline in the secondary sector arises from the virtually inevitable shift of demand from the goods produced by that sector to the services of the tertiary sector can be examined in (at least) two ways. The first is to make some international comparisons. The argument here would be that if the decline in the secondary sector is inevitable, then it would be expected to afflict most if not all developed economies. Whereas in relative terms, *manufacturing* employment peaked in UK in 1955, it peaked rather later in most other countries, for example in 1970 in Germany. However, over the decade to 1983, the share of employment accounted for by manufacturing declined in virtually all advanced capitalist economies.[1,2]

The second way is to consider the composition of demand rather than of supply. The share of manufacturing output may decline for a variety of reasons. It may be, as suggested above, that the (relative) demand for manufactured products declines whilst the (relative) demand for services increases. There are, however, at least two other reasons. First, (as will be seen below) productivity tends to increase faster in manufacturing than elsewhere in the economy. This would mean that (relative) employment would tend to decline in manufacturing as employment would grow more

[1] The information in these paragraphs is taken from R.E.Rowthorn and J.Wells, *De-Industrialization and Foreign Trade* (Cambridge University Press, 1987).
[2] Of nineteen countries on which Rowthorn and Wells report, the share of manufacturing employment rose in only three small economies (Finland, Iceland and New Zealand).

slowly (or decline more rapidly) in manufacturing than elsewhere for any given growth of output. Further, the relative price of manufactured products would be expected to decline to reflect the faster growth of labour productivity. The share of manufactured products is given by $p_M \cdot M/$ $(p_M \cdot M + p_R \cdot R)$ where p_M is price of manufactured products and p_R are other prices, and the output of manufactured products is M and of other goods and services, R. The fall in the relative price of manufactured products (p_M/p_R) would, *ceteris paribus*, lead to a fall in the share of manufactured products.[1]

Second, the data used refer to the domestic output of manufactured goods. The domestic demand for manufactured goods is split between domestic and foreign supply, and domestic output supplies both domestic demand and exports. Thus it is possible that a (relative) decline in the output of manufactured goods represents a combination of a shift in the composition of demand away from British-made goods to foreign-made goods, and a failure of British manufactured industry to meet the demand. The move from a surplus to a deficit on international trade in manufactures, discussed below, would be consistent with this view.

Whilst many countries have experienced a decline in the relative importance of manufacturing, the British experience of a failure of manufacturing output to grow to any significant extent since 1973 is unusual. Over the period 1973–86, the growth of manufacturing net output averaged -0.6% per annum, compared with a rate of 3.0% in the period 1960–73. In contrast, the growth of manufacturing output in the OECD area averaged 2.3% over the period 1973–86 (much lower than the average rate of 6.1% over the period 1960–73).[2]

Concern over the size of the British manufacturing sector has arisen in two particular ways. The first relates to the rate of productivity growth in the secondary sector compared with the rate elsewhere in the economy (which is dominated by growth of productivity in the tertiary sector). The basic argument is that production in many service industries is labour-intensive and the substitution of capital equipment for labour and technological change would be difficult to implement. Thus service industries would tend to display low (or even zero) rates of growth of productivity. In contrast, manufacturing and other production industries can benefit from technological change, from the exploitation of economies of scale and from the substitution of capital equipment for labour. All of these features aid productivity growth.

Some relevant statistics are given in table 4.1. These clearly indicate that distribution, hotels, repairs and catering have a productivity record much below those of the other sectors. It could be expected that these industries are ones in which the arguments of the previous sector relating to the service sector would particularly apply. Thus as the relative size

---

[1]   For further discussion and evidence see Rowthorn and Wells, *op. cit.*, Appendix 3.
[2]   Data taken from OECD, *Historical Statistics, 1960–1986*.

TABLE 4.1

Productivity Statistics: Trend growth of output per (full-time equivalent) person employed (annual rates)

	1971–85	*1979–85*
All industries and services	1.79	2.38
Manufacturing	2.19	4.73
Distribution, hotels, repairs and catering	−0.03	0.82
Transport	1.72	3.05
Communications	3.47	3.44
Banking, finance and insurance	2.57	2.81

Source: D.G.Mayes, 'Does Manufacturing Matter?', *NIER*, no. 122, November 1987 (based on unpublished work by A.Murfin).

of the service sector increases, it would be expected that the average growth rate of productivity would decline. This may be an inevitable consequence of a change in the composition of demand away from manufactured goods towards services.

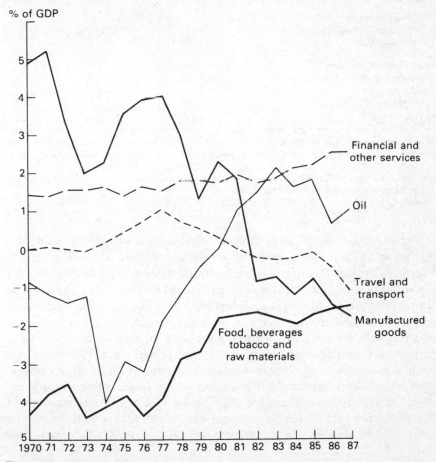

Figure 4.2   Net Trade Balance (expressed as per cent of GDP) by type of commodity, 1970–1987. (*Source:* Calculated from *United Kingdom Balance of Payments* (The CSO *Pink Book*).)

TABLE 4.2

International Trade Statistics

	1977	1982	1987
Exports			
Share (%) of:			
Food, beverage and tobacco	5.0	5.4	5.1
Basic materials	2.3	1.9	2.1
Oil	4.8	15.4	8.1
Semi-manufactures	23.0	19.1	20.9
Finished manufactures	36.0	32.0	35.5
Services	26.8	24.2	26.1
Imports			
Share (%) of:			
Food, beverage and tobacco	12.7	9.6	8.3
Basic materials	8.3	5.0	4.4
Oil	11.5	10.4	5.2
Semi-manufactures	19.8	19.1	21.4
Finished manufactures	26.4	32.4	39.4
Services	20.2	21.9	20.0
Net balance (£m) in:			
Food, beverage and tobacco	−3,212	−2,585	−3,799
Basic materials	−2,536	−2,041	−2,722
Oil	−2,815	+4,118	+2,944
Semi-manufactures	+1,510	+ 999	−1,579
Finished manufactures	+4,364	+1,280	−5,911
Services	+3,037	+2,762	+5,638
Goods and services	+ 713	+4,980	−4,524
Current Account Balance	− 150	+4,685	−2,504

Notes: Services include financial services, tourism. Figures in first two parts do not sum to 100% because of rounding and from the omission of a category not classified. Net balance is positive if exports exceed imports, negative otherwise. Total balance also includes the net balance of a not classified category. Current account balance also includes transfers, net receipts of interest, dividends and profits.

Source: Calculated from *United Kingdom Balance of Payments 1988* (The CSO *Pink Book*).

The second concern arises from the international trade implications,[1] and some of these can be seen by reference to figure 4.2 and table 4.2. Figure 4.2 traces the net balance on trade (exports minus imports) for a number of categories measured relative to GDP since 1970. The position shown in figure 4.2 for the seventies is indicative of the general experience of Britain up to that time. Deficits on foods, basic materials and oil were offset by surpluses on manufactured goods and services (of which financial services are an important element). In the period since 1970 there has been a general tendency for a decline in the deficit on food, beverages, tobacco and basic materials. The impact of the quadrupling of the price of oil in late 1973 on the oil deficit can be clearly seen as can that of the exploitation of North Sea oil and gas, which meant that during the 1980s Britain has gained a balance of trade surplus on oil. The emergence

---

[1] For a full discussion see House of Lords, *Report from the Select Committee on Overseas Trade*, HL 238 (HMSO, 1985).

of a deficit on travel and transport is a reflection of, *inter alia*, the growth of overseas holidays and the decline of the British merchant navy. There has been some upward trend in the surplus on trade in financial and other services.

The importance of the manufacturing sector arises, in part, from its importance in international trade, which is reflected in table 4.2. It can be seen that manufactures accounted (in 1987) for over 56% of exports but also nearly 61% of imports. Thus the significance of manufacturing is much larger in international trade than it is in national output. Since it is likely, given climatic and geological conditions, that Britain will remain a net importer of primary products then it would follow that to achieve a balance on the current account Britain would have to run a surplus on the combined manufactured goods and invisible items account.

However, the main concern has been over the steady decline in the net balance on manufactured goods during the eighties. The surplus on trade in manufactured goods averaged the equivalent of 3.4% of GDP during the seventies. As the House of Lords Select Committee on Overseas Trade noted, 1983 was the first year in which Britain had run a deficit on trade in manufactured goods.[1] Since 1983 the deficit on manufactured goods has tended to widen.

The optimistic interpretation of this deterioration of the manufacturing net balance is that it is the other side of the coin of the emergence of a net surplus on oil. In so far as foreign trade has to be in balance, then the surplus on one part of the trade account will have to be balanced by deficits elsewhere.[2] On this basis, a trade surplus on manufactured goods will re-emerge as production of oil declines. This will come about through some adjustment of the exchange rate and by the movement of resources back into manufacturing industry as they are released from oil production.

The pessimistic interpretation is that there is a fundamental weakness in British manufacturing such that it is unable to compete successfully in international markets. It can be noted that the net deficit on manufactures is not simply the obverse of a surplus on oil in that there has been a trend during the second half of the eighties particularly for the current account balance to deteriorate. In 1987 the current account deficit had reached £4½bn, and at the time of writing was estimated to have been over £14bn in 1988 and forecast to be around the same level or larger in 1989.

Britain was the first country to industrialize and for much of the nineteenth century was the leading industrial nation. But by the end of the nineteenth century, its decline relative to other industrial countries had begun with competition being felt in industries such as textiles, chemicals and iron and steel from other countries notably Germany and the United

---

[1] House of Lords, *ibid.*
[2] As the United States experience during the eighties has shown, it may be possible to run a trade deficit for many years with an inflow of capital required to balance the trade deficit.

States. But it was only in the 1960s that the extent of the relative decline became fully apparent as one country after another overtook Britain in terms of living standards. Indeed during the long post-war boom lasting into the early 1970s many industrialized countries grew at around twice the rate of Britain (with the notable exception of the United States).

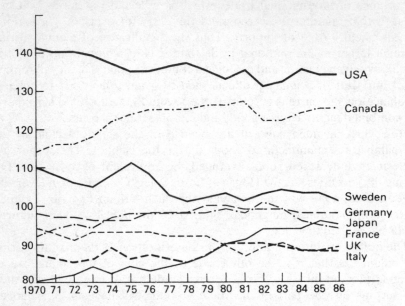

Figure 4.3   Comparison of International Living Standards, 1970–1986. GDP per head in purchasing power parity terms (OECD average = 100).
(*Source:* OECD *National Accounts 1960–1986.*)

Figure 4.3 provides some information on relative living standards (as measured by GDP per capita) since 1970 for a range of industrialized countries. For each year, the OECD average is taken as 100. There figures refer to purchasing power parity exchange rate calculations. This means that differences in the level of prices between countries have been taken into account.[1] The figures underlying figure 4.3 suggest that the relative decline of Britain's living standards has continued through the 1970s and into the 1980s.

Since the failure of the British economy to match the growth performance of other industrialized countries became apparent in the early 1960s, successive governments have tried a wide range of economic and industrial policies to seek to reverse the trend. The present government has loudly proclaimed that it has indeed succeeded in reversing the trend. A full con-

---

[1]   It can be seen from figure 4.3 that the GDP per head in Japan in 1986 on the purchasing power parity basis was below the OECD average and was just over 70% of the USA level. The gap between Japan and the USA in GDP per head terms when actual exchange rates are used is much less. Indeed it has been estimated that on this basis Japan overtook the USA in 1988.

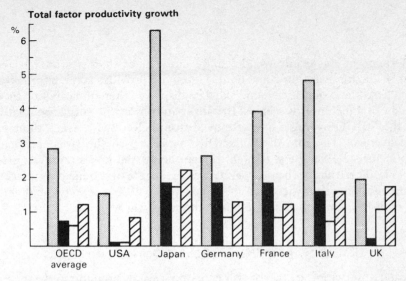

Total factor productivity growth

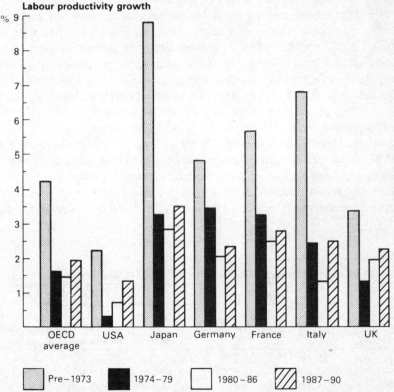

Labour productivity growth

Pre–1973   1974–79   1980–86   1987–90

Figure 4.4 Productivity Trends in Selected Countries (business sector, compound annual growth rates).

Notes: The pre-1973 period differs across countries and the starting year varies from 1960 to 1964. Data for 1987 to 1990 are OECD estimates and projections.

Total factor productivity is real gross value added at factor cost divided by total factor inputs (at 1985 weights). Labour productivity is real gross value added divided by private sector employment including self-employed.

OECD average is weighted average of 19 countries (including six reported here) based on 1985 business sector output at 1985 prices and exchange rates.

Source: OECD, *Economic Outlook*, December 1988, Table 20.

sideration of this claim would require more space than is available, and our discussion is rather condensed. Figure 4.4 provides some information which may help our discussion. The data displayed there indicate that there has been some improvement of Britain's productivity performance relative to the OECD average, having moved from below the average to above the average. The rate of productivity increase (whether total factor or labour) since 1980 does, though, remain below the levels achieved prior to 1973. There has been a sharper decline in the rate of productivity increase in many other countries than in Britain (since 1973), thereby leading to an improvement in Britain's relative productivity growth record.

3   FIRM SIZE AND INDUSTRIAL CONCENTRATION

Casual observation of the British economy reveals an enormous range in the size of firms, from one-person businesses through to firms employing over 50,000 people. Some idea of the range of size of firms can be seen from table 4.3, which relates to manufacturing industries only. Firms employing less than 200 workers have sometimes been defined as small firms. On that definition, nearly 128,000 small firms employed nearly one and a half million workers in manufacturing industries in 1986, amounting to over 30% of total employment. At the other end of the scale, four firms employed over 50,000 workers with an average of over 70,000 employees. Firms employing over 7,500 workers, of which there were 114 in 1986, employed almost as many workers as the small firms. Over the past decade there appears to have been a substantial growth in small firms with an increase of around 40,000 firms recorded, and an increase in the share of employment in manufacturing industries of seven percentage points.

TABLE 4.3

Size Distribution of Enterprises in Manufacturing Industries, 1978 and 1986

Size of enterprises (employees)	1978		1986		
	Number of enterprises	Share of employment (%)	Number of enterprises	Number of establishments	Share of employment (%)
1– 99	84,518	17.4	125,503	129,656	24.0
100– 199	2,650	5.5	2,239	3,561	6.5
200– 499	1,578	7.3	1,449	3,217	9.4
500– 999	619	6.5	508	1,787	7.4
1,000– 4,999	590	18.8	430	3,761	17.9
5,000–19,999	142	19.5	94	2,479	18.8
over 20,000	37	25.1	20	1,313	16.1

Source: Calculated from *Census of Production*, 1978, 1986.

It would be expected that the typical size of firms in an industry would be strongly influenced by the cost conditions under which that industry operates. When there are substantial economies of scale, then it would be expected that there would be a few large firms (since small firms would be at a significant cost disadvantage *vis-à-vis* large firms). Conversely, when there are diseconomies of scale, then a predominance of small firms would be expected.

The theory of perfect competition assumes a large number of firms each of which is a price-taker and free entry into the industry concerned. The profit-maximization condition under perfect competition is the equality between price and marginal cost. The theory of monopoly refers to an industry dominated by one firm where there are substantial difficulties facing new entrants into the industry. The profit maximizing condition here is marginal revenue equal to marginal cost, which can be rewritten as:

$$p \cdot (1 - 1/e) = m.c.$$

where p is price, e is the elasticity of demand and $m.c.$ is marginal cost.[1] This yields a price of $p = (e/e - 1) \cdot m.c.$, which implies that price would be higher (relative to marginal cost) under a situation of monopoly than under a situation of perfect competition. We return later to this comparison of perfect competition and monopoly with a discussion of its policy implications. For our purposes here it is sufficient to note that this view suggests that the structure of an industry is of some significance. The structure of an industry would include the number of firms in an industry, the inequality of size amongst those firms, and the ease or difficulty of entry into the industry.

One purpose of measuring industrial concentration is to have some idea of where along the spectrum between perfect competition and monopoly an industry lies. A low level of concentration would indicate the atomistic competition end of the spectrum and a high level the monopoly end. There are numerous measures of industrial concentration which can be used.[2] The simplest, and the one which is used here, is the *n*-firm concentration ratio. This is the share of the largest *n* firms in the industry concerned. The value of *n* is generally determined by data availability rather than any indication from economic theory. In the case of table 4.3 below, the value of *n* is five. The share of the largest *n* firms can be measured in a variety of ways, e.g. in terms of sales, employment, capital stock. Since the concentration ratio is intended to reflect market power within a product market, the use of sales would appear the 'natural' variable to use, but once again data availability often forces the choice.

---

[1] The profit-maximization condition is marginal revenue equal to marginal cost. The marginal revenue, $\Delta(pq)/\Delta q$ where Δ signifies a small change, which can be expanded as $p \cdot q/q + p$. This can be written as $p \cdot (1 + \Delta p \cdot q/\Delta q \cdot p)$ which is equal to $p \cdot (1 - 1/e)$. Hence $p \cdot (1 - 1/e) = m.c.$

[2] For further discussion of measures of concentration, see L. Hannah and J. Kay, *Concentration in Modern Industry* (Macmillan, 1977) and M. Sawyer, *The Economics of Industries and Firms* (Croom Helm, 1985), Chapter 3.

Concentration can be reported at the industry (or market) level[1] and at the aggregate level. The discussion above linking concentration measures to the perfect competition/monopoly spectrum would suggest that the industry (market) level would be the appropriate one. But a large firm typically operates in a range of industries, which may enable it to co-ordinate decisions across a range of industries. Concern over the centralization of decision-making in an economy (e.g. over prices, investment, employment) leads to measuring aggregate concentration.

Table 4.4 provides some statistics on the level of concentration in manufacturing industries in 1986. In view of the increasing importance of the tertiary sector it is regrettable that recent statistics are not available for that sector.

The statistics given in table 4.4 refer to the group level (sometimes referred to as the three digit level). On this basis, the manufacturing sector has 105 industries (of which data are available on 102). Even so, these industries may be too broad for our purposes and contain a number of separate markets (industries). For example, one of these industries is soap and toilet preparations, which covers products such as soaps, soap powder, shampoos, toothpaste etc. It could reasonably be argued that a lower level of aggregation would be more appropriate so that, for example, the market for soaps would be treated separately from that of toothpaste.

TABLE 4.4

Concentration Figures: Manufacturing Industries, 1986

Range of five-firm concentration ratio (%)	Number of industries	Share in employment (%)
0– 9.9	4	7.0
10–19.9	16	28.5
20–29.9	14	11.1
30–39.9	24	17.6
40–49.9	15	18.4
50–59.9	11	4.0
60–69.9	7	2.3
70–79.9	4	6.6
80–89.9	5	4.1
90–100	2	0.5

Averages for 102 industries
Weighted average
Share of largest five firms (ranked by employment) in:
employment   34.7%
sales   42.1%
net output   39.5%

Source: Calculated from *Census of Production*, 1986.

---

[1] In the text the terms *market* and *industry* are used interchangeably.

The lower part of table 4.4 indicates that on average in 1986 the largest five firms in an industry (when ranked in terms of employment) accounted for 34.7% of employment, and 42.1% of sales (which suggests that larger firms tend to have higher labour productivity than smaller firms). These averages mask considerable variations between industries. In the seven separately identified industries falling within the timber and wooden furniture sector, the largest five firms account, on average for 15% of employment, whilst in the seven motor and other transport vehicles industries the largest five firms average a share of 67%. The spread of concentration ratios is also indicated in table 4.4 which shows that there were four industries accounting together for 7% of employment in which the five-term concentration ratio was below 10%. At the other end of the scale, there were five industries (with 4.1% of employment) in which the largest five firms employed between 80 and 90% of the industry workforce and two industries (with only ½% of employment) where the concentration ratio was over 90%.

The level of concentration has generally risen during this century. This can be conveniently summarized by the course of aggregate concentration.[1] The share of the largest 100 firms in manufacturing net output was estimated to be 16% in the first decade of this century, around 22–24% in the inter-war period, and then rose steadily from a level of 22% in 1949 to 41% in 1968. Since then, the share of the largest 100 firms has been rather steady, and was 38% in 1985.[2] For the whole economy, Hughes and Kumar[3] estimate that the largest 100 companies accounted for 24.7% of employment in 1968, 24.5% in 1975 and 25.1% in 1980.

3.1   Acquisitions and Mergers

A major route by which the structure of an industry and the size of firms change is by acquisitions and mergers. There is a technical difference between an acquisition (where one firm takes over another) and a merger (where two or more firms fuse together to form a new company), but in line with common usage we do not make any distinction between acquisition and merger below. Figure 4.5 illustrates the variation in merger activity in Britain over the past twenty years. The number of firms acquired has averaged nearly 700 a year, with a total of nearly 15,000 firms acquired

[1]   The trends in industrial concentration are summarized in M. Sawyer, *op. cit.*, Chapter 3; for discussion of concentration outside of manufacturing, see S. Aaronovitch and M. Sawyer, *Big Business* (Macmillan, 1975).

[2]   There are complications arising from some (rather slight) changes in the definition of the manufacturing sector and from nationalization and privatization of firms. The figures in the text refer to private firms only.

[3]   A. Hughes and M. Kumar, 'Recent Trends in Aggregate Concentration in the United Kingdom Economy: Revised Estimates', *CJE*, vol. 8 (1984).

over the twenty year period. Around three-quarters of these acquisitions involve the purchase of independent companies, whilst the remainder involve the sale of subsidiaries by one company to another.

Expenditure on acquisitions fluctuates substantially. The number of firms acquired in the most active acquisition year is around three times the number in the least active year. But the variation in terms of the expenditure is much greater. Even after deflating for variations in share prices, expenditure on acquiring subsidiaries in 1988 was nearly ten times the value in 1975.

The early years of the period (1968–72) witnessed a merger boom, which was larger than any previous merger boom but this was followed by a decade during which merger activity was rather subdued. This could be seen as a response to a general disenchantment with the benefits of mergers.[1] However, there was a dramatic upswing in merger activity beginning in 1985 and continuing up to the time of writing. The scale of merger activity over the four years 1985–88 well surpassed the levels reached in the last merger boom of 1968–72.

The scale of merger activity can be gauged by comparing expenditure on acquiring subsidiaries with total investment in fixed capital assets (plant, machinery and buildings). For example, amongst limited companies, expenditure on acquiring subsidiaries in 1985 was equivalent to 30% of the expenditure on fixed assets.[2] The relevance of this comparison is twofold. First, the figures for total investment provide an appropriate benchmark and put the large numbers involved in merger activity into perspective. Second, and more important, the comparison draws attention to the use to which firms put their investment resources. Whereas investment in plant and equipment and so on represents the creation of new resources and an addition to the productive potential of the economy, expenditure on acquisitions does not add to the productive capacity but rather is a change of ownership of existing assets.

The direction of merger activity is indicated to some extent by the figures in table 4.5, which refer to the proposed mergers considered by the Office of Fair Trading as part of mergers policy (see below). These figures refer to relatively large potential mergers, and most large firms are already diversified. A merger is regarded as horizontal if the two (or more) firms involved are operating in the same industrial sector, whereas it would be regarded as vertical if the firms were in a purchaser/supplier relationship with each other. The diversified merger category covers remaining cases. There is no discernible trend in the figures shown in table 4.5, with horizontal

---

[1]   The disenchantment was perhaps a reaction to the claims made for the benefits of mergers made during the merger boom of 1968/72. The alleged advantages of mergers (and the resulting larger scale of firms) lay behind the establishment of the Industrial Reorganisation Corporation mentioned below. The disenchantment was aided by academic work such as G. Meeks, *Disappointing Marriage: A Study of Gains from Merger* (Cambridge University Press, 1977), which strongly suggested that mergers did not on average raise profitability and efficiency.

[2]   The source of data is Business Monitor MA3, *Company Finance* (HMSO).

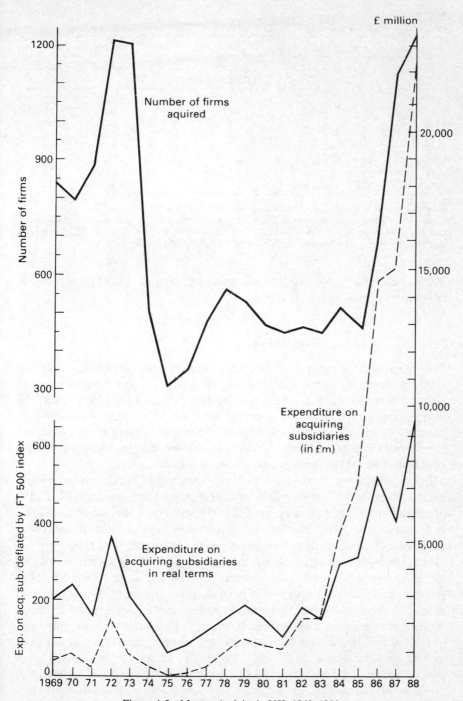

Figure 4.5   Merger Activity in UK, 1969–1988
Note: Expenditure in real terms is expenditure in money terms divided by share price index (FT500).
Source: Calculated from *Business Monitor* M7, *FS*.

TABLE 4.5

Proposed Mergers Classified by Type of Integration

Year	Horizontal		Vertical		Diversified	
	Number	Value	Number	Value	Number	Value
			(Percentages of total)			
1970/4	73	65	5	4	23	27
1975/8	65	67	9	8	26	25
1979/82	61	68	6	3	34	30
1983	71	73	4	1	25	26
1984	63	79	4	1	33	20
1985	58	42	4	4	38	54
1986	69	74	2	1	29	25
1987	67	80	3	1	30	19

Source: Annual Reports of the Director-General of Fair Trading.
Note: 'The allocation of mergers to these three categories involve an element of judgement and this should be kept in mind when interpreting these figures' (Review of Monopolies and Mergers Policy, *A Consultative Document*, Cmnd. 7198 (HMSO, 1978)).

mergers accounting for two-thirds or more of mergers, and vertical mergers being rather unimportant.

3.2   Multinational Enterprises

Most large firms operating in Britain are multinational enterprises (MNEs). In the minority of cases, the firm is owned by foreigners and most of its activities take place outside the United Kingdom. In the other cases, the firm is mainly owned by UK nationals with the larger part of its activities based in Britain. Amongst the largest 100 manufacturing firms (based on net output) in Britain 20 are foreign-owned, but the vast majority of the remaining largest 100 firms operate internationally.[1]

In 1985 there were 1,515 manufacturing enterprises under foreign ownership, amounting to just over 1% of enterprises. They accounted for 14% of employment, 20% of sales and 22% of capital expenditure in the manufacturing sector. Over half of the enterprises were American and these accounted for two-thirds of the net output of foreign-owned firms.

Foreign-owned companies are not evenly spread across all sectors of the economy. They tend to be sparsely represented in what could be considered the less dynamic sectors of manufacturing industry. Foreign-owned companies account for less than 5% of employment in metal manufacturing, manufacture of other transport equipment, textile industries, manufacture of leather and leather goods, footwear and clothing industries and timber and wooden furniture industries. The sectors where foreign-owned companies account for more than 15% of employment are the chemical industry, mechanical engineering, manufacture of office machinery and data process-

---

[1]   For some estimates see K. Cowling and R. Sugden, *Transnational Monopoly Capitalism* (Wheatsheaf Books, 1987).

ing equipment, electrical and electronic engineering, manufacture of motor vehicles and parts thereof, instrument engineering and processing of rubber and plastics.

The arrival of a multinational enterprise is often welcomed by the host government. The establishment of a multinational enterprise will generally involve new investment and the creation of employment.[1] Further, multi-national enterprises may bring new technology. However, in order to attract multinational enterprises, governments (national and local) often offer sub-stantial investment subsidies, tax exemptions and the like. The competition between countries and regions of countries tends to lead to a bidding up of the subsidies offered to MNEs, with obvious benefit to the MNEs con-cerned. Further, decisions on employment, production etc. are then taken by people based well outside the country concerned. A feature of many MNEs is that they are willing and able to move production from one country to another which would mean that inward investment made in response to the offer of subsidies etc. may move out in response to subsidies else-where.

4   INTRODUCTION TO INDUSTRIAL POLICIES

We now turn to some consideration of industrial policies. These policies can range from changing the form of ownership of a firm or industry (i.e. nationalization and privatization), the encouragement or discouragement of mergers through to legislation governing the relationship between firms (e.g. limiting collusion between firms). There are many other policies which influence the behaviour and performance of firms and industries. For ex-ample, macro-economic policies influence the general economic environ-ment within which firms operate, and the price, employment and investment decisions of firms are likely to be strongly influenced by macro-economic conditions. Further, taxation and subsidy policies are often designed to influence what firms do. But macro-economic and taxation policies are discussed elsewhere in this book, so that discussion here is restricted to industrial policy, by which we mean policies designed to change the behav-iour and performance of specific firms and industries.

The appropriate role of the State in industrial matters has always been a matter of controversy, and the sharp differences between the role of the State as viewed by the Labour government of 1974/79 and as viewed by the current Conservative government illustrate that controversy. At the risk of over-simplification, it may be useful to consider three broadly defined views on the role of the State in connection with the operation of firms and industries. These can be labelled the market failure approach, the Austrian school, and the developmental State view. The first of these

---

[1]   This would not be the case when the multinational enterprise arrives through the acquisition of an established domestic firm. The employment creation effect may be overstated in so far as employment elsewhere in the economy is displaced.

has been the dominant view amongst economists, whilst the second has had considerable influence on the policies of the current government. The third view has not had as much influence in Britain as in countries such as Japan and France, but some elements of this view can be seen as reflected in policies pursued by the Labour governments of 1964/70 and of 1974/79.

4.1   The Market Failure Approach

The market failure approach has two basic elements. The first is the proposition that a system of perfect competition would, under certain assumptions, generate a desirable (Pareto optimal) outcome.[1] The second is that when some of those assumptions are not (or cannot) be met, then there is a role for government. This role may be to try to bring about the conditions of perfect competition (e.g. by increasing the number of firms in an industry); or it may be to alleviate the consequences of the impossibility of achieving perfect competition. The discussion now turns to an elaboration of these ideas, along with some examples.

It is convenient to consider an industry in which production takes place subject to constant costs so that average costs and marginal costs are equal. This assumption allows a simplification of the analysis without losing anything of importance for this discussion. With constant costs, the unit costs in an industry are not affected by the number of firms in that industry, and hence the average (and marginal) cost curve can be drawn as a horizontal line without reference to the number of firms. This has been done in figure 4.6, where the average cost curve is labelled as *ac*. The demand curve facing the industry is drawn as *D*. If the industry was perfectly competitive, then each firm would equate price with marginal cost (as a condition of profit maximization) and the normal profit requirement would be that price (average revenue) equal average cost. The output produced, with price equal to marginal cost, would be Q_c.

The outcome of price equal to marginal cost is seen to have some desirable features. The demand curve for a product indicates how much consumers are willing to pay per unit for different quantities. It is intended to represent the consumers' marginal evaluation of the product as the scale of output varies. The marginal cost is the incremental cost of production. In a fully employed economy, greater production of one good requires less production of some other goods. Assuming that the marginal costs of production reflect the opportunity cost of reducing production elsewhere, then the marginal cost is equal to the consumers' evaluation of the foregone alternative production. When consumers value the product under consideration more than the alternative, then price exceeds marginal cost, and economic welfare can be increased by shifting resources into its production. This would continue up to the point where price is equal to marginal cost. This

---

[1]   A Pareto-optimal outcome is one from which it is not possible to make some people better off without making others worse off.

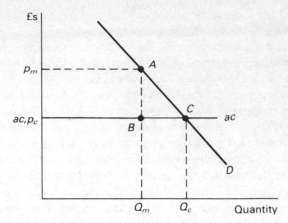

Figure 4.6   Monopoly Welfare Loss

argument forms the basis of the idea that perfect competition would generate a desirable outcome, since price would there equal marginal cost.

A situation of monopoly can also be represented in figure 4.6. The profit maximizing position of a monopolist is the equality of marginal revenue and marginal cost, and this would yield an output of Q_m and a price of p_m. It can be readily seen that price is higher and output lower under monopoly than under perfect competition (when both face the same cost and demand conditions). The loss to consumers of the higher price under monopoly is given (approximately) by the area p_mACBp. The basis of this approximation is as follows. Consider a consumer who would have been willing to pay an amount p_a for the good in question. At a competitive price this consumer would gain to the extent of $p_a - p_c$ as the excess of the value of the good to that consumer over the price which is paid. As the price is raised from the competitive level to the monopoly level, a range of consumers withdraw from purchase of this good, and their individual loss is the excess of the price they would have been prepared to pay over the competitive price. This excess summed over all the relevant individuals gives the area p_mACBp. This welfare loss can be divided into the rectangle p_mABp_c and the triangle ABC. The former is the monopoly profits (excess of price over average cost times output), and represents a transfer from consumers to producers (as compared with perfect competition). Subtracting this transfer, it is the triangle ABC which represents the net welfare loss of monopoly (again as compared with perfect competition).

The estimates of the size of monopoly welfare loss have ranged from the trivially small to the substantial.[1] The original estimate made by Harberger[2] for the American economy in 1929 was that the loss was less

---

[1]   For survey of monopoly welfare loss and its estimation, see M. Sawyer, *op. cit.*, Chapter 14.
[2]   A. C. Harberger, 'Monopoly and Resource Allocation', *AER*, vol. 44 (1954).

than $\frac{1}{10}\%$ of GDP, and a number of studies arrived at estimates of a similar order of magnitude. However, some recent estimates have placed the losses at a much more significant level. For example, Cowling and Mueller[1] estimate the welfare loss from monopoly in the range 3% to 7% of gross corporate product for the United Kingdom in the mid-sixties.[2]

The implication that the welfare costs of monopoly are (or could be) substantial (as compared with perfect competition) underlies many ideas on anti-monopoly policies. At a minimum, it suggests that monopoly may involve losses, and that situations of monopoly require some monitoring. British monopoly policy is discussed below, but two points should be noted here. First, our discussion has concerned the extreme cases of monopoly and perfect competition, whereas most industries in reality lie somewhere between the two. Monopoly policy in practice is not concerned with firms which are complete monopolists (in the sense of being the only supplier) since there are virtually no firms in such a position but rather with firms which have a considerable market share (in the British case a share of more than 25%). Second, the only aspect of performance which has been considered has been pricing (and the consequences for output). There are many other dimensions of performance (e.g. technical progress, advertising) which are important, and in which monopolies and oligopolies may have advantages over atomistic competition. An oligopolist with a reasonably secure market position and a flow of profits may be in a better position to finance and undertake research than a competitive firm in an insecure position with only a competitive level of profits. Research and development (and production in general) may be subject to some economies of scale providing further advantages for an oligopolistic structure over a competitive one.

The idea that perfect competition has certain desirable properties and the related idea that price should equal marginal cost for an optimal outcome relies on a range of restrictive assumptions, and some of those are now briefly considered. First, the equality achieved by perfectly competitive firms would be between price and marginal *private* cost, whereas the welfare requirement would be for an equality between price and marginal *social* cost. The difference between private and social costs arises from the existence of externalities. The pollution from a factory is suffered by many people, and some or all of the costs of pollution are borne by people other

---

[1]   K. Cowling and D. Mueller, 'The Social Costs of Monopoly Power', *EJ*, vol. 88 (1978).

[2]   There are a number of reasons for the differences in the orders of magnitude of the estimates of Cowling and Mueller (and others) from those of Harberger (and others). Cowling and Mueller assume joint profit maximization and estimate the elasticity of demand from the observed price-cost margin by applying a formula similar to that given in the footnote on page 239 above. Harberger assumed a unit elasticity of demand in all markets. A further major difference arises from the estimation of the competitive level of prices. Harberger used the average rate of profit with the consequence that some actual prices were below the calculated competitive level. Cowling and Mueller used an estimate of the opportunity cost of capital.

than the firm which generated the pollution.[1] An extra traveller on a crowded road imposes further congestion on other travellers. Although further discussion of this point falls outside the range of this chapter, it can be seen that the differences between private and social costs would lead to policy suggestions of imposing taxes and subsidies to remove (or at least reduce) the difference between private and social costs.

Second, there is the presumption of full employment of workers and machinery in the economy. The withdrawal of resources from the industry under consideration is assumed to lead to the use of those resources elsewhere in the economy. Thus re-deployment rather than unemployment of resources (including labour) is assumed.

Third, consumers (and indeed firms as well) are assumed to be well informed on the quality of the product which they are buying as well as the price which they are paying. But for many products, their quality can only be judged by use. It may not be possible to judge the safety of a product (e.g. an electrical good) or to know the conditions under which a product was produced (e.g. whether food has been hygienically made). When a product malfunctions and requires repair, most of us are not technically equipped to judge what repairs are necessary (and that applies whether we are thinking of cars or of ourselves). Prices may be quoted in a misleading manner (e.g. the price offered compared with some notional recommended price). Much consumer protection legislation is devoted to imposing minimum standards on products. Codes of practice have been negotiated with a range of industries. The Consumer Protection Act 1987 makes it an offence to give misleading price indications. Thus, much public policy is designed to overcome problems arising from difficulties which consumers face in acquiring necessary information to judge quality and price.

Fourth, unit costs are assumed to be constant (as in our example) or to increase as the scale of production rises. In other words, production is assumed to involve constant or increasing costs. However, in some industries production involves decreasing costs. Industries such as railways, gas and electricity, which have often been labelled 'natural monopolies' are seen as operating subject to decreasing costs. It would, for example, be wasteful of resources to have two railway lines linking city A with city B unless there was sufficient traffic to warrant both of them.

In a situation of decreasing costs, marginal costs are below average costs and so marginal cost pricing is not viable in the sense that price would be less than average costs and losses would result. Further, perfect competition would not be viable under such a situation for the largest firm would have the lowest costs and be able to undercut its rivals. This would enable the largest firm to expand further, operate subject to even lower costs and eventually reach a monopoly position.

The dilemma which this presents is clear. Technical efficiency would

---

[1] This would depend on the nature of the laws governing pollution; e.g. whether those who suffer from pollution can seek legal redress from the polluter.

require a single firm, but one firm would possess monopoly power. There have been a range of policy responses to this dilemma. In Britain as in many other countries (the USA being the notable exception), the 'natural monopolies' of public utilities (postal service, telephone, gas, electricity, water, railways, television and radio) have until recently been under public ownership.

The second response, followed in the USA and now for the newly privatised 'natural monopolies' in Britain, has been to subject the firms to regulatory control, especially of prices and profits. Some of the difficulties of regulation are considered below.[1]

The third response, which has been developed in the past decade or so, argues that the number of firms in an industry is largely irrelevant, and that attention should be directed to the ease of entry into and exit from an industry. This line of argument has been associated with the theory of contestable markets, though it can also be linked with the Austrian approach discussed below. The general argument can be illustrated by reference to figure 4.6. The implicit assumption in arriving at the conclusion that a monopolist would charge a price of p_m was that its position was not threatened by the prospect of other firms being able to enter the industry. The entry of other firms into the industry would increase total output and reduce prices and profits. The existence of substantial monopoly profits would provide a strong incentive for other firms to seek to enter the industry concerned.

Baumol and his co-workers[2] define a market as perfectly contestable if there are no barriers to entry or to exit. The absence of barriers to entry would mean that any new entrant could compete with the existing firms without any handicap. The absence of barriers to exit would mean that there are no financial or other penalties for leaving an industry. This would mean, for example, that any equipment which was used in that industry could be readily re-sold for use elsewhere. The relevance of the ease of exit is that firms considering entry into an industry are not put off by the difficulties of leaving the industry. This leads to the possibility of 'hit-and-run' entry; that is a firm entering an industry briefly, forcing down prices and then leaving the industry. Baumol and others argue that under conditions of free entry and exit an incumbent firm (even with a monopoly position) would not dare to raise price above the competitive level. For if the firm were to do so, then other firms would immediately enter (seeking the available profits) and that would force down prices.

The policy implications of this line of argument are clear, namely that

---

[1]   For an extensive discussion of regulation and its difficulties see M.Waterson, *Regulation of the Firm and Natural Monopoly* (Blackwell, Oxford, 1988).

[2]   W.J.Baumol, 'Contestable Markets: An Uprising in the Theory of Industrial Structure', *AER*, vol. 72 (1982), and W.J.Baumol, J.Panzar and R.D.Willig, *Contestable Markets and the Theory of Industrial Structure* (Harcourt Brace Jovanovich, New York). For further discussion see M.Sawyer, *op. cit.*, pp. 250–52.

regard should be paid to entry and exit conditions and not to monopoly positions *per se*. A monopolist which seeks to secure its position by raising entry and exit barriers would be condemned.

The final response considered has operated to some degree in commercial television, and government proposals currently under discussion would seek to widen its operation. This response is for the government to auction off the right to operate in a particular market. In the case of commercial television, franchise to operate has been granted to a single company in each of the television regions, though the granting of the franchise has been based on company plans for programme quality, range of programmes etc. The proposals current at the time of writing are for the sale to the highest bidder of rights to operate television and radio services. The basis of this response can again be illustrated by reference to figure 4.6. A monopolist would gain profits of p_mABp_c, and a firm would be prepared to pay up to that amount for the right to have the monopoly position. If several firms compete for the right to be the monopolist, then the price paid for that right would be bid up to the level of the monopolist profits. When the price is bid up to that level, in effect the monopoly profits are gained by the firm with the licence but paid over to the government. There would still be some loss of consumer welfare as compared with the atomistic competition case, though with decreasing costs (which underpin the 'natural monopoly' case) atomistic competition would not be viable for the reasons explained above.

4.2   The Austrian School

The view of competition which is embedded in the traditional approach is that of the static equilibrium of atomistic competition with a large number of small firms. In contrast the Austrian approach views competition as a dynamic process taking place against a background of change and uncertainty. The existence of profits, particularly high profits, is seen as an indicator that the firms concerned are particularly efficient both in terms of productive efficiency and of producing goods which consumers wish to buy. In particular, high profits are not seen as associated with market power, though there may be an association between high market shares and profits. But the link is not from high market share indicating monopoly to high profits, but rather that above average efficiency generates a high market share and large profits.

The prospect of high profits is seen as the necessary inducement for firms to introduce new ideas, products and techniques and to pursue efficiency. A firm which is particularly successful will indeed earn high profits. However, high profits are seen as always under threat from the entry of other firms. A firm with high profits may be able to maintain those profits, but only if it can remain more efficient than its rivals (potential as well as actual). It is the threat of new entry into an industry which keeps the incumbent firms on their toes. This leads to an emphasis on the importance of entry conditions into an industry, rather than the number of firms in the industry. One firm in an industry may appear to be a situation of monopoly, but if there are a number of firms ready to enter that industry if the existing firm allows its prices to rise above their level of costs then the incumbent firm is highly constrained in its pricing.

In the analysis of monopoly welfare loss, it was implicitly assumed that the excess profits arose from the possession of monopoly power. In contrast, the Austrian approach would argue that the profits were temporary and are the necessary spur to innovation and efficiency. Thus Littlechild[1] considers that an innovating monopolist 'generates a social gain given by his own entrepreneurial profit plus the consumer surplus'.

Another important element of the Austrian approach is the importance of property rights and of the entrepreneur. If the entrepreneur is to seek after profits, then (s)he must have the claim to the profits generated, and hence, it is argued, the property rights to the profits must be assigned to the entrepreneur. The single entrepreneur is seen to be willing to take risks, to strive for lower costs etc., because (s)he will be the beneficiary of any resulting profits. In an organization with a large number of owners, the link between effort and profits is much diluted. The essential difficulty of nationalized industries, workers' co-operatives and also of large manager-controlled corporations is seen to be that ownership is dispersed.[2]

These lines of arguments can be seen to have influenced the policies of the present government. The stress on property rights, with a strongly implied preference for private ownership over public ownership is reflected in the privatization programme discussed below. The emphasis on competition as a process and the focus on conditions of entry into an industry rather than the number of incumbent firms have influenced monopolies and mergers policies.

4.3   Developmental State

A quite different view of the appropriate roles of private firms, markets and the State is given by a set of ideas which we include under the heading of the developmental state. The 'market failure' approach discussed above focuses on government intervention when markets in some sense fail, and could also be described in a number of respects as the regulatory view

---

[1]   S. Littlechild, 'Misleading Calculations of the Social Cost of Monopoly Power', *EJ*, vol. 91 (1981).
[2]   There may be cases such as mutual organizations like building societies where the ownership of the assets of the organization may be very difficult to define.

of the state (e.g. regulating monopolies). The developmental state view is seen as complementary with the regulatory view.[1]

Marquand[2] argues that 'the state has played a central part in economic development in virtually all industrial societies, with the possible exception of early nineteenth-century Britain. Even in Britain, moreover, the state played an important facilitating role' in passing a variety of Acts of Parliament which allowed for example the building of the railways and the necessary infrastructure.

There are numerous examples of the developmental state in the post-war era, and here three (Japan, France and Italy) are briefly discussed to indicate the type of policies which a developmental state may follow.

The economic success of Japan in the last four decades is well known. Whilst Japan has operated a market economy, there has been much government influence on the direction of development of the economy. Much of this was undertaken through the Ministry of International Trade and Industry (MITI). The essential objective of industrial policy was to move Japan from a relatively backward economy specializing in labour-intensive products to an advanced industrial power. This meant moving the economy away from the production of goods and services in which it had a comparative advantage to the production of industrial products (initially products such as ships, steel, and later cars and computers). It involved targeting certain key sectors of the economy for development. A barrage of policy devices was used to protect the key sectors and to ensure their development. These included 'the extensive use, narrow targeting and timely revision of tax incentives; the use of indicative plans to set goals and guidelines for the entire economy; the creation of numerous, formal and continuously operating forums for exchanging views, reviewing policies, obtaining feedback and resolving differences; the assignment of some government functions to various private and semi-private associations . . . ; an extensive reliance on public corporations, particularly of the mixed public–private variety, to implement policy in high-risk or otherwise refractory area; the creation and use by the government of an unconsolidated "investment budget" . . . ; the orientation of anti-trust policy to developmental and international competitive goals rather than strictly to the maintenance of domestic competition; government-conducted or government-sponsored research and development (the computer industry); and the use of the government's licensing and approved authority to achieve developmental goals'.[3]

The route initially followed in France was the use of national plans (which influenced the National Plan drawn up for the UK in the mid-sixties). One feature of the French approach has been that the plan 'is at one and

---

[1] This distinction is drawn by R.Dore, 'Industrial Policy and How the Japanese do it', *Catalyst*, Spring 1986, and K.Cowling, 'An Industrial Strategy for Britain: the Nature and Role of Planning', *IRAE*, vol. 1 (1987).

[2] D.Marquand, *The Unprincipled Society* (Fontana Press, 1988).

[3] Chalmers Johnson, *MITI and the Japanese Miracle: The Growth of Industrial Policy, 1925–1975* (Stanford University Press, Stanford, 1982).

the same time comprehensive and passive. The plan provides a coordinating structure plus information flows but the planners are left in a peripheral position in relation to crucial strategic decisions . . .'.[1]

One of the intentions of such a national plan is that it presents a consistent economic scenario against which individual firms can make their investment and other decisions. Investment decisions are geared to future growth prospects, and one intention of 'indicative planning' is that firms share common expectations about those growth prospects. There is an element of expectations becoming self-fulfilling: the expectation of fast growth becomes translated into a high level of investment which then enables the growth to occur. Another aspect of 'indicative planning' is the identification of constraints on economic growth and the direction of resources to overcome those constraints.

French governments have generally pursued policies of support for 'national champions' in certain strategic, high-technology industries. Assistance has been provided to such industries on a highly selective basis, and can range from provision of subsidies, protection from foreign competition and the use of public procurement programmes etc.

State-holding companies in Italy (particularly the Institute for Industrial Reconstruction, IRI) have been important instruments in industrial development. The development of an Italian steel industry and telecommunications industry came largely from the initiative of IRI. There has been a heavy involvement of the public sector in trading activities, and these have included partial ownership of trading companies. In recent years, there has been an emphasis on the promotion of investment, research and innovation through subsidies and other incentives.

The general idea of the developmental state is that the private market will not produce the best possible outcome. It identifies a range of ways by which state intervention can operate to improve the operation of markets. Some industrial policies pursued in Britain over the past thirty years can be seen as influenced by that general idea. The creation of the National Plan in the mid-sixties was to some degree based on the French experience. Similarly, the original idea of the National Enterprise Board was strongly influenced by the Italian experience with state holding companies.

5   COMPETITION POLICY: AN INTRODUCTION

From 1948 onwards, British governments have operated, with a varying degree of vigour, evolving competition policies. It is convenient for purposes of discussion to divide these policies into five different types. The first to emerge was monopoly policy (starting from the 1948 Monopoly and Restrictive Practices Act), which originally covered restrictive practices as well. The restrictive practices policy was separated from monopoly policy

---

[1]   Cowling, *op. cit.*

with the passage of the Restrictive Trade Practices Act 1956. Some control over mergers and acquisitions was added in 1965, and the Office of Fair Trading, created in 1973, is heavily involved in the administration of competition policy.

5.1   Monopoly Policy

The previous discussion suggested that a situation of monopoly offered some advantages over a comparable situation of perfect competition but also some disadvantages. A situation of monopoly provides the monopolist with substantial market power. This power could be used to raise prices and lower output (as compared with a situation with more firms). It may enable more research and development to be undertaken and economies of scale exploited. In addition, though, the monopolist can in effect take the monopoly profits by allowing costs to rise above those technically necessary.

Monopoly policy since 1973 has had the following structure. A firm (or group of firms acting in concert) can be referred to the Monopolies and Mergers Commission (MMC hereafter) for investigation when its market share is thought to exceed 25%. Thus the statutory definition of monopoly is a market share of 25%. The MMC is required to first investigate whether the firm (or firms) concerned do indeed have a market share of 25%. The major part of their work is to investigate whether the actions and performance of the monopolist have been in the public interest. The public interest is not precisely defined and its interpretation has indeed varied. However, successive Acts since 1948 have indicated that regard should be paid, *inter alia*, to efficient production and distribution, a balanced distribution of industry and employment within the United Kingdom, increase of efficiency and the encouragement of new enterprise. The only change of significance has been the explicit mention of the desirability of competition *per se* in the Fair Trading Act of 1973.

British monopoly policy operates on a discretionary basis. The Secretary of State for Trade and Industry has discretion over whether a firm (or group of firms believed to be acting together) are referred to the MMC for investigation. In practice, there are many firms with market shares of over 25% which have not been referred for investigation. Further, the MMC has considerable discretion over the interpretation of the public interest. There is no explicit build-up of case law.

In its reports the MMC gives its judgement and usually makes recommendations for changes in the firm's behaviour, though the implementation of any such recommendations is in the hands of the Secretary of State for Trade and Industry. In the overwhelming majority of cases, the MMC has made some criticisms of the practices of the firms under investigation. Predominant in terms of number of times reported amongst the practices which have been condemned are restriction of sale of competitors' goods,

price notification agreements, monopoly pricing and profits and discriminatory pricing.[1] Most of the practices found to be against the public interest
were aspects of behaviour which either operated to make life more difficult
for (actual or potential) competitors without benefiting consumers through
the supply of 'better' products or the charging of lower prices. These types
of behaviour include supplying a retail outlet only if that outlet agreed
not to sell competitors' goods and the favouring of some firms at the expense
of others by discriminatory pricing. Excessive profits and prices have generally been condemned, particularly when reinforced by entry barriers and
restrictions on competition. In the past few years, increasing attention has
been given by the MMC to the effects which an existing monopoly or
oligopoly position has on competition and on the possibility of new entry
into the industry concerned. The majority of those recent MMC reports
on monopoly situations which have found activities as against the public
interest have included the restriction of competition amongst the activities
against the public interest.

In none of their reports did the MMC condemn a monopoly position
as such and recommend structural change. The nearest the MMC came
to recommending structural change was in the case of roadside advertising
services.[2] Ten companies had set up and owned a company called British
Posters Ltd., and the MMC made the recommendation, which was carried
out, that this company be disbanded. In March 1989, the MMC recommended that brewers be limited to the ownership of 2,000 public houses,
and six brewers operated more than this number (with Bass operating the
most at 7,100).[3]

5.2   Merger Policy

Since 1965, a proposed merger which would create or enhance a monopoly
position or which involves the acquisition of assets above a specified size,
is evaluated by the government. The definition of a monopoly position
is that used in the monopoly policy, i.e. a market share of more than
25%. The size requirement for a merger to be evaluated was initially set
at £5m, raised to £15m in 1980 and further raised to £30m in mid-1984.
The initial evaluation of a proposed merger is made by a panel of civil
servants (the Mergers Panel), who consider whether there should be a
referral of the merger to the MMC for further investigation. The final
decision on referral is made by the Secretary of State for Trade and Industry,
with advice from the Director-General of Fair Trading (DGFT). A firm
contemplating a merger can seek confidential guidance from the OFT on

[1]   For a summary of practices found against public interest, see Review of Monopolies and
Mergers Policy, *A Consultative Document*, Cmnd. 7198 (HMSO, 1978).
[2]   Monopolies and Mergers Commission, *Roadside Advertising Services: A Report on the
Supply in the UK of the Roadside Advertising Services* (HMSO, 1981).
[3]   Monopolies and Mergers Commission, *The Supply of Beer* Cmnd. 651 (HMSO, 1989).

its likely attitude to the proposed merger. The bidding firm can also respond to such guidance by designing the takeover bid in such a way as to reduce the chances of referral of the merger to the MMC. For example, a firm may seek to acquire another but state its intention to re-sell part of the firm acquired to avoid the creation of a monopoly position. Any investigation by the MMC is normally expected to be completed within six months, during which time the takeover bid usually lapses (under the conditions of the Stock Exchange Takeover Code).

The thrust of the current policy has been described by the then Secretary of State for Trade and Industry (N. Tebbit) in July 1984 in the following terms: 'I regard mergers policy as an important part of the government's general policy of promoting competition within the economy in the interests of the customer and of efficiency and hence of growth and jobs. Accordingly my policy has been and will continue to be to make references primarily on competition grounds.' The report of this speech continues by saying that '[i]n evaluating the competitive situation in individual cases Mr Tebbit said he would have regard to the international context: to the extent of competition in the home market from non-UK sources; and to the competitive position of UK companies in overseas markets.'[1]

The limited impact of merger policy is evident from the proportion of proposed mergers investigated by the MMC. During the period 1965–78, about $2\frac{1}{2}\%$ of proposed mergers covered by the Fair Trading Act were referred to the MMC for more detailed consideration, with the remainder allowed to proceed. In the period 1979–87, 2,070 mergers fell within the scope of the legislation, of which 64 potential mergers were referred to the MMC, amounting to just over 3% of total.[2] In the period 1979–87 of the 64 mergers referred to the MMC, 19 were declared against the public interest, 29 were declared as not against the public interest and 16 were abandoned by the firms involved before the MMC reported and the referral was withdrawn.[3]

5.3   Restrictive Practices

Restrictive practices cover matters such as agreement between firms over prices to be charged, over sharing out a market (e.g. agreeing that each geographical area be supplied by only one firm) etc. The major legislation on restrictive practices dates from 1956. There are two notable contrasts between the restrictive practices policy and those on monopolies and mergers. The first is that the body which is charged with the operation of the restrictive practices legislation is part of the judiciary, namely the

[1]   The quote in the text is taken from a speech by the then Trade and Industry Secretary Norman Tebbit, as reported in *British Business*, 13 July 1984, p. 381.
[2]   There were a number of instances when a single company was subject to more than one takeover proposal.
[3]   The corresponding figures for the period 1965 to 1978 were 14 declared against the public interest, 14 not against the public interest, and 15 abandoned before a report was made.

Restrictive Practices Court (hereafter RPC). This means that there is a build up of case law on restrictive practices, in contrast to the situation with monopolies and mergers policy. The second is that there is a presumption in the legislation that restrictive practices are against the public interest unless proved otherwise (whereas the merger legislation has the presumption in favour of mergers). This presumption against restrictive practices has been reinforced by the way in which the RPC has interpreted the legislation. There are eight 'gateways' through which a restrictive practice can pass in order to continue.[1]

Initially the restrictive practices legislation covered only goods, but was extended to cover services in 1976. The application of the restrictive practices legislation to the operation of the Stock Exchange led eventually to the re-organization of the Stock Exchange in October 1986 in the 'Big Bang' (see Chapter 2). The restrictive practices operated by the Stock Exchange were referred to the RPC but the matter was taken out of their hands by the government. An act of parliament was enacted to exempt the Stock Exchange from the restrictive practices legislation in exchange for a number of concessions by the London Stock Exchange, the most important of which was the scrapping of minimum commission rates.

Resale price maintenance (RPM) is one type of restrictive practice which is separately dealt with under the Resale Prices Act 1976. RPM operates when a supplier makes a condition of supply of goods to retailers that the retailers charge consumers at least some minimum price. Under the Act, such a condition is generally illegal. This legislation contains the presumption against RPM, with the possibility of exemptions being granted by the RPC. Although RPM has declined substantially, firms may resort to practices such as stating recommended prices which can have similar effects. The Office of Fair Trading receives around 30 complaints a year to the effect that producers are imposing conditions on the minimum price to be charged by retailers or wholesalers. In the past few years, investigation of these complaints has led to a few firms (around four to five a year) being required to give undertakings to desist from imposing minimum prices to be charged as a condition of supply.

5.4   Anti-competitive Practices

The Competition Act of 1980 signalled a number of important changes in the approach of government to industrial policy and, as the title of the Act would suggest, reflected the new Conservative government's declared belief in the benefits of competition and of the use of the market over government intervention. One aspect is the control of anti-competitive practices, which are defined as 'a course of conduct which has or is intended

---

[1]   These gateways included the defence that removal of the restrictive practice would cause unemployment, lead to public injury or a fall in exports.

to have or is likely to have the effect of restricting, distorting or preventing competition in the United Kingdom'.[1] The DGFT can initiate an investigation into any activities which (s)he believes may amount to anti-competitive practices. The findings of such investigations are published with recommendations on the next steps to be taken. When no anti-competitive practices or practices with only insignificant effect are found, then the investigation is at an end. In other cases, the DGFT can seek an undertaking from those identified as engaging in anti-competitive practices to desist from those practices. In the event of an undertaking being given, then the DGFT monitors the observance of the undertakings given (which have generally been given for periods of five to ten years). In the event of no undertaking being given, the case is referred to the MMC, for a view on whether the anti-competitive practices are against the public interest. Finally, if the MMC finds that the practices are against the public interest, those involved can, if necessary, be legally compelled to desist from those practices by order of the Secretary of State for Trade and Industry. There have been rather few investigations by the DGFT into possible anti-competitive practices, with an average of less than four a year.

5.5   Consumer Protection

Some other limitations on the activities of firms come from legislation relating to consumer protection, much of which is enforced by the DGFT and by Trading Standards Officers. The DGFT has a duty to collect and assess information on commercial activities, so that trading practices which may affect consumers' interests may be discovered. The DGFT has sought to draw up codes of practice in a range of industries (covering, for example, direct selling, double glazing, motor trade and credit) and can set in motion procedures which can lead to the banning of specified trade practices. Under the Fair Trading Act 1973, the DGFT can seek assurances on future good conduct when traders persistently disregard their obligations under the law in a manner detrimental to consumers, and if such assurances are not given or given and then broken the DGFT can bring proceedings to obtain a court order (breach of which may result in action for contempt of court). In the 15 years up to 1987, the DGFT had sought assurances, court undertakings and orders in connection with 603 traders, with the five sectors of car and motoring, electrical, home improvements, mail order and carpets and furniture accounting for 444 of these cases.

Another area of regulation and consumer protection which is overseen by the Office of Fair Trading is credit licensing. However, that aspect as well as the regulation of financial markets in general has already been discussed in Chapter 2.

---

[1]   This is taken from the preamble to the Competition Act 1980.

6   STRUCTURAL REORGANIZATION

The policies on monopolies, mergers and restrictive practices can have impacts on industrial structure, even if those impacts are to prevent change occurring as would be the case with mergers policy. Whilst the present Conservative government has sought to withdraw from direct intervention in industrial structure and behaviour, this represents a significant change from previous practice. In this section we briefly review the structural reorganization policies which have been pursued. It should be noted first that a number of industries (e.g. coal-mining, steel, railways), which appear to be in long-term decline in most industrialized countries, have been under public ownership in Britain. The contraction of these industries has then been largely in the hands of government. In some cases (e.g. steel) there were many companies involved in the industry at the time of nationalization, but the privatization of these industries has resulted in only one company in each industry (British Steel) being returned to the private sector.

The re-structuring (which usually means fewer firms) of the cotton industry, the aircraft industry and the shipbuilding industry was encouraged by government assistance during the late fifties and early sixties. In the case of cotton and shipbuilding, this was largely a response to excess capacity in the face of growing international competition.

The major agency designed to promote general structural change was the Industrial Reorganization Corporation (hereafter IRC) which came into existence in December 1966, its operation effectively ending four years later. The IRC operated mainly through the promotion of mergers, and its aims have been summarized as 'threefold. First, they aimed to increase productivity by improving the logical structure of industry ... Secondly, they aimed to promote (or at least not harm) regional development. Thirdly, they aimed at retaining company control in the UK.[1] In contrast to the philosophy underlying existing merger policy (and industrial policy more generally) the IRC was based on the view that market forces were inadequate. McClelland[2] stated that one of the propositions 'on which the case for the IRC rests is that market forces would not have cured these structural inadequacies quickly enough. In theory, where there are economies of scale to be exploited, or where one company's management is inadequate, the stock market provides a mechanism whereby a takeover bid will occur. In practice, the mechanism is often ineffective. Shareholders are inadequately informed, directors have vested interests; having regard to the risks for any particular party, finance may not be forthcoming'. The IRC sought to use a combination of persuasion and money (to help finance take-over bids) to encourage mergers.

The National Enterprise Board formally existed from 1975 until 1981

---

[1]   A. Graham, 'Industrial Policy' in W. Beckerman (ed.), *The Labour Government's Economic Record* (Duckworth, 1972).
[2]   W. G. McClelland, 'The Industrial Reorganisation Corporation 1966/71: An Experimental Prod', *TBR*, no. 94 (1972).

though its effective role was ended in 1979. Although it had been conceived originally as part of a considerable extension of public ownership and government intervention, it actually performed two rather different roles. The first one, which involved the bulk of its funds, was to act as a holding company for the government stake in companies such as British Leyland and Rolls Royce, which had come into public ownership through government rescue of large companies in danger of going bankrupt. The second role was that of filling a gap in the capital market through the provision of finance to firms involved in areas of advanced technology and to medium-sized firms to foster regional development.

6.1   Policies towards Small Businesses

The present government has placed considerable emphasis on the promotion and formation of small businesses. There is no precise definition of small business, and the promotion of small business is often undertaken on the grounds that today's successful small business is tomorrow's large business. Following the Bolton Committee,[1] independent businesses employing less than 200 people have been regarded as small businesses, though many would regard that size limit as too high especially when applied outside the manufacturing sector.

The Enterprise Allowance Schemes (EAS) began in 1982 to encourage the formation of new businesses by the unemployed. A payment of £40 a week is made for a year under the scheme, with recipients required to provide at least £1,000 in start-up capital (which can be borrowed). In the five-year period ending 1987/88, there were 330,000 entrants to the scheme, of whom over 47,000 dropped out before the end of the year for which an allowance would be provided.[2] It has been estimated that of every 100 aided under the EAS, 57 are still operating after 3 years, and those surviving firms provide a further 65 jobs. The estimation of the effect of any policy designed to create or protect employment is fraught with difficulties. The policy may appear to help the creation of jobs which would have been created anyway. Further, the jobs created may be at the expense of jobs elsewhere in the economy. The establishment of a new business will to some degree attract custom from existing firms. The Department of Employment assumes that half of the EAS businesses displaced existing business, but admit that there is no firm statistical basis for this estimate.

The Loan Guarantee Scheme is designed to fill a perceived gap in the availability of finance for small and medium sized firms. Application for

---

[1]   *Report of the Committee of Inquiry on Small Firms*, Cmnd. 4811 (HMSO, 1971), often referred to as the Bolton Committee Report after the name of chair of the committee.
[2]   This and subsequent information has been taken from National Audit Office, *Department of Employment/Training Commission: Assistance to Small Firms*, HC 655 (HMSO, 1988).

finance is made direct to a bank which is responsible for the appraisal of the scheme, but subject to final approval by the Department of Employment. In the case of default on the loan, the bank can call on the guarantee provided (on a proportion of the loan) by the Department of Employment. The borrower is charged an interest rate premium (over that which would be charged by the bank). In the first phase of operation (lasting for three years up to May 1984), loans to the value of £486m were guaranteed to nearly 15,000 businesses. There was a high rate of default with banks calling in the guarantee in 29% of cases on loans totalling 40% of those guaranteed. The rules on granting loans were tightened, and in the year 1986/87, only a thousand loans to the value of £40m were guaranteed. In the past few years, the rules on eligibility have been relaxed leading to the guaranteeing of more loans. The Business Expansion Scheme (BES) provides tax relief on money invested in business (with a limit of £500,000 on the total amount invested in a single company within a year). The intention of this scheme is to encourage the supply of venture capital and the financing of relatively small firms.

The Training for Enterprise programme covers a variety of schemes designed to provide start-up training for new businesses and help for existing business people. At a cost of around £18m, during 1987/88, over 115,000 people were provided with training. An Information and Advisory Service deals with around a quarter of a million enquiries a year, with nearly 40,000 counselling sessions provided.

The figures in table 4.3 suggest significant recent growth in the number of small businesses in manufactured industries. The number of self-employed has grown from around 2 million in 1980 to 3 million in 1988. How far these changes are a result of the types of policies described above and how far a result of changing market and technological conditions is a matter of considerable debate.

6.2   Informal Planning

The present government has displayed considerable hostility towards any idea of planning and government intervention. There had, however, been a variety of attempts during the sixties and seventies to have government involvement in the co-ordination of economic activity. The establishment of the National Development Council (NEDC) in 1962 as a tripartite body representing employers, trade unions and government, supported by a permanent staff, was the first major move. Whilst the NEDC continues in existence, it has played little role over the past decade. The general idea behind the establishment of the NEDC was to build a consensus between the various parties involved with the problems facing the British economy. The establishment of EDCs covering individual industries was intended to provide a forum within which impediments to faster growth could be identified and overcome.

The industrial strategy[1] pursued by the 1974/79 Labour government sought to build on this structure. The first stage of that strategy was to analyse difficulties facing particular sectors and search for ways of overcoming those difficulties. Some sectors of the economy were viewed as particularly important for future success, and the idea behind the strategy was to identify and then aid those sectors which were important and potentially successful. Sector Working Parties (SWPs) were tripartite bodies involving government, business and trade unions established to aid the implementation of the strategy. A major problem which this approach faces is that of the implementation of the remedies for the difficulties identified for the tripartite bodies do not have powers of implementation.

The Industry Act 1972 provided powers for government to provide selective financial assistance to industry. An example of such assistance was the wool textile scheme which was designed to encourage new investment and the rationalization of existing capacity. This Act was used by the industrial strategy to finance sectoral schemes such as the provision of assistance for investment. Fifteen sectoral schemes were supported under section 7 of the 1972 Industry Act as part of the industrial strategy, and the government estimated that these had led to the creation of 150,000 new jobs and the protection of 90,000 others,[2] though the point made above on the difficulties of the estimation of impact of such policies on jobs would also apply here.

7   PRIVATIZATION

The major programme of nationalization in the post-war period was undertaken by the Labour Governments of 1945–51. During that period, industries such as coal-mining, railways, part of road haulage (later denationalized), gas, electricity and the Bank of England were nationalized. Nationalization in the sixties and seventies was concentrated on industries in long-term decline (such as steel, shipbuilding and aerospace). Individual firms such as British Leyland and part of Rolls-Royce, came into public ownership more by accident than design as a response by the government to the threat of the extinction through bankruptcy of those firms.

The general trend in the direction of nationalization has been sharply broken over the past decade. Whilst there was some limited sale of nationalized firms during the period of Conservative government in 1970–74, these were restricted to the sale of a travel agency (Thomas Cook) and state-owned public houses in the Carlisle area. During the period of the Conservative governments from 1979 onwards, privatization, which started off in a rather low key way has grown in importance particularly since 1984.

The term 'privatization' has been used to cover a number of different policies. It is convenient to distinguish three policies which have sometimes

---

[1]   *An Approach to Industrial Strategy*, Cmnd 6315 (HMSO, 1975).
[2]   Trade and Industry, 24.11.1978, p. 383.

been included under the heading of privatization.[1] The first type of policy is the sale of assets which the government had previously owned, and this would constitute the narrow definition of privatization (and the sense in which the term will be used below). In some cases, as in the first stages of the privatization programme, the assets sold were largely those which had been relatively recently acquired by the government and often as part of a rescue programme. This part of privatization was largely a selling off of those assets which had been acquired by the National Enterprise Board under the preceding Labour government. In other cases (notably the sale of part of British Telecom), the privatization involved sale of firms which had been nationalized for long periods of time.

The second type of policy, often labelled 'contracting-out', is the provision to public bodies (government departments, nationalized industries, publicly owned hospitals and schools) of certain goods and services by private firms, which had previously been provided by the public bodies themselves. Public bodies have always purchased goods and services from the private sector, and this policy of 'contracting-out' aims to increase the extent to which that is done. An example of 'contracting-out' is the use of private contract cleaning firms by hospitals instead of the hospitals hiring their own cleaning staff.

The third type of policy included under this heading does not necessarily involve any change of ownership that would be implied by the term privatization and could be more accurately labelled de-regulation or liberalization. This policy involves the removal of some of the restrictions on which firms can provide certain types of goods or services (for example, limits on companies which are able to provide local bus services). The link between privatization and de-regulation is that the firms eligible to provide the goods and services have often been publicly owned.

TABLE 4.6

Proceeds from the Sale of Public Assets (£bn)

1979/88	0.4	1980/81	0.4	1981/82	0.5	1982/83	0.5
1983/84	1.1	1984/85	2.1	1985/86	2.7	1986/87	4.4
1987/88	5.2	1988/89	6.0 (est.)	1990/91	5.0 (proposed)		

Source: The Government's Expenditure Plans 1988/9–1990/1 (Cmnd. 288), Autumn Statement 1988, HC 695.

The scale of the privatization programme in terms of the receipts from sales is indicated in table 4.6. It can be seen that in the early eighties, the receipts from privatization were relatively modest, but rose in 1984/85 with the first part of the proceeds from the sale of British Telecom. From

---

[1]   For further discussion of privatization see, e.g. Symposium on Privatization and After, *FSt*, vol. 5 (1984), J.Kay and A.Silerston, 'The New Industrial Policy – Privatisation and Competition', *MBR*, Spring 1984 (1984), J.Kay and D.Thompson, 'Privatisation: A Policy in Search of a Rationale', *EJ*, vol. 96 (1986), J.Vickers and G.Yarrow, *Privatization: An Economic Analysis* (M.I.T. Press, 1988).

1986/87 onwards the proceeds from privatization has been around £5bn, and are projected around that level for the next few years. Since the sale of assets is counted as negative public expenditure, these sales were useful for a government committed to the reduction of public expenditure and of the budget deficit. The scope of the privatization programme is also indicated in table 4.7 which provides a list of the main asset sales.

TABLE 4.7

Main Asset Sales by British Government, 1979–1988

Sale of shares
Amersham International
Associated British Ports
British Aerospace
British Airports Authority
British Airways
British Gas
British Steel
British Telecom
Britoil
Cable and Wireless
Enterprise Oil
Jaguar Cars
Rolls-Royce

Other Sales
Royal Ordnance and Rover Cars sold to British Aerospace
Sealink sold to British Ferries
National Freight sold to consortium of managers, employees and company pensioners
National Bus Company (sold as 72 separate companies)
British Shipbuilders (warship yards)
Sale of minority shareholdings in British Sugar, British Petroleum, ICL, Ferranti and British Technology Group
Sale of property etc. of Crown Agents Holdings, Forestry Commission, New Town Development Corporation

The setting of the issue price of the shares in the to-be privatized firms presents a dilemma.[1] The government wishes to secure proceeds from the sale which are as great as possible but at the same time wishes to ensure that the sale is successful. The spread of share ownership amongst individuals has also been one of the aims of the Conservative government,[2] and this points in the direction of a lower price (to encourage sales). Indeed,

---

[1] In a number of cases (e.g. sale of the Rover group to British Aerospace) shares were not offered to the public and the company was sold as a going concern to another company. In such cases, the consideration in the text do not apply.

[2] The proportion of shares owned directly by individuals has tended to decline throughout the post-war period, whilst ownership by financial institutions (mainly banks, unit trusts, pension funds and insurance companies) tended to rise. This may well have continued throughout the eighties (P.Grout, 'The Wider Share Ownership Programme', *FSt*, vol. 8 (1987)). One effect of the privatization programme appears to have been to increase the number of shareholders; estimates vary but from something of the order of 5–7% of the adult population to around 20%. However, the impact here of privatization appears to be of shareholders with a small holding of shares in one or two companies.

the observation that the shares of privatized firms have traded immediately after privatization at levels above the issue price suggests that the issue price has been set too low.[1] The privatized public utilities have been sold with their monopoly position largely intact. This would be expected to lead to higher profits and a higher market valuation as compared with the break-up of the public utilities into competing firms. Thus, striving for a higher price for the firm conflicts with the aim of increased competition.

There has not yet been a full evaluation of the effect of privatization in the UK. Our discussion considers, first, the theoretical issues and then refers to the general evidence on comparisons between the performance of private and public sector companies.

In the first phase of privatization, the companies which were privatized were mainly companies which had been in competition with private sector companies even when nationalized. Some of this privatization was the sale of assets which had been acquired by the National Enterprise Board under the preceding Labour government. In the second phase the focus shifted to the sale of public utilities, beginning with British Telecom, continuing with British Gas, and at the time of writing the prospect is for the sale of electricity and water companies.

The issues raised by privatization are rather different for the sale of companies in competition with others and for the sale of public utilities. The managers of a company operate under a variety of constraints, but two sets of constraints are generally emphasized by economic analysis. The first is that which derives from the nature of the market in which the firm operates. It is generally argued that the more competition the less discretion the managers have and the greater the pressure to strive for maximum profits. The second arises from the capital market and relates to takeovers. The argument is that if the current management fail to make the best use of the assets at their disposal, then the company is likely to become the target of a hostile takeover bid. Others will see that they can put the assets to more profitable use and launch a takeover bid. Suppose that on the basis of the existing management and expected profits and dividends the stock market values firm A at V_a. Further, suppose that another company (or set of potential owners) believe that the value of firm A would be V_b, then they would be prepared to pay up to V_b for firm A. In order to be successful, a take-over bid has to offer a price substantially above the existing stock market valuation; and premia of 20–30% are common. There are also significant costs associated with launching a take-over bid (e.g. cost of advice from merchant bank, press advertising campaign directed to shareholders of target company).

---

[1] For some details see Vickers and Yarrow, *ibid.*, pp. 173–80. Their Table 7.1 (covering sales up to the end of 1987) indicates that where the sale was at a set price (rather than by tender offer) the gross proceeds to the government were £16,782m. The estimated undervaluation on these sales is £3,517m (using the share price at the end of the first day of trading for these estimates), i.e. over 20% of the gross proceeds.

It is debatable whether most take-overs are of the hostile form which this line of argument would indicate, and also whether the effect of take-overs is to raise the efficiency and profitability of the assets acquired (see fn. 1, p. 242). In the case of a number of privatized firms, the government has retained a so-called golden share which prevents a takeover (for example, a 'special share' in Rolls Royce would enable the Secretary of State for Trade and Industry to limit foreign and individual ownership, which in effect blocks a takeover). In the case of British Telecom, the government has initially retained a 49% stake. A merger may not come to fruition because of an adverse judgement by the MMC, and it is arguable whether a government would be prepared to allow the acquisition of companies such as, say, British Gas or British Telecom especially if the acquiring firm were foreign.[1]

The nature of the market in which a firm operates is generally seen to place constraints on what the firm can and cannot do. It is, of course, usually argued that a firm in a monopoly position has much more freedom of manœuvre than a firm in a situation of atomistic competition. Many firms which have been privatized such as the Rover Group, Jaguar, National Freight Corporation etc. were operating in competition with many other firms even when nationalized. The act of privatization has not changed the nature of the market in which they operate.

When public utilities have been privatized with their monopoly position largely intact, then their activities have been subject to regulation. At the time of writing, this applies to British Gas (BG) and British Telecom (BT), and it is proposed that similar arrangements will apply to the proposed privatization of the electricity and water industries. The regulatory authorities are the Office of Gas Supply (OFGAS) and of Telecommunications (OFTEL), with possible referral of the monopoly situation to the MMC.

The regulation has three aspects to which attention is drawn here. The first relates to price. In the case of gas, prices for domestic consumers are allowed to change to fully reflect changes in the cost of gas whereas any rise in non-gas costs can only be reflected in price to the extent of 2% below the rise in the retail price index (RPI). Similarly, the price of an index of BT's services is limited to a rise of 3% below the rise in the RPI, but since this applies to an index of all services the price of some services can be increased much more.[2] This approach involves certain difficulties. The public utilities have little incentive to keep price increases below the limit set. The limitation of price increases to 2 or 3% below the rate of increase of the RPI is presumably based on an assumption

---

[1] The Kuwait Investment Office (owned by the Kuwait government) built up a stake of 20% in the oil company BP following the sale of the final British government stake in BP (which at one time had been 49%). This was referred to the MMC and the KIO was required to reduce its stake substantially.

[2] This restriction on price increases is part of the licence under which British Telecom operates, but operated initially for the five year period ending 31 July 1989. At the time of writing the arrangements after that date were not known.

about the rate of productivity increase which can be achieved. But that productivity increase is likely to vary over time and to depend on investment decisions made by the utility. There is also the difficulty for the regulatory authority of securing the relevant information. This is illustrated by the following quotation from the Director General of Gas Supply:[1] 'Condition 3 of the authorisation stipulates that, at the time of any change in its published tariffs, British Gas must provide OFGAS with a written forecast of the maximum average price per therm, together with its components, for the year in which the change is to take effect and the following year. These forecasts should contain sufficient information as to the assumptions underlying the forecasts to enable the Director General to be reasonably satisfied that the forecasts have been properly prepared on a consistent basis. Initially British Gas refused to provide sufficient information for the Director General to be so satisfied. This resulted in OFGAS giving notice in August that it proposed to make an order under section 28 of the Gas Act requiring BG to produce the necessary information'. Eventually information was provided and undertakings were given that information would be provided in future.

The second aspect concerns the general control over the possible use of monopoly power in other areas than those covered immediately above. This has largely related so far to the prices charged for the supply of gas or telephone services other than those subject to regulatory control. British Gas was referred to the MMC over pricing and supply of gas to contract customers (broadly speaking non-domestic customers). The MMC concluded that '[w]e have found extensive discrimination by BG in the pricing and supply of gas to contract customers. We believe that this is attributable to the existence of the monopoly situation and operates or may be expected to operate against the public interest. First, BG's policy of price discrimination imposes higher costs on customers less well placed to use alternative fuels or to obtain such fuels on favourable terms. ... Second, BG's policy of relating prices to those of alternatives available to each customer places it in a position selectively to undercut potential competing gas suppliers. This may be expected to deter new entrants and to inhibit the development of competition in this market. Third, the lack of transparency in pricing creates uncertainty in the minds of customers about future gas prices and renders more risky the business environment in which they operate'.[2]

The third aspect relates to a range of unprofitable activities which the public utility is obliged or expected to undertake. This would include, for example, the provision of public call-boxes, (free) directory enquiries.

The difficulties which confront the regulatory agency include obtaining the information necessary to perform their function (as indicated above). This may be exacerbated by the relative small number of staff which they

---

[1] Quote from the *Report of the Director General of Gas Supply 1987*, HC 293 (HMSO, 1988)

[2] Monopolies and Mergers Commission, *Gas*, Cmnd. 500 (HMSO, 1988).

have, 30 in the case of OFGAS and 117 in the case of OFTEL. A problem which has been identified from American experience is that of 'agency capture'. This simply means that the personal contacts and interchange of personnel between the regulatory agency and the regulated firm as well as deliberate attempts by the regulated firm can lead the agency to act in the interests of regulated firms.

We turn now to the empirical question of whether ownership and control does make any difference to the efficiency of a firm. Making comparisons between the performance and efficiency of private and public sector companies is not a straightforward exercise. There are some general difficulties in making useful comparisons between companies which are in different situations (here of private or public ownership). There may be reasons why the firms are in different situations and those reasons can influence the comparisons. For example, a company may be in the public sector because it failed under private ownership but was judged to be too important to be allowed to go bankrupt. In such a case, a poor performance by a company under public ownership may not arise because it is in the public sector, but rather it is in the public sector because it is a poor performance company. Comparisons between public sector companies and private sector ones are also complicated by differences in the objectives of the two types of companies. Public sector companies may be required to maintain unprofitable services, be encouraged to maintain employment (particularly in periods of substantial unemployment) and be limited in their range of activities (e.g. British Rail is largely restricted to operating a railway service and not to diversify into other forms of transport).

Millward and Parker[1] conduct a wide ranging survey on the available evidence, and indicate the extensive difficulties in making comparisons between privately owned and publicly owned firms. They conclude that 'while the results are rather mixed, there is some evidence that competition does reduce the costs of public firms and regulation raises the costs of private firms. Neither finding is inconsistent with the finding about the effects of "ownership" on costs – namely that, . . . there is no general indication that private firms are more cost efficient than public firms'.

Ferguson[2] summarizes 15 comparisons of public and private sector efficiency. Eight of these refer to American electricity generation with the following conclusions. Two studies report no difference between the sectors, three report the public enterprise as more efficient and one reports private firms more efficient. One study finds both types of firm with costs $2\frac{1}{2}\%$ above the competitive level, and the final study reports that private firms sell wholesale electricity at higher prices and buy in at lower prices (than public sector firms). The results of the other seven studies (covering water, rail and airlines) are similar in tone.

1   R. Millward and D. M. Parker, 'Public and Private Enterprise: Comparative Behaviour and Relative Efficiency' in R. Millward *et al.*, *Public Sector Economics* (Longmans, 1983).
2   P. Ferguson, *Industrial Economics: Issues and Perspectives* (Macmillan, 1988).

Yarrow[1] concludes that '... private sector monitoring [i.e. private ownership] is more efficient where the relevant firm faces strong competition and other forms of product and factor market failure are relatively unimportant. ... The evidence on comparative performance in cases where product and factor markets inefficiencies are substantive is much less clear cut. Indeed, in examples such as electricity supply it tends to point in the other direction, towards better performance by public firms'.

Contracting-out by the public sector has particularly affected local authorities and the health service.[2] In the near future, local authorities will be compelled to seek competing tenders (i.e. bids from private companies as well as estimates from their own work-force) for refuse collection, street and building cleaning, vehicle and ground maintenance etc. Thus contracting-out can be viewed as a move from a monopoly supply situation (e.g. where a local authority always employed its own work-force for, say, refuse collection) to one of some competition (with a number of firms bidding for the contract).

One survey has concluded 'that in areas such as refuse collection and cleansing services, the available evidence points to privately owned firms being cheaper on average than the municipal operations by a significant amount'.[3] This conclusion is based mainly on American experience, though some limited British evidence points in the same direction. A study of competitive tendering in refuse collection[4] in Britain estimated that costs under private contracting for refuse collection were 22% below those with local authority provision. However, in those cases where refuse collection had been put out to tender but the tender had been won by the local authority refuse department, costs were also lower; in this case to the extent of 17%. The same group of authors[5] find rather similar results for hospital domestic services, namely private contracting of such services resulted in a cost reduction of 34% and of in-house provision after competitive tendering of 22%. However, there was some evidence of private contractors offering unsustainably low prices ('loss-leaders') to secure entry into this market. These studies would be consistent with the view that it is competition rather than the form of ownership which is relevant for efficiency.

A lower cost service is not necessarily more efficient than a higher cost one, in that the lower costs may have been achieved by the payment of lower wages and by a lower quality service. In particular, the British studies

---

[1]   G. Yarrow, 'Privatization in Theory and Practice', *EP*, 1986.
[2]   For extensive discussion see K. Ascher, *The Politics of Privatisation: Contracting out Public Services* (Macmillan, 1987).
[3]   M. Waterson, *op. cit.*
[4]   S. Domberger, S. A. Meadowcroft and D. J. Thompson, 'Competitive Tendering and Efficiency: The Case of Refuse Collection', *FSt*, vol. 7 (1986).
[5]   S. Domberger, S. A. Meadowcroft and D. J. Thompson, 'The Impact of Competitive Tendering and the Costs of Hospital Domestic Services', *FSt*, vol. 8 (1987).

referred to above do not make much allowance for possible lower quality and wages.[1]

Liberalization and de-regulation has not followed a uniform pattern. There have been some areas of de-regulation and liberalization. One area of increased regulation has been that of financial services, as discussed in chapter 2. During the eighties there has been, partly under the impact of changing technology, some liberalization in the telecommunications area. This has included, for example, the abolition of British Telecom's exclusive right to supply customer telephone apparatus (though the equipment has to be approved by the British Approvals Board for Telecommunications or the Secretary of State for Trade and Industry). The Secretary of State can also licence firms other than British Telecom to run telecommunications system. Mercury (a subsidary of the recently privatized Cable and Wireless) has been granted such a licence (indeed the government has decided that this will be the only licence granted before 1990). The effectiveness of Mercury in competing with British Telecom depends on the terms on which their network is connected in with the British Telecom network (since the vast majority of telephones are in that network). OFTEL has ruled that there must be full interconnection between the two networks.[2]

The Road Traffic Act 1930 brought in the regulation of bus services. Quality was regulated by, for example, the setting of standards for vehicles and for drivers and this continues. The quantity of bus services was also regulated with licences required to be able to operate a particular route. These restrictions were lifted for inter-city bus services in 1980 and for most other bus services in 1986. One study on the de-regulation of the inter-city services[3] found that prices of express bus services initially fell dramatically with many prices dropping to half their previous level. Prior to 1980, the right to operate many of the most important inter-city routes was held by the publicly owned National Bus Company. However, companies who had previously provided contract coach services provided a ready source of new entrants, helping to generate the substantial price fall. The National Bus Company was able to reassert its dominant position in a few years. Prices have since risen, and in many cases prices of express services have returned to close to their level (in real terms, that is relative to the retail price index) prior to de-regulation. This study found that there were some gains in efficiency following de-regulation. There was also some re-arrangement of the provision of bus services with increased frequency on some routes and reduced frequency on others. A report on the de-regulation of local bus services found that the facilities, reliability, availability of information and the quality of the ride all declined or remained static. It

---

[1] For some critical comments on one of these studies see J. Gurley and J. Grahl, 'Competition and Efficiency in Refuse Collection: A Critical Comment', *FSt*, vol. 9 (1988).

[2] For further discussion see Vickers and Yarrow, *op. cit.*, Chapter 8.

[3] S. A. Jaffer and D. J. Thompson, 'Deregulating Express Coaches: A Reassessment', *FSt*, vol. 8 (1987).

indicated that whilst there was improvement to services in some areas, there had been a general loss of confidence in local bus services in many areas.[1]

8 PUBLIC ENTERPRISES

The nationalized industries contributed 9% of GDP in 1979, and under the impact of privatization this figure had declined to 5½% in 1987. In 1987 these industries employed around 800,000. These figures refer only to public corporations and hence exclude public ownership in other types of companies. Privatization has been more extensive in connection with those forms of state ownership.

The three main forms of public ownership in Britain have been:

(i) the public corporation, which is a corporate body established by statute and free to manage its own affairs without detailed Parliamentary control. The relevant government minister can give general directions to the public corporation and appoints most or all of the board of management;

(ii) sole or majority state shareholding in an otherwise conventional commercial company;

(iii) organization of an industry as a department of state under the direct control of a government minister. The Post Office was the only significant example of this approach, but was turned into a public corporation in 1969.

The framework within which public corporations operate has been subject to a number of changes in the post-war period. During the first phase the public corporations were largely required to break even on average. This requirement did not encourage efficiency. The 1961 White Paper[2] introduced financial targets for public corporations, with target rates of return specified for each industry but varying between industries depending on factors such as demand conditions and the degree to which the corporation was required to provide unprofitable services. The 1967 White Paper[3] brought in a number of innovations. These included:

(i) the setting of prices to reflect long-run marginal costs;

(ii) subjecting investment to a test discount rate (initially set at 8%, later increased to 10%);

(iii) identifying and seeking government funding for any non-commercial activities (e.g. rural train services).

---

[1] Buswatch Survey reported in the *Guardian*, 26 October 1988.

[2] *Financial and Economic Obligations of the Nationalised Industries*, Cmnd. 1337 (HMSO, 1961).

[3] *Nationalised Industries: A Review of Economic and Financial Objectives*, Cmnd. 3437 (HMSO, 1967).

In addition, it was determined that industries would continue to be required to meet a financial target.

Linking prices to marginal costs is seen as desirable for the reasons indicated in our previous discussion (pp. 246–250). There has also been a move towards having a structure of prices which reflects short-run marginal costs. The implementation of marginal cost pricing faces a variety of difficulties of which two are mentioned here. First, the identification and measurement of marginal costs present substantial problems. Second, when production takes place subject to increasing returns, average costs are below marginal costs, and hence pricing according marginal cost would lead to financial losses.

The implementation of the 1967 changes was limited by the operation of government macro-economic policies, particularly those involving price and wage controls. Clearly the imposition of limits on price may interfere with both with the policy of aligning price with marginal cost and the achievement of financial targets.

The 1978 White Paper[1] signalled a substantial downgrading of the linking of price with marginal cost. It also led to the framework of control which is currently in use. This framework has a number of elements. Strategic objectives are agreed by the relevant government department with each industry and these provide the framework within the financial controls and industrial planning procedures are set. Investment is usually required to secure a 5% rate of return in real terms (i.e. after allowing for inflation) before taxes and interest payments. In some industries, public enterprise may have little discretion over prices through competition with other firms. In those industries where nationalized industries do have discretion, 'the financial targets will determine the level of prices in the light of general objectives, their control of costs and the need to cover the continuing cost of supply including an adequate return on capital'.[2] Financial targets are set usually for three years ahead. The targets as in place in early 1988 are given in table 4.8. Finally, external financing limits (EFLs) are imposed. These limits in effect cover the cash flow (difference between revenue and the sum of current and capital expenditures) of the public corporations, which means that there is an additional constraint which largely bites on the investment programme of the public corporations. These EFLs may be negative (which means that the public corporation concerned is required to make a net contribution to the Exchequer), or positive. The government's concern with the public sector borrowing requirement (of which the EFLs are part) has given the EFLs particular importance.

Since 1980, public bodies have been subject to efficiency investigations by the MMC. These investigations have covered a wide range of issues including costs, productivity, service quality, pricing and investment poli-

1   *The Nationalised Industries*, Cmnd. 7131 (HMSO, 1978).
2   *The Government's Expenditure Plans 1988/9–1990/1*, Cmnd. 288 (HMSO, 1988).

TABLE 4.8

Financial Targets of Nationalized Industries, 1988

British Coal	By 1988/89 Break even after social grants
British Rail	By 1989/90 Public Sector obligation down to £555m
British Shipbuilders	None
British Waterways	1987/88 Break even
Civil Aviation Authority	1985/6–1987/8 7% rate of return
Electricity	1988–89 3.75% rate of return 1989/90 4.75% rate of return
Girobank	1985/6–1987/8 average 22% rate of return on assets at historic cost
London Regional Transport	1984/5–87/8 Reduce revenue support to £95m
North of Scotland Hydro-electric	1987/88 2.7% rate of return
South of Scotland Electricity	1988/89 2.8% rate of return
Post Office	1986/87–88/9 3.25% return on turnover

Scottish Transport Group
  (i) road passengers
  (ii) shipping
  (iii) other
	
	1986–90 Average 4% rate of return
	Break even after grant
	8% trading surplus on turnover

Water Authorities	1987/88 1.875% rate of return 1988/89 2.24% rate of return

Note: The rate of return is the ratio profits before tax and interest divided by net assets at current cost (unless otherwise stated).
Source: The Government's Expenditure Plans 1988/9–1990/1, Cmnd. 288 (HMSO, 1988).

cies. The referrals of public bodies to the MMC on this basis have averaged around three a year.

The recent productivity performance of (formerly and currently) nationalized industries represents a substantial improvement over the performance during the seventies. Some relevant figures for individual industries are given in table 4.9. Calculations for those industries which were in public ownership at the end of 1987 indicate that their growth rate of productivity from 1979/80 to 1986/7 averaged an annual rate of 4.7%, a percentage point above the average for manufacturing industry.

9   TECHNOLOGY AND RESEARCH AND DEVELOPMENT

In table 4.10 some (highly summary) statistics are provided on the scale and financing of research and development in the United Kingdom and six other industrialized countries. Whereas in the 1960s the scale of R&D in the UK was, relative to GDP, amongst the highest, by 1985 this was not the case. The deterioration in the position of the UK is greater than at first indicated by table 4.10 in that over the period 1963–1985 GDP in the UK grew more slowly than elsewhere so that the absolute level of R&D in France, West Germany and Japan will be greater than in Britain

TABLE 4.9

Productivity Trends in Selected Nationalized Industries, 1968–85

	Output per head		Total factor productivity	
	1968–78	*1979–85*	*1968–78*	*1979–85*
British Rail	0.8	3.9	n.a	2.8
British Steel	−0.2	12.6	−2.5	2.9
Post Office	−1.3	2.3	n.a	1.9
British Telecom	8.2	5.8	5.2	0.5
British Coal	−0.7	4.4	−1.4	0.0
Electricity	5.3	3.9	0.7	1.4
British Gas	8.5	3.8	n.a	1.2
National Bus	−0.5	2.1	−1.4	0.1
British Airways	6.4	6.6	5.5	4.8

Source: R.Molyneux and D.Thompson 'Nationalised Industry Performance: Still Third-rate?', *FSt*, vol. 8, 1987.

(as has always been the case for the USA). In absolute terms over the slightly different period of 1964–86, industry research and development expenditure grew from £1,400m (in 1975 prices) to £1,883m.

TABLE 4.10

Statistics Relating to Research and Development

	Expenditure on Research and Development as % of GDP		Government Defence-finance as related % of total	
	1963	*1985*	*1963*	*1985*
United Kingdom	2.2	2.3	43.1	49.2
Japan	1.4	2.6	19.1	n.a
Sweden	1.2	2.8	34.0	26.0
West Germany	1.5	2.7	36.7	12.1
Italy	n.a	1.1	51.7	8.5
France	n.a	2.3	52.9	32.7
United States	3.1	2.8	50.3	69.4

Composition of Research and Development Expenditure, UK			
	Civil	*Defence*	*Total*
Basic	36.7	—	18.2
Strategic	27.6	1.7	14.5
Applied	24.8	14.9	19.8
Development	10.9	83.5	47.5

Sources: OECD, *Science and Technology Indicators* (1984); Cabinet Office, *Annual Review of Government Funded Research and Development* (HMSO, 1988).

The involvement of government in the financing of research and development in most industrialized countries is also apparent from table 4.10. However, the USA and the UK stand out as having particularly high proportions of research and development in areas which are related to defence. The division of research and development expenditure into four categories in table 4.10 is based on the following distinctions. Basic research is that undertaken primarily to acquire knowledge and with no specific application in mind, whereas strategic research is undertaken with eventual practical application in mind even though these cannot be clearly specified. Applied research is that which is directed primarily towards specific practical aims or objectives, and finally development is systematic work drawing on existing knowledge to produce new products, processes etc.

The three approaches to industrial policy suggested above can be applied to the case of research and technology. The 'market failure' approach has to be extended to introduce research and development. Research has a number of key features. First, research is the exploration of the unknown so that calculations on the benefits and costs of an avenue of research are particularly difficult to make. This uncertainty may militate against firms undertaking research with firms tending to opt for less risky ventures. There are often very long lags between the start of a research programme and the commercial implementation of the fruits of that programme. The combination of uncertainty and long lead times is seen to discourage research and also the provision of finance for research programme. There may be a transfer of knowledge generated by research programmes so that, despite the patent laws, firms other than the one undertaking the research benefits from the discoveries made. This line of argument is that there will be a systematic tendency for there to be under-investment in research and development. This is reflected in estimates that the rate of return on research and development is much higher than rates of return on other investment projects.[1]

Second, research is not homogeneous, and a crude division would be between basic and strategic research as defined above and applied research and development. The former could be seen as research undertaken in the pursuit of knowledge without any thought of commercial or other application, whereas the latter is undertaken for commercial reasons. However, the basic research of one era provides the platform for applied research of the next era. For example, those scientists who discovered the principles of electricity could be seen as undertaking basic research whereas those who have used those principles to develop say washing machines are engaged in applied research. The distinction between basic and applied is, of course, not a hard and fast one but useful for our discussion. Basic research is particularly prone to the difficulties identified above, namely uncertainty of outcome and long lead times. Yet such research is necessary for future progress. Further, the output from basic research should be spread as quickly as possible so that it can be drawn into applied research.

---

[1]   One estimate puts the social rate of return at 56% on research and development as compared with a private rate of return of 25%, both of which would be above the rate of return on investment in general: see E. Mansfield, 'Measuring the Social and Private Rates of Return on Innovation' in *Economic Effects of Space and Other Advanced Technologies* (Strasbourg, Council of Europe, 1980).

Third, knowledge is costly to produce, but once it has been produced it can be spread at very low cost. This sets up the following conflict. An individual will only undertake costly research if the benefits will eventually exceed the estimated costs (of course mistakes are often made). From that perspective, the individual can be encouraged to undertake research by being able to reap the gains. But once the discovery has been made, it would appear beneficial for that knowledge to be passed on to others (since it can be spread at virtually zero marginal cost); in which case the discoverer would not benefit. The patent laws have been seen as an attempt to strike a balance by giving inventors certain rights over the use of their invention for a specified period (generally 16 years in the United Kingdom). The patent holder can be compelled to grant licences for the use of the invention if the patentee is abusing the monopoly position granted by, for example, not working the invention commercially.

The Austrian school draw on the work of Schumpeter particularly.[1] Schumpeter argued that a (temporary) monopoly position often arose out of a successful research programme and the discovery of new products. Hence monopoly profits were often the return to previous research and development, though in turn these profits provide a source of funds for further investment in research and development. But these high profits do not last for ever for there is a 'perennial gale of creative destruction' which threatens the monopolist's position. The prospect of profits provides the spur to undertake research and development, but competition from others (e.g. development of close substitutes) will eat away at those profits. Thus there is an interplay between a temporary monopoly position (arising from successful innovation) and the background of competition. Schumpeter suggested that the benefits of (temporary) monopoly were to aid the pace of research and development and to more than offset the short-run costs of monopoly in terms of higher price and lower output, as suggested in figure 4.6.

Another element of the Austrian approach (as indicated above) would be the view that '[f]irms themselves are best able to assess their own markets and to balance the commercial risks and rewards of financing R&D and innovation. The government should not take on responsibilities which are principally those of industry'.[2]

The developmental state perspective would to some degree draw on the arguments outlined to the effect that the private market will systematically under-invest in research and development. It would further note that competition between firms and between countries in the late twentieth century often takes the form of technical innovation rather than price. This general view is reflected in the argument that '[t]he government has . . . a general

---

[1] See, for example, J. Schumpeter, *Capitalism, Socialism and Democracy* (Allen and Unwin, 1954).
[2] Department of Trade and Industry, *DTI – the Department for Enterprise*, Cmnd. 278 (HMSO, 1988).

responsibility to support science and technology because this is fundamental to the social and economic well-being of the country'.[1]

The present government has generally sought to reduce industrial subsidies and assistance, and this is reflected in the virtual halving (in real terms) of expenditure on industrial support.[2] However, whilst regional and selective assistance was cut (in 1979/80 prices) from £509m in 1979/80 to £159m in 1987/88 and support for aerospace, shipbuilding, steel and vehicle manufacture from £338m to £80m, there was a rise in the support of technology. This support was nearly doubled from £142m to £240m (and to £417m in current prices). However, the government's view of its own policy is that 'innovation policy should be focused primarily on the circumstances when research is necessary before commercial applications can be developed, or where the benefits of the research are likely to be widespread, and on technology transfer'.[3]

There are a large number of government programmes which can be placed under the heading of the encouragement and support of industrial research and development. Most of them, however, account for very small sums of public expenditure. The bulk of public expenditure in this area (as can be seen from table 4.9) relates to research in defence-related industries. It has also been estimated[4] that around 30% of Britain's highly qualified scientists and engineers are employed in the defence sector. One particular difficulty which arises here is that the secrecy which surrounds defence-related work limits the spread of knowledge arising from this type of research work. The industrial spin-offs benefiting other sectors of industry are then likely to be limited. It has been argued that 'technological spin-offs from the military sector, while obviously tangible, are generally few and far between and thus represent a poor return on R&D compared to equivalent civilian outlays. This is partly because Britain's particularly tight security laws inhibit the flow of knowledge from military laboratories, but it stems as much from the qualitative difference between military and civilian technology'.[5]

In non-defence areas, government support of research and development can be conveniently divided under three heads. The first heading is that of single company support, of which the bulk of expenditure is taken by the general support for industry programme. This is designed to provide general financial support to encourage beneficial R&D projects which represent a significant advance for the industry or sector concerned. Other programmes operating in the mid-eighties under this head included: the software products scheme (SPS) under which support of up to 25% of

[1]   House of Lords, *Report of Select Committee on Science and Technology*, HL 20 (HMSO, 1986).
[2]   See J. Shepherd, 'Industrial Support Policies', *NIER*, no. 122, November 1987.
[3]   Department of Trade and Industry, *op. cit.*
[4]   M. Kaldor, M. Sharp and W. Walker. 'Industrial Competitiveness and Britain's Defence', *LBR*, no. 162 (October 1986).
[5]   M. Kaldor *et al.*, *ibid.*

the eligible development and marketing costs of innovative software products can be provided; the microelectronics industry support programme (MISP) which is designed to develop UK capability in microelectronics technology; the fibre optic and opto-electronics scheme (FOS) which is designed to stimulate novel product development in the electronic and fibre optics industries. However, as part of reduced provision for support of projects in individual companies, the MISP and FOS schemes are in the process of being phased out.

The second heading is that of collaborative project support. The major programme here has been the ALVEY project which was designed 'to stimulate [information technology] research through a programme of collaborative pre-competitive projects fitting into the strategies developed for the key technologies of intelligent knowledge based systems (IKBS), the man/machine interface (MMI), software engineering, very large scale integration (VLSI) and computing architectures'.[1] The government met 50% of the project costs.

Over the five years beginning in 1988, government departments expect to spend around £200m on the LINK scheme. This scheme is designed to speed the commercial exploitation of research by encouraging academic–industry collaboration in strategic areas of science and technology. These areas cover, for example, advanced semiconductor materials, molecular electronics.

The EUREKA project was a French inspired agreement, adopted by 18 EEC and EFTA nations and the EEC Commission in November 1985. It seeks to encourage industry-led collaborative projects in advanced technologies leading to innovative products, processes or services. There is no central fund and each government is responsible for financial support of its own firms. The British participation is described as designed to 'improve the competitiveness of British firms in world markets in civil applications of new technologies by encouraging European industrial and technological market-led collaboration in R and D'.[2] The extent of government support is 50% of the costs of applied research projects and up to 25% of the costs of development projects. In mid-1988 there were some 160 EUREKA projects which had been agreed of which British participants were involved in 57.[3]

SMART (Small Firms Merit Award for Research and Technology) is a competition (with a 100 winners in 1988) for small firms (under 200 employees). In 1988 the prize from the competition was a 75% grant (up to £37,500) for a feasibility study lasting up to a year, with further grants for some of the prizewinners. The intention is to encourage the development of high risk projects and the start-up of high technology firms, and the

---

[1] J.Shepherd, *op. cit.*
[2] J.Shepherd, *op. cit.*
[3] At the EEC level, the ESPIRIT II programme (at a cost to the European Commission of around £500m) is designed to make European IT competitive. The programme covers micro-electronics, information processing systems and information technology.

competition looks for the best novel ideas, particularly in biotechnology, information technology, advanced materials technology and advanced manufacturing technology.

The third heading covers consultancy, advice and awareness pro-grammes. These programmes range from the provision of IT equipment in schools through to business and technical advisory service (BTAS). They are mainly linked to micro-electronics and information technology.

10   EUROPEAN ECONOMIC COMMUNITY AND INDUSTRIAL POLICIES

Britain has been a member of the European Economic Community since 1973, and that membership has had a number of effects on British industry and the conduct of industrial policy. The composition of international trade has moved towards the EEC and hence away from the more traditional markets of the British Commonwealth. In this section we discuss two aspects of the impact of EEC membership on British industry. The first part con-cerns the impact of the Treaty of Rome which established the EEC on industrial policies. The second part considers some of the consequences of the proposed establishment of a 'single market' by the end of 1992.

The EEC has operated (under Articles 85 and 86 of the Treaty of Rome of 1957) a monopoly and mergers policy to which British firms have in principle been subject. The relevant parts of the Treaty of Rome are Articles 85 (dealing with cartels and restrictive trade practices) and 86 (monopoly). These articles refer to inter-state trade, which would appear to exclude any cartels or monopolies affecting only within-country trade, but agree-ments and actions which serve to limit imports from one EEC country to another would be covered by these articles.

The implementation of competition policy is in the hands of the European Commission with cases which appear to break Articles 85 or 86 being taken to the European Court of Justice. There is a similarity with British policy in the area of cartels and restrictive practices in that there is a presumption that they are against the public interest with the possibility of exemptions being granted. Article 85 covers agreements, decisions and concerted prac-tices which may affect trade between member states and which have the effect of restricting or distorting competition. The article specifically men-tions agreements and practices which fix prices, limit production, share out markets between firms or which charge discriminatory prices. In prac-tice, the Court and Commission have placed a 'tough' interpretation on Article 85. However, the implementation of the article is subject to a *de minimis* rule under which agreements involving firms with a combined mar-ket share below 5% or with a combined annual turnover below 50 million ECU (around £30m) are excluded from consideration. Firms do not have to register any restrictive trade agreements, but may notify the Commission of agreements. The incentive to notify an agreement 'since if they do not do so there can be no question of their agreement being exempted' and if 'the agreement is duly notified it enjoys a provisional or temporary validity'.[1]

Article 86 deals with the abuse of market dominance rather than with monopoly *per se*, and with those abuses which affect trade between member states. In the Article, particular abuses mentioned are:

'(a) directly or indirectly imposing unfair purchase or selling prices or other unfair trading conditions;
(b) limiting production, markets or technical development to the prejudice of consumers;
(c) applying dissimilar conditions to equivalent transactions with other trading parties, thereby placing them at a competitive disadvantage;
(d) making the conclusion of contracts subject to acceptance by the other parties of supplementary obligations which, by their nature or according to commercial usage, have no connection with the subject of such contracts'.[2]

The Treaty of Rome does not define dominance but the Court has looked at both market share and actions before arriving at a view as to whether there is dominance in a particular case. A market share as low as 40% has been used as partial evidence of dominance. There is the problem of finding an appropriate definition of the market, and this problem is exacerbated in the EEC context since the question arises as to whether the appropriate market area is the whole of the EEC or is one particular country or region.

Mergers are not explicitly covered by the Treaty of Rome, and indeed there has been debate over whether mergers were covered. However, the European Court has ruled that Article 86 does cover mergers, partly on the grounds that Article 85 (on restrictive practices) could be side-stepped by firms merging (rather than operating illegal agreements amongst themselves). However, there has not actually been a formal decision of the Court prohibiting a merger.

The conduct of industrial policy (particularly in the realm of subsidies) has probably been more affected by the rules limiting national governments providing 'unfair' advantages to their own firms. Articles 92 to 94 of the Treaty of Rome restrict state aid to firms. The range of state aid which is covered has been defined to be constituted not only by grants 'but also by loans on more favourable terms than are available on the market, guarantees, tax concessions, relief of social security contributions, and by the State putting up new capital for enterprises in circumstances in or on terms which a private investor would not do so'.[3] Part of Article 92 makes

[1] D. Swann, *The Economics of the Common Market* (Penguin Books), sixth edition.
[2] Quote is from Article 86 of the Treaty of Rome.
[3] Commission of the European Communities, *Fourteenth Report on Competition Policy* (Office for Official Publications of the European Communities, Brussels, 1985).

State aid which distorts (or threatens to distort) competition by favouring some firms or industries in so far as trade between member countries is affected incompatible with the common market. Article 93 leads to State aid being kept under constant review, with member countries having to report plans on State aid.[1] The rules have impinged on British government policy in terms of the extent of financial assistance offered. Further, the terms governing the sale by the government of the Rover Group to British Aerospace were similarly influenced by the European Commission.[2]

The effect of British membership of the EEC on British industry and industrial policy is likely to be much greater in the next few years than it has been in the past 16 years. This will be a consequence of the so-called single market, sometimes referred to by the year by which it is intended to have full implementation, namely 1992. There are three particular aspects of the single market in the EEC context to which attention should be drawn. First, there is the removal of customs barriers affecting the movement of goods between one member country and another (which will mean the disappearance of duty-free shopping on journeys between member countries). Second, each member country sets product standards for specific goods and services sold within its borders. These product standards may be of a general form (e.g. that a good be of 'merchantable quality') but also of a specific form. There are, for example, laws governing the required contents of different types of food, laws on the pollution levels from cars etc., etc. Third, government (central and local) of each member country often favours the purchase of goods and services produced within its borders or by its firms.

The intention of the single market is that each of these three impediments to inter-country trade should be eliminated. However, these impediments to trade will still apply (and indeed may be intensified) in regard to trade between member countries and non-member countries. Further, transport costs, differences in national tastes and so on, will obviously still remain and there will also be differences in VAT rates etc., though there is pressure toward the 'harmonization' of these tax rates.

The 'official' estimate of the effect of removing these impediments to trade between member countries (the first two items in table 4.11) is for a gain amounting to around $2\frac{1}{2}\%$ of GDP. There are two points to note on these estimates. First, a reduction in employment is counted as a gain since it is a reduction in costs. Thus, the reduction in employment of customs officers is viewed as a reduction in costs (largely in this case costs incurred by governments) and hence counted as a gain. But this assumes (implicitly)

---

[1]   For further details see D. Swann, *op. cit.*

[2]   Although it was described as a sale, the terms of the transfer of ownership of the Rover Group from the government to British Aerospace (BAe) made it more like a gift. The government sold the Rover Group to BAe for £150m. However, the government offered £800m to write off the company's debts, which was subsequently reduced to £547m at the insistence of the European Commission.

TABLE 4.11

Estimated Benefits of a Single Market in the EEC

	ECU (billions)	% GDP
Gains from removing barriers affecting trade	8–9	0.2–0.3
Gains from removal of barriers affecting overall production	57–71	2.0–2.4
Gains from exploiting economies of scale more fully	61	2.1
Gains from intensified competition reducing inefficiencies and monopoly profits	46	1.6
Total (for seven member states)	127–187	4.3–6.4
Total for all 12 member states	164–258	4.3–6.4
Central estimate	216	

Notes: Monetary value of benefits expressed in billions of European Currency Units (ECU) in 1985 prices. 1 ECU was equal to about 0.67p at the time of writing.

There is overlap between categories of gains from exploiting economies of scale and gains from intensified competition: it is assumed that the range for these two categories combined is 62–107 billion ECUs.

The detailed studies were mainly undertaken for seven member states which were Belgium, France, Germany, Italy, Luxembourg, Netherlands, and United Kingdom, and the estimated gains for seven member states refer to these countries. These seven states account for 88% of total EEC GDP. The figures for twelve member states assume the same proportionate gain in the additional five states as in the seven for whom the calculations were made.

Source: P. Cecchini, *The European Challenge 1992: The Benefits of a Single Market* (Wildwood House, 1988).

that customs officers find employment elsewhere in the economy. If, in contrast, they remain unemployed (or whilst the customs officers find employment they replace others) then the gain is zero or may be negative (when the customs officer values being employed).

Second, national and local governments will be unable to express preference in their procurement policies for goods and services which have been domestically produced. There appears a gain on public expenditure in that governments will have to purchase at the lowest price (from a community-based supplier) rather than from domestically based suppliers. Thus, governments will not be able to use their purchasing power to help stimulate local employment nor to encourage technical advance through their procurement policies.

The impact of these changes on prices, output and technical efficiency has been described as follows: 'highlights of the 1992 picture include a substantial gain for consumers (consumer surplus) as prices drop and product choice and quality increase under the impact of open competition. Producers face a more mixed outlook. In the short term, profits (particularly those resulting from monopoly and protected positions) may be squeezed. But in the longer run, business as a whole is expected to respond to the new competitive climate by making various adjustments – e.g. scaling up production ('economies of scale of production'), gaining experience of how to produce more efficiently ('economies of scale of learning' or 'learning curve effects'), eliminating management inefficiencies ('X-inefficiency' to the economist), and by improved capacity to innovate. Gains from these and other adjustment, when netted out, lead to an increase in the community's "net economic welfare".[1]

The estimated impact of these changes in economic welfare is given by the third and fourth items in table 4.11. These estimates are clearly substantial, and in total suggest an increase of around 6% in the GDP of the EEC countries. Our discussion of these estimates has two parts. The first is to indicate the nature of these estimates, and the second is to suggest that there are reasons for thinking that the benefits will not be as large as indicated (with particular reference to UK).

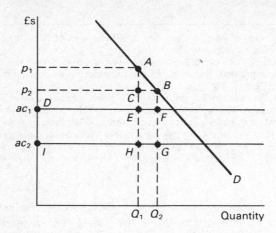

Figure 4.7   The Impact of Lower Unit Costs on Welfare

The basis of the estimates of the gains of the single market can be seen by reference to figure 4.7. The existing price is taken as p_1, at which Q_1 is purchased, the average costs of production are ac_1. After the single market, the price is assumed to fall on the basis that there will be an increase in effective competition. Customs barriers and other impediments to trade have the effect of providing some protection for firms in their domestic market, and this allows price to be somewhat higher than otherwise. Price is also assumed to fall because costs fall (as indicated in the quote above and for reasons to be discussed below). The overall effect on price is represented by a fall in price from p_1 to p_2. Following the line of argument given above, the gain of economic welfare to consumers of the lower price (and the related increase in quantity consumed) is p_1ABp_2, of which p_1ACp_2 represents a reduction in profits, leaving ABC as the net gain from lower prices.

The reduction in costs is argued to arise from the combination of three sources. The first is the further exploitation of economies of scale (decreas-

[1]   P. Cecchini, *The European Challenge 1992: The Benefits of a Single Market* (Wildwood House, 1988).

ing unit costs). This assumes that firms are currently prevented from fully exploiting the available economies of scale through an inability to sell the resulting output. A firm may find that the average costs of producing 50,000 units would be £10 and of producing 100,000 units would be £9. But if the market for its output is only 50,000 units then it clearly would not be worthwhile to fully exploit the available economies of scale. However, if another market now becomes available in which a further 50,000 can be sold, then it would be worthwhile to expand productive capacity to meet that extra demand at a lower unit cost. The basis of this argument is further discussed below.

The second basis is 'learning curve effects'. The general notion here is that as experience of a particular production process builds up, ways of improving the production process are gradually discovered and put into effect. There has been debate over whether experience is better measured by the amount of (cumulative) output produced or by the length of time during which the process has been used. In the cumulative output case, it is usually argued that many of the learning or experience effects can be summarized by an equation of the form $\log UC = a + b \log Q$, where UC is the unit cost (of output produced to date) and Q the cumulative output; b is expected to be negative. A value of $b = -0.32$ for example would indicate that for each doubling of output, unit costs decline by 20%.[1]

The third basis is the reduction of X- (or technical) inefficiency.[2] The general idea here is that firms often operate with some technical inefficiency (though economists often assume technical efficiency), and that an increase in effective competition will force firms to operate in a more efficient manner.

These three effects are represented in figure 4.7 by a reduction in the average cost curve from ac_1 to ac_2.[3] The profits in the industry are initially p_1AED and become p_2BGI. The change in profits is thus $DFGI + CBFE - p_1ACp_2$. The last term has already been discussed above. Of the change in profits, the area $DEHI$ corresponds to lower costs on the initial output.

These estimates of the gains from a single market have been subject to a number of challenges, some of which we now briefly discuss. It can be seen by reference to table 4.10 that the gains from economies of scale are estimated as just over 2% of GDP, providing around two-fifths of the estimated gains. It should be first noted that the estimation of economies of scale is fraught with difficulties.[4] Further, policies such as those pursued

---

[1] See Review of Monopoly and Mergers Policy, *op. cit.*
[2] The term X-inefficiency comes from H. Leibenstein, 'Allocative Efficiency vs. X-efficiency', *AER*, vol. 56 (1966).
[3] Economies of scale would mean, of course, declining unit costs, whereas figure 4.7 assumes constant unit costs. Drawing in declining unit costs would complicate the figure and the analysis. However, figure 4.7 can be interpreted as saying that the industry in question could have operated on a cost curve lower than ac^1 before (reflecting economies of scale) but did not do so since the resulting output could not be sold.
[4] For further discussion see M. Sawyer, *op. cit.*, Chapter 4.

by the IRC during the sixties were strongly influenced by the notion that British firms were 'too small', and the resulting larger firms were not noticeably successful.

The concentration of production which is associated with the exploitation of economies of scale involves costs which are often omitted from the calculations. On average, the distance between the point of production and the eventual sale is increased, thereby raising transport costs. It is also argued that industrial relations become more fraught in large factories. For these and other reasons, firms may not wish to build factories of the size indicated by studies of economies of scale.

The exploitation of economies of scale will usually involve the emergence of a smaller number of large firms at the level of the EEC. This would involve some firms going out of business, with the remaining firms able to expand and satisfy the demand previously met by the firms which have now disappeared. The exact effect of this on competition is difficult to estimate. On the one hand, there is seen to be more competition arising from the reduction of trade barriers; but on the other hand, the number of firms gradually declines. If the latter effect is significant and as a consequence effective competition declines it would be expected that prices would rise, thereby offsetting some of the gains of the single market.

The concentration of production also raises the question of the geographical location of that production. There will be a further tendency for production to be located towards the geographical centre of the EEC area. Further, since richer consumers have a higher level of demand, it would be expected that production would tend to move towards the more prosperous regions of the EEC. Some have spoken of a 'golden triangle' within the EEC with apexes of (approximately) London, Hamburg and Milan. Movement of industry towards the geographical centre and towards the richer areas would mean a movement away from most of the regions of the United Kingdom (with the exception of London and the South-East).

11   CONCLUDING REMARKS

The prospects for British industry in the next few years are likely to be strongly influenced by two sets of issues which have been discussed in this chapter. The deteriorating balance of trade position may force a prolonged period of slow growth and policy responses to correct the trade deficits. If, however, British industry is 'leaner and fitter' then the trade deficit may be corrected through a rising demand for British exports. The movement towards the 'single market' which place further competitive pressures on British industry. The pessimistic view touched on at the end of the previous section would indicate a shift of industrial activity away from most regions of Britain towards other countries. The optimistic view of the EEC would suggest a new era of prosperity for Britain and the rest of the EEC.

SUGGESTIONS FOR FURTHER READING
General Texts on Industrial Economics

R.Clarke, *Industrial Economics* (Blackwell, 1985)

D.Hay and D.Morris, *Industrial Economics, Theory and Evidence* (Oxford University Press, 1979)

M.Sawyer, *The Economics of Industries and Firms* (second edition, Croom Helm, 1985)

Recent Developments

C.Mayer, 'Recent Developments in Industrial Economics and their Implications for Policy, *OREP*, vol. 1 (1985)

Manufacturing Sector and Foreign Trade

R.E.Rowthorn and J.Wells, *De-Industrialization and Foreign Trade* (Cambridge University Press, 1987)

House of Lords, *Report from the Select Committee on Overseas Trade*, HL 238 (HMSO 1985)

Competition Policy

D.Hay and J.Vickers, 'The Reform of U.K. Competition Policy', *NIER*, no. 125, August 1988

Privatization and Regulation

J.Vickers and G.Yarrow, *Privatization: An Economic Analysis* (M.I.T. Press, 1988)

K.Ascher, *The Politics of Privatisation: Contracting out Public Services* (Macmillan, 1987)

M.Waterson, *Regulation of the Firm and Natural Monopoly* (Blackwell, 1988)

Research and Development

Symposium on Technical Progress, *OREP*, vol. 4, no. 4 (1988)

Single Market and 1992

P.Cecchini, *The European Challenge 1992: The Benefits of a Single Market* (Wildwood House, 1988).

5

Labour

Geraint Johnes and Jim Taylor

1 EMPLOYMENT

1.1 The Labour Force and Economic Activity Rates

The most obvious and useful starting point for a detailed investigation of the labour market is the labour force itself. This consists of all persons who are in employment plus all those who are seeking work or are on a government employment or training scheme. We can see from table 5.1 that Great Britain's civilian labour force has grown by over two million since 1971 and that this was almost entirely due to the increase in the number of females. The male labour force has remained virtually static throughout this period. In 1971, females accounted for 37.3% of the workforce; by 1991, this figure is expected to rise to 42.5%.

There have been several fundamental changes in the labour force of Great Britain in recent years. The percentage of males who are economically active (i.e. in a job or seeking one), for example, fell from 80.5% to 73.7% between 1971 and 1987 (see table 5.1). This fall in the male activity rate was more than offset by a simultaneous increase in the male population of working age, thus giving rise to a small increase in the male labour force. The situation for males contrasts sharply with that for females: the percentage of females of working age who are economically active increased from 43.9% in 1971 to 50.0% in 1987. This is expected to increase to 53.0% by 1995. Much of this increase in the female activity rate has been associated with an increase in part-time employment, particularly for married women. The combined effect of this increase in the female activity rate and the increase in the population of working age is reflected by the increase of 2.4 million in the female labour force during 1971–87, an increase of 25%.

The contribution of the growth in the population of working age and changes in the activity rate to the overall change in the labour force are given in table 5.2. This shows in detail the changes which have occurred since 1971. The most outstanding features are the loss of over 600,000 males from the economically active population during 1981–86 and the addition of nearly 800,000 females to the economically active population during 1971–76. These two examples vividly demonstrate that fundamental changes in the labour force can occur over relatively short periods.

Economic activity rates vary not only between males and females but also between different age groups and between people with different ethnic

TABLE 5.1

The Civilian Labour Force and Activity Rates in Great Britain: by Sex

	Civilian labour force (millions)			Activity rates (%)	
Year	Males	Females	Total	Males	Females
Estimates					
1971	15.6	9.3	24.9	80.5	43.9
1976	15.6	10.1	25.7	78.9	46.8
1981	15.6	10.6	26.2	76.5	47.6
1987	15.7	11.6	27.3	73.7	50.0
Projections					
1991	16.0	12.2	28.2	73.7	51.9
1995	15.9	12.4	28.3	73.3	53.0

Note: The activity rate is the civilian labour force expressed as a percentage of the resident population aged 16 or over.
Sources: ST 19, 1989, pp. 67–68; *DEG*, April 1989, pp. 159–172.

origins. For males, the activity rate reaches its peak for the 25–44 age group whereas for females the activity rate is very similar across all age groups between 16 and 54 (see table 5.3). This flattening out of the female activity rate is a very recent trend and is a consequence of the much quicker return to work after child-bearing in the 1980s than has traditionally been the case. The greater availability of part-time jobs for women has facilitated this trend towards higher activity rates for females in the child-bearing age groups (mainly 20–44).

One of the most outstanding features of UK activity rates is the stark difference in long-run trends between males and females. In particular, the difference between male and female activity rates has diminished considerably during the past few decades. Between 1971 and 1987, for example, the difference between male and female activity rates fell from 36.6 percentage points to 23.7 percentage points and this difference is likely to continue falling during the 1990s (see table 5.1). These long-run trends in the male and female activity rates raise an interesting and important question: why has the male activity rate declined whilst the female rate has been increasing? Before searching for answers to this question, it is important to realize that the long-run trend in the activity rate has differed considerably according to age group. This is true for both males and females (see table 5.3). The activity rate for males aged 16–19, for example, has actually increased rather than fallen as was the case for males in most other age groups. The most dramatic fall in the male activity rate occurred in the 60–64 age group; it fell from 82.9% in 1971 to 56.4% in 1988 in this group. Since this accounts for a substantial proportion of the fall in the overall male activity rate, it can be inferred that earlier retirement has been a major cause of the falling long-run trend in the male activity rate.

As far as the female activity rate is concerned, the long-run trend has been upwards for all age groups below 60. The upward trend has been particularly steep for females in the 25–44 age group, increasing from 52.4% in 1971 to 69.8% in 1988. Substantial increases have also occurred in other

TABLE 5.2

Contribution of Population Growth and Changes in the Activity Rate to Changes in the Civilian Labour Force in Great Britain: by Sex

Time period	Males (thousands)			Females (thousands)		
	Contribution of population growth	Contribution of changes in the activity rate	Total change	Contribution of population growth	Contribution of changes in the activity rate	Total change
Estimated						
1971–76	170	−148	22	−8	794	786
1976–81	396	−337	59	328	153	481
1981–86	518	−663	−145	335	311	646
Projected						
1986–91	295	−76	217	100	174	274

Notes:

1. This is the change in the civilian labour force which would have occurred if the activity rate in each age group had remained at its initial value in each of the periods shown.

2. This is the change in the civilian labour force minus the contribution of population growth.

Source: ST 18, 1988, p. 67.

TABLE 5.3

Economic Activity Rates in Great Britain: by Age and Sex

Age group	Males (%)				Females (%)			
	1971	1981	1988	1991*	1971	1981	1988	1991*
16–19	69.4	72.4	75.4	75.6	65.0	70.4	74.0	75.1
20–24	87.7	85.1	86.2	86.1	60.2	68.8	70.1	71.0
25–44	95.4	95.7	94.4	94.2	52.4	61.7	69.8	72.2
45–59 (45–54)	94.8	93.0	87.7	87.7	62.0	68.0	71.1	71.8
60–64 (55–59)	82.9	69.3	56.4	56.0	50.9	53.4	54.1	55.1
65 and over								
(60 and over)	19.2	10.3	7.3	6.2	12.4	8.3	6.6	6.4
All	80.5	76.5	74.0	73.7	43.9	47.6	50.8	51.9

Notes:
( ) = females.
* = projected.
Sources: *ST 19*, 1989, p. 70: *DEG*, April 1989, pp. 159–72.

age groups. The reasons for this long-run upward trend in the female activity rate are still the subject of debate, but recent research suggests that plausible explanations can be found on both the supply side and the demand side of the labour market. The main explanations on the supply side are that the female activity rate has increased because of:

– a reduction in sexual discrimination against females
– a change in social attitudes towards mothers returning to work after childbirth
– the rapid growth of nurseries and playschools
– and the introduction of household products such as the fully-automatic washing machine, the microwave oven and fast food.

All these have helped to liberate females (and some males!) from domestic chores. In addition, it may even have been the case that husbands have become more tolerant of their wives working, particularly as family income has been boosted as a result.

There are three primary demand-side explanations for the long-run increase in female economic activity. Firstly, very high levels of labour demand for over three decades following the Second World War led employers to search for additional labour reserves. Secondly, a rising real wage has increased the opportunity cost of not working in paid employment, thereby inducing more women to take a job. Thirdly, in their search for cheaper labour, employers have provided more opportunities for short-time working and this has been found to be particularly popular among married women. Research in recent years has tended to support these various explanations of the long-run upward trend in the female activity rate.

Finally, table 5.4 shows how economic status varies according to ethnic origin. White males are more likely to be in employment and less likely to be unemployed than non-white males. For females, those with an Indian/

Pakistani/Bangladeshi origin are far less likely to be economically active than either white or West Indian females; and West Indian females are nearly twice as likely to be out of work than was the case for white females.

1.2   Recent Changes in Employment: Industrial and Regional Aspects

The UK's industrial base has undergone radical re-structuring since the 1970s. Four of the more prominent structural changes are discussed in this section. The first is the shift in jobs between the main industrial sectors. Since 1979, two million jobs have been lost in the manufacturing sector while 2.4 million have been created in the service sector (see table 5.5). The banking, finance and insurance sector alone has provided an extra one million jobs during 1979–88, an increase of 55% in just nine years. This switch from manufacturing jobs to service jobs during the 1980s is part of a much longer-term trend which began in the mid-1960s. After reaching an all-time peak of over nine million workers in 1966, manufacturing employment has continued to decline throughout the 1970s and 1980s while employment in the service sector has continued to expand except for a slight drop in the early 1980s (see figure 5.1). These long-term structural changes in the industrial base of the UK are reflected by the decline in the manufacturing sector's share of total employment from 33.9% in 1971 to 21.4% in 1988. The service sector's share of total employment rose from 53.2% to 68.1% in the same period. These changes demonstrate just how quickly industrial re-structuring has been occurring in the UK.

The second major structural change which has occurred in the UK labour market during the 1980s is the rapid growth in the number of self-employed workers since 1979. Between 1979 and 1988, the number of self-employed workers increased by over a million, from 1.9 million to 3.0 million. This occurred across a wide range of industries, the most substantial increases being in the construction and service sectors.

The third prominent structural change in the UK labour market in the 1980s has been the shift in employment in favour of females. The most rapidly declining industries have been dominated by males while the most rapidly expanding industries have been dominated by females. Furthermore, many of the new jobs have been part-time rather than full-time. Between 1981 and 1988, the number of male employees in employment fell by 500,000 whereas the number of female employees in employment increased by over 900,000. Over a half of these extra jobs for females were created during 1986–88.

The major shifts in employment which have been occurring between industries have been accompanied by less dramatic, though still substantial shifts in employment between regions. This shift in jobs between regions is the fourth major structural change which has occurred during the 1980s. Since the 1960s, the southern regions of the UK have increased their share of total employment from 47.6% to 52.9% (see table 5.6). The structural

TABLE 5.4

Economic Status of the Population of Working Age in Great Britain : by Sex and Ethnic Group, 1985–87

Economic status	Males (%)			Females (%)		
	White	West Indian	Indian, Pakistani, Bangladeshi	White	West Indian	Indian, Pakistani, Bangladeshi
In employment	79	65	64	61	59	34
Out of employment	9	18	16	7	13	8
Economically inactive	12	16	20	32	27	58
Total	100	100	100	100	100	100

Note: Errors in summation due to rounding.
Source: *ST 19*, 1989, p. 71.

TABLE 5.5

Employment in the United Kingdom: by Industry

Industrial sector	Employment in thousands			% change	
	1971	*1979*	*1988*	*1971–79*	*1979–88*
Agriculture, forestry, fishing	764	666	582	−12.8	−12.6
Energy and water	798	723	460	−9.4	−36.4
Manufacturing	8,196	7,394	5,362	−9.8	−27.5
Construction	1,549	1,590	1,598	2.6	0.5
Distribution, hotels, repairs	4,433	4,909	5,391	10.7	9.8
Transport and communications	1,622	1,567	1,538	−3.4	−1.9
Banking, finance, insurance	1,488	1,795	2,792	20.6	55.5
Other services	5,315	6,435	7,364	21.1	14.4
All industries	24,165	25,078	25,087	3.8	0.0
Self-employed	2,026	1,905	2,984	−6.0	56.6
Employees	22,139	23,173	22,103	4.7	−4.6
% self-employed	8.4	7.6	11.9	—	—

Source: ST 19, 1989, pp. 73–4.

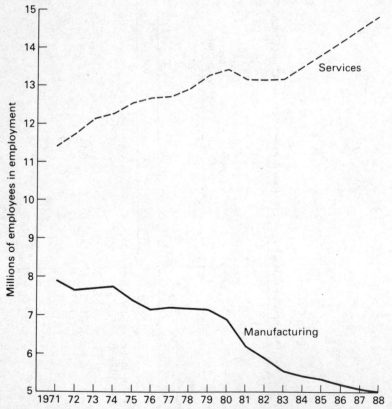

Figure 5.1   Changes in Manufacturing and Service Sector Employment in GB, 1971–88. (*Note:* Figures refer to June each year.) (*Sources: DEG*, Historical Supplement 1, February 1987; *DEG*, January 1989.)

changes in the industrial distribution of employment and in the regional shift in employment are not, of course, unrelated. The most severe job losses since the early 1970s have been in traditional industries such as ship-building, textiles and heavy engineering, all of which have been relatively more important sources of employment in the northern than in the southern regions. The structural decline of the older staple industries is only part of the story, however, since jobs in private services have been expanding more rapidly in the south than in the north.

TABLE 5.6

Employment in the Regions of the United Kingdom: Long-term Trends

Region	Numbers employed in thousands			% of total UK employment		
	1965	1973	1987	1965	1973	1987
South East	8,190	8,240	8,618	32.6	33.0	34.5
East Anglia	670	750	952	2.7	3.0	3.8
South West	1,572	1,652	1,915	6.3	6.6	7.7
East Midlands	1,509	1,555	1,742	6.0	6.2	7.0
'Southern' regions	11,941	12,197	13,227	47.6	48.8	52.9
West Midlands	2,480	2,416	2,283	9.9	9.7	9.1
Yorkshire/Humberside	2,198	2,122	2,058	8.8	8.5	7.8
North West	3,121	2,971	2,549	12.4	11.9	10.4
North	1,371	1,358	1,201	5.5	5.4	4.8
Wales	1,145	1,121	1,027	4.6	4.5	4.1
Scotland	2,275	2,215	2,093	9.1	8.9	8.4
Northern Ireland	566	584	561	2.3	2.3	2.2
'Northern' regions	13,156	12,787	11,722	52.4	51.2	47.1
United Kingdom	25,097	24,984	24,999	100	100	100

Source: Department of Employment.

1.3 Hours Worked by Employees

Average weekly hours worked in the UK has been on a steady downward trend since the mid-1950s. For male manual workers, average hours worked has fallen from around 48 hours per week in the mid-1950s to between 44 and 45 hours per week in the 1980s (see figure 5.2). For females, hours worked fell sharply from the mid-1950s to the late 1960s but has been very stable since the early 1970s. The long-run downward trend in hours worked seems to have halted for females, at least for the time being. The almost continuous downward trend in hours worked for male workers reflects an increasing preference for leisure as real income increases. Thus, although an increase in real wages may be expected to induce workers to work longer hours, this has apparently been more than offset by an increase in the desire for more leisure as income increases. Leisure is more useful if income is high enough to enjoy it.

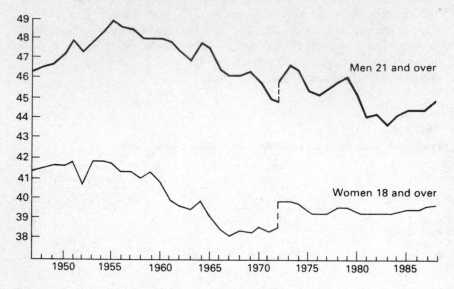

Figure 5.2   Average Weekly Hours Worked by UK Manual Workers (April each year). (*Note:* From 1972, average hours worked excludes those whose pay was affected by absence.) (*Sources: British Labour Statistics, Historical Abstract 1886–1968; DEG.*)

A further interesting feature of the hours worked time series shown in figure 5.2 is that it fluctuates pro-cyclically. This means that hours worked increase when the economy is in a boom phase of the economic cycle (as in 1955, 1964, 1973, 1979 and 1988) and decrease during slumps. The effect of the 1979–81 depression on the hours worked by males is particularly well marked; weekly hours worked fell from 46.2 in 1979 to 44.2 in 1981 and then to 43.8 in 1983 before eventually rising strongly as the economy grew rapidly in the mid-1980s. The 1980s' slump and subsequent boom had a much greater effect on male hours than on female hours. This was probably a result of the far greater impact of the slump on the male-dominated manufacturing sector than on the service sector, which is more 'female intensive' in its use of labour.

The time series of average hours worked for UK workers as a whole (shown in figure 5.2) conceals considerable variation between industries. These differences in hours worked are particularly large for males. For example, non-manual males in banking, finance and insurance worked only 37.4 hours per week compared to 47.7 hours by manual workers in transport and communications.

2 UNEMPLOYMENT
2.1 Labour Market Stocks and Flows

To understand the causes of unemployment, it is useful to begin by examining the relationship between labour market stocks and flows. Basically, there are three primary stocks: the stock of employed workers, the stock of unemployed and the stock of those who are not economically active. As figure 5.3 shows, the stock of economically inactive persons includes those not in the working population (e.g. students, mothers with young children and those who are sick or retired). Each of these three stocks is connected to the other two by means of flows of persons between them. The unemployment stock, for example, is connected to the employment stock because redundant workers flow from the employment stock to the unemployment stock; and also because unemployed people who get jobs flow in the opposite direction. It should be clear that the unemployment stock will increase whenever the inflow into this stock exceeds the outflow from it, as happens during recessions when firms are releasing more workers than they are taking on.

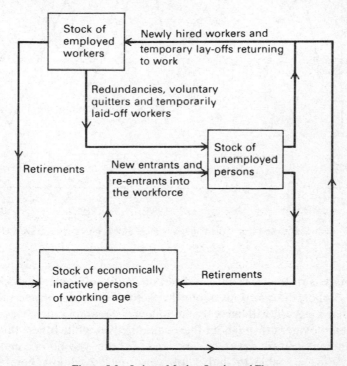

Figure 5.3   Labour Market Stocks and Flows

The relationship between inflows into the unemployment stock (and outflows from it) is shown in figure 5.4 for the period 1984–88. Two observations can be made about these inflows and outflows. Firstly, the inflows into and out of the unemployment stock are of a similar order of magnitude; and they tend to rise and fall together. Secondly, since the inflows are very large in relation to the stock, it takes only small differences between the inflow and the outflow to cause a substantial change in the unemployment stock. The inflow exceeded the outflow, for example, during the first half of the 1980s with the result that the unemployment stock rose from under 1.1 million in 1979 to over 3.1 million in 1986. The reverse happened between 1986 and 1989 with the result that the unemployment stock fell by over a million (from 3.1 to 2.0 million) in just under three years.

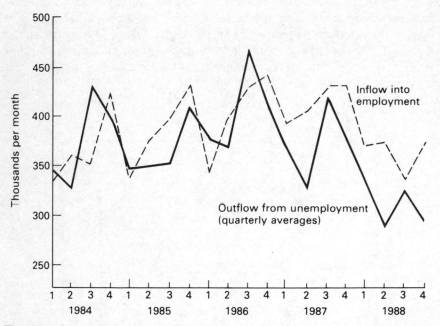

Figure 5.4   Inflows Into and Out of the Unemployment Stock: quarterly averages, UK (1984–88). (*Source: DEG.*)

An analysis of the flows into and out of the unemployment stock raises crucially important questions about the factors which determine the probability that a person will become unemployed. Some people never experience unemployment throughout their working lives while others find themselves unemployed for several years; and of those who do become unemployed, some are able to find a job very quickly while others are less fortunate. Figure 5.5 shows that in 1988, 45% of unemployed males had been unemployed for over a year compared to 24% who had been unemployed for under 13 weeks. The situation is more favourable for females: 30% had been unemployed for over a year and 31% for under 13 weeks.

The question therefore arises whether certain types of people are more

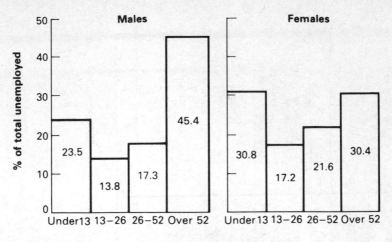

Figure 5.5   Duration of unemployment in the UK (at July 1988).
(*Source: DEG*, November 1988.)

likely to become unemployed than others; and if a person does become unemployed, what factors affect the speed at which they are able to get a job? The first question is most easily answered by seeing how the likelihood of becoming unemployed varies between different groups of people. Information is also available which shows how the likelihood of leaving the unemployment stock varies between different groups of unemployed people.

The likelihood of becoming unemployed: The chances that anyone will become unemployed are strongly influenced by demographic and socio-economic factors. These include a person's age, sex, geographical location, qualifications, skills and the general economic health of the economy. In addition, the likelihood of leaving the unemployment stock is closely related to the length of time a person has been unemployed.

The likelihood of becoming unemployed is defined as the inflow into the unemployment stock divided by the working population. The effects of a person's age and sex on the likelihood of becoming unemployed are shown in table 5.7, which indicates a sharp decline in the likelihood of becoming unemployed as a person gets older (up to the mid-30s). This can be expected to happen since younger workers are generally more mobile between jobs than older workers, who are often reluctant to move because of the loss of seniority rights which they have built up with their existing employer. Younger, less experienced workers are also more likely to be made redundant when firms are reducing their employment levels. The only noteworthy difference between males and females is that females have a slightly lower likelihood of becoming unemployed in all age groups.

Another factor which affects a person's likelihood of becoming unemployed is their location. The likelihood of becoming unemployed is sub-

TABLE 5.7

The Likelihood of Becoming Unemployed and Ceasing to be Unemployed in Great Britain: by Age and Sex

Age group	Males (%)		Females (%)	
	Likelihood of becoming unemployed Oct. 87–Jan. 88	Likelihood of ceasing to be unemployed Oct. 87–Jan. 88	Likelihood of becoming unemployed Oct. 87–Jan. 88	Likelihood of ceasing to be unemployed Oct. 87–Jan. 88
Under 18	11.5	69.5	9.3	67.6
18–19	11.4	54.2	8.8	60.0
20–24	7.7	47.8	6.4	57.8
25–29	5.0	43.0	4.7	54.9
30–34	3.7	37.3	3.0	55.1
35–44	2.8	34.8	1.9	51.8
45–54	2.6	28.4	1.6	34.5
55–59	2.8	22.6	0.9	20.2
60 and over	2.3	54.5		
All ages	4.4	39.6	3.5	50.9

Notes:

a. The likelihood of becoming unemployed is the inflow expressed as a percentage of the labour force (employees, unemployed, self-employed and HM forces).

b. The likelihood of ceasing to be unemployed is the outflow expressed as a percentage of the unemployed.

c. 55 and over for females.

stantially higher (for both males and females) in the north than in the south. The likelihood of employed males becoming unemployed in the South East, for example, was 3.4% in 1987 compared to over 6% in the North and in Scotland. Regional differences in the likelihood of becoming unemployed are slightly smaller for females.

A person's educational background, qualifications and skills can be expected to exert a substantial influence on the likelihood that they will become unemployed. In addition to enhancing a worker's value to employers, more highly educated and better qualified workers can expect to be more mobile and therefore have a wider range of job opportunities available to them. This is confirmed by data obtained from the 1987 Labour Force Survey. Table 5.8 shows that unemployment rates varied between under 3% for males with higher educational qualifications to over 15% for males with the lowest level of school-leaving qualifications. For those whose highest qualification was A-level or its equivalent, the unemployment rate of 6.1% for males was twice as high as those with a degree but was just over half the rate of those with CSE below grade 1. The change in unemployment between 1984 and 1988 in each qualification group indicates that the cyclical upturn had a greater impact on the unemployment rate of those with lower qualifications, particularly for males. The reduction in male unemployment from 11.9% to 8.9% between 1984 and 1988 resulted in a fall of 6.8 percentage points for those with CSE below grade 1. This compares with a fall of less than one percentage point for those with a degree. An upturn in the economy therefore reduces the difference in unemployment rates between groups with different qualifications.

TABLE 5.8

Unemployment Rates in Great Britain, 1984 and 1988: by Highest Qualification Attained

| | *% unemployed* | | | |
| | *males* | | *females* | |
Highest qualification attained	*1984*	*1988*	*1984*	*1988*
First or higher degree	3.5	2.6	7.4	4.8
Higher education below degree level	3.7	2.8	6.2	3.1
A-level or equivalent	8.2	6.1	10.6	7.5
O-level or equivalent	11.2	7.2	10.6	7.8
CSE below grade 1	18.6	11.8	18.9	12.6
No qualifications	18.2	15.4	13.4	11.0
All persons	11.9	8.9	11.7	8.5

Source: DEG, April 1989, p. 193.

Further evidence that the likelihood of becoming unemployed is related to qualifications is indicated by a survey of nearly 8,000 UK graduates undertaken in 1986/87. This survey provides information about their employment status at two points in time: six months after their graduation (in 1980) and again six years later (in 1986). The results given in table

5.9 show that the unemployment rate of graduates six months after their graduation increases as the class of degree falls. The unemployment rate for those with third-class degrees, for example, was 16.1% compared to an unemployment rate of only 4.2% for those with a first-class degree. The situation six years after graduation, however, suggests that the effect of degree class on the likelihood of becoming unemployed wears off over time. The differences in unemployment rates between the various degree classes are very small six years after graduation, though the rate is still highest for those with a third-class degree.

TABLE 5.9

Unemployment Rates of UK Graduates: by Degree Class

| | % unemployed | |
Degree class	6 months after graduation	6 years after graduation
First	4.2	2.9
Upper second	8.4	2.4
Undivided second	8.8	3.6
Lower second	12.1	3.1
Third	16.1	5.3
Other type	9.0	2.1
All classes	10.1	2.9

Note: 'Other type' includes pass degrees and ordinary degrees.
Source: National Survey of 1980 Graduates and Diplomates (1987), ESRC Data Archive.

The likelihood of ceasing to be unemployed: We have shown that the likelihood of *becoming unemployed* varies considerably between different types of people. The same is true for those in the unemployment stock: the likelihood of *leaving* the unemployment stock can be shown to vary according to age, sex, location and the length of time for which a person has been unemployed.

For males, the likelihood of leaving the unemployment stock declines sharply as age increases (with the exception of those in the 60 and over age group, the majority of whom retire on leaving the unemployment stock). For females, the decline in the likelihood of leaving the unemployment stock as age increases is far less marked and a sharp fall only occurs after the age of 45 (see table 5.7). Young workers of both sexes are therefore far more likely to leave the unemployment stock during any given period of time than are older workers (with the exception of males over 60). This is probably because employers generally have a preference for younger workers and also because younger workers are likely to be less choosy about their choice of job than are older workers, who are more likely to be set in their ways and more reluctant to try new types of work.

A person's location also affects the likelihood of leaving the unemployment stock. Those unemployed in the south of England are more likely to leave the stock than those living elsewhere in Britain. The difference between the north and the south is particularly marked for unemployed males. Comparing East Anglia and the North West, for example, over 50% of unemployed males left the unemployment stock in East Anglia (during the last quarter of 1987) compared to under 35% in the North West. A further factor which affects the likelihood of leaving the unemployment stock is the length of time a person has already been unemployed. The likelihood of leaving the unemployment stock is much higher for those who have been unemployed for only a short period of time. It becomes increasingly difficult to get out of the unemployment stock the longer a person is in it (see figure 5.6).

Figure 5.6 Outflow from Employment for Persons Unemployed for Different Amounts of Time. (*Sources:* Layard and Nickell (1986a) and *DEG*.)

There are two reasons why the probability of leaving the unemployment stock falls as the time spent unemployed increases. First, as the duration of unemployment increases, the unemployed become discouraged and consequently search for a job with less enthusiasm. Second, employers are more reluctant to hire those who have been unemployed for long periods compared to those who have been unemployed for only a short time. This is partly because employers believe that the long-term unemployed have failed to find a job because they are in some sense inferior; their job applications have already been rejected by employers, perhaps several times. The long-term unemployed are also less attractive to employers because of the deterioration of skill levels and work habits as the duration of their unemployment increases. It is not so much that the unemployed lose their skills but rather that the appearance of new products and new processes require those in jobs to learn new skills. Those in work are constantly amending their skills. The skill gap between the employed and the unemployed consequently widens as the time spent in the unemployment stock increases. The consequence of an increase in the duration of unemployment is therefore an increasing mismatch between the skills required by employers and the skills offered by the unemployed.

2.2   Some Problems in Measuring Unemployment

Unemployment is usually defined by economists as referring to anyone who is seeking and is available for work at wages currently being paid to comparable persons who are in work. This is not the definition currently used to measure unemployment in the UK. The current unemployment count includes only those who are claiming unemployment benefit. It therefore excludes all those seeking work but who are *not* claiming unemployment benefit. According to the annual Labour Force Survey (a sample survey of those over 16 years of age), about 870,000 people who were seeking work in 1986 were not claiming benefit because they were not entitled to do so. Many married women who are looking for work fall into this category. This is reflected in the consistently higher unemployment rate for males than for females (see figure 5.7). On the other hand, the official unemployment count included 860,000 persons who were not looking for work or who were not available for work even though they were claiming benefit. The official unemployment count based on benefit claimants also included a small (but unknown) number of fraudulent claimants who are working in the black economy. Conversely, it excludes unemployed people who fail to claim benefit even though they are entitled to it.

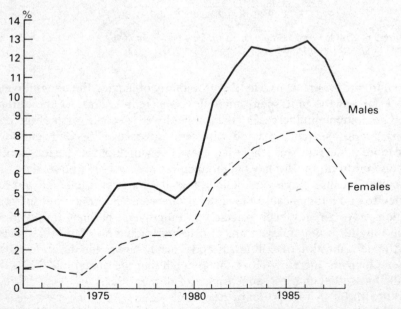

Figure 5.7   Male and Female Unemployment Rates in the UK: June each year (seasonally adjusted). (*Source: DEG*, December 1988.)

Estimates of the unemployment rate therefore vary substantially according to how the unemployed are counted. According to Johnson (1987), the official unemployment rate of 11.7% in 1986 (based on benefit claimants) fell considerably short of the more realistic rate of 14.3% which included those seeking work but not claiming benefit. It might also be noted that the unemployment *rate* has been reduced by changing the way in which the rate is measured. Prior to 1986, the unemployment rate was calculated by including the employed and the unemployed in the denominator. Since 1986, the unemployment rate has included the self-employed and HM forces in the denominator together with the employed and the unemployed. The immediate effect of this change was a reduction in the unemployment rate by about 1.5 percentage points.

The official definition of unemployment has been changed several times during the 1980s. According to estimates made by the Department of Employment, these changes have led to a reduction in the unemployment total of around half a million below the level that would have occurred at the 1980s unemployment peak (in 1986) if the changes had not been made. Two changes which were estimated to have reduced unemployment (by 190,000 and 162,000 respectively) are, first, the replacement of the old method of counting all those registered as unemployed at jobcentres by the count based on benefit claimants only; and second, the effective lowering of the early retirement age for men to sixty by replacing unemployment benefit by supplementary benefit. A more recent change in the method of counting the unemployed is the removal of all 16–17-year-olds from the unemployment count following the withdrawal of their entitlement to unemployment benefit in October 1988. This has reduced the unemployment count by over 50,000 – again by changing the unemployment benefit rules.

Less obvious and less quantifiable changes have occurred in recent years which have affected the unemployment count. First, unemployment benefit offices have tightened up the 'availability for work' tests in order to discourage those claimants who are not genuinely seeking work. The 1988 Social Security Bill specifies that a person will have to be 'actively seeking work' in order to be eligible for unemployment benefit. This means that they will be expected to be applying for job vacancies and to be registered with a job agency. Second, the number of workers on government employment and training programmes have reduced the unemployment total, perhaps substantially, since without access to such programmes many would not be employed or in training. Nearly 230,000 people were on employment and training schemes (such as the Community Programme) or were receiving the Enterprise Allowance in 1988; and nearly 300,000 youths were on the Youth Training Scheme (see section 2.6 below). How many of these would have been unemployed if the scheme had not existed is unknown.

On the other hand, it has been argued that a substantial number of unemployed persons are not interested in finding a job because they are supplementing their unemployment benefit by working in the black economy. This view is supported by a Department of Employment Survey of 2,700 unemployed people in London in 1988 which concluded 'that a significant minority of the capital's 280,000 unemployed were claiming benefit while working in the black economy' (*Financial Times*, 13 October 1988).

Nevertheless, on balance, it seems likely that the current method of measuring unemployment in the UK seriously underestimates the economist's definition of unemployment, which includes all persons out of work who are looking for a suitable job at current wages and conditions of employment.

2.3 International Comparisons

Between 1948 and 1968, the annual unemployment rate in the UK averaged 1.8% and never rose above 2.6%. The following two decades witnessed a remarkably different story, especially during the 1980s when a new dimension was added to the post-war history of UK unemployment. The unemployment rate rose from 2% in 1974 to 4% in 1979. This was followed by a remarkably sustained increase to over 11% in 1986, when more than three million people were recorded as claiming unemployment benefit – and perhaps an additional million others were unemployed but not entitled to benefit and so were not recorded in the unemployment total.

The UK was not alone in experiencing high unemployment during the 1980s as can be seen from figure 5.8. All the major industrialized nations experienced substantial increases in their unemployment rates in the early 1980s. Closer inspection of the long-run trends in unemployment in the major industrialized countries reveals two substantial upward shifts in the unemployment rate, the first in 1974 and the second in the early 1980s. The two exceptions to this general pattern are Japan and France, where unemployment increased fairly steadily after 1974 until peaking in 1987. The fact that these two upward shifts in unemployment were so widespread across the world's major trading nations suggests the existence of a common cause. Both cases were marked by a sharp decline in world trade as a direct result of concerted international action to deal with two serious and related economic problems. Firstly, the sharp and unprecedented increase in the price of oil in 1973/74 from three dollars to ten dollars per barrel had serious adverse effects on the balance of payments of the major industrial nations, all of which relied heavily on imported oil. This oil price increase also provided an unwelcome impetus to inflation, which was already increasing in these countries. In order to rectify their balance of payments deficits on current account and to deal with the threat of inflation, these nations deflated their economies by operating more restrictive fiscal and monetary policies. Similar policies were introduced in the aftermath of the increase in oil prices in 1979/80, this time from 13 dollars to 29 dollars per barrel.

The effect of these two worldwide recessions on the UK unemployment

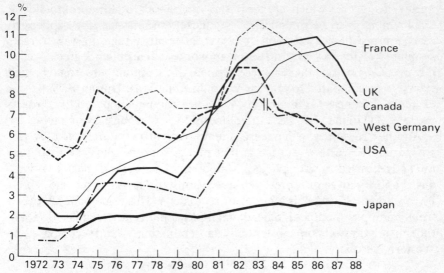

Figure 5.8   Unemployment Rates: International Comparisons.
(*Sources: OECD Economic Outlook 43* and *DEG*, December 1988.)

rate was an increase from 2.2% in 1974 to 5.2% in 1977; and an increase
from 4.5% in 1979 to 11.3% in 1983. It may be asked why the UK should
have suffered such a large increase in unemployment at a time when it
became a net exporter of oil. The UK's balance of payments should have
been helped by the oil price increase of 1979/80. The answer is that the
sudden increase in the value of the UK's oil reserves coupled with the
very tight monetary policy during 1980–81 caused a substantial appreciation
of the sterling exchange rate. The dollar/sterling rate, for example, rose
from 1.74 dollars per pound in 1977 to 2.32 dollars per pound in 1980
(annual averages). This led to a sharp decline in the UK's export competitiveness which had particularly harmful effects on the manufacturing sector,
as indicated by the unprecedented fall in manufacturing employment by
22% between 1979 and 1983. An interesting question which is posed by
the long-term unemployment trends in figure 5.8 is why Japan has managed
to keep its unemployment rate so low during the 1980s compared to most
other industrialized nations. The answer to this question helps to throw
some light on the high levels of unemployment experienced by the UK
during the 1980s, since one of the reasons for the low unemployment rate
in Japan is that wages there are far more flexible during recessions than
they are in most Western European labour markets. In Japan, wages contain
a much larger bonus element than is the case in Western Europe. The
result is that any decline in profits quickly feeds through into a corresponding reduction in wages. Indeed, the lifetime employment system which
flourishes in Japan's major industrial companies *requires* much greater wage
flexibility than occurs in other countries. The bonus system allows a great
deal of flexibility without workers feeling that their status has been eroded

by the wage cuts which are necessary in periods of low profitability if employment is to be maintained. Japanese workers therefore appear to place a much higher value on employment security than on wage targets compared to many Western European workers. This high degree of wage flexibility has helped the Japanese economy to maintain a reasonably high growth rate compared to other industrialized nations. During 1979–87, for example, Japanese GDP grew by 4.0% per annum compared to a growth rate of 2.0% in the UK, 1.8% in France and 1.7% in West Germany.

Another reason why Japanese unemployment rates are generally low compared to Western Europe is that many workers who lose their jobs are not recorded as unemployed. Many part-time workers, such as house-wives and older semi-retired workers, simply disappear from the labour force when they lose their jobs during recessions. This discrepancy between 'true' unemployment and 'official' unemployment is not peculiar to Japan, though it may well be substantially larger in that country compared to Western Europe.

2.4   Long-run Unemployment Trends in the UK

The underlying long-run trend in UK unemployment has risen strongly during the post-war period. Some researchers have argued that this upward trend is the result of an increase in the *natural rate of unemployment*, which is defined as the unemployment rate which exists when the labour market is in equilibrium. Labour market equilibrium only exists when the actual rate of unemployment equals its natural rate. This concept of a natural rate of unemployment has been extended in recent years to allow for the persistent increase in wages and prices, even during recessions. The equilibrium unemployment rate is now usually defined as the rate that is consistent with a constant rate of inflation. If unemployment is below its natural rate, inflation will rise; if unemployment is above its natural rate, inflation will fall; only if unemployment is at its natural rate will inflation remain constant. This special rate of unemployment is often referred to as the non-accelerating inflation rate of unemployment – or NAIRU for short. The fairly steady inflation rate of around 5% in the UK during 1983–87 suggests that the UK unemployment rate was at its NAIRU level during this period. The sharp fall in unemployment since 1986, followed by the increasing rate of inflation, seems to suggest that unemployment has recently fallen below its NAIRU level. It should be noted that the NAIRU itself is not a constant and can be expected to change over time.

The most detailed investigation of the UK unemployment rate has been undertaken by Layard and Nickell (1986a). They identify seven factors which have had varying degrees of influence on the unemployment rate from the mid-1950s to the mid-1980s. These are as follows.

(1) *Demand Factors*. Unemployment will increase if the national demand for goods and services falls. This can occur as a result of contractionary

monetary and fiscal policies, a fall in world trade or a decline in competitiveness.

(2) *Trade Union Militancy.* An increase in trade union militancy can cause unemployment to increase by forcing wages up beyond the level warranted by increases in labour productivity. This is sometimes referred to as 'classical' unemployment since it is caused by the real wage being held above its market clearing level.

(3) *Employment Taxes.* Firms have to pay national insurance contributions for every worker they employ (provided they earn more than a certain amount per week). Any increase in this tax on employment can be expected to reduce the demand for labour since it raises labour costs for the employer.

(4) *Mismatch Unemployment.* Unemployment occurs when there is a mismatch between the demand for labour and the supply of labour. The unemployed may have the required skills to fill a job vacancy but may not be located in the same geographical labour market area as the vacancy. There is a *geographical* mismatch in this case. Likewise, job vacancies and unemployment may occur within the same geographical labour market but the unemployed may not have the required skills to fill those vacancies. There is a *skill* mismatch in this case. Both a geographical mismatch and a skill mismatch can, of course, occur simultaneously. Mismatch unemployment is more likely to occur during periods of severe structural change, as in the early 1980s when the collapse of many manufacturing industries led to the loss of predominantly male jobs, many of which were located in the northern and western parts of the UK. At the same time as male manufacturing jobs were being lost in the north, new jobs were beginning to appear (especially in the mid-1980s) in the south – but mainly in the service sector and mainly for females. These structural changes in UK industry during the 1980s could have led to a serious mismatch between labour demand and labour supply.

(5) *Unemployment Benefit.* Unemployment benefit may alter the level of unemployment in three ways. First, an increase in unemployment benefit (or other income support measures) relative to earnings available from work will induce some workers to become unemployed. Alternatively, an increase in benefits will encourage those who become unemployed (perhaps through no fault of their own) to spend more time unemployed than they would have done if benefits had been lower.

Second, an increase in benefits may raise the floor to the wage which employers can offer potential workers, thus causing unemployment. A more elaborate version of this wage floor argument, put forward by Patrick Minford (1983), stresses the interaction of trade union power with the benefit floor. Strong trade unions raise wages in the unionized sector of the economy, thus reducing the demand for labour in that sector. Surplus labour from the unionized sector then transfers to the non-unionized sector, thus reducing wage levels in this sector towards the wage floor set by unemployment benefit (and supplementary payments such as rent rebates).

Third, substantial changes have been made, particularly during the 1980s, to the rules governing the payment of unemployment benefit. A recent example of this is the Restart Programme, which requires all those unemployed for over six months to attend a Restart interview, the primary intention of which is to provide special guidance for the long-term unemployed. A further aim, however, is to encourage the long-term unemployed to seek out and accept job offers more eagerly. This approach is to be strengthened in 1989 by withdrawing unemployment benefit from anyone who refuses to accept a 'reasonable' job offer, even if this means accepting lower pay than in the person's previous job. Another recent change to the unemployment benefit rules was the raising of the waiting period, for those who quit their job voluntarily, from six weeks to thirteen weeks before becoming entitled to unemployment benefit. Changes in the eligibility rules could have substantial effects on the level of unemployment.

(6) *Incomes Policy.* Successive governments from 1961 through until the end of the 1970s tried to reduce inflation by using various methods of restraining pay increases. These ranged from gentle persuasion to statutory controls on wage increases. Although incomes policies do not seem to have had much success in holding down inflation (except temporarily), there is less evidence available about their effect on unemployment. The main aim was to reduce the unemployment rate which is consistent with non-accelerating inflation (i.e. the NAIRU). Most research suggests that incomes policies have had little effect on both inflation *and* the unemployment rate.

(7) *Import Prices.* The sharp increase in import prices due to the sudden surge in oil prices in 1973 and 1974 was immediately followed by demands by workers for higher wages in order to maintain their real wage. The UK labour force was unwilling to adjust to the new terms of trade which had been imposed on the industrialized world by oil exporters (through OPEC). Real wages had to fall if competitiveness was to be maintained and workers were not willing to accept this new fact of life. The consequence was a loss of competitiveness and a deterioration in the performance of Britain's export industries.

To what extent have these various factors contributed to the long-run upward trend in the UK unemployment rate? After estimating the statistical relationship between each of these factors and unemployment in the UK over a period of three decades, Layard and Nickell are able to compute the extent to which each factor contributed to the long-term upward trend in the male unemployment rate. Estimates are provided for two separate time periods during 1956–83 (see table 5.10). These show that the most important factor contributing to the increase in unemployment during 1956–66 to 1975–79 was an insufficient increase in the demand for goods and services. The other main factors which have contributed to the long-term upward trend in unemployment are higher employment taxes and an increase in the mismatch between labour demand and labour supply. It is also worth noting that the positive effect of unemployment benefit on unemployment in the first period was reversed in the second period. One reason for the poor results obtained for the unemployment benefit explanation is the sharp decline in the unemployment benefit/earnings ratio after 1977. Recent research at the National Institute of Economic and Social Research adds further support to the view that unemployment benefit has played very little part in explaining the high unemployment levels reached in the 1980s (Hall *et al.*, 1987). The National Institute's researchers conclude that a low level of demand for goods and services was primarily responsible for the large increase in unemployment during the early 1980s.

TABLE 5.10

Factors Contributing to the Increase in Male Unemployment, 1956–83

Factor	Contribution to the change in unemployment 1956–66 to 1975–79	1975–79 to 1980–83
Demand factors	0.7	6.6
Trade union militancy	2.4	0.8
Employment taxes	0.6	0.4
Mismatch	0.4	0.5
Unemployment benefit	0.5	−0.1
Incomes policy	−0.4	0.5
Import prices	0.9	−0.9
Total change	5.1	7.8
(Actual change)	(4.8)	(7.0)

Sources: R.Layard and S.Nickell, 'The causes of British unemployment', *NIER*, February 1985; 'Unemployment in Britain', in *The Rise in Unemployment*, edited by C.Bean, R.Layard and S.Nickell (Basil Blackwell, 1986).

Although the detailed empirical work by Layard and Nickell may provide useful insights into the causes of the long-run upward trend in UK unemployment, the relative importance of the factors which they identify as the main determinants may have changed radically in the second half of the 1980s. One factor which could be of considerable importance is the mismatch between labour demand and labour supply. It is now widely accepted that the upward leap in unemployment between 1979 and 1982 was caused mainly by a sharp fall in both domestic and foreign demand for UK goods and services. When the economy began to recover after 1982, however, the new jobs were taken mainly by females and not by males: a fundamental structural change was occurring in the UK labour market. Unemployment which was initially caused by a contraction of demand was subsequently converted into structural unemployment as the recovery produced new jobs which could not be filled by the unemployed due to a skill or geographical mismatch or a combination of both.

One commonly held view about the causes of unemployment has not yet been mentioned. It is widely believed that unemployment is caused by the replacement of workers by machines. New technology destroys jobs through the replacement of labour-intensive production methods by capital-intensive methods. But historical experience does not support the view that new technology leads to a loss of jobs *nationally*. It needs to be remembered that there is no reason to expect the *total* demand for labour to fall when labour-saving techniques are introduced into particular sectors of the economy. Indeed, new technology permits more to be produced with the same inputs. It also provides opportunities to supply entirely new products, therefore creating new markets. Technical change is necessary if firms and industries are to remain competitive in world markets. Firms and industries which are reluctant to keep pace with new technology are unlikely to stay in business for long.

2.5   Regional Unemployment Disparities

The severity of the north–south divide in Britain is best reflected by regional differences in unemployment rates, which have been greater during the 1980s than at any time since the depression of the 1930s. It is because of these persistent differences in unemployment rates between regions that successive governments have tried to create additional jobs in areas of high unemployment. Before explaining the main elements of regional policy, it will be useful to have a look at some of the longer-term labour market trends in UK regions.

TABLE 5.11

Changes in Employees in Employment by Broad Sector, 1979–86

	Change in employees in employment (thousands)			% change in employees in employment		
	Manu-facturing	*Non-manu-facturing*	*Total*	*Manu-facturing*	*Non-manu-facturing*	*Total*
North[1]	−1,340	−92	−1,432	−32.4	−1.2	−12.1
South[2]	−666	498	−168	−21.3	6.1	1.5

Notes:
[1] North = West Midlands, Yorkshire and Humberside, North West, Northern region, Wales, Scotland and Northern Ireland.
[2] South = South East, East Anglia, South West and East Midlands.

One of the most visible effects of the severe recession in the early 1980s was the widening of the north–south divide. This is strikingly illustrated by the greater collapse of manufacturing employment in the north than in the south (see table 5.11). The north lost over 1.4 million jobs in total between 1979 and 1986, a drop in employment of 12% compared to a job loss of only 168,000 in the south, a fall of less than 2%. The job losses in the north were mainly concentrated in the manufacturing sector and although the south suffered from a loss of 660,000 manufacturing jobs, this was largely offset by a gain of nearly 500,000 jobs in service industries. The north was not so lucky. That the north suffered far more from the recession than the south is clearly evident from the very sharp increase in regional differences in unemployment rates during the 1980s (see figure 5.9). Unemployment in the Northern region, for example, increased by 7.4 percentage points (from 8.0 to 15.4%) between 1980 and 1985 while it increased by 4.9 percentage points (from 3.1 to 8.0%) in the South East. In spite of strong employment growth in many regions since 1983, much of this has been concentrated in the south (see table 5.12). Regional disparities in unemployment have therefore failed to narrow. The north–south divide remains one of the Government's major economic headaches.

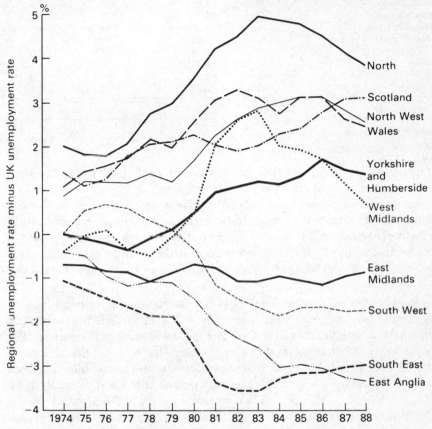

Figure 5.9   Regional Unemployment Differences: GB regions 1974–88. (*Source: DEG.*)

It is important not to become obsessed with the north–south divide. Unemployment black spots exist in *all* parts of the UK – even in regions where the unemployment rate is relatively low. In the South West, for example, Cornwall's unemployment rate is higher than the rate in all UK regions except for Northern Ireland. The wide disparities in unemployment rates within each UK region can be seen in table 5.13. These spatial differences in unemployment become even greater as smaller and smaller areas are compared. The inner city areas, for example, usually have the highest

TABLE 5.12

Recovery from the 1979–83 Recession: Employment Growth in GB Regions, 1983–87

Region	Civilian employed labour force (in thousands)		Change in civilian employed labour force (in thousands)	
	1983	1987	1983–87	%
South East	7,812	8,475	663	8.5
East Anglia	782	923	141	18.0
South West	1,728	1,871	143	8.3
East Midlands	1,583	1,718	135	8.5
West Midlands	2,119	2,260	141	6.7
Yorkshire/Humberside	1,941	2,038	97	5.0
North West	2,526	2,541	15	0.6
North	1,148	1,198	50	4.4
Wales	1,014	1,011	−3	−0.3
Scotland	2,078	2,080	2	−0.1
Great Britain	22,730	24,117	1,387	6.1

Source: DEG.

unemployment rates, and suburban areas and smaller towns tend to have lower unemployment rates (within each county).

Another dimension to the regional problem which is often overlooked is that the *quality* of jobs tends to be better in the south than the north. This is reflected by the greater concentration of high technology jobs in the south and by the higher proportion of workers employed in high skill industries such as producer services and research and development (R&D).

Regional policy: A wide range of policy instruments have been used by successive governments since the early 1930s in an attempt to reduce regional unemployment disparities. The rapid widening of these disparities in the early 1980s suggests that these policies have been unsuccessful. It should be realized, however, that expenditure on regional policy has been extremely low for most of the post-war period and has only rarely risen above 0.5% of GDP. In 1987/88, expenditure on regional policy by the Department of Industry was under £400m (barely 0.1% of GDP). There are no plans to increase this in the near future. It should also be realized that a large number of jobs have been created in the assisted areas as a result of regional policy, though many of these are jobs which have been diverted from other regions such as the South East and the West Midlands. Economists at the University of Cambridge have estimated that over 780,000 jobs were created in the assisted areas during 1960–81 and that 600,000 of these were still in existence in 1981 (Moore, Rhodes and Tyler, 1986). There can be little doubt that the assisted areas would have been in an even worse position in the 1980s if regional policy had not been in operation during the 1960s and 1970s.

For the first three post-war decades, regional policy was based upon

TABLE 5.13

Unemployment Rates in the Counties of Great Britain, November 1988

SOUTH EAST		WEST MIDLANDS		NORTH	
Bedfordshire	4.3	Hereford and Worcester	6.2	Cleveland	15.1
Berkshire	2.8	Shropshire	7.6	Cumbria	7.5
Buckinghamshire	2.9	Staffordshire	7.0	Durham	12.2
East Sussex	5.6	Warwickshire	6.0	Northumberland	11.4
Essex	5.3	West Midlands Conurbation	10.0	Tyne and Wear	13.4
Hampshire	4.6				
Hertfordshire	3.1	EAST MIDLANDS		WALES	
Isle of Wight	10.0	Derbyshire	8.7	Clwyd	10.5
Kent	5.8	Leicestershire	5.4	Dyfed	13.0
Oxfordshire	2.9	Lincolnshire	8.2	Gwent	11.2
Surrey	n/a	Northamptonshire	4.5	Gwynedd	14.2
West Sussex	2.5	Nottinghamshire	9.2	Mid-Glamorgan	13.1
Greater London	6.6			Powys	7.5
				South Glamorgan	9.0
EAST ANGLIA		YORKS AND HUMBERSIDE		West Glamorgan	11.8
Cambridgeshire	3.9	Humberside	10.6		
Norfolk	6.3	North Yorkshire	6.6	SCOTLAND	
Suffolk	4.2	South Yorkshire	13.2	Borders	6.4
		West Yorkshire	8.5	Central	12.0
SOUTH WEST				Dumfries and Galloway	10.8
Avon	6.6	NORTH WEST		Fife	12.2
Cornwall	12.2	Cheshire	8.3	Grampian	6.7
Devon	8.5	Lancashire	10.3	Highland	12.2
Dorset	5.3	Greater Manchester	9.0	Lothian	9.2
Gloucestershire	5.0	Merseyside	15.9	Strathclyde	14.3
Somerset	5.8			Tayside	10.8
Wiltshire	4.6			Orkney Islands	10.7
				Shetland Islands	6.5
				Western Islands	21.9

Note: Figures are not given for Surrey.
Source: DEG.

three types of assistance: controls on the location of manufacturing industry; investment subsidies for manufacturing firms locating new plant and equipment in designated assisted areas; and labour subsidies (during 1967–76) for manufacturing firms located in assisted areas. Controls on the location of industry were vigorously enforced in the immediate post-war years and again in the late 1950s and early 1960s. Their influence waned in the 1970s, however, since the government began to believe that discouraging investment in the South East could be harmful to the longer-term growth prospects of the national economy. Location controls were ultimately abolished in 1982.

From 1972, the Industry Act distinguished between two types of universal subsidy. The Regional Development Grant was available as of right to manufacturing firms investing in the assisted areas. This *automatic* investment grant became the linchpin of regional policy during the 1970s and early 1980s. The Regional Development Grant was supplemented by a second type of investment subsidy: the Regional Selective Assistance scheme provided grants to firms located in assisted areas on a *discretionary* basis. The size of these discretionary grants was (and still is) decided after detailed negotiations between the individual firm and Department of Industry officials.

Between 1967 and 1976, a labour subsidy was paid to all manufacturing firms located in the assisted areas. This Regional Employment Premium was a blanket subsidy paid on all employees, with different rates being paid for males, females and juveniles. At its peak, expenditure on the Regional Employment Premium amounted to about 0.2% of GDP (in 1968/69). This compares with a peak expenditure of just over 0.4% of GDP for regional investment grants in 1975/76. The Regional Employment Premium was ultimately abolished at the end of 1976 at the request of the European Community under its rules on Competition Policy, which do not permit *permanent* input subsidies to be paid by individual member states.

The traditional approach to regional policy has been modified extensively during the 1980s. The Regional Development Grant was amended in the 1984 reforms to regional policy and was subsequently abolished in 1988. The main thrust of the 1984 reforms was to make regional policy expenditure more cost effective. Among the main proposals was, firstly, the reduction in the maximum grant available from 22% to 15% and, secondly, the imposition of a ceiling on the total amount of grant available to individual firms. This was done by linking it to the number of jobs created. For all firms with 200 or more workers, a cost-per-job limit of £10,000 was imposed. In addition, certain service industries (such as business services) became eligible for the Regional Development Grant. There was also a switch in expenditure from automatic to discretionary grants.

This shift in emphasis from automatic to discretionary investment grants was finally completed in 1988 when the Regional Development Grant was abolished. This marks an important watershed in UK regional policy since it now means that *all* regional policy expenditure by the Department of Industry is entirely discretionary. Under the Regional Development Grant scheme, the government had no option but to pay grants to firms on demand. It is the desire for more centralized control over public expenditure which motivated the shift away from automatic grants. The hope is that each pound's worth of expenditure will produce greater benefits under a discretionary system of payments as the automatic obligation to support developments which might have taken place in the region anyway is avoided. The main components of the new regional policy introduced in 1988 are shown in table 5.14.

TABLE 5.14
Summary of the 1988 Reforms to Regional Policy

1. Regional Development Grant abolished. Savings in expenditure to be transferred (at least initially) to other regional assistance schemes such as Regional Selective Assistance.

2. Small firms under 25 employees:
   (i) eligible for 25% investment grant up to a maximum of £15,000;
   (ii) eligible for an innovation grant of 50% up to a maximum of £25,000 to support new products and new methods of production.

3. Firms with under 500 employees:
   – will qualify for grants to meet the cost of employing management consultants under the Business Development Initiative Scheme; two-thirds of the cost to be met by the government (compared to one-half in non-assisted areas).

4. Regional Selective Assistance:
   – more money to be made available to offset the reduced expenditure on Regional Development Grants. Only projects that would not otherwise go ahead to be supported.

Source: DTI – The Department for Enterprise, Cmnd. 278 (HMSO, 1988).

In addition to eliminating automatic investment grants, current regional policy puts far more emphasis on stimulating the growth of small firms than was the case with traditional regional policy. This inevitably means concentrating more resources and more effort on encouraging firms already located in areas of high unemployment to invest more heavily rather than inducing industry to move from other more prosperous areas to the assisted areas as was the case with regional policy in the 1960s and 1970s. Whether this new approach to regional policy will be more successful than the traditional approach (based on location controls and automatic investment grants) remains to be seen.

The government has not been alone in developing new forms of regional policy. Radical new developments have been introduced in the 1980s at three different organizational levels: local government, regional agencies and the European Community have all made significant strides towards becoming more involved in regional development issues. Local authorities in many parts of the UK responded to the recession of the early 1980s by establishing their own economic development initiatives, which included clearing derelict land, building small workshops and setting up industrial development bureaux to provide business advice to small and medium-sized firms, especially new start-ups. Many county authorities have also created enterprise boards (or enterprise agencies) which have wide-ranging powers to raise capital and buy shares in small companies in order to stimulate their growth. At the regional level, the two best-known agencies in GB are the Scottish and Welsh Development Agencies, both of which were set up in 1976. They have extensive powers to assist private industry in order to create more jobs in their respective countries. Other regional organizations in Scotland and Wales with a primary interest in job creation include the Highlands and Islands Development Board and Mid-Wales Development. Similar organizations exist in Northern Ireland: the Local Economic Development Unit provides business advice and financial assistance to small firms and the Industrial Development Board does the same for larger enterprises.

Finally, the European Community has become increasingly involved in regional policy issues since the establishment of the European Regional Development Fund (ERDF) in 1975. So far, the vast proportion of ERDF funds (about 80%) has gone to public infrastructure projects, such as roads and telecommunications, rather than into private sector investment. This may change in the 1990s, however, since the ERDF intends to earmark a greater proportion of its increasing expenditure on development programmes directed at regenerating industrial growth in high unemployment areas. The ERDF is expected to play an increasing role in regional economic development in the 1990s in response to the additional strains which the complete elimination of barriers to trade within the EC is likely to place on many peripheral (high unemployment) areas after 1992.

2.6 Employment and Training Schemes

In an effort to get the unemployed back into jobs, especially those unemployed for over six months, many different types of unemployment and training programmes have been implemented since the mid-1970s. In 1976, less than 100,000 were on employment and training programmes; by 1988, the number had increased to over 500,000. Between 1983 and 1988, the main schemes in operation were the Youth Training Scheme (YTS), the Community Programme, the Enterprise Allowance Scheme and several smaller programmes such as the Job Release Scheme, Community Industry and the New Workers Scheme. The number of people on these schemes during 1984–88 is given in table 5.15.

The YTS has been by far the largest of the employment and training programmes and has recently been expanded even further by converting it from a one-year to a two-year scheme for those leaving school at sixteen. A place on the YTS is guaranteed for all school-leavers and is widely supported by employers because of the large element of government subsidy. Thus, although youth training measures were originally introduced in order to induce employers to take on unemployed youths, participation

TABLE 5.15

People on Work-related Government Employment and Training Programmes

Type of scheme	Total persons on each scheme (in thousands)				
	1984	1985	1986	1987	1988[3]
Youth Training Scheme[1]	214	268	229	266	290
Community Programme	72	82	124	171	148
Other schemes[2]	29	47	43	52	81
Total	315	396	396	488	519

Notes:
[1] Number in training, Spring each year.
[2] These include: Enterprise Allowance, Job Release Scheme, New Workers Scheme, Community Industry, Jobstart Allowance and Jobshare.
[3] Provisional.
Source: DEG, April 1989, p. 189.

in the YTS for school-leavers is now the norm (unless they are proceeding to further education).

The Community Programme was directed specifically at the long-term unemployed. Most of the work undertaken by those on the programme was concerned with improving either the urban or rural environment in some way, such as clearing derelict sites, re-building walls and constructing adventure playgrounds. By far the most serious criticism directed at the scheme, was that it was not training people for permanent jobs. It merely reduced the unemployment rate by providing temporary work which would be of little value to those participating on the scheme over the longer term.

Finally, the Enterprise Allowance Scheme is designed to help the unemployed to set up their own businesses and is open to all persons between eighteen and retirement who are receiving unemployment benefit. In addition to a weekly allowance of £40, they are offered information and guidance from business consultants. Surveys of those who have participated in the Enterprise Allowance Scheme indicate that those who remain in business for over two years after the allowance has terminated are likely to have the following characteristics: males over thirty, unemployed for under three months prior to joining the scheme, a spouse in paid employment and an intention to invest a large amount in the business. The educational qualifications of the participants were found to be unrelated to the survival of the business.

2.7 The 1988 Revisions to the Employment Training Programme

The Employment Training (ET) programme became operational in September 1988, replacing all previous schemes and programmes directed at the long-term unemployed. ET integrates all previous schemes into a single programme in order to provide training places for about 600,000 people each year (with 300,000 places being available at any one time). It is open to anyone who has been unemployed for more than six months.

. The centrepiece of ET is the direct involvement of employers, the purpose of this being to relate training more closely to the needs of employers. The programme is designed such that each trainee will spend at least part of the training period at the workplace with an employer. The primary aim is to shift the emphasis away from job creation schemes, which offer only temporary jobs, towards training for permanent jobs. Since ET is intended to provide training for the long-term unemployed, the main route into the programme is through a Restart interview, which is a requirement for all people unemployed for over six months. In order to induce the unemployed onto these training programmes, participants will receive a training allowance of between £10 and £12 on top of their unemployment benefit. Those who complete their training will also receive a cash bonus of up to £80 (and up to £200 for those obtaining vocational qualifications). An annual budget of £1.5bn has been set aside to fund the training programme, which will be operated by a wide range of approved organizations in both the public and the private sector. These include local authorities, colleges, private training organizations and Chambers of Commerce – all of which were involved in the Community Programme.

The ET programme faces three major problems. First, many trainees are unable to find suitable placements after completing their training. Second, the scheme experienced high drop-out rates (around 50% in some districts) immediately after its introduction (*Financial Times*, 1 September 1988). It was therefore proving difficult to entice the long-term unemployed onto ET schemes. Many training managers have consequently fallen behind schedule in filling places on training courses, thus reducing the financial viability of the scheme. Third, the government initially failed to obtain the co-operation of the trade union movement in implementing the scheme, basically because trade union leaders regarded ET as a way of reducing unemployment without creating permanent jobs. They also believed that the training on offer was likely to be of low quality. Whether the ET programme succeeds, however, will depend very heavily on the underlying growth of the economy, since finding permanent jobs for those who are enticed onto an ET scheme will be determined by the overall growth in employment.

Looking further into the future, the government has recently proposed a programme which will integrate all government training schemes with various business enterprise schemes. These schemes will be run by Training and Enterprise Councils (TECs), which will be based upon areas with a working population of around 250,000 and will have an average budget of about £20m. In addition to their task of providing training schemes for the unemployed and for school leavers, the TECs will administer various business enterprise schemes such as the Enterprise Allowance, the Small Firms Service and the Business Growth Training Scheme. Each of the TECs (of which there will be about 100) will be encouraged to supplement the funding they receive from the government by raising money from local employers and other sources. Whether they will be successful remains to be seen.

2.8   Inner City Unemployment: The Urban Action Programme

In 1988, the government introduced its Action for Cities programme, the primary aim of which is to rejuvenate inner cities. Long-term unemployment is particularly severe in the inner city areas of many large towns, particularly the major conurbations such as London, Birmingham, Glasgow, Liverpool, Manchester, Leeds, Newcastle, Bristol and Belfast. Long-term unemployment in inner cities is linked to other problems such as sub-standard housing, high crime rates, poverty and a high concentration of dependants relative to those in work. Even when new jobs are created in inner cities the residents often find that they are unable to compete with suburban and out-of-town residents due to lack of relevant skills and work experience.

Action for Cities aims to remove the labour market disadvantages of inner-city residents by co-ordinating the activities of numerous government departments and government agencies. This targeting of government programmes on inner cities is already occurring to some extent in so far as employment and training policies are aimed principally at the long-term unemployed. But these policies are being supplemented by the work of the Urban Development Corporations and the Inner City Task Forces. The Urban Development Corporations are concerned with improving the physical environment in the inner city while the Inner City Task Forces have been set up to provide a focal point for finding ways of stimulating economic development in inner-cities. This involves co-ordinating the activities of government departments, local agencies and local private enterprise as well as helping to target resources on particularly disadvantaged groups, especially ethnic minorities.

A further aim of the Action for Cities programme is to use public funds to stimulate private sector investment. In 1988–89, about £3bn will be spent on supporting urban regeneration in Britain and it is intended that this will bring in several times that amount in private investment. We should be careful to note, however, that this £3bn mainly consists of expenditure on employment policies such as Employment Training run by the Training Agency. The Action for Cities programme simply helps to target the expenditure of several government programmes on the most depressed and deprived areas of the UK.

3   INCOME AND EARNINGS

In this section the distributions of income and earnings are discussed. Various explanations of the distribution of income between households and the pattern of earnings between workers are examined. This leads to a consideration of the factors which influence earnings. These are seen to include occupation, industry, gender, ethnic origin, education and family background. Finally, the 1988 reforms to the social security system are discussed.

3.1 Distribution of Income

Table 5.16 shows the composition of UK personal incomes in 1987. Pay makes up around three-fifths of total personal income. This proportion varies inversely with unemployment, so that as the unemployment rate increases, the contribution of pay to total personal income falls and the contribution of social security benefit rises.

TABLE 5.16

Composition of UK Personal Incomes, 1987

Source	%
Pay	61
Income from self-employment	8
Rents, dividends, and interest	7
Private pensions, annuities, etc.	8
Social security benefits	13
Other current transfers	3

Source: Social Trends 19, 1989, table 5.2.

The distribution of household incomes in 1986 is shown in table 5.17. While the spread of original income is very wide indeed – many of the bottom fifth have zero original income and rely on benefits – a combination of a progressive tax system and a programme of social security ensures that the final income distribution is much narrower. Nevertheless the average net income of households in the top fifth of the distribution is more than four times that of households in the bottom fifth.

TABLE 5.17

Distribution and Redistribution of Household Income, 1986

	Original income		Final income	
	Average per household (£)	*% of total*	*Average per household (£)*	*% of total*
Bottom fifth	130	0.3	4,130	6
Next fifth	2,800	6	5,150	11
Middle fifth	8,030	16	7,020	17
Next fifth	13,180	27	9,940	24
Top fifth	24,790	51	17,260	42
Total all households	9,790	100	8,700	100

Note: Final income is original income *minus* income and other taxes *plus* social security cash benefits and benefits in kind such as education and health.
Source: ST 19, 1989, tables 5.17 and 5.18.

Between 1983 and 1986, the ratio of average final incomes of households in the top fifth to those in the middle fifth rose from 208% to 246%. This was due primarily to an increase of 11% in 1985/86 in the earnings of the main earner in top quintile households. Overall, earnings of the main earner rose by only 7% in that year.

Many of the households in the top quintiles receive part of their income in the form of a return on their stock of wealth. The return from investments in housing or shares is an example of this. In 1985, the most wealthy 10% of the population owned 54% of marketable wealth. Total marketable wealth was estimated to be £863bn at this time.

Since 1981 the share of the bottom 40% of households in original income has fallen from 9% to 6%, and the share of the top 40% has risen from 73% to 78%. Over the same period the share of the bottom 40% in final income fell from 20% to 17% and that of the top 40% rose from 63% to 66%. There has therefore been a widening in the dispersion of income in recent years. We shall see later that a similar widening has occurred in the dispersion of earnings.

3.2   Distribution of Earnings

Since it is impossible to earn a negative amount, and since there is virtually no upper limit on how high earnings can rise, it should not be surprising to learn that the distribution of earnings is highly skewed. The provision of a system of welfare payments guarantees a lower limit to earnings. Consequently, there exists a bunching of workers who earn amounts just above the benefit level. While many workers earn more than this, few earn less.

The distribution of earnings in April 1987 is shown in table 5.18. The skew is highlighted by the fact that 10% of the male workforce earn less than three-fifths of median earnings. The top 10%, on the other hand, earn more than one-and-three-quarter times median income. It appears, then, that those on high earnings enjoy a position which is further away from the median than those on low earnings. The bunching of earnings at relatively low levels is further evidenced by comparison of the difference between the extreme deciles and quartiles above and below the median. In the case of men, 15% of all earners have earnings which lie just £15.84 either side of £134.64, while another 15% earn amounts which lie as much as £87.12 on either side of £263.34. The picture is much the same for women. Table 5.18 also shows the distribution of earnings in 1980. It is interesting to note that in 1980 the values below the median were all higher than in 1987, while the values above the median were all lower than in 1987. This is indicative of a widening distribution of earnings during the 1980s.

One reason underlying the skew of the distribution of earnings has already been mentioned – the existence of a lower bound, but no upper bound, on earnings. A number of other reasons have been advanced to explain

TABLE 5.18

Distribution of Earnings, April 1980 and April 1987

	Median earnings per week (£)	As a % of median			
		lowest decile	lower quartile	upper quartile	highest decile
1980					
Men	113	66	81	127	162
Women	72	69	82	126	163
1987					
Men	198	60	76	133	177
Women	133	64	78	134	171

Source: New Earnings Survey.

this skew, however, and we turn now to a consideration of these.

The first explanation concerns the productivity-enhancing effects of training. Investment by workers in their own human capital raises their productivity. In a market which has at least some of the hallmarks of competition, training and education therefore must lead to increased earnings. Now if, as seems to be the case, workers with more natural ability invest more heavily than others in training and education, then earnings at the top end of the ability distribution will be boosted more than those at the bottom end. Even though the distribution of ability is unskewed, the distribution of productivity will still have a positive skew.

The above explanation begs the question of why those with less innate ability invest less heavily than others in education and training. One reason must be that fewer doors are open to these groups. Educational and training opportunities are greatest for those with most ability, since ability is needed to obtain entrance qualifications. Even if all workers had equal natural ability, social and cultural factors – such as class differences or family background – might make it relatively rare for members of certain social groups to achieve high earnings.

Second, a division of the labour market into two sectors – union and non-union – might lead to a positive skew in the earnings distribution. If unions push up the wage in the union sector, employment in that sector will be reduced and workers will be displaced into the non-union sector where wages are pushed down. This leaves a relatively large number of workers in low-wage non-union jobs, while a smaller group occupy comparatively well-paid jobs in the union sector.

Third, it is important to note that earnings and productivity are determined by a whole host of factors, some of which may themselves have skewed distributions. The earnings enjoyed by an individual can be predicted with a reasonable degree of accuracy given information about the worker's characteristics and about the labour market within which he or she is employed. This being so, it is sensible to proceed by investigating the determinants of earnings. If relatively few workers are employed in labour markets in which – other things being equal – the forces of demand and supply generate high wages, and if relatively few workers have the characteristics which attract high rates of return, then the positive skew of the wage distribution is easily explained.

3.3 The Determinants of Wage Structure: Occupation, Industry and Region

(1) Wage structure by occupation: Suppose all workers are alike and compete in a single labour market which operates perfectly. In such a world, workers engaging in unpleasant tasks would have to be compensated to the extent that they would be indifferent between their present job and more enjoyable but less well-paid jobs. The return – in terms of both financial reward and the psychic disutility of work – to all occupations would be equal. This principle, introduced into economics by Adam Smith, is that of compensating wage differentials.

Compensating wage differentials are to a large extent observed in the world within which we live. Workers can expect wage bonuses in return for working unsocial hours. Workers employed in a dangerous environment can expect to earn higher wages than they would receive in a safer situation.

Reasons other than compensating wage differentials also help to explain the spread of earnings between occupations. First consider the exceptionally high wages earned by some sportsmen, actors, musicians, and other entertainers. In general these workers supply non-rival goods. Many people can attend a sports event, film, play or concert at the same time, and so the productivity of such workers is very high even though the individual tickets may be inexpensive. This means that high wages can be paid to artists of this kind. However, the high returns are available only to unusually talented individuals, and so competition on the supply side of the labour market for entertainers is limited. Hence entertainers can exploit their own scarcity value and earn an economic rent. This rent allows them to earn sums over and above what is needed to induce them to stay in their present occupation; for instance, top soccer stars can earn a wage which more than compensates them for bruises, broken bones, short careers and the pressures of being in the public eye.

Second, competition in the labour market may not be perfect. A world where unions bargain with large firms or even with employers' associations is far removed from the textbook model of demand and supply. Minimum standards or qualifications are often set by either employers (who wish to guarantee quality of service) or unions (who wish to restrict the supply of labour so as to boost wages), and these activities hinder free competition in labour markets. Contracts made between firms and their workers typically restrict wage movements for the duration of the agreement (usually 12 months in the UK). Welfare benefits set a floor below which earnings cannot normally fall; minimum wage legislation can have a similar effect. In large organizations, wages are often determined by internal politics, and, where the career path of workers within the firm is clearly defined, wages for some jobs may be set without reference to a worker's earnings potential outside the firm.

The distribution of earnings by broad occupational category as at April 1987 is shown in Table 5.19. As can be seen, the spread is very wide, with hourly wage rates varying between £3.05 for farm workers and £5.48 for security workers. The low wages paid to farm labourers are partly explained by the payment in the agricultural sector of benefits in kind, in the form of meals. Other explanations include the low demand for labour in rural areas which depresses wages in these local labour markets. Security workers, on the other hand, require compensation for the danger inherent in their job. It is also the case that non-manual workers generally earn more than manual workers. This reflects the tendency for those employed in non-manual jobs to have sacrificed earnings potential in favour of education and training at an earlier stage in their lives.

TABLE 5.19

Earnings by Occupation, Full-time Adult Men, April 1987

	Average gross weekly earnings (£)	Average gross hourly earnings (£)
Non-manual		
Professional and related in management and administration	328	—
Professional and related in education, welfare and health	261	—
Literary, artistic and sports	284	—
Professional and related in science, engineering and technology	267	—
Managerial	266	—
Clerical	181	447
Selling	201	502
Security	239	548
Manual		
Catering, cleaning, hairdressing	148	331
Farming, fishing and related	134	305
Materials processing (excluding metals)	190	412
Making and repairing (excluding metals and electrical)	194	425
Processing, making and repairing (metal and electrical)	204	447
Painting, repetitive assembling, product inspection	179	401
Construction, mining	184	408
Transport operating	183	380
Miscellaneous	171	377
Total: manual	186	404
Total: non-manual	266	679
Total: all occupations	224	526

Source: New Earnings Survey.

The imperfections of the labour market receive a lot of attention in the economics literature. This being so it is easy to forget that – considering the difficulty of the task – the labour market usually performs rather well in allocating jobs to a mass of uncoordinated workers. In 1988 many employers were complaining of a shortage of professional mechanical engineers. Yet there were strong signs that the labour market was responding to this shortage. Between April 1987 and April 1988 the average gross weekly earnings of such workers rose by 13%; this compares with a rise of just 10.6% in all non-manual occupations, and a rise of 9.7% in all (manual and non-manual) occupations.

To some extent it is inevitable that inter-occupational differences in earnings are the result of differences in the characteristics of the workforce rather than differences in the nature of the job itself. To illustrate this, it is helpful to compare nurses and judges. Pay differences may to some extent be due to differences in the job specifications, but it should be borne in mind that differences in the average age, experience, years of education and sex composition of employees in each occupation can influence average earnings too. Using 1973 data, Shah (1983) has estimated that even if all these factors were constant across occupations, judges would, on average, earn an annual salary about 70% higher than that of nurses. This reflects, in part, a strong job preference on the part of nurses.

More recently, Blanchflower and Oswald (1989) have found that between 1983 and 1986, non-manual workers earned 19% more per hour than manual workers. This estimate assumes that such factors as personal characteristics, education, region of residence, industry within which they work, are all constant. In other words, even if occupational choice were the only respect in which workers differed, non-manual workers would still be paid 19% more per hour than manual workers.

Clearly, then, the distribution of wages between occupations is determined by many factors. Chief amongst these are the personal characteristics of the workers themselves, the educational and training requirements for entry into the occupation, and the desirability of the job.

(2) Wage structure by region: As can be seen in table 5.20, wages vary substantially across regions within the UK. Wages are highest in the South East region, and lowest in the South West. As will be seen later, the South West region has an industrial structure which holds wages in that area below those earned elsewhere. It is rather surprising to observe that the North, North West and Wales are – besides the South East – the highest wage regions; apart from Scotland these are the three British regions with the highest unemployment rates. This may be due in part to the uneven manner in which unemployment affects various groups in the work force. Unskilled and unqualified workers are disproportionately represented in the unemployment stock. In areas of low unemployment, the low wages earned by these disadvantaged groups pulls down the average figure for the wages of those in work. Where unemployment is high, on the other hand, relatively few low wage jobs remain, so the average wage of those in work appears high.

TABLE 5.20

Earnings by Region, Full-time Manual Men, April 1987

	Pence per hour	Relative to South East
South East	422.4	100
East Anglia	391.6	93
South West	382.4	91
West Midlands	397.5	94
East Midlands	393.3	93
Yorkshire and Humberside	396.5	94
North West	404.6	96
North	415.6	98
Wales	401.0	95
Scotland	394.2	93

Source: New Earnings Survey.

But much of the inter-regional variation in wages discussed above is likely to be due to differences in the industry mix or occupation mix of regions. The relatively high wage financial sector is strongly represented in the South East, for example. In 1987, 14.8% of male employees in this region were employed in financial services compared with just 9.9% for the UK as a whole. This is not the only reason, however, for the existence of regional disparities in earnings. The South East has been able to outpace other regions in terms of output and employment growth. In 1986, the South East achieved regional income growth of 11.7%, compared with aggregate UK growth of 6.4%. This trend is likely to continue with the opening of the Channel Tunnel. Wages have been forced up in the South East in order to encourage workers from other areas to move there. The hourly earnings of full-time male workers rose by 10.5% in the year up to April 1987 in Greater London. This compares with an increase of 8.1% in the UK as a whole. Consequently it is no surprise to find wages elsewhere in Britain lagging behind those in the South East, even after allowance has been made for inter-regional differences in industry and occupation mix.

Blanchflower and Oswald find that, other things being equal, hourly wages outside the South East were, for 23-year-old workers in 1981, typically between 4 and 8% lower than in the South East. In Greater London, the wages were, on average, 11% higher than in the South East as a whole, other things being equal. High property prices and the considerable costs of travelling long distances to work clearly go a long way towards explaining these disparities.

Although average wages are higher in the South East than in any of the nine remaining regions of Britain, only two regions – East Anglia and the South West – can be said to have a particularly adverse industry mix.

Even in these cases the impact on the average wage is very small (only about 1%).

3.4 The Determinants of Wage Structure: Worker Characteristics

A vast number of personal characteristics have a role to play in determining an individual's earnings. These include gender, race, family composition, employment history, union membership, health and education. In this section we deal with each in turn.

Gender: In mid-1988, 46% of all employees in employment in Great Britain were females. Despite their obvious importance in the labour force, it remains the case that women are, on average, paid substantially less than men. In 1987, men were 3.5 times more likely than women to be earning over £5 per hour. This is largely, but not solely, the consequence of differences in the kind of work men and women do. It is easily seen from table 5.21 that even within each broad occupational class men earn hourly wages well in excess of those earned by women.

TABLE 5.21

Male and Female Hourly Earnings, Full-time Workers, April 1987

	Female (p)	Male (p)	Female/Male (%)
Total manual	287	404	71
Total non-manual	416	679	61
Total all occupations	386	526	73
Occupations: manual			
Catering, cleaning, hairdressing	276	331	83
Materials processing (excluding metals)	288	412	70
Making and repairing (excluding metals and electrical)	279	425	68
Processing, making and repairing (metals and electrical)	315	447	70
Repetitive assembling, etc.	296	401	74
Transport, etc.	310	380	82
Occupations: non-manual			
Clerical	366	447	82
Selling	294	502	59
Security	542	548	99

Note: Data refer to adult workers whose pay in the survey week was not affected by absence, and excludes the effect of overtime.
Source: New Earnings Survey.

A number of reasons explain gender differences in earnings. First, women tend to be less strongly committed to membership of the labour force than men. Counter examples abound, of course, but it remains the case that a large proportion of women drop out of the labour force to have children and then return to work some years later. Now, work experience is a characteristic which carries a high reward in the labour market. Experience keeps individuals up to date with new techniques and maintains familiarity with the ways of the workplace. On average, earnings of both men and women rise by about 3% per year when they are in work. Earnings potential drops by some 3%, however, for every year a woman is out of the labour force. This means that older women who have returned to work after ten years raising a family can expect to earn just under half as much as an otherwise identical man.

Second, labour turnover amongst women tends to be higher than is the case amongst men. This is partly due to the weak labour force attachment of women referred to above. In September 1988 the engagement rate for males in manufacturing was 1.8% and the leaving rate was 1.7%; the corresponding figures for women were 2.8% and 2.5% respectively. This relatively high turnover carries penalties for firms employing many women. Turnover costs firms money; persistently heavy recruitment caused by high turnover rates means that firms must employ a relatively large number of personnel management staff. The costs attached to this are frequently passed on to women in the form of lower wages. Furthermore, where labour turnover is high there is little incentive for the firm to use training programmes to invest in the human capital of its workers. Consequently, women tend to be trained to a lesser extent than their male counterparts.

A third reason why female earnings are relatively low is because of geographically isolated labour markets. Employers in remote areas enjoy a degree of monopsony power over female workers where the latter cannot move to find work because their husbands are tied to a job.

Since 1976, the Equal Pay Act (passed in 1970) has required that women performing similar tasks to men, or performing work of equal value to that of men, must be treated equally to men. The Sex Discrimination Act of 1975 requires that men and women should be guaranteed equality of opportunity. As can be seen from table 5.22, these Acts had an immediate impact on the minimum rates of pay set in collective agreements (column 1). The effect of the Acts on hourly earnings is not so easy to assess, however. Certainly female earnings have risen relative to male earnings since the implementation of the Acts. While full-time women earned, on average, 64% of male hourly earnings in 1970, this proportion rose to 73% in 1976 and has remained at about that level ever since. But it is not possible unambiguously to attribute this improvement to the new legislation without first considering some alternative explanations.

First, demand factors might explain the change. The demand for female employment might have risen during the mid-1970s, thereby pushing wages up. However, a short-run cyclical upswing is not sufficient to explain the figures of table 5.22 because the hourly earnings ratio remained at historically high levels despite the recession of the early 1980s. (The persistence of relatively high female earnings into the late 1980s also casts doubt on the theory that the rise in the female:male earnings ratio was due to the partially flat-rate incomes policies of the 1970s. Were this the case, the

TABLE 5.22

Relative Female/Male Pay and Employment (%)

April	Full-time workers			Part-time females, full-time males	
	Hourly wage rates $W_f W_m$	*Hourly earnings* $W_f W_m$	*Employ-ment* F/M	*Hourly earnings* $W_f W_m$	*Employment* F/M
1970	83	64	40	—	—
1973	87	64	41	51	10
1976	100	73	42	59	11
1980	100	71	46	58	12
1984	100	73	47	58	12
1987	100	73	49	56	12

Note: W_f is wage or earnings of females; W_m is wage or earnings of males; F and M are, respectively, employment of females and males. Data for part-time workers are expressed as full-time equivalents. The hourly wage data refer to the weighted average of minimum rates of manual workers laid down in collective agreements.
Sources: Tzannatos and Zabalza (1984), and authors' own calculations from the *New Earnings Survey*.

removal of these policies in 1978 should, by now, have allowed relativities to settle back to their equilibrium levels.) It is possible that the increase in the demand for female labour was not purely cyclical, and that women's relative pay rose as a result of changes in the composition of demand which caused a movement of women from low wage sectors into higher wage sectors. Nevertheless in all sectors of the economy except one (Public Administration) female relative pay rose over the decade 1970–80.

The second alternative explanation is that female labour supply might have declined over the 1970s, thereby forcing female wages up. As can be seen from column 3 of table 5.22, however, the ratio of female employment to male employment has been rising steadily since 1970. On the basis of labour supply movements, the differential between male and female wages should have increased, whereas in fact – as we have seen – it fell substantially during the 1970s.

In the absence of any convincing alternative, it seems fair to conclude that the Equal Pay Act has contributed to the narrowing of gender differences in rates of pay. It is clear from table 30 that much more remains to be achieved. Female hourly earnings are still well below those of men. This remains the case even if education, experience, hours of work, industry mix and other variables are held constant between the sexes. Blanchflower and Oswald (1989) estimate that 23-year-old women in 1981 earned 23% less per hour than their male counterparts, other things being equal. It would appear, therefore, that women remain unable to climb as high as men up the career ladder. Since education and experience have been controlled for, this indicates that some degree of discrimination remains.

Race: Non-whites, like women, suffer from discrimination in the labour market. Blackaby (1986) has estimated that in 1975, other things being equal, non-white males earned approximately 9% less than white males. This estimate holds constant such important determinants of earnings as education, experience, family composition and unemployment history. To the extent that racial discrimination adversely affects employment opportunities among the ethnic minorities, this figure will be an underestimate.

A substantial part of the racial wage gap is due to the fact that non-whites find it difficult to enter occupations which have high wages. The 1982 Policy Studies Institute (PSI) Survey reveals that there is a concentration of ethnic minorities in manual jobs, particularly in semi-skilled and unskilled occupations. Sixteen per cent of the employed white work force, for example, fell into the semi-skilled and unskilled categories compared to 40% for non-whites.[1] This is partly the consequence of ethnic differences in qualifications. Workers of West Indian origin, for example, are less highly qualified in terms of both academic and vocational training than are their white counterparts. Asian workers are a less homogeneous group, and they tend to fall into one of two extremes. On the one hand, there are the highly educated, and on the other hand there is a large group who have received very little formal education. While on average Asians have better academic qualifications than either West Indians or whites, they have benefited relatively little from vocational training. Johnes and Taylor (1989), however, show that non-white graduates earned as much as white graduates, on average, after six years in the job market.

In all regions, white males earn more than non-white males, and the gap is especially pronounced in the North West and the East Midlands. Overall, the gap in England and Wales amounts to 17%. Comparing this with Blackaby's 9% estimate, it can be deduced that around one-half of the total gap between the earnings of whites and non-whites in Britain is due to such factors as education and occupation; this has obvious implications for education policy. The other half is pure discrimination.

Education: It is not at all surprising to find that education has a positive influence on an individual's earnings capability. Indeed, were this not the case, people would not sacrifice years of earnings in order to acquire post-compulsory education.

After controlling for other determinants of earnings, Blanchflower and Oswald (1989) compare the earnings of 23-year-old workers in 1981 who have no educational qualifications with those who do. As might be expected, it is broadly the case that more education leads to higher earnings. Those workers who have between one and four O-level passes earn an average premium of around 5% per hour. Those with five or more O-level passes earn a premium of 9% per hour. A worker with two or more A levels earns, on average, 14% more per hour than one with no qualifications,

---

[1]   Brown, 1984.

and the premium rises to 18% for those with degrees.

These figures may not seem very high at first sight, but it should be remembered that they are based on the assumption that all other determinants of earnings are held constant across all workers. To the extent that highly educated workers choose to enter relatively well-paid occupations, tend to have relatively good promotion prospects and stable employment histories, the above estimates understate the true differential between the earnings of highly educated workers and others. The usefulness of the estimates lies in the fact that they indicate the extent to which an improvement in education alone (without changes in occupation, etc.) can raise earnings.

Family composition: Married workers tend to earn more than single workers, other things being equal. One reason for this is that the responsibility and expense of a family imposes the discipline of a stable work habit. This has two effects: first, a worker might work harder in order to earn more, and second, men (in particular) will become more attractive to firms upon marriage and will therefore be in a position to move to higher-paying jobs. The most rigorous work on this topic using British data has been that of Dolton and Makepeace (1987) who analyse the 1977 salaries of workers who graduated from universities, polytechnics and colleges of higher education in 1970. They find that marriage raises male earnings by around 6%, other things being equal. The impact on male earnings of child rearing is negligible, however. For women the results are somewhat different. For women who continue to work after marriage, their earnings fall by around 4%. If they have children, their earnings may fall by a further 25%.

Other determinants of earnings: Amongst 23-year-olds in 1981, the following variables were amongst the most important determinants of earnings, other things being equal. First, union membership raised the hourly wage by 7%. (The union mark-up on wages will be discussed at greater length in section 4.)

Second, those who work unsocial hours are paid a premium of 11% on average. It is clear that leisure is worth more to people at certain times of the day than at others. If workers must be on duty during the evening or at night, they cannot enjoy various leisure activities, such as a night out at the theatre, movies or pub; moreover the amount of time that they can spend with their families is reduced. Such a reduction in the utility of their leisure must be compensated for in the form of higher wages.

Third, if a worker has a history of unemployment experience, his or her wage is, on average, likely to be 5% lower than would otherwise be the case. As has already been mentioned, experience of work raises earnings potential whereas periods out of work lead to a depreciation of human capital and hence productivity. A history of unemployment also – rightly or wrongly – sends signals to an employer about certain of the worker's other characteristics, such as motivation, aptitude and tenacity.

Fourth, workers who are employed in jobs which are part of a well-established career structure earn a premium of 8%. Such workers might be regarded as members of the 'primary' work force. Firms which fill vacancies in senior positions exclusively from within the ranks of their own workforce will be keen to hold on to their best workers. Consequently, wages tend to be higher where a promotion ladder exists.

Fifth, registered disabled persons earn, on average, 28% less than other workers. This may in part be due to inevitable constraints on the type of tasks that they can perform and the efficiency with which they can carry out their duties at work. Although earnings of disabled people are lower than earnings of people in good health, the difference in their *incomes* need not be so great since many of these workers will qualify for disability benefit.

Finally, an increase in local unemployment rates puts downward pressure on average earnings, other things being equal. In areas of high unemployment the supply of labour is plentiful in relation to demand, and so firms are able to bid down the wage. There is, however, considerable evidence to suggest that this effect tapers off at very high levels of unemployment.

3.5   Changes in Earnings Over Time

Figure 5.10 shows the rate of growth of hourly earnings of male manual workers. In 1980, a short burst of inflation occurred which was largely stimulated by an oil price rise, an increase in the rate of value-added tax, and the award of substantial pay increases in the public sector. Since then the rate of growth of earnings has slowed down considerably, though there is evidence to suggest that wage inflation was rising once more by late 1988.

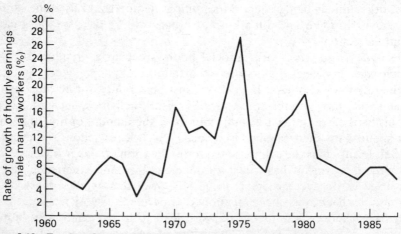

Figure 5.10   Earnings Growth, Male Manual Workers.
(*Sources:* Layard and Nickell (1986), *DEG*.)

Productivity has been rising rapidly since 1980. The stagnation experienced at the turn of the decade was followed by dramatic increases in output per head, especially in manufacturing. This has been, in part, the result of the shake-out of labour during the years of recession, and partly due to the outcome of changes in the structure of industry. The improvement of labour productivity in the manufacturing sector has occurred at a time when the capital stock has been rising very slowly. Growth of capital stock in manufacturing averaged less than 1% per annum over the years 1980–87. This compares with 2.3% during 1973–79. The low levels of net investment cast doubt over the sustainability of productivity growth over the longer run.

3.6   Social Security

Having considered the determinants of earnings, we now turn to an examination of another important component of total personal income, namely social security. The system of social security in the UK underwent radical reform in 1988 and this has inevitably caused some degree of controversy.

Several catalysts prompted this reform. First, the old system had become extremely complex and unwieldy. There were 30 types of benefit but no consistent definition of need was used between these. Different definitions of income (gross or net) were used for different benefits and some benefits involved the use of very complicated rules in calculating eligibility. The new system reduces the number of benefits available, thus making it considerably simpler. Second, the old system was out of date in that it had not adapted over the years in response to changes in social trends and to changes in demography. Single-parent families were inadequately catered for, as were low-income families with children. Third, the State Earnings Related Pension Scheme (SERPS), introduced in 1978, required reform, since it had become clear that this scheme would be extremely burdensome for taxpayers in the next century. Fourth, a major problem of poverty traps and unemployment traps existed with the old system. The main difficulty attached to supporting the poor by a system of taxes and benefits is that the assistance provided might discourage low-income workers from working harder. The poverty trap is an extreme case of this since by working longer hours or by securing a wage increase (perhaps by changing jobs), a worker loses so much via the loss of benefits and increase in tax that he would have been better off before his earnings rose. In some cases, the poverty trap may discourage an unemployed person from taking up an offer of employment. The latter case is an example of the unemployment trap. It was almost inevitable, with a system as complex as that which existed until 1988, that poverty traps and unemployment traps would be common. Although they have not been removed entirely, these traps now affect many fewer people than was formerly the case.

Having set out above the reasons for the change in the social security system, each of the benefits now in place will be discussed in turn.

(1) Housing Benefit: Housing Benefit entitles families on low incomes and with little wealth to claim up to 100% of their rent and up to 80% of their local tax bills (i.e. rates or the community charge). For social security purposes, a 'family' corresponds to the unit which is liable for income tax. No assistance is provided with mortgage interest payments for those who are buying their own homes. Such individuals may, however, be able to claim financial help under the Income Support scheme. Housing Benefit cannot be paid if the applicant's stock of capital (savings) exceeds £8,000.

The Housing Benefit scheme uses a system of tapers to ensure that as net income rises entitlement to support decreases gradually. Up to a critical level of net income the applicant is entitled to the maximum support levels indicated above. In the 1989–90 tax year, the critical level is £2,709.20 per annum (*Hansard*, 27 October 1988). If net income exceeds this level, then assistance with rent is reduced by 65% of the difference. Thus a family with a net income of £3,000 per annum which claims assistance for rent payments receives £189.02 less in Housing Benefit than one with a net income below the critical level. Assistance with rates also tapers off as net income rises above £2,709.20 per annum, but in this case help is reduced by 20% of the excess.

(2) Family Credit: Family Credit is available to low-income families in full-time work who have children. Claimants receive an adult credit plus additional credits for each child. The magnitude of these credits depends on the age of the children. No Family Credit is payable if the claimant's stock of capital exceeds £6,000. As is the case with Housing Benefit, a taper system operates to ensure that Family Credit entitlements are reduced gradually as net income rises. The critical level of net income in this case is £2,849.60 per annum for the tax year 1989–90. As net income rises above this level, Family Credit payments are reduced by 70% of the excess.

(3) Income Support: Income Support replaced Supplementary Benefit in 1988. This is available to low-income families not in full-time work. For the purposes of social security, full-time work implies a working week of 24 hours or more. Income Support is not payable if savings exceed £6,000. Claimants receive a personal allowance which rises with the number of dependants. Families with children, single parents, the old, sick and disabled are entitled to premiums in addition to their personal allowances. Claimants who are unemployed may also be entitled to unemployment benefit, which in the tax year 1989–90 amounts to £34.70 per week.

In addition to Housing Benefit, Family Credit and Income Support, a variety of benefits remain which have not been subject to substantial modification in the wake of the 1986 Social Security Act. These include sickness benefit, unemployment benefit, industrial disablement pensions, severe disablement allowances, and the flat-rate retirement pension.

The old system of social security allowed one-off payments to be made to claimants facing exceptional needs. Major household items such as furniture and general maintenance could be financed in this way. This scheme had, by 1988, become expensive and difficult to administer. It was therefore replaced by the Social Fund. This is a system of grants and loans which are designed to meet unexpected short-term needs of low-income families. Mandatory grants are available to finance funeral expenses; these are available to those claiming Housing Benefit, Family Credit or Income Support. Mandatory maternity grants can also be claimed by those receiving Family Credit or Income Support. Other grants, which are awarded at the discretion of the local social security officers, are available to assist in the rehabilitation of individuals who are returning to the community after a period of residential care.

The most controversial aspect of the Social Fund has been the introduction of interest-free loans as a means whereby families on low incomes can raise the finance to meet urgent needs. Such loans are awarded at the discretion of local officers and are normally repayable at a rate of 15% of weekly benefit over a maximum period of 18 months. The loans are not available to families with savings in excess of £500.

The loans system introduced as part of the Social Fund has already been the focus of intense public debate. Three features have attracted particular concern. First, the discretionary nature of the loans can lead to inequities as claimants in different areas are treated differently. Second, claimants who are suffering the greatest hardship, and who therefore need the loans most, might be refused a loan on the grounds that they will not be able to afford the repayments. Third, although over £160 million is being spent on the Social Fund in the tax year 1988–89, the loans element of the scheme is intended eventually to be self-financing. This redistributive impact of this aspect of the reforms is not yet clear.

The final component of the social security system which underwent major reform in 1988 is the provision of pensions. Changes in this area were geared towards reducing the cost of the SERPS. This was achieved by making the SERPS less appealing in two ways. First, the benefits of the SERPS were reduced. Thus a pensioner's entitlement is now based on average earnings throughout his or her working life. (Before 1988 the pension was linked with earnings averaged over the twenty years in which the worker enjoyed the highest earned income.) Moreover, since 1988 a spouse inherits only one-half of the full pension, not (as before) the full amount. Second, since 1988 people have been given financial incentives to contract out of the SERPS and into private personal pension schemes.

The amounts spent on various social security schemes and the number of recipients are shown in table 5.23. As can be seen, these benefits contribute a major component of total government expenditure. The total budget of the Department of Social Security in 1988–89, at £47.5bn, represents

26% of all government expenditure, and is more than twice as high as that of the other large departments, such as Health, Defence, or Education and Science.

TABLE 5.23

Social Security Benefits; Public Expenditure and Estimated Number of Recipients, 1988–89

	Expenditure (£m)	Recipients (thousands)
National Insurance Benefits		
Pension benefits		
Retirement pensions	19,312	9,735
Invalidity benefit	3,211	1,040
Industrial disablement benefit	439	205
Widow's benefit and industrial death benefit	928	395
Lump-sum payment to contributory pensioners	108	10,900
Other benefits		
Unemployment benefit	1,481	755
Sickness benefit	167	90
Maternity allowance	43	25
Non-contributory benefits		
Pension benefits		
Non-contributory retirement pension	44	35
War pension	592	255
Attendance and invalid care allowances	1,065	770
Severe disablement allowance	307	265
Mobility allowance	663	540
Lump-sum payment to non-contributory pensioners	7	700
Other benefits		
Income support	8,584	4,925
Child benefit	4,528	12,015
Family credit	409	470
One-parent benefit	169	665
Housing benefit (rent rebates and allowances)	3,874	4,465
Social fund	164	?

Source: ST 19, 1989, table 5.8

Having described the reforms introduced by the 1986 Social Security Act, it is instructive to examine the extent to which they have been successful in relieving the poverty trap. An illustration of the manner in which the severity of the poverty trap has been reduced is given in figure 5.11. Before 1988, a man with dependent wife and two children would have been in a poverty trap if he earned £100 per week. If he were to increase his earnings, his net income would be reduced. If he managed to increase his earnings by one pound, he would lose more than a pound in extra tax payments and through the loss of benefits. He therefore had a disincentive to work harder. In the wake of the reforms he still has little incentive to increase his work input, but at least the effective marginal tax rate has now fallen below 100%, and he gains three pence if he earns an extra pound.

A particularly severe aspect of the poverty trap before the reforms was the adverse effect on couples with two children. Families of this type with gross earnings between £80 and £120 per week experienced either no incentive or a disincentive to increase earnings. This was a matter of considerable concern since, as we saw in table 5.18, the lowest decile of the male earnings distribution lies towards the upper end of this range. A considerable number of families are therefore likely to have been caught in this poverty trap. Since 1988, however, this situation has been remedied. Effective marginal tax rates do exceed 100% between £50 and £60 per week (see figure 5.11), but income support and unemployment benefit levels render it extremely unlikely that many families will be caught in this new trap.

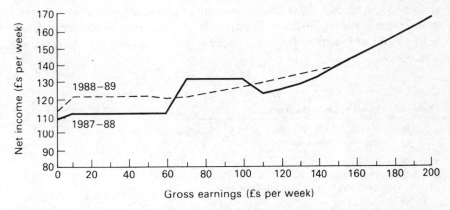

Figure 5.11 Gross and Net Income Before and After the 1988 Social Security Reforms, Married Couple with Two Children. (*Source:* Dilnot and Webb (1988).)

In the absence of a massive increase in social security expenditure, it was not possible to achieve this virtual elimination of poverty traps without making some workers worse off. Married couples with two children and gross weekly earnings of between £75 and £110 are amongst those who lost out as a result of the reforms. Lone parents with two children and gross weekly earnings between £50 and £100 also suffered a fall in net income, other things being equal. Childless couples with gross earnings of less than £140 per week fall into the same category. The burdens imposed on these groups by the 1988 reforms explain to a large degree the bitter controversy which surrounded the transfer to the new system. In all, it is estimated that 1.4 million people will gain from the reforms, while 1.7 million will lose.

4   TRADE UNIONS, INDUSTRIAL RELATIONS AND INCOMES POLICIES
4.1   Trade Unions

Trade union membership in the UK has been declining since 1979, when nearly 13.29 million workers were members. At the end of 1986 there were nearly 10.54 million union members, and this represents a fall of over 20% in seven years. This is the most marked fall in union membership since before the depression of the 1930s and warrants more detailed investigation.

The first possible explanation for the decline of union membership is that workers leave unions on becoming unemployed. Since unemployment rose by 1.9 million over the years in question, it is hardly surprising that fewer workers should be members of unions. Unemployment can only be a partial answer, however, since the fall in membership of 2.75 million was greater than the rise in unemployment. In 1986 the proportion of employees in employment who were union members fell below 50% for the first time since 1970. Nonetheless, unemployment may also influence union membership indirectly. In particular, if unions are believed to price workers out of jobs then they may become less attractive to workers during a recession.

TABLE 5.24

Trade Union Membership by Industry

Industry in which most members are deemed to be employed	*Membership (in thousands)*		*% change*
	1985	*1986*	
Agriculture, forestry and fishing	—	—	—
Energy and water supply	323	311	−3.7
Extraction, manufacture of metals, minerals and chemicals	91	87	−4.4
Metal goods, engineering, vehicles	404	392	−3.0
Other manufacturing	650	635	−2.3
Construction	254	254	0.0
Distribution, hotels and catering, repairs	424	420	−0.9
Transport and communication	712	686	−3.7
Banking, finance, insurance	344	352	+2.3
National government	480	488	+1.7
Local government	1,509	1,499	−0.7
Education	793	779	−1.8
Health	686	694	+1.2
Other	161	172	+6.8
Membership of unions covering several industries	3,992	3,769	−5.6
GRAND TOTAL	10,824	10,539	−2.6

Note: Union membership is less than 1,000 in agriculture, forestry and fishing.
Source: DEG, May 1988.

A second reason for the fall in the number of union members is that there has been a change in the structure of industry. Declining industries tend to be more heavily unionized than growing industries, so overall union density falls over time. Table 5.24 indicates that changes in membership broadly corresponds to shifts in employment; only in some service industries is union membership rising. The influence of industrial structure on union membership can be seen from table 5.25, which shows actual union density in each GB region together with the union density that would have been observed had each region had the same industry mix as GB as a whole.

It is clear from table 5.25 that inter-regional differences in union density would be considerably smaller if all regions had the same industry mix. Nevertheless, the broad pattern remains unchanged. The northern regions would still have the highest union densities even if the industry mix were identical in all regions.

A third possibility is that a change in the sex mix of employees in employment explains the collapse of union membership. If women are less likely to join unions than are men, then the change in membership may be due to the increase in the female participation rate. This is unlikely to be the case, however, since in 1985 women represented between 35% and 36% both of union membership and full-time employees in employment.

TABLE 5.25
Union Density by GB Region in 1984, Adjusted for Industrial Structure

Region	Actual density (%)	Density adjusted for industrial structure (%)
East Anglia	40	54
Greater London	47	54
Rest of South East	43	58
South West	55	57
East Midlands	61	58
Scotland	63	61
West Midlands	65	60
Yorkshire and Humberside	67	59
Wales	71	58
North West	71	59
North	72	60

Source: DEG, May 1988.

A final factor which might explain the fall in union membership is the political climate. Carruth and Disney (1988) find that, other things being equal, union density is around 2.5 percentage points lower when a Conservative government is in power than at other times.

Although union density is now less than 50%, the influence of unions on bargaining remains wide. The proportion of employees in employment whose pay was affected by collective agreements in 1985 was 64.1%. Amongst manual male workers, only 29% are not covered by some kind of collective agreement. Thus, union coverage is considerably greater than union density.

One aspect of union–firm relations which has received particular attention is the closed-shop. A closed-shop occurs when union membership becomes a condition of employment. It can take one of two forms. The first is the pre-entry closed-shop, which is rather rare, and which requires a worker to be a union member before he or she can be hired. More common is the post-entry closed-shop, in which a worker must join the union upon recruitment. While the closed-shop is often regarded as anti-libertarian, it should be borne in mind that it usually comes into being only where union density is already high. Firms have often welcomed the more structured format of industrial relations which the closed-shop offers. Finally, in the absence of a closed-shop, unions are often frustrated by the ability of non-members to enjoy the benefits gained by the sacrifices of union members; this implies that – owing to such 'free riding' – unions suffer from being under-resourced where a closed-shop does not exist.

It has been estimated (Millward and Stevens, 1986) that closed-shops covered between 3.5 and 3.7 million workers, almost one-fifth of all employees in 1984. Between 1980 and 1984 the proportion of manual workers covered by closed-shop agreements fell from 40% to 30%, and so it would appear that the closed-shop is rapidly becoming less common.

Throughout most of the present century there has been a steady fall in the number of unions. This has continued through the 1980s. At the end of 1986 there were 335 unions in Britain, down from 470 in 1975. Many of these are very small. No fewer than 63 unions had less than 100 members. These tiny unions include the Society of Shuttlemakers (around 40 members) and the London Society of Tie Cutters (which had 84 members in 1977). At the other extreme, 24 unions in 1986 had at least 100,000 members. These include the Transport and General Workers' Union (1,377, 944 members in 1986) and the Amalgamated Engineering Union (857,559 members). Just over a quarter of all unions are affiliated to the Trades Union Congress (TUC), but since most of the largest unions are affiliated, the TUC represents 88% of all union members.

4.2   The Union Mark-up

Much recent research has focused on the magnitude of the union : non-union wage differential (see Metcalf, 1988). This is the difference which two workers would expect to obtain between their rates of pay if they were identical to one another in every respect except union membership. It is, of course, to be expected that union members will receive greater remuneration than non-members since a major aim of unions is to secure higher wages for their members, and if they failed in this task many members might consider withdrawing their financial support from their union.

Estimates of the union mark-up are presented in figure 5.12. It is clear that until the early 1980s, the trend in this differential had been upward. The sharp rise in the mark-up between 1979 and 1981 coincided with the sudden increase in unemployment. While this might be interpreted as confirmation of the argument put forward by new classical economists that an increase in trade union power during 1979–81 helped to raise the unemployment rate, it should be noted that the rise in the mark-up could just as easily be a consequence as a cause of the rise in the number of jobless. Union members who were made unemployed around 1980 will have raised the supply of labour in the non-union sector thereby reducing

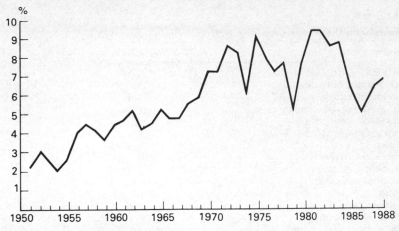

Figure 5.12   Estimated Mark-up of Union over Non-union Wages.
(*Source:* Layard and Nickell.)

wages in that sector relative to the non-union sector; this in itself will have caused the mark-up to increase.

Since 1982, the mark-up has declined once more, and although the differential rose slightly in the 1980s, it remains well below the high levels obtained in the depths of the recession. This is likely to be due largely to the decline in union membership over the period and to the impact of recent union legislation.

The mark-up varies considerably across occupations and industries. Blanchflower (1984) finds a mark-up of around 10% for semi-skilled workers in 1980, but his estimate of the differential for skilled workers does not significantly differ from zero. Stewart (1983) found that in 1975 the mark-up in the shipbuilding industry was 18% while that in electrical engineering was only 2%. His estimates are reproduced in table 5.26.

A number of variables are likely to influence the magnitude of the union: non-union wage differential. Beenstock and Whitbread (1988) argue that the differential will rise if union density and the real value of unemployment benefit increase. Moreover, they find that the mark-up is some five percentage points lower under a Labour government than under a Conservative government. This last observation implies that unions respond more to government calls for wage restraint when Labour is in office. There is, however, no evidence to suggest that incomes policies influence the magnitude of the mark-up.

The time series estimates of the union mark-up reported above have been used by Layard and Nickell (1986a) in an attempt to explain the growth in unemployment between the late 1970s and the early 1980s. Although unemployment rose by seven percentage points over this period, only 0.8 percentage points can be attributed to the growth of the union mark-up. Most of the rise in unemployment was found to be due to a deficiency of demand.

TABLE 5.26

Estimates of the Union : Non-union Wage Differential by Industry, 1975

Industry	Mark-up (%)
Shipbuilding and marine engineering	18.2
Paper, printing and publishing	11.4
Other manufacturing industries	10.9
Metal goods not elsewhere specified	10.7
Clothing and footwear	10.1
Chemicals and allied industries	9.6
Vehicles	9.6
Timber and furniture	9.1
Instrument engineering	8.6
Food, drink and tobacco	6.6
Textiles	6.6
Metal manufacture	5.4
Mechanical engineering	4.1
Bricks, pottery, glass, cement	2.4
Electrical engineering	2.0

Source: Stewart (1983).

4.3　　Strikes

An important weapon in the armoury of trade unions is the ability to strike. Despite the publicity which attaches to strike action when it occurs, the incidence of industrial stoppages is remarkably low; on average, UK employees lost less than one hour in 1986 through striking. There is considerable variation across countries in strike activity. Britain loses proportionately less time through striking than the USA, Canada and Italy, but more than France and Germany.

The passion typically aroused by strikes often serves to obscure the fact that remarkably little is known about what causes them. While on strike, workers sacrifice their incomes and their employers suffer output losses; it seems that everybody loses out. This being so, it is remarkable that strikes ever happen at all. A number of possible explanations can, however, be suggested (Johnes, 1985).

First, a strike may serve to convey information to the negotiating teams on both sides of the dispute about the strength of resolution of each side. Perhaps a stoppage, expensive though it may be, is the most efficient means available whereby such information can be conveyed. The role of the strike is therefore to remove uncertainty, and the stoppage is the price paid for not removing this uncertainty by other means.

A closely related explanation of strikes is the view that strikes are analogous to road accidents. Accidents are, in general, avoidable; for instance they could be prevented by slower driving. But since the probability of having an accident is relatively small, drivers are willing to take risks. The same may be true of negotiators in an industrial dispute. In this case the cost of an error is a strike.

Another view of strikes is that they occur in response to a breakdown of communications between the union's leadership and the rank and file members. The latter may find that their leaders have underestimated their demands, and in the absence of an efficient institutional framework for communication between members, strikes send quick signals to the leaders.

The above models all have in common the characteristic of removing faults or mistakes in the bargaining process. For this reason they may be considered as members of the same family of models – the 'error removal' models.

The second main theory of strikes is the 'externalities' model. Parallels may be drawn between strikes on the one hand and either martyrdom or military conflict on the other. In all cases suffering is volunteered. An obvious explanation of martyrdom is that the martyr believes that good will come of his death. An oft-quoted reason for war is that one nation cannot tolerate a minor act of aggression by another because of the implications this might have for democracy (or some other high principle) elsewhere in the world. Similarly, it may be possible to rationalize strikes by reference to positive externalities which are generated by the dispute. An example of such an externality is the case of a union which, by striking, sends signals to employers throughout the economy that the union movement as a whole may be increasing its militancy; this would strengthen the hand of other unions in negotiations. The striking union would, of course, require a *quid pro quo* from these third parties. This may take the form of tacit agreements that the burden of striking is spread across unions over time.

Third, a firm which is making losses in the short term may wish to engineer a strike in order to reduce these losses. It may do this by making offers in negotiations which the union is sure to reject. The firm can then share its savings from the strike with the union, in the form of an improved wage deal, once the strike is over. This kind of stoppage may be described as a 'loss reduction' strike.

The development of empirical work on strikes has been largely independent of theoretical research. Nevertheless much is by now known about the environment within which strikes are relatively likely to take place. Blanchflower and Cubbin (1986) identify a number of significant determinants of the strike propensity of establishments using 1980 data. First, single establishment firms are less likely to suffer strike action than multi-establishment firms. Moreover, strikes become increasingly likely as the number of employees at the establishment increases, but less likely as the size of the whole firm increases.

Second, unionization affects strike proneness in a number of ways. The propensity to strike at an establishment rises as the proportion of full-time manual workers who are union members increases. The presence at the establishment of manual shop stewards also raises the propensity to strike, as does an increase in the number of manual unions represented at the establishment. The latter variable is likely to influence strike proneness positively because of inter-union competition. This will take the form of demarcation disputes between unions and a desire on the part of each union to convince workers of its own effectiveness. In addition, the presence of a large number of unions complicates negotiations with the employer and makes it difficult to resolve disputes peacefully.

Third, the adoption of payments by results schemes raises the probability of a strike within an establishment. Such schemes lead to uncertainty concerning remuneration levels and this can cause frustration on the part of the workforce.

Fourth, strike proneness varies between industries. Other things being equal, there tends to be a lower incidence of strikes in the public sector than elsewhere, but a higher incidence in manufacturing industries, especially engineering.

It is worth noting at this stage that a strike is by no means the only form of industrial action which unions can take. In 1984, establishments which suffered industrial action by manual workers were equally likely to experience non-strike and strike action. This is shown in table 5.27. The commonest forms of non-strike action are overtime bans and the work to rule.

TABLE 5.27

Percentage of Establishments Affected by Industrial Action in 1980 and 1984, by Type of Dispute

	Manual or Non-manual		Manual		Non-manual	
	1980	1984	1980	1984	1980	1984
Strike action	13	19	11	8	4	14
Non-strike action	16	18	10	8	8	12
Strike or non-strike action	22	25	16	13	11	18
Strike action lasting						
Less than one day	6	14	4	5	2	10
One day or more	9	12	7	5	3	9
One day but less than a week	n/a	11	n/a	5	n/a	9
One week or more	n/a	1	n/a	1	n/a	—
Non-strike action:						
Overtime bans/restriction	10	11	7	6	5	6
Work to rule	7	8	4	2	4	6
Blacking of work	5	3	2	2	3	2
Lockout	1	—	1	—	—	—
Go-slow	1	—	1	—	—	—
Other pressure	1	2	1	1	1	2

Source: Millward and Stevens (1986).

4.4   Industrial Relations

The shape of British industrial relations has changed substantially over the last decade, largely as the result of a number of changes in legislation.

The Employment Acts of 1980, 1982 and 1988, together with the 1984 Trade Union Act, are likely to have altered the balance of power fundamentally between unions and firms. A brief examination of British employee relations as they stand at present will therefore prove instructive.

Pay bargaining in Britain traditionally takes place at national level. National unions negotiate with large employers or with associations of employers in order to set a wage which is then allowed to vary little from area to area. Since the price of housing is considerably greater in the South East, a 'London allowance' is frequently paid by large employers to employees who work in this region. For a given job type, this is often the full extent of inter-regional wage differences within a single organization. Both free competition and the existence of employers' organizations serve to equalize rates of remuneration across different firms. This means that the main source of inter-regional variation in wage rates in Britain has traditionally been small firms and differences in industry mix. Things have changed more recently, though. Brown (1985) notes that 'the post-war period has seen the weakening, at first slowly but in the 1970s very rapidly, of industry-wide bargaining in the private sector, and consequently in the role of employers' associations.

It is usual for unions and employers to bargain over pay deals which are of twelve months in duration. There are exceptions to this rule, of course, and these exceptions have in recent years been occurring more frequently, especially in cases where bargains have been late in being struck. Moreover, many issues which do not concern pay (for instance, tea breaks, working hours, overtime rates) are renegotiated much less frequently than once a year.

The dependants of those workers who are on strike are in certain cases able to claim state benefits. Thus a striking worker has in the past been deemed to be unemployed when his dependants have entered claims. Since 1982, however, the state has assumed that the striking worker receives £17 per week in strike pay from his union. This has the effect of reducing benefit payments made to the dependants of striking workers. The total amount of dispute benefit paid by all unions to their members in 1985 was £14.7m (Annual Report of the Certification Officer, 1986). This amounted to £2.30 per worker per day of strike. The corresponding figure for 1984 (when the coal strike severely affected strike statistics) was just 46 pence. It is clear, then, that the state's assumption considerably overestimates the true position.

Strikes in the UK can legally take place only after a ballot of members has been conducted. Political strikes are illegal, as are strikes in support of 'union only' contracts such as the closed-shop. The strike may occur at any time during the negotiating process. Employers and unions may agree to take the dispute to arbitration; the Arbitration and Conciliation Service (ACAS) is frequently employed in such a role. In such cases the parties normally agree beforehand that the arbiter's decision will be binding. A strike, if one occurs, therefore normally precedes arbitration in the UK.

Since the Simmons versus Hoover case of 1977, the law has regarded a strike as constituting a breach of contract on the part of the union. This being so, the 1982 Employment Act allows the union to be fined. In extreme cases, the union may even have its funds sequestrated. By the same token employers may dismiss striking workers and can employ alternative labour. Within a period of three months the employer may not selectively re-employ workers who have been dismissed in this way – either all sacked workers must be re-employed or none. If the employer breaks this rule then unfair dismissal charges may be made. After the period of three months has expired, however, the employer may legally engage in the selective re-employment of dismissed workers. The dismissal of workers by a firm during a strike is similar in effect to a lockout, though in the latter instance even non-strikers are prevented by the firm from working during the period of the dispute. In the UK, lockouts are included in the statistics on strike activity and no separate data are collected.

Another important aspect of industrial relations is that of employee participation. In the UK, this form of industrial democracy is not legally required, but various tax incentives have been introduced in order to encourage firms to introduce share ownership schemes and profit-related pay. Since 1982 firms employing over 250 workers have been required by law to report annually to the authorities on progress which has been made in the field of employee participation; this, of course, represents only a mild form of encouragement. In view of all this, it is not surprising that worker participation has not been very widely adopted in the UK. Of firms employing more than 25 workers, only around a quarter use joint consultative committees as a tool of decision making within the organization.

The most important union body in Britain is the Trades Union Congress (TUC) which in 1986 comprised 87 affiliates. The TUC is composed of a wide variety of organizations, and frequently suffers the problems which are typical of such heterogeneous groupings. Inter-union jealousies can cause severe difficulties, and the system of negotiations where several unions must at once liaise with one employer (or group of employers) renders the bargaining system complicated. This system also gives rise to opportunities for the employer to play unions off against one another, a practice which hinders the rapid and peaceful resolution of problems.

It has frequently been argued that an important determinant of the state of industrial relations in a country is the degree of corporatism apparent in that country. By corporatism is meant the practice whereby wage settlements are achieved by involvement in the negotiating process of the government as well as unions and firms. The aim of this intervention is generally to ensure that wage deals are arrived at in a manner broadly in accord with the public interest. Consequently wage settlements which would result in high levels of involuntary unemployment would be unlikely in a corporatist economy. Such a system of negotiation involves a tripartite arrangement between government, unions and firms. This system does not now operate in Britain, although some elements of tripartism remain from a more corporatist past. In particular, the National Economic Development Council (NEDC or 'Neddy') draws on the experience of representatives of both sides of industry as well as of government. Nonetheless, as Newell and Symons (1987) state, 'British corporatism, such as it was, collapsed in 1979'.

The overall picture which emerges of British industrial relations is one of somewhat unstructured activity. A large number of unions bargain, mainly at national level, with a large number of employers, and settle wages which, on the whole, take incomplete account of inter-regional differences in economic climate, and which therefore fail to clear markets in some regions.

REFERENCES

M. Adams, 'The distribution of earnings, 1976–1986' (Department of Employment Research Paper 64, 1988).

H. Armstrong and J. Taylor, *Regional Policy and the North–South Divide* (Employment Institute, Black Prince Road, London, 1988).

M. Beenstock and C. Whitbread, 'Explaining changes in the union mark-up for male manual workers in Great Britain, 1953–83' (1988).

D. Blackaby, 'An analysis of the male racial earnings differential in the UK', *Applied Economics*, 18, 1233–1242 (1986).

D. Blanchflower, 'Union relative wage effects', *BJIR*, 22, 311–332 (1984).

D. Blanchflower and J. Cubbin, 'Strike propensities at the British workplace', *Oxford Bulletin of Economics and Statistics*, 48, 19–40 (1986).

D. Blanchflower and A. Oswald, 'The wage curve', paper presented at conference on 'Unemployment – inflation trade-offs in Europe' (Saltsjobaden, Stockholm, 1989).

C. Brown, *Black and White Britain: the Third PSI Survey* (Heinemann, 1984).

W. Brown, 'The effect of recent changes in the world economy on British industrial relations', in H. Juris, M. Thompson and W. Daniels (eds.), *Industrial relations in a decade of economic change* (Industrial Relations Research Association, 1985).

A. Carruth and R. Disney, 'Where have two million trade union members gone?', *EC*, 55, 1–20 (1988).

W. Daniel and N. Millward, *Workplace Industrial Relations in Britain* (Heinemann, 1983).

A. Dilnot and S. Webb, 'The 1988 Social Security reforms', *FSt*, 9, 26–53 (1988).

P. Dolton and G. Makepeace, 'Marital status, child rearing and earnings differentials in the graduate labour market', *EJ*, 97, 897–922 (1987).

J. L. Fallick and R. F. Elliott, *Incomes Policies, Inflation and Relative Pay* (Allen and Unwin, London, 1981).

C. Greenhalgh, 'Labour supply functions for married women in Great Britain', *EC* (August, 1977).

S.Hall *et alia*, 'The UK labour market', *LBR* (July, 1987).

G.Johnes, 'Error removal, loss reduction and external effects in the theory of strikes', *Australian Economic Papers*, 24, 310–325 (1985).

G.Johnes and J.Taylor, 'Ethnic minorities in the graduate labour market', *New Community* (July, 1989).

C.Johnson, 'The meaning of unemployment', *Lloyds Bank Economic Bulletin*, Number 105 (September, 1987).

H.Joshi, R.Layard and S.Owen, 'Why are more women working in Britain?', *Journal of Labour Economics* (January, 1985).

R.Layard and S.Nickell, *An Incomes Policy to Help the Unemployed* (Employment Institute, Black Prince Road, London, 1986).

R.Layard and S.Nickell, 'Unemployment in Britain', *Economica*, 53, supplement. Also published in C.Bean, R.Layard and S.Nickell (eds.), *The Rise in Unemployment* (Blackwell, 1986a).

R.Layard and S.Nickell, *An Incomes Policy to Help the Unemployed* (Employment Institute, 1986b).

R.Layard and S.Nickell, 'The performance of the British labour market', in R.Dornbusch and R.Layard (eds.), *The Performance of the British Economy* (Oxford University Press). Expanded version is also available as DP249 of the Centre for Labour Economics, London School of Economics (1987).

D.Metcalf, 'Trade unions and economic performance: the British evidence' (London School of Economics, 1988).

N.Millward and M.Stevens, *British Workplace Industrial Relations, 1980–84* (Gower, 1986).

N.Millward and M.Stevens, 'Union density in the regions', *DEG*, 286–295 (1988).

P.Minford, *Unemployment: Cause and Cure* (Martin Robertson, 1983).

B.Moore, J.Rhodes and P.Tyler, *The Effects of Government Regional Economic Policy* (Department of Trade and Industry, HMSO, 1986).

A.Newell and J.Symons, 'Corporatism, laissez-faire and the rise in unemployment', *European Economic Review*, 31, 567–614 (1987).

P.Paci, 'Tax-based incomes policies: will they work? have they worked?', *FSt*, 9, 81–94 (1988).

A.Shah, 'Professional earnings in the UK', *EC*, 50, 451–462 (1983).

M.Stewart, 'Relative earnings and individual union membership in the UK', *EC*, 50, 111–125 (1983).

Z.Tzannatos and A.Zabalza, 'The anatomy of the rise of British female relative wages in the 1970s', *BJIR*, 22, 177–194 (1984).

Statistical Appendix

TABLE A-1

UK GROSS DOMESTIC PRODUCT, EXPENDITURE (at 1985 prices), 1977–88 (£m)

Year	Consumers' Expenditure Total	Of which, Durables	General Government Final Consumption	Gross Domestic Capital Formation Total	Of which, Dwellings	Value of Physical Increase in Stocks and Work in Progress	Exports of Goods and Services	Total Final Expenditure at Market Prices[2]	Imports of Goods and Services	Adjustment to Factor Cost[1]	Gross Domestic Product at Factor Cost[2]
1977	176,016	12,525	66,926	53,307	12,811	3,193	83,987	383,974	−73,737	−41,076	268,386
1978	185,950	14,338	68,466	54,914	12,913	2,882	85,554	398,336	−76,582	−45,203	276,531
1979	193,794	16,171	69,943	56,450	13,363	3,325	88,789	412,902	−84,019	−46,610	282,322
1980	193,806	15,417	71,050	53,416	13,379	−3,357	88,963	403,713	−81,185	−45,305	277,238
1981	193,832	15,707	71,269	48,298	10,304	−3,191	88,205	397,812	−78,922	−44,246	274,614
1982	195,561	16,504	71,826	50,915	10,962	−1,289	89,000	405,733	−82,847	−44,895	277,989
1983	204,318	19,579	73,282	53,476	12,247	1,306	91,092	423,474	−88,119	−46,390	288,965
1984	207,927	19,442	73,897	58,075	12,571	1,072	97,029	438,000	−96,687	−48,514	292,799
1985	215,535	20,433	73,955	60,283	11,928	569	102,782	453,124	−99,166	−49,521	304,437
1986	227,757	22,249	75,398	61,293	12,809	689	106,607	471,744	−105,521	−51,893	314,330
1987	240,100	23,920	76,198	66,373	13,486	916	112,355	495,942	−113,370	−54,767	327,805
1988	255,624	26,329	76,612	74,219	14,727	1,945	111,195	519,595	−126,894	−56,412	336,289

Sources: BB, 1988; *ET*, April 1989.

Notes:

[1] This represents taxes on expenditure less subsidies valued at constant prices.

[2] Expenditure estimate: for years up to and including 1982, totals may differ from the sum of their components.

TABLE A-2

UK PRICES, EARNINGS AND PRODUCTIVITY, 1977–88: Index Numbers (1985 = 100)

Year	Retail Prices (All items)	Average Earnings (whole economy)	Average Earnings (manufacturing)	Average Earnings (services)	Wages and Salaries per unit of output (whole economy)	Wages and Salaries per unit of output (manufacturing)	Output per Person Employed (whole economy)	Output per Person-Hour Worked (manufacturing)
	1	2	3	4	5	6	7	8
1977	48.8	41.3	—	—	49.3	50.1	85.7	78.4
1978	52.8	46.6	—	—	54.5	56.8	87.9	79.4
1979	59.9	53.8	—	—	62.0	65.5	89.4	79.7
1980	70.7	65.0	61.5	66.1	76.1	80.1	87.4	78.6
1981	79.1	73.3	69.6	75.4	83.4	87.5	89.3	82.3
1982	85.9	80.2	77.4	81.3	87.4	91.2	93.1	86.7
1983	89.8	87.0	84.4	88.4	90.7	91.6	97.0	93.4
1984	94.3	92.2	91.7	94.0	94.6	94.3	98.4	97.8
1985	100.0	100.0	100.0	100.0	100.0	100.0	100.0	100.0
1986	103.4	107.9	107.7	107.7	105.5	104.5	102.3	103.3
1987	107.7	116.3	116.3	116.0	110.1	106.1	104.9	109.4
1988	113.0	126.4	126.2	126.2	118.3	109.2	106.1	114.6

Sources: ET(AS), 1988; *ET*, April 1989; *MDS*, March 1989.

TABLE A-3

UK PERSONAL INCOME, EXPENDITURE AND SAVING, 1977–88 (£m, current prices)

	PERSONAL INCOME BEFORE TAX							
Year	Wages and Salaries	Forces Pay	Employers' Contribu- tions	Current Grants from Public Authori- ties	Other Personal Income	Total[1]	UK Taxes on Income (Payments)	National Insurance and Health Contribu- tions
	1	*2*	*3*	*4*	*5*	*6*	*7*	*8*
1977	73,411	1,506	11,655	15,031	23,401	125,004	18,149	9,503
1978	84,001	1,645	13,197	17,871	27,023	143,737	19,460	10,101
1979	98,424	2,020	15,422	20,917	33,228	170,011	21,586	11,526
1980	116,569	2,436	18,634	25,524	37,776	200,939	25,683	13,939
1981	127,884		21,700	31,242	41,537	222,363	28,969	15,916
1982	136,245		22,376	36,584	46,954	242,159	31,396	18,095
1983	145,469		24,111	39,843	52,120	261,543	33,230	20,780
1984	155,118		24,980	43,020	56,154	279,272	34,576	22,320
1985	168,566		26,048	46,792	60,848	302,254	37,535	24,251
1986	182,677		26,988	50,823	65,457	325,945	40,995	26,125
1987	198,515		27,964	52,553	70,425	349,457	43,610	28,363
1988	221,890		29,823	54,312	79,555	385,580	48,729	31,551

Sources: ET, April 1989; *BB*, 1988.

Notes:
[1] Before providing for depreciation and stock appreciation.
[2] Before providing for depreciation, stock appreciation and additions to tax reserves.
   Column 6 = 1 + 2 + 3 + 4 + 5.
   Column 10 = 6 − 7 − 8 − 9.
   Column 13 = 14 − 11.
   Column 15 = 10 − 14.

		CONSUMERS' EXPENDITURE				PERSONAL SAVINGS		
Other Current Transfers	*Total Personal Disposable Income*[2]	*Durable Goods*		*Other*				
		Amount (£m)	*As % of PDI*	*Amount (£m)*	*Total*	*Amount (£m)*[2]	*As % of PDI*	*Year*
9	10	11	12	13	14	15	16	
795	96,557	7,754	8.0	79,133	86,887	9,670	10.0	1977
1,052	113,124	10,168	9.0	90,051	100,219	12,905	11.4	1978
1,178	135,721	13,087	9.6	105,565	118,652	17,069	12.6	1979
1,308	160,009	13,495	8.4	124,401	137,896	22,113	13.8	1980
1,234	176,244	13,942	7.9	139,624	153,566	22,678	12.9	1981
1,387	191,281	15,439	8.1	153,106	168,545	22,736	11.9	1982
1,401	206,132	18,248	8.9	166,371	184,619	21,513	10.4	1983
1,477	220,899	18,779	8.5	178,715	197,494	23,405	10.6	1984
1,664	238,804	20,433	8.6	195,102	215,535	23,269	9.7	1985
1,879	256,946	23,003	9.0	214,637	237,640	19,306	7.5	1986
2,098	275,386	26,139	9.5	233,827	259,966	15,420	5.6	1987
2,249	303,051	30,836	10.2	259,870	290,706	12,345	4.1	1988

TABLE A-4

UK POPULATION, WORKING POPULATION, UNEMPLOYMENT AND VACANCIES, 1977-88 (thousands)

Year	Total Population (mid-year estimate)	Workforce[1]	Workforce in employment[2]	Unemployed[3]	Unemployment Rate (%)[4]	Vacancies at job centres[5]
	1	2	3	4	5	6
1977	56,190	26,224	24,865	1,162.7	4.4	154.5
1978	56,178	26,358	25,014	1,145.7	4.3	210.3
1979	56,240	26,627	25,393	1,075.8	4.0	241.3
1980	56,330	26,839	25,327	1,365.7	5.1	134.2
1981	56,352	26,741	24,346	2,173.6	8.1	91.1
1982	56,306	26,677	23,908	2,546.7	9.5	113.9
1983	56,347	26,610	23,626	2,790.5	10.5	137.3
1984	56,460	27,265	24,235	2,920.6	10.7	149.8
1985	56,618	27,797	24,618	3,035.7	10.9	161.7
1986	56,763	27,985	24,756	3,107.2	11.1	188.1
1987	56,930	28,211	25,306	2,822.3	10.0	234.9
1988	n.a.	28,090	25,749	2,294.5	8.0	247.8

Sources: MDS, March 1989; ET, April 1989, ET(AS), 1988; DEG, April 1989.

Notes:
[1] The workforce is the sum of those in employment (including self-employed), the unemployed (claimants), the armed forces and participants in work-related government training programmes. Mid-year figures.
[2] Employees in employment, self-employed, armed forces, those on work-related government training programmes and the unemployed (claimants).
[3] Annual average of seasonally adjusted figures pertaining to claimants aged 18 or over. Wider definitions are inconsistent through time. See DEG, December 1988.
[4] Unemployed as per cent of workforce.
[5] Average of monthly figures.

TABLE A-5

UK GENERAL GOVERNMENT : CURRENT ACCOUNT, 1975-87 (£m)

	1975	1976	1977	1978	1979	1980	1981	1982	1983	1984	1985	1986	1987
RECEIPTS													
Taxes on income	16,758	18,969	20,490	22,623	25,238	31,001	30,249	40,392	43,484	46,791	51,603	52,158	55,601
Taxes on expenditure	14,036	16,284	19,834	22,754	29,670	36,475	42,465	46,467	49,460	52,585	56,724	62,700	67,980
National Insurance, etc. contributions	6,848	8,423	9,503	10,101	11,526	13,939	15,916	18,095	20,780	22,312	24,191	26,033	28,449
Gross Trading Surplus	126	152	183	216	180	180	236	216	50	-92	256	105	-177
Rent, etc.[1]	1,524	1,942	2,256	2,517	3,173	4,251	4,715	4,857	4,836	5,373	5,510	4,078	4,313
Interest and dividends, etc.	1,996	2,357	2,687	2,851	3,353	3,954	4,456	5,292	5,097	5,128	6,276	5,890	5,859
Miscellaneous current transfers	73	118	136	151	134	169	177	187	222	217	229	262	317
Imputed charge for consumption of non-trading capital	778	925	1,045	1,182	1,433	1,739	1,935	1,999	2,056	2,162	2,350	2,582	2,732
Total	42,157	49,170	56,134	62,395	74,677	91,708	106,149	117,505	125,985	134,476	147,139	153,808	165,074
EXPENDITURE													
Current expenditure on goods and services	22,353	26,117	28,424	32,224	37,434	47,283	53,522	58,447	63,817	67,722	71,645	77,103	83,040
Non-trading capital consumption	778	925	1,045	1,182	1,403	1,739	1,935	1,999	2,056	2,162	2,350	2,582	2,732
Subsidies	3,686	3,438	3,386	3,775	4,643	5,719	6,369	5,811	6,269	7,538	7,202	6,106	5,762
Grants to personal sector	10,263	12,748	15,031	17,781	20,917	25,524	31,242	36,584	39,843	43,029	46,757	50,729	52,478
Current grants abroad (net)	337	776	1,033	1,664	2,016	1,780	1,607	1,789	1,930	2,099	3,332	2,233	3,287
Debt interest	4,127	5,293	6,238	7,093	8,671	10,873	12,703	13,973	14,189	15,756	17,474	17,191	17,667
Total current expenditure	41,544	49,297	55,257	63,809	75,134	92,918	107,378	118,603	128,104	138,306	148,760	155,944	164,966
Balance: current surplus[2]	613	-127	877	-1,414	-457	-1,210	-1,229	-1,098	-2,119	-3,830	-1,621	-2,136	108
Total	42,157	49,170	56,134	62,395	74,677	91,708	106,149	117,505	125,985	134,476	147,139	153,808	165,074

Sources: BB, 1986, 1987, 1988.

Notes:
[1] Includes royalties and licence fees on oil and gas production.
[2] Before providing for depreciation and stock appreciation.

TABLE A-6

UK MONETARY AGGREGATES, PUBLIC SECTOR BORROWING REQUIREMENT (£m), INTEREST RATES AND EXCHANGE RATES, 1977–88

Year	The Wide Monetary Base MO[1,2]	M3[1,3]	M4[1,4]	Public Sector Borrowing Requirement	Yield on UK Treasury bills (%)	Gilts[5] (%)	Dollar Exchange Rate ($/£)[6]	Sterling Effective Exchange Rate[7]
	1	2	3	4	5	6	7	8
1977	8,495	42,704	74,208	5,466	6.39	12.73	1.7455	84.6
1978	9,751	49,273	85,310	8,195	11.91	12.47	1.9197	84.9
1979	11,013	55,340	97,363	12,551	16.49	12.99	2.1225	90.9
1980	11,635	65,536	114,089	11,786	13.58	13.78	2.3281	100.0
1981	11,863	76,230	137,901	10,507	15.39	14.74	2.0254	98.9
1982	12,251	89,878	154,444	4,880	9.96	12.88	1.7489	94.2
1983	13,043	99,851	174,897	11,605	9.04	10.80	1.5158	86.7
1984	13,789	109,904	198,759	10,281	9.33	10.69	1.3364	81.9
1985	14,261	124,481	224,879	7,476	11.49	10.62	1.2976	81.5
1986	15,000	150,135	261,040	2,420	10.94	9.87	1.4672	75.8
1987	15,738	184,507	303,766	−1,438	8.38	9.47	1.6392	75.6
1988	16,399	222,911	357,971	−11,668	12.91	9.36	1.7796	79.7

Sources: ET(AS), 1988; ET, April 1989; NIER, February 1989; FS.

Notes:

[1] Figures quoted are for the seasonally adjusted level as at the end of the last quarter of each year.

[2] The monetary base consists of notes and coins together with bankers' operational balances at the Bank of England.

[3] M3 is a wide monetary aggregate, consisting of notes and coins together with the deposit liabilities of banks.

[4] M4 is a wider aggregate consisting of M3 together with deposits held at building societies (less building societies' holdings of notes and coin and bank deposits).

[5] The yield on long-dated (20-year) British Government bonds.

[6] Average of daily Telegraphic Transfer rates in London.

[7] As calculated by the IMF; indexed on 1980 = 100. A decline in the index indicates an overall depreciation of sterling.

TABLE A-7

UK BALANCE OF PAYMENTS, 1976–88 (£m)

CURRENT ACCOUNT[1]

| | Visible Trade | | | Invisibles (balance) | | | | |
| | Exports (f.o.b.) | Imports (f.o.b.) | Visible Balance | Services | Transfers | Interest Profits and Dividends | Total Invisible Balance | Current Balance |
Year	1	2	3	4	5	6	7	8
1976	25,082	29,041	−3,959	2,244	1,560	−786	3,018	−941
1977	31,682	34,006	−2,324	3,037	265	−1,128	2,174	−150
1978	34,981	36,574	−1,593	3,542	806	−1,791	2,557	964
1979	40,470	43,868	−3,398	3,907	1,205	−2,210	2,902	−496
1980	47,147	45,794	1,353	3,949	−196	−1,984	1,769	3,122
1981	50,668	47,318	3,350	3,923	1,210	−1,547	3,586	6,936
1982	55,330	53,112	2,218	2,762	1,446	−1,741	2,467	4,685
1983	60,698	61,773	−1,075	3,721	2,847	−1,600	4,968	3,893
1984	70,263	74,843	−4,580	3,942	4,432	−1,717	6,657	2,077
1985	77,988	80,334	−2,346	5,962	2,747	−3,008	5,701	3,355
1986	72,656	81,365	−8,700	5,631	5,356	−2,136	8,851	151
1987	79,421	89,594	−10,173	5,333	5,387	−3,452	7,268	−2,905
1988	80,157	100,714	−20,557	3,473	6,001	−3,582	5,892	−14,665

TRANSACTIONS IN UK EXTERNAL ASSETS AND LIABILITIES[1]

Year	Direct Investment UK Investment Overseas	Overseas Investment in UK	Portfolio Investment UK Investment Overseas	Overseas Investment in UK	Net Banking Transactions	Official Reserves[2]	Other Government Transactions	Other[3]	Net Transactions	Balancing Item
	9	10	11	12	13	14	15	16	17	18
1976	−2,419	95	1,653	1,032	−708	853	−453	302	355	586
1977	−2,399	12	2,546	1,910	2,270	−9,588	736	621	−3,892	4,042
1978	−3,520	−1,073	1,962	−139	−1,986	2,329	−886	442	−2,871	1,907
1979	−5,889	−887	3,030	1,549	3,646	−1,059	−354	−779	−743	1,044
1980	−4,866	−3,310	4,355	1,499	936	−291	−243	−1,952	−3,872	570
1981	−6,005	−4,468	2,932	323	−659	2,419	−113	−1,800	−7,371	277
1982	−4,091	−7,563	3,027	225	3,785	1,421	246	598	−2,352	−2,333
1983	−5,417	−7,193	3,386	1,888	2,743	607	−1,062	49	−4,361	468
1984	−6,003	−9,866	−181	1,419	10,425	908	−783	−3,668	−7,749	5,672
1985	−8,800	−19,440	3,784	7,121	7,626	−1,758	−707	2,669	−9,505	6,510
1986	−11,290	−25,644	4,846	8,066	9,912	−2,891	−332	3,482	−13,851	13,700
1987	−18,775	1,526	8,108	9,665	2,525	−12,012	778	−1,266	−9,451	12,356
1988	−14,937	−10,872	7,114	4,134	14,446	−2,761	−403	2,717	−562	15,227

Sources: ET(AS), 1988: *ET*, April 1989.

Notes:

[1] All items listed represent a positive flow if not otherwise indicated; for transactions in assets and liabilities a positive flow represents an increase in UK assets (decrease in liabilities). The relationship between columns is as follows: Col 3 = Col 1 − Col 2; Col 7 = Cols 4 + 5 + 6; Col 8 = Col 3 + Col 7; Col 17 = Cols 9 + 10 + 11 + 12 + 13 + 14 + 15 + 16; Col 18 = (with sign reversed) Col 8 + Col 17.

[2] Borrowing from, less lending to, overseas residents by UK banks.

[3] Borrowing from, less lending to, overseas residents by UK residents other than banks and government.

TABLE A-8

PRODUCTION IN INDUSTRY, 1978–1988 (Index Numbers, 1985 = 100)

	1978	1979	1980	1981	1982	1983	1984	1985	1986	1987	1988
Energy	70.8	83.7	83.3	86.4	91.6	96.8	88.8	100.0	105.0	103.9	99.7
Manufacturing											
Food, drink and tobacco	98.2	99.7	99.0	97.3	98.9	100.0	100.8	100.0	100.9	103.3	105.8
Chemicals	91.1	93.4	84.0	83.5	84.9	91.4	96.8	100.0	101.8	109.1	114.1
Metals	112.1	116.8	88.7	94.1	95.2	93.9	93.6	100.0	99.9	108.6	121.3
Engineering and Allied inds.	105.9	103.6	96.2	88.3	90.4	92.3	96.8	100.0	99.3	104.0	112.2
Building materials	118.3	117.3	105.7	94.2	93.5	96.6	100.4	100.0	101.3	106.8	117.6
Textiles, clothing	117.1	115.7	98.1	91.0	89.2	92.5	95.9	100.0	100.8	103.3	102.4
Other manufacturing	110.6	113.0	101.0	94.1	90.5	93.5	98.4	100.0	104.5	114.6	126.5
Total Manufacturing	105.7	105.5	96.3	90.6	91.1	93.7	97.6	100.0	100.9	106.6	114.1
Consumer goods	104.6	104.5	96.5	93.1	92.4	95.3	98.1	100.0	101.6	106.5	112.4
Investment goods	103.1	101.6	97.0	88.6	91.3	91.8	95.8	100.0	99.0	103.3	111.2
Intermediate goods	88.1	95.8	88.8	88.1	90.4	95.4.	93.2	100.0	103.5	106.3	107.9

Sources: NIER, February 1989; MDS, March 1989. The headings are those of the 1985 Standard Industrial Classification (SIC).

TABLE A-9
GDP BY INDUSTRY[1]

	1973		1980		1987	
	£m	%	£m	%	£m	%
Agriculture, forestry and fishing	2,006	3.0	4,246	2.1	5,901	1.7
Energy and water supply	3,018	4.6	19,368	9.7	24,184	6.8
Manufacturing	20,919	31.7	52,954	26.6	85,552	24.1
Construction	4,995	7.6	12,053	6.0	21,524	6.1
Distribution, hotels and catering; repairs	8,982	13.6	25,654	12.9	48,963	13.8
Transport	3,248	4.9	9,554	4.8	16,227	4.6
Communication	1,608	2.4	4,762	2.4	9,688	2.7
Banking, finance, insurance, business services and leasing	4,709[2]	7.1	24,776[2]	12.4	63,903[2]	18.0
Ownership of dwellings	3.525	5.3	12,147	6.1	20,180	5.7
Public administration, national defence and compulsory social security	4,220	6.4	24,522	7.3	24,895	7.0
Education and health services	5,276	8.0	17,965	9.0	31,681	8.9
Other services	3,507	5.3	10,674	5.4	22,366	6.3
GDP at factor cost (income definition)	66,013	100.0	199,377	100.0	354,519	100.0

Sources: *BB*, 1985, 1988.

Notes: [1] The contribution of each industry to GDP before providing for depreciation but
after providing for stock appreciation. Comparisons across years may be affected
by revisions in SIC definitions of industries or sectors.
[2] After deducting financial companies' net receipts of interest.

TABLE A-10

REGIONAL UNEMPLOYMENT RATES (%), 1976–88

	1976	1977	1978	1979	1980	1981	1982	1983	1984	1985	1986	1987	1988
South East	3.1	3.3	3.0	2.6	3.1	5.5	6.7	7.5	7.8	8.0	8.2	7.1	5.2
East Anglia	3.5	3.8	3.5	3.1	3.8	6.3	7.4	8.0	7.9	8.0	8.1	6.8	4.8
South West	4.7	4.9	4.6	4.0	4.5	6.8	7.8	8.7	9.0	9.3	9.5	8.2	6.3
East Midlands	3.5	3.6	3.6	3.3	4.5	7.4	8.4	9.5	9.8	9.9	9.9	9.0	7.2
West Midlands	4.3	4.2	4.0	4.0	5.5	10.0	11.9	12.9	12.7	12.7	12.6	11.1	8.5
Yorkshire and Humberside	3.9	4.0	4.2	4.1	5.3	8.9	10.4	11.4	11.7	12.0	12.4	11.3	9.5
North West	5.1	5.3	5.3	5.0	6.5	10.2	12.1	13.4	13.6	13.8	13.9	12.7	10.7
North	5.3	5.9	6.4	6.5	8.0	11.8	13.3	14.6	15.3	15.4	15.2	14.0	11.9
Scotland	5.1	5.9	5.9	4.7	7.0	9.9	11.3	12.3	12.6	12.9	13.3	13.0	11.2
Wales	5.3	5.6	5.7	5.3	6.9	10.5	12.1	12.9	13.2	13.8	13.9	12.5	10.5
Northern Ireland	7.1	7.8	8.1	7.9	9.4	12.7	14.4	15.5	15.9	16.1	17.6	17.6	16.4
United Kingdom	4.2	4.4	4.3	4.0	5.1	8.1	9.5	10.5	10.7	10.9	11.1	10.0	8.0

Sources: Unemployment Statistics – seasonally adjusted series, *DEG*, Historical Supplement No. 1, April 1989.

Note:

The unemployment rate is the number of unemployed claimants aged 18 and over expressed as a percentage of the estimated workforce (employed employees and unemployed claimants + self-employed + HM Forces).

Index